The World Bibliography of Armed Land Conflict

from
Waterloo to World War I

WARS   CAMPAIGNS   BATTLES   REVOLUTIONS   REVOLTS

COUPS D'ETAT   INSURRECTIONS   RIOTS   ARMED CONFRONTATIONS

by
Dale E. Floyd

Volume 1

Michael Glazier, Inc.
Wilmington, Delaware

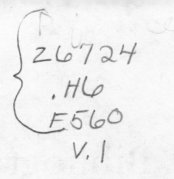
First published in 1979 by Michael Glazier, Inc.
1012A King Street, Wilmington, Delaware 19801

Copyright © 1979 by Dale E. Floyd

Library of Congress Card Catalogue Number: 79-54082
International Standard Book Number: 0-89453-147-6

Printed in the United States of America

For
Gayle, Betty and Donald

TABLE OF CONTENTS

ACKNOWLEDGEMENTS

During the many years that I have been working on this bibliography, I have received assistance from numerous individuals and institutions. First, I wish to express my gratitude to Dallas D. Irvine who originally suggested that I undertake such a project, although, at the time, he had something else in mind. Also, the preparation of this bibliography would have been impossible had it not been for the numerous bibliographies and footnotes in the various publications that I have consulted over the years. The following institutions kindly allowed me to enter their stacks and read the shelves to locate pertinent books and articles: the National Archives Library, the U.S. Military Academy Library, the U.S. Army Military History Institute, the University of Maryland Library, the George Mason University Library and the Army Library. The Library of Congress was helpful in bringing books and articles to its Main Reading Room where I could examine them and loaned many publications through interlibrary loan. A hardy thanks is also deserved by the Ministry of Defence Library (Central and Army) in London, England which graciously sent me numerous "Book Lists" from its series on various subjects. The following librarians were most helpful to me in my search for publications: Sara Strom of the National Archives Library, Alan C. Aimone of the U.S. Military Academy Library and John Slonaker of the U.S. Army Military History Institute. Various individuals offered valuable suggestions and citations including Mike Musick of the National Archives, John Jessup of George Mason University, George Stansfield of the National Defence University and Robert S. Allen of Parks Canada.

For the actual preparation of the bibliography I wish to thank Kristen Leedom, who in spite of many adversities including giving birth to a baby, typed the manuscript. Also, Jodi Wysong, Courtney Sullivan, David Floyd and Eric Floyd helped by alphabetizing hundreds of index cards. Finally, I wish to thank my wife, Gayle, a librarian, who helped in various ways including searching the Library of Congress' National Union Catalog to find correct citations and for taking over many of my duties as husband and father so that I could work on the bibliography.

In conclusion, I wish to state that any errors and omissions in this bibliography are not the fault of anyone but myself.

Dale E. Floyd
Springfield, Virginia

INTRODUCTION

This bibliography began as a personal aid for the compiler who found it helpful in his work as an archivist in the Navy and Old Army Branch at the National Archives and for his private reading and research. Of course, there is no substitute for original, primary sources which should be consulted by anyone who desires to write a definitive study on a particular subject. Thus, a diligent and thorough researcher should visit the various archives, manuscript repositories and libraries throughout the world that have custody of pertinent source materials depending on the research topic. Unfortunately, many researchers do not have the economic and/or foreign language capabilities to undertake such trips. Also, in some instances, the researcher only needs a short precise account of a particular incident or event and he will, therefore, look for a printed source that is readily available. This bibliography has been compiled for historians, military history buffs, war gamers, military miniature painters and relic collectors, and other interested researchers who simply seek references to printed sources in the English language that will quickly provide them with the information that they require.

A Bibliography of Nineteenth Century Armed Land Conflict is a listing of books, scholarly theses and dissertations, pamphlets, government publications and periodical articles in the English language relating to armed land conflict throughout the world that occurred between 1815, after the Battle of Waterloo, and 1914, when World War I broke out (or later for those countries that became involved in the conflict sometime after it began). Armed land conflict in this bibliography includes air warfare but not naval combat on the water.

This bibliography is divided into three main parts: General Military History; Continents, Smaller Land Areas and Countries; and Armed Confrontations. The Introduction to each part describes the type of sources it includes. Each part is then divided into various sections. Generally each section is arranged in alphabetical order except that Mc's and Mac's come before M's. However, a few sections do not include lists but simply provide cross-references to publications listed elsewhere by giving the part and number assigned them in the bibliography. Cross-references are also given at the end of many sections that do have lists of publications.

Some of these cross-references are to publications listed in the Addendum which can be found in the back of the second volume. The Addendum includes publications that were published after the particular sections in which they should appear were prepared, those that were overlooked before and others that were only recently discovered by the compiler. The user is advised to consult these cross-references because many of them are useful.

At the end of each volume, the user will find a page headed Corrections of Errors. Although the compiler and typist attempted to make as few errors as possible in the preparation of this bibliography, perfection was impossible. Subsequent editing caught many of these errors but some escaped detection and others were too complicated to correct easily. Thus, some important changes can be found in Corrections of Errors and the user is strongly urged to consult it irregardless of the subject of interest.

Naturally, this compilation is not comprehensive and many users may discover after consulting it that publications with which they are familiar are not included. Some publications were simply unknown by the compiler and others were not included at his discretion for one reason or another. The compiler found it most difficult in selecting publications to include which relate to weapons and uniforms. A phenomenal number of publications pertaining to weapons and uniforms have been published but, unfortunately, many of them are poorly researched and written and contain erroneous information.

This bibliography is simply meant to be a guide to the study of Nineteenth Century armed land conflict and is only a beginning for the serious researcher who wishes to consult all pertinent publications relating to his subject which have been written in the English language. However, as an aid to further study, sources that include a good bibliography and/or footnotes are indicated with an asterisk (*) preceeding the citation.

Citations

Citations provided in this bibliography are as complete as is necessary for the user to locate the desired publications. In most instances, entries for books, pamphlets and government publications cite first editions as they are listed in the National Union Catalog compiled by the Library of Congress which should make it simple for anyone to borrow them through interlibrary loan. Many of the books, pamphlets and government publications cited here are in print or have been reprinted. To determine whether or not a particular publication is presently available for purchase, consult the latest issue of Books in Print which can be found in many libraries and bookstores. Other publications may be purchased from used book dealers. Some used book dealers will attempt to locate an out of print publication for you by advertising. This search service will cost a fee over and above the price of the book but, despite the expense, this proceedure may be the only way to obtain a copy of the publication. Many used book dealers including those who provide out of print search services advertise in publications such as The New York Times Book Review. Generally, Congressional and parliamentary publications of the various countries are not included in this bibliography due to the extreme difficulty of locating them in the National Union Catalog.

References to articles in scholarly journals and popular magazines have been included. However, the articles cited here are only a few of the great number that can be found. For further study, the user is hereby advised that articles appearing in thousands of journals and magazines are a valuable research source. Generally, article citations provide the author's name, the title of the article, an abbreviation denoting the journal or magazine in which it appeared, the volume number, the number of the issue or season/month and year and the page numbers. In a few instances, the compiler was unable to locate the full citation to certain valuable articles but due to their importance he included them with an incomplete reference. The full titles of journals and magazines for which abbreviations have been given in the citations can be found on pages xiv-xx. Some individuals are convinced that articles appearing in popular magazines such as American History Illustrated and History Today are not worth consulting because they include erroneous information and do not provide footnotes. However, many factual, precise articles written by competent historians and other writers have appeared in popular magazines and are exactly what some users need--short, concise and accurate accounts of specific events or subjects. Therefore, some citations to articles appearing in popular magazines have been included in this bibliography.

Numerous useful and informative scholarly theses and dissertations have been written on subjects relating to Nineteenth Century armed land conflict. Reproductions of most American Ph.D. dissertations can be purchased from University Microfilm of Ann Arbor, Michigan. American M.A. theses are not as readily available but they usually may be borrowed through interlibrary loan from the library at the school where they were accepted for a degree. Similarly, theses and dissertations written in Canada, Great Britain and other countries can usually be obtained in one way or another through interlibrary loan and reproductions may be available for purchase from the appropriate university for a fee.

Peculiarities

This bibliography is not annotated, although the compiler originally intended to do so, but in most instances the subtitles of publications have been given which, in many circumstances, clarifies the subject. Similarly, the compiler intended to omit all nobility and military titles when providing the authors' names but the plan went awry and some are included. Also, some publications have been cited twice by accident but in a few instances they are given more than once because of their relationship to different subjects.

As stated before, the compiler provides citations to books, government publications and pamphlets as they appear in the National Union Catalog. Many publications which the compiler originally planned on including do not appear because they could not be found in the National Union Catalog. Thus, practically all of the publications cited in this bibliography can be found somewhere in the United States. Likewise, the user is advised that some very worthwhile publications not cited in this bibliography may be found in other countries. In addition, citations to diplomatic, political, social, and economic historical studies are not included in this compilation.

Generally, this bibliography does not include citations for regimental histories. Likewise, because of the great number of English language publications relating to such countries as the United States and Great Britain, those pertaining to specific cities, regions and military posts have not been cited in most cases.

ABBREVIATIONS FOR PERIODICALS

A	Assembly (Association of Graduates of the U.S. Military Academy)
A&N	The Army and Navy Magazine
AAAPSS	The Annals of the American Academy of Political and Social Sciences
AAHSJ	The American Aviation Historical Society Journal
AAJ	Australian Army Journal
AC	Air Clues
ACQR	The American Catholic Quarterly Review
AEH	The Aerospace Historian
AERON	Aeronautics
AFA	African Affairs: Journal of the Royal African Society
AFAR	African Arts
AFD	The American Funeral Director
AFJAG	The United States Air Force JAG Law Review
AFS	Armed Forces and Society
AFSR	African Studies Review
AH	American Heritage
AHI	American History Illustrated
AHQ	The Alabama Historical Quarterly
AHR	The American Historical Review
AHS	African Historical Studies
AHY	The Austrian History Yearbook
AI	The Annals of Iowa
AID	The Army Information Digest
AIRP	Air Pictorial
AJIL	The American Journal of International Law
AJLH	The American Journal of Legal History
AJN	The American Journal of Nursing
AJPH	The Australian Journal of Politics and History
AM	Americana
AMAR	The American Archivist
AMERS	The Americas: A Quarterly Review of Inter-American Cultural History
AMERW	The American West
AMME	The American Mercury
AMQT	The American Quarterly
AMR	The American Rifleman
ANEP	The American Neptune; A Quarterly Journal of Maritime History
ANQ	Antiques
APH	The Airpower Historian
AQ	The Army Quarterly (now The Army Quarterly and Defence Journal)
AR	The Alabama Review
ARF	The American Rifleman
ARIZ	Arizoniana (now the Journal of Arizona History, JAZH)
ARMOR	Armor (formerly the Journal of the United States Cavalry Association JUSCA, The Cavalry Journal, and the Armored Cavalry Journal)

ARMY	Army
ARR	The American Review of Reviews
ARTS	Arts; The Proceedings of the Sydney University Arts Association
ASA	Asian Affairs
ASEER	The American Slavic and East European Review (formerly the Slavonic and East European Review, American Series)
ASR	The American Sociological Review
ASTI	American Studies International
ATLM	The Atlantic Monthly
AUR	The Air University Review
AUSO	Australian Outlook
AUSQ	The Australian Quarterly
AW	The Annals of Wyoming
AZHR	The Arizona Historical Review
AZW	Arizona and the West
BHI	British History Illustrated
BHR	The Bulgarian Historical Review
BIHR	The Bulletin of the Institute of Historical Research
BJS	The British Journal of Sociology
BKS	Balkan Studies
BLM	Blackwood's Magazine
BMHS	Bulletin, The Military Historical Society
BP&P	Bengal; Past and Present
BV&A	By Valor and Arms
BZMGS	Byzantine and Modern Greek Studies
CAJ	The Canadian Army Journal
CAM	The Colored American Magazine
CAMP	Periodical: The Journal of the Council on Abandoned Military Posts
CAR	The Central Asian Review
CARJ	The Coast Artillery Journal
CATHR	The Catholic Historical Review
CDQ	The Canadian Defence Quarterly
CE	The Christian Examiner
CEH	Central European History
CFJ	The United States Army Combat Forces Journal (formed by the combination of the Field Artillery Journal, FARJ, and the Infantry Journal, IJ, which was also titled the Journal of the United States Infantry Association, JUSIA)
CH	The Chautauquan
CHJ	The China Journal
CHQ	The California Historical Quarterly
CHR	The Canadian Historical Review
CIMM	The Century Illustrated Monthly Magazine
CJ	The Cavalry Journal (British)
CJAC	The Canadian Journal of Arms Collecting
CJEPS	The Canadian Journal of Economics and Political Science
CJH	The Canadian Journal of History
CM	Colorado Magazine

COK	The Chronicles of Oklahoma
COSM	The Cosmopolitan Magazine
CR	Contemporary Review
CS	Caribbean Studies
CSSH	Comparative Studies in Society and History
CSTSH	Contemporary Studies of Social History
CUH	Current History
CV	The Confederate Veteran
CWH	Civil War History
CWTI	Civil War Times Illustrated
D	Daedalus (formerly Proceedings of the American Academy of Arts and Sciences)
DARM	Daughters of the American Revolution Magazine
DE	The Developing Economies
DH	Delaware History
DMJ	The Defense Management Journal
ECHR	The Economic History Review
ECJ	The Economic Journal
EEQ	The East European Quarterly
EHR	The English Historical Review
EP	(El) Palacio
ER	The Edinburgh Review, or Critical Journal
ES	Every Saturday: A Journal of Choice Reading Selected from Foreign Current Literature (title varies)
EUSR	European Studies Review
EXEH	Explorations in Economic History
FA	Foreign Affairs; An American Quarterly Review
FARJ	The Field Artillery Journal
FCHQ	The Filson Club Historical Quarterly
FEQ	The Far Eastern Quarterly
FES	The Far Eastern Survey
FHS	French Historical Studies
FLHQ	The Florida Historical Quarterly
FR	The Fortnightly Review
FRO	The Frontier
G	The Galaxy; A Magazine of Entertaining Reading
GAHQ	The Georgia Historical Quarterly
GEOR	The Geographical Review
H	Horizon (New York)
HAG	The Hawaiian Guardsman
HAHR	The Hispanic American Historical Review
HIS	History; The Quarterly Journal of the Historical Association
HJ	The (Cambridge) Historical Journal
HJAS	The Harvard Journal of Asiatic Studies
HMPEC	The Historical Magazine of the Protestant Episcopal Church
HNMM	Harper's New Monthly Magazine
HSANZ	Historical Studies: Australia and New Zealand
HST	The Historian; A Journal of History
HT	History Today
IA	IA, The Journal of the Society for Industrial Archaeology

IJ	Infantry Journal (also titled the Journal of the United States Infantry Association, JUSIA, along with the Field Artillery Journal, FARJ became the United States Army Combat Forces Journal, CFJ)
IJH&P	The Iowa Journal of History and Politics (The Iowa Journal of History)
IJAHS	The International Journal of African Historical Studies
INFQ	The Infantry Quarterly
INHM	The Indiana Magazine of History
INMH	The International Magazine of History
INTJ	The International Journal
IS	The Irish Sword
IY	Idaho Yesterdays
JAFH	The Journal of African History
JAFS	The Journal of African Studies
JAJ	The Judge Advocate Journal
JAS	The Journal of Asian Studies
JASFLH	The Journal of the American Society of the French Legion of Honor
JASH	The Journal of Asian History
JASS	The Journal of Asiatic Studies
JAZH	The Journal of Arizona History
JBS	The Journal of British Studies
JCEA	The Journal of Central European Affairs
JCH	The Journal of Contemporary History
JCMVA	The Journal of Comparative Medicine and Veterinary Archives
JCONH	The Journal of Contemporary History
JCR	The Journal of Conflict Resolution
JFI	The Journal of the Franklin Institute
JHI	The Journal of the History of Ideas
JHM	The Journal of the History of Medicine
JI-AS	The Journal of Inter-American Studies (later The Journal of Inter-American Studies and World Affairs)
JI&CH	The Journal of Imperial and Commonwealth History
JIDH	The Journal of Interdisciplinary History
JISHS	Journal of the Illinois State Historical Society
JLAS	The Journal of Latin American Studies
JLIBH	The Journal of Library History
JMH	The Journal of Modern History
JMSH	The Journal of Mississippi History
JMSI	The Journal of the Military Service Institution
JNE	The Journal of Negro Education
JNH	The Journal of Negro History
JOUQ	The Journalism Quarterly
JP	The Journal of Politics
JPMS	The Journal of Political and Military Sociology
JRA	The Journal of the Royal Artillery
JRAMC	The Journal of the Royal Army Medical Corps
JRUSI	The Journal of the Royal United Service Institution
JSAH	The Journal of the Society of Architectural Historians
JSAHR	The Journal of the Society for Army Historical Research
JSEAS	The Journal of Southeast Asian Studies

JSOCH	The Journal of Social History
JSH	The Journal of Southern History
JSS	The Journal of the Siam Society
JUSCA	The Journal of the United States Cavalry (also titled the Cavalry Journal and the Armored Cavalry Journal, now Armor, ARMOR)
JUSIA	The Journal of the United States Infantry Association (also titled the Infantry Journal, IJ, along with the Field Artillery Journal, FARJ, became the United States Army Combat Forces Journal, CFJ)
JUSII	The Journal of the United Service Institution of India
JWEST	The Journal of the West
JWH	The Journal of World History (Cahiers d'Histoire Mondiale)
KANHQ	The Kansas Historical Quarterly
LABH	Labor History
LARR	Latin American Research Review
LBIYA	The Leo Baeck Institute Year Book
LENCK	Leatherneck
LINCH	The Lincoln Herald
LUR	The Laurentian University Review
McM	McClure's Magazine
MA	Military Affairs (formerly the Journal of the American Military History Foundation and the Journal of the American Military Institute)
MAM	The Mariners' Mirror
MAN	Man
MARM	Marines Magazine
MAS	Modern Asian Studies
MCG	The Marine Corps Gazette
MC&H	The Military Collector and Historian
ME	The Military Engineer
MES	Middle Eastern Studies
METM	The Metropolitan Magazine
MH	The Magazine of History
MH&E	The Military Historian and Economist
MHJ	The Military History Journal (South Africa)
MHM	The Maryland Historical Magazine
MHT&SW	The Military History of Texas and the Southwest
MICH	Michigan History
MID-A	Mid-America
MIL	Militaria (South Africa)
MK	Mankind: The Magazine of Popular History
MLR	The Military Law Review
MM	MacMillan's Magazine
MMED	Military Medicine
MM&I	Marines Magazine and Indians
MMWH	Montana; The Magazine of Western History (formerly the Montana Magazine of History)
MN	Monuments Nipponica
MNH	Minnesota History
MNHB	The Minnesota History Bulletin
MOHR	The Missouri Historical Review

MR	Military Review
MSJC	The Medical Service Journal of Canada
MSUR	The Military Surgeon
MVHR	The Mississippi Valley Historical Review (now the Journal of American History)
MWJ	The Midwest Journal
NAR	The North American Review
NATOL	The NATO Letter
NC	The Nineteenth Century (later the Nineteenth Century and After)
NCHR	The North Carolina Historical Review
NDH	North Dakota History (formerly the North Dakota Historical Quarterly)
NE	The New Englander
NEBH	Nebraska History
NEQ	The New England Quarterly
NHSJ	The Nevada Historical Society Journal
NMHR	The New Mexico Historical Review
NWCR	The Naval War College Review
NYH	New York History
NYHSQ	The New York Historical Society Quarterly
NZJH	The New Zealand Journal of History
OH	Ontario History
OHQ	The Oregon Historical Quarterly
OM	The Overland Monthly
P	Parameters: The Journal of the Army War College
P&P	Past and Present; A Journal of Historical Studies
PACNW	The Pacific Northwest Quarterly
PAFJ	The Pan-African Journal
PAL	Palimpsest
PAPS	Proceedings of the Academy of Political Science
PH	Pennsylvania History
PHR	The Pacific Historical Review
PMHB	The Pennsylvania Magazine of History and Biography
POQ	The Public Opinion Quarterly
PPHR	The Panhandle-Plains Historical Review
PROL	Prologue: The Journal of the National Archives
PSQ	The Political Science Quarterly
QQ	The Queen's Quarterly
QMR	The Quartermaster Review
RIHM	The Revue Internationale d'Histoire Militaire
RIPEH	The Review of Iranian Political Economy and History
RMSSJ	The Rocky Mountain Social Science Journal
RO	The Reserve Officer
RP	The Review of Politics
RPH	Romania: Pages of History
RR	The Russian Review
RUSM	Russell's Magazine
RW	Railroad World
S	Scribner's Magazine
S&S	Science and Society
SAQ	The South Atlantic Quarterly
SDH	South Dakota History

SEER	The Slavonic and East European Review
SH	Saskatchewan History
SHSP	The Southern Historical Society Papers
SLM	The Southern Literary Messenger
SLR	The Slavic Review
SLS	Sierra Leone Studies
SMJH	The Smithsonian Journal of History
SS	Social Science
SWSSQ	The Southwestern Social Science Quarterly
T&C	Technology and Culture
THQ	The Tennessee Historical Quarterly
TQH&GM	Tyler's Quarterly Historical and Geneaology Magazine
TRHS	Transactions of the Royal Historical Society
UHQ	The Utah Historical Quarterly
UHR	The Utah Humanities Review
USAS	U.S. Air Services
US	United Service; A Quarterly Review of Military and Naval Affairs
USM	United Service Magazine (also United Service Journal)
USNIP	United States Naval Institute Proceedings
VCAV	The Virginia Cavalcade
VHM	Victorian Historical Magazine (Australia)
VMHB	The Virginia Magazine of History and Biography
VS	Victorian Studies
VTH	Vermont History
WAHQ	The Washington Historical Quarterly
WECHH	The Westchester Historian
WEHUR	The Western Humanities Review
WHQ	The Western Historical Quarterly
WMH	The Wisconsin Magazine of History
WPHM	The Western Pennsylvania Historical Magazine
WSJHQ	The Western States Jewish Historical Quarterly
YLR	The Yale Law Review
YR	The Yale Review

ABBREVIATIONS

Brig.	Brigadier
Capt.	Captain
Col.	Colonel
compl.	compiler
compls.	compilers
ed.	editor
eds.	editors
et.al.	and others
Gen.	General
Lt.	Lieutenant
Maj.	Major
n.d.	no date given
n.p.	no place given
no.	Number
pgs.	pages
pseudo.	pseudonym
pts.	parts
trans.	translator
vols.	volumes

PART I: GENERAL MILITARY HISTORY

This part of the bibliography includes, mainly, citations for publications relating to general military subjects. General histories, bibliographies, encyclopedias, dictionaries, atlases, manuals, guides and indexes
pertaining to more than one continent and/or conflict are referenced here.
If citations to more specific subjects are required, turn to the following
two parts of the bibliography. However, there are two sections in this part
that are fairly specific: "The Background of Nineteenth Century Warfare"
and "Events Leading Up to World War I." Also there is a large section
entitled "Miscellaneous Studies" containing references to publications that
could not be included under other subject headings and did not warrant a
separate one. Almost any topic given below requires additional research.
Fortunately, some recent research has been done on formerly neglected subjects
such as guerilla-primitive warfare and socio-psychological studies of warfare
and the military. Some subjects remain neglected that are exemplified by
the fact that there has not been a good atlas published which adequately
covers Nineteenth Century warfare in general.

BACKGROUND OF NINETEENTH CENTURY WARFARE

The few references given here to publications on pre-Nineteenth Century
(Waterloo and before) warfare and military developments are meant to be only
a meager beginning for anyone interested. Quite naturally, Napoleon and his
concepts on warfare exerted a great influence throughout the Nineteenth
Century. Probably the best one-volume study of Napoleon and his methods is
David Chandler's The Campaigns of Napoleon, cited below.

1. Betts, Raymond F., ed. The Scramble for Africa; Causes and
    Dimensions of Empire. (Boston, 1966).

2. *Chandler, David G. The Campaigns of Napoleon. (New York, 1966).

3. Esposito, Vincent J. and John Robert Elting. A Military History
    and Atlas of the Napoleonic Wars. (New York, 1964).

4. Gardner, Brian. The African Dream: From Cape to Cairo, the Epic
    Adventure of the Conquest of Africa. (New York, 1970).

5. Glover, Richard. Peninsular Preparations: The Reform of the
    British Army, 1795-1809. (New York, 1963).

6. Jacobs, James R. The Beginning of the U.S. Army, 1783-1812.
    (Princeton, 1947).

7. Kierman, Frank A., Jr. and John K. Fairbanks, eds. Chinese Ways
    in Warfare. (Cambridge, Massachusetts, 1974).

8. *Lynch, John. The Spanish-American Revolutions, 1808-1826.
    (New York, 1973).

9. Madariago, Salvador de. The Rise of the Spanish American Empire.
    (2 vols.,New York, 1947).

10. Mahon, John K. "Anglo-American Methods of Indian Warfare, 1676-1794."
    MVHR 45 (September 1958), 254-275.

11. *Mahon, John K. The War of 1812. (Gainesville, Florida, 1972).

12. Morton, Louis. "The End of Formalized Warfare." AH 6 (August 1955),
    12- 9 and 95.

13. Nutting, Anthony. Scramble for Africa; The Great Trek to the Boer
    War. (New York, 1971).

14. Paret, Peter. "Colonial Experience and European Military Reform
    at the End of the Eighteenth Century." BIHR 37 (May 1964), 47-59.

15. Paret, Peter. Yorck and the Era of Prussian Reform, 1807-1815.
    (Princeton, 1966).

16. Quimby, Robert S. The Background of Napoleonic Warfare: The Theory
    of Military Tactics in Eighteenth Century France. (New York, 1957).

17. Richardson, Hubert N.B. A Dictionary of Napoleon and His Times.
    (New York, 1920).

18. Rothenberg, Gunther E. The Art of Warfare in the Age of Napoleon.
    (Bloomington, Indiana, 1978).

19. Shanahan, William O. Prussian Military Reforms, 1783-1813.
    (New York, 1945).

20. Smith, Robert S. Warfare and Diplomacy in Pre-Colonial West Africa.
    (New York, 1977).

21. Spaulding, Oliver L., Hoffman Nickerson, and John W. Wright.
    Warfare: A Study of Military Methods from the Earliest Times.
    (Washington, D.C., 1957).

22. Strage, Mark. Cape to Cairo: Rape of a Continent. (New York, 1973).

23. Uzoigive, G.N. "Pre-Colonial Military Studies in Africa." JAFS 13
    (September 1975), 469-81.

24. *Albion, Robert G. Introduction to Military History. (New York, 1929).

25. Chandler, David. The Art of Warfare on Land. (New York, 1974).

26. Falls, Cyril. The Art of War from the Age of Napoleon to the Present Day. (New York, 1961).

27. *Falls, Cyril. A Hundred Years of War. (London, 1953).

28. Fuller, John F.C. Conduct of War, 1789-1961; A Study of the Impact of the French, Industrial, and Russian Revolutions on War and Its Conduct. (London, 1961).

29. Fuller, John F.C. A Military History of the Western World. (3 vols., New York, 1954-56.)

30. Fuller, John F.C. War and Western Civilization, 1832-1932; A Study of War as a Political Instrument and the Expression of Mass Democracy. (London, 1932).

31. Gibbs, Norman H. "Armed Forces and the Art of War. A. Armies." in C.W. Crowley, ed. War and Peace in an Age of Upheaval, 1793-1830. Volume 9 of the New Cambridge Modern History. (New York, 1965), 60-76.

32. Graham, James J. Elementary History of the Progress of the Art of War. (London, 1858).

33. Kendall, Paul Murray. The Story of Land Warfare. (London, 1957).

34. Leckie, Robert. Warfare; A Concise, Provocative Survey of Armed Conflict. (New York, 1970).

35. Macksey, Kenneth. The Guiness History of Land Warfare. (Enfield, Middlesex, England, 1973).

36. Magrath, Richard N. An Historical Sketch of the Progress of the Art of War. (Dublin, 1838).

37. Maguire, Thomas M. A Summary of Modern Military History with Comments on the Leading Operations. (London, 1887).

38. Maguire, Thomas M. Summary of Modern Military History. (London, 1900).

39. Mitchell, William A. Outlines of the World's Military History. (Washington, D.C., 1931).

40. *Montgomery, Bernard L. A History of Warfare. (London, 1968).

41. *Montross, Lynn. War Through the Ages. (Revised and Enlarged Edition, New York, 1960).

42. Nickerson, Hoffman. The Armed Horde, 1793-1939: A Study of the Rise, Survival and Decline of the Mass Army. (New York, 1940).

43. Perris, George H. A Short History of War and Peace. (New York, 1911).

44. *Preston, Richard A. and Sydney F. Wise. Men in Arms: A History of Warfare and Its Interrelationships with Western Society. (Second Revised Edition, New York, 1970).

45. *Ropp, Theodore. War in the Modern World. (Revised Edition, New York, 1962).

46. Turner, Gordon B. A History of Military Affairs Since the Eighteenth Century. (New York, 1956).

47. Zook, David H., Jr. and Robin Higham. A Short History of Warfare. (New York, 1966).

GENERAL HISTORIES OF NINETEENTH CENTURY WARFARE, WAR AND THE ART OF WAR

48. Bond, Brian. "War and Peace: Mechanized Warfare and the Growth of Pacifism." in Asa Briggs, ed., The Nineteenth Century: The Contradictions of Progress. (New York, 1970), 186-214.

49. Browning, Oscar. Wars of the Century and the Development of Military Science. (Philadelphia, 1901).

50. Greene, Francis V. "Recent Changes in the Art of War." Proceedings of the New York State Historical Association. Vol. 15 (1916), 156-75.

51. Greene, Francis V. "The Important Improvements in the Art of War During the Past Twenty Years and Their Probable Effect on Future Military Operations." JMSI 4, No. 13 (1883), 1-54.

52. Howard, Michael. "The Armed Forces." in F.H. Hinsley, ed., Material Progress and Worldwide Problems, 1870-1898. Volume 11 of the New Cambridge Modern History. (New York, 1962), 204-42.

53. Lazelle, Henry M. "Important Improvements in the Art of War During the Past Twenty Years and Their Probable Effect on Future Military Operations." JMSI 3, No. 11 (1882), 307-373.

54. Liddell Hart, Basil H. "Armed Forces and the Art of War: Armies." in J.P.T. Bury, ed., The Zenith of European Power, 1830-70. Volume 10 of the New Cambridge Modern History. (New York, 1960), 302-30.

55. *McElwee, William. The Art of War: Waterloo to Mons. (Bloomington, Indiana, 1974).

56. Merritt, Wesley. "Important Improvements in the Art of War in the Last Twenty Years and Their Probable Effect on Future Military Operations." JMSI 4, No. 14 (1883), 172-89.

57. "Recent Changes in the Art of War." ER 123 (January 1866), 95-130.

58. Wisser, J.P. "A Decenniums of Military Progress." JMSI 18 (March 1896), 235-54.

AERONAUTICS

59. *Brockett, Paul. Bibliography of Aeronautics. (Washington, D.C., 1910).

60. Collier, Basil. A History of Airpower. (New York, 1974).

61. Dickerman, Joseph. Balloons in War: A Lecture Delivered Before the Class of Officers at the U.S. Infantry and Cavalry School, Fort Leavenworth, Kansas, March 27, 1894. (Fort Leavenworth, Kansas, 1896).

62. *Dickson, Katherine M., compl. History of Aeronautics and Astronautics: A Preliminary Bibliography. (Washington, D.C., 1967).

63. Earle, Edward M. "The Influence of Air Power Upon History." YR 35 (June 1946), 577-93.

64. Glassford, William A. "Military Aeronautics." JMSI 18 (May 1898), 561-76.

65. Greely, Adolphus W. "Balloons in War." HNMM 101 (June 1900), 33-56.

66. Hargreaves, Reginald. "Conflict Goes Aloft." AQ 83 (January 1962), 205-13.

67. *Higham, Robin. <u>Air Power: A Concise History</u>. (New York, 1972).

68. Infield, Glenn B. <u>Unarmed and Unafraid: The First Complete History of Men, Missions, Training and Techniques of Aerial Reconnaissance</u>. (New York, 1970).

69. Payne, L.G.S. <u>Air Dates</u>. (London, 1957).

70. Robertson, Bruce. <u>Aircraft Camoflage and Markings, 1907-1954</u>. (Letchworth, England, 1961).

71. Taylor, John W.R., compl. <u>Combat Aircraft of the World; From 1909 to the Present</u>. (New York, 1969).

72. Taylor, John W.R. <u>A History of Aerial Warfare from Early Reconnaissance Balloons to the Lethal Weaponry of the Nuclear Age</u>. (New York, 1974).

73. Whitehouse, Arthur G.J. <u>The Military Airplane: Its History and Development</u>. (Garden City, New York, 1971).

74. Wragg, David W. <u>Dictionary of Aviation</u>. (New York, 1974).

See also: Part I: 668; Addendum: 19, 67, 116, 130.

ARTILLERY

75. Batchelor, John and Ian Hogg. <u>Artillery</u>. (New York, 1972).

76. Bishop, Harry G. <u>Field Artillery, the King of Battles</u>. (Boston, 1935).

77. Comparato, Frank E. <u>Age of Great Guns: Cannon Kings and Cannoneers Who Forged the Firepower of Artillery</u>. (Harrisburg, Pennsylvania, 1965).

78. Downey, Fairfax. <u>Cannonade; Great Artillery Actions of History, the Famous Cannons and the Master Gunners</u>. (Garden City, New York, 1966).

79. Ferry, J.P., Col. "The Rebirth of the Military Rocket and its Development as an Artillery Weapon, 1900-1945." <u>Royal Artillery Historical Society Proceedings</u> 4 (January 1976), 47-65.

80. <u>Guns: An Illustrated History of Artillery</u> by Erich Egg and others. Edited by Joseph Jobe. (Greenwich, Connecticut, 1971).

6

81. Hime, Henry W.L. The Origin of Artillery. (New York, 1915).

82. Hogg, Ian V. A History of Artillery. (London, 1974).

83. *Hogg, Oliver F.G. Artillery; Its Origin, Heyday, and Decline. (Hamden, Connecticut, 1970).

84. Hohenlohe-Ingelfingen, Karl A.E. Friedrich. Letters on Artillery. Translated by Maj. N.L. Walford. (London, 1888).

85. Johnson, Curt. Artillery. (London, 1975).

86. Kosar, Franz. A Pocket History of Artillery: Light Field Guns. (London, 1974).

87. Lallemand, Henry. A Treatise on Artillery. (New York, 1820).

88. Lemly, Henry R. Essay on Changes Wrought in Artillery in 19th Century and Their Effect Upon the Attack and Defense of Fortified Places. (Fort Monroe, Virginia, 1886).

89. Lloyd, Edward W. and A.G. Haddock. Artillery: Progress and Present Position. (New York, 1893).

90. MacDougall, Patrick R. Modern Warfare as Influenced by Modern Artillery. (London, 1864).

91. Manucy, Albert. Artillery Through the Ages: A Short Illustrated History of Cannon, Emphasizing Types Used in America. (Washington, D.C., 1949).

92. May, Edward S. Achievements of Field Artillery. (Woolwich, England, 1893).

93. May, Edward S. Field Artillery With the Other Arms: Its Employment, Illustrated from Military History, and its Re-armament with Quick-firing Guns Discussed. (London, 1898).

94. May, Edward S. Guns and Cavalry: Their Performances in the Past and Their Prospects in the Future. (London, 1896).

95. *Miller, Lester L., Jr. The Development of Artillery as Reflected in Writings, a Period Listing. (Fort Sill, Oklahoma, 1976).

96. *Miller, Lester L., Jr. An Historical Listing of Artillery Indicated by Size: Guns and Howitzers: A Bibliography of Periodical Articles. (Fort Sill, Oklahoma, 1975).

97. *Miller, Lester L., Jr. An Historical Listing of Artillery Indicated by Size: Mortar: a Bibliography. (Fort Sill, Oklahoma, 1975).

98. Miller, Lester L., Jr. An Historical Listing Covering Schematic Developments in Artillery. (Fort Sill, Oklahoma, 1974).

99. Owen, Charles H. Elementary Lectures on Artillery, Prepared for the Use of the Gentleman Cadets of the Royal Military Academy. (3rd. Edition, Woolwich, England, 1861).

100. Porrino, Michael F. "Development of Pack Artillery and its Significance in Modern Warfare." MA 20 (Spring 1956), 28-34.

101. Rifled Field Pieces. A Short Compilation of What is Known of the New Field Artillery of Europe, with Some Account of Our Own. (Washington, D.C., 1862).

102. Rogers, Hugh C.B. Artillery Through the Ages. (London, 1971).

103. Schenck, Alexander D. Comparisons of the Armaments of European Nations, Describing Their Systems of Artillery. (Fort Monroe, Virginia, 1886).

104. Stevens, Phillip H. Artillery Through the Ages. (New York, 1965).

105. Tennent, James Emerson. The Story of the Guns. (London, 1864).

106. United States, Ordnance Department. Railway Artillery. A Report on the Characteristics, Scope of Utility, Etc., of Railway Artillery. by Lt. Col. H.W. Miller. (2 vols., Washington, D.C., 1921-22).

107. Wilson, A.W. The Story of the Gun. (Woolwich, England, 1944).

     See also: Part I: Weapons, and 155; Addendum: 115.

ATLASES

108. Banks, Arthur. A World Atlas of Military History, 1861-1945. (London, 1978).

109. Williams, John. Atlas of Weapons and War. (New York, 1976).

110. Atteridge, Andrew H. Famous Land Fights: A Popular Sketch of the History of Land Warfare. (Boston, 1914).

111. Atteridge, Andrew H. Famous Modern Battles. (New York, 1911).

112. Atteridge, Andrew H. The Wars of the Nineties: A History of the Warfare of the Last Ten Years of the 19th Century. (New York, 1899).

113. Barker, A.J. Famous Military Battles. (London, 1974).

114. Battles of the Nineteenth Century. Described by Archibald Forbes, George A. Henty, Arthur Griffiths and other well-known writers. (7 vols., New York, 190(?)).

115. Belfield, Eversley. Defy and Endure; Great Sieges of Modern History. (New York, 1967).

116. Borthwick, John D. The Battles of the World or Cyclopedia of Battles, Sieges and Important Military Events. (Montreal, 1886).

117. *Carnegie Endowment for International Peace, Library. Wars of the World: List of Wars, Quotations on Comparative War and Peace Years, and References to Books on the History of War. Compiled by Mary Alice Matthews. (Washington, D.C., 1939).

118. Colin, Jean Lambert Alphonse. The Great Battles of History. Translated from French by Henry Spenser Wilkinson. (London, 1915).

119. Crane, Stephen. Great Battles of the World. (Philadelphia, 1901).

120. *Eggenberger, David. A Dictionary of Battles. (New York, 1967).

121. Falls, Cyril, ed. Great Military Battles. (London, 1964).

122. Fuller, John F.C. Decisive Battles: Their Influence Upon History and Civilization. (New York, 1940).

123. Garrett, Richard. Clash of Arms; the World's Great Land Battles. (New York, 1976).

124. Harbottle, Thomas B. Dictionary of Battles from the Earliest Date to the Present Time. (London, 1904).

125. Hargreaves, Reginald. The Enemy at the Gate; A Book of Famous Sieges, Their Cause, Their Progress, and Their Consequences. (London, 1945).

126. Holmes, Richard. Epic Land Battles. (Secaucus, New Jersey, 1976).

127. Knox, Thomas W. Decisive Battles Since Waterloo: The Most
Important Military Events from 1815 to 1887. (New York, 1887).

128. Maurice, John F., compl. Hostilities Without Declaration of War,
An Historical Abstract of the Cases in Which Hostilities Have
Occurred Between Civilized Powers Prior to Declaration or Warning,
from 1700 to 1870. (London, 1883).

129. Melegari, Vezio. The Great Military Sieges. (New York, 1972).

130. Melegari, Vezio. Great Sieges. (New York, 1970).

131. Robinson, Maj. Gen. Charles W., and others. Wars of the 19th
Century. (London, 1914).

132. Selby, John M. Stories of Famous Sieges. (London, 1967).

133. Shaw, Roger. One Hundred and Seventy-five Battles by Land, Sea
and Air, from Marathon to the Maine and After. Edited by Samuel
C. Vestel. (Harrisburg, Pennsylvania, 1937).

134. *Sutton, Antony C. Wars and Revolutions: A Comprehensive List of
Conflicts, Including Fatalities, Part One: 1820 to 1900. (Stanford,
California, 1971).

135. Welsh, Charles, ed. Famous Battles of the Nineteenth Century.
(4 vols., New York, 1903).

136. Whitton, Frederick E. The Decisive Battles of Modern Times.
(London, 1923).

137. Wilberforce, Archibald, ed. The Great Battles of All Nations from
Marathon to the Surrender of Cronje in South Africa, 490 B.C. to
the Present Day. (2 vols., New York, 1900-01).

138. *Young, Peter. A Dictionary of Battles, 1816-1976. (London, 1977).

See also: Addendum: 32.

BIBLIOGRAPHIES

139. Commission Internationale D'Histoire Militaire. Bulletin de
Bibliographie: Selection, 1974-1976. (English and French
Annotations), (Lausanne, Switzerland, 1978).

140. Holabird, S.B. "Subjects for a Military Library." Ordnance Note No. 299, June 12, 1883, in United States, Ordnance Department, Ordnance Notes. (12 vols., Washington, D.C., 1873-84).

141. Lanza, Conrad H. List of Books on Military History and Related Subjects. (Fort Leavenworth, 1923).

142. Maggs Brothers, London. Four Centuries of Military Books. Catalogue No. 915. (London, 1969).

143. Mahon, John K. "Doctoral Dissertations on Military History." MA 17 (Fall 1953), No. 3, 140-2.

144. "Military Literature" in John Frederick Maurice, War. (London, 1891), 93-123.

145. Millett, Allan R. and Benjamin F. Cooling, III. Doctoral Dissertations in Military Affairs; A Bibliography. (Manhattan, Kansas, 1972).

146. Millis, Walter. Military History. (Washington, D.C., 1961).

147. Newcombe, Hanna, compl. Bibliography on War and Peace. (Dundas, Ontario, 1963).

148. Paret, Peter. "The History of War." D 100 (Spring 1971), 376-96.

149. Ropp, Theodore. "Military Historical Scholarship Since 1937." MA 41 (April 1977), 68-74.

150. "A Selected List of Books of which it May be Useful to Know the Correct Titles." Appendix in John Frederick Maurice, War. (London, 1891), 125-44.

151. Spaulding, Thomas and Louis C. Karpinski. Early Military Books in the University of Michigan Libraries. (Ann Arbor, Michigan, 1941).

152. United States, Military Academy, West Point, Library. Bibliography of Military History. Compiled by Alan C. Aimone. (Third Edition, West Point, New York, 1978).

153. United States, U.S. Army Military History Institute. Some Suggested Readings for New Dimensions in Military History. Volume 5 in Essays in Some Dimensions of Military History. Compiled by Benjamin Franklin Cooling. (Carlisle Barracks, Pennsylvania, 1977).

See also: Part I: 265.

BIOGRAPHY

154. Berger, Martin Edgar. "War, Armies, and Revolution: Friedrich Engel's Military Thought." Ph.D. Dissertation, University of Pittsburgh, 1969.

155. Borden, Morton. "Friedrich Engels on Rifled Cannon." MA 21 (Summer 1957), 75-7 and (Winter 1957), 193-8.

156. Earle, Edward M., ed. Makers of Modern Strategy; Military Thought from Machiavelli to Hitler. (Princeton, New Jersey, 1943).

157. Elting, John R. "Jomini: Disciple of Napoleon?" MA 28 (Spring 1964), 17-26.

158. Engels as Military Critic; Articles Reprinted from the Volunteer Journal and the Manchester Guardian of the 1860's. Introduction by William H. Chaloner and William O. Henderson. (Manchester, England, 1959).

159. "General Jomini." ES 7 (May 1, 1869), 565-7.

160. Howard, Michael. "Jomini and the Classical Tradition in Military Thought," in Michael Howard, ed., The Theory and Practice of War. (London, 1965), 5-20.

161. *Keegan, John and Andrew Wheatcroft. Who's Who in Military History. (New York, 1976).

162. Kitchen, Martin. "Friedrich Engel's Theory of War." MA 41 (October 1977), 119-24.

163. McClellan, George B. "Jomini." G 7 (June 1869), 874-88.

164. Paret, Peter. Clausewitz and the State. (New York, 1976).

165. Parkinson, Roger. Clausewitz: A Biography. (New York, 1970).

166. *United States, Military Academy, West Point, Library. Antoine-Henry Jomini; A Bibliographical Survey. Compiled by John I. Alger. (West Point, New York, 1978).

167. United States, Military Academy, West Point, Department of Military Art and Engineering. Jomini, Clausewitz and Schlieffen. (West Point, New York, 1951).

168. Windrow, Martin C. and Francis K. Mason. A Concise Dictionary of Military Biography: Two Hundred Years of the Most Significant Names in Land Warfare, 10th - 20th Century. (Reading, England, 1975).

THE CAUSES OF WAR

169. Bakeless, John E. The Economic Causes of Modern War; A Study of the Period, 1878-1918. (New York, 1921).

170. Bernard, Luther L. War and Its Causes. (New York, 1944).

171. *Blainey, Geoffrey. The Causes of War. (New York, 1973).

172. Carr, Albert H.Z. A Matter of Life and Death; How Wars Get Started or Prevented. (New York, 1966).

173. Richardson, Lewis F. Arms and Insecurity; A Mathematical Study of the Causes and Origins of War. Edited by Nicolas Rashevsky and Ernesto Trucco. (Pittsburgh, Pennsylvania, 1960).

174. Robbins, Lionel C. The Economic Causes of War. (London, 1939).

175. Russett, Bruce M., ed. Peace, War, and Numbers. (Beverly Hills, California, 1972).

176. Turner, Tell A. Causes of War and the New Revolution. (Boston, 1927).

See also: Addendum: 164.

CAVALRY AND ARMOR

177. Ambrus, Victor G. Horses in Battle. (New York, 1975).

178. Bernhardi, Federick A.J. von. Cavalry in War and Peace. Translated by George T.M. Bridges. (London, 1910).

179. Brereton, John M. The Horse in War. (New York, 1976).

180. Carter, William H. Horses of the World; The Development of Man's Companion in War Camp, On Farm, in the Marts of Trade, and in the Field of Sports. (Washington, D.C., 1923).

181. Childers, Erskine. War and the Arme Blanche. (London, 1910).

182. Denison, George T. A History of Cavalry from the Earliest Times, with Lesson for the Future. (Second Edition, London, 1913).

183. Denison, George T. Modern Cavalry: Its Organization, Armament and Employment in War. With an Appendix Containing Letters from General Fitzhugh Lee, Stephen D. Lee, and T.L. Rosser, of the Confederate State's Cavalry, and Col. Jenyn's System of Non-Pivot Drill in Use in the 13th Hussars. (London, 1868).

184. *Elliot, George H., compl. Cavalry Literature: A Bibliographical Record of Works on the History, Organization, Tactics, and Administration of Cavalry. (Calcutta, 1893).

185. Ellis, Christopher and Dennis Bishop. Vehicles at War. (Cranbury, New Jersey, 1977).

186. Ellis, John. Cavalry; The History of Mounted Warfare. (New York, 1978).

187. Gibley, Walter. Small Horses in Warfare. (London, 1900).

188. Great Britain, War Office, Intelligence Division. Equipment of Cavalry, by Henry M. Hozier. (London, 1865).

189. Haig, Douglas. Cavalry Studies: Strategical and Tactical. (London, 1907).

190. Halle, Armin and Carlo Demand. An Illustrated History of Fighting Vehicles. (London, 1971).

191. Hohenlohe-Ingelfingen, Karl A.E. Friedrich. Letters on Cavalry. Translated by Lt. Col. N.L. Walford. (Second Edition, London, 1889).

192. Hooper, Frederick. The Military Horse. (Cranbury, New Jersey, 1976).

193. Icks, Robert J. Tanks and Armored Vehicles, 1900-1945. Edited by Phillip Andrews. (Old Greenwich, Connecticut, 1970).

194. James, Walter H. The Role of Cavalry as Affected by Modern Arms of Precision. (Aldershot, 1894).

195. *Kutz, Charles R. War on Wheels: The Evolution of an Idea. (London, 1942).

196. Lawford, James. The Cavalry. (Indianapolis, Indiana, 1976).

197. Layriz, Otfried. Mechanical Traction in War for Road Transport, with Notes on Automobiles Generally. Translated by Robert B. Marston. (London, 1900).

198. Lumley, J.R. "Mounted Riflemen," Ordnance Note No. 169, November 2, 1881, in United States, Ordnance Department, Ordnance Notes. (12 vols., Washington, D.C., 1873-84).

199. Lunt, James. *Charge to Glory! A Garland of Cavalry Exploits*. (London, 1960).

200. Lunt, James D. "The Passing of L'Arme Blanche." *HT* 9 (January 1959), 40-.7.

201. Maude, Frederic N. *Cavalry Versus Infantry*. (Fort Leavenworth, Kansas, 1894).

202. Nolan, Louis Edward. *Cavalry: Its History and Tactics*. (London, 1853).

203. Ogorkiewicz, Richard M. *Armor: A History of Mechanized Forces*. (New York, 1960).

204. Robertson, Lt. S. "The Cavalryman and His Horse." Ordnance Note No. 297, May 7, 1883 in United States, Ordnance Department, *Ordnance Notes*. (12 vols., Washington, D.C., 1873-84).

205. Roemer, Jean. *Cavalry: Its History, Management, and Uses in War*. (New York, 1863).

206. *Taylor, William L. "The Debate Over Changing Cavalry Tactics and Weapons, 1900-1914." *MA* 28 (Winter 1964), 173-83.

207. Trench, Charles Chenevix. "Horsemanship in History." *HT* 20 (November 1970), 771-81.

208. Tylden, Geoffrey. "Lancers." *JSAHR* 13 (Summer 1945), 44-6.

209. United States, Adjutant General's Office, Military Information Division. *Target Practice and Remount Systems Abroad* by Eaton A. Edwards and Capt. Joseph S. Herron. (Washington, D.C., 1902).

210. Wagner, Arthur L., ed. *Cavalry Studies from Two Great Wars*. (Kansas City, Missouri, 1896).

211. White, Brian T. and John Wood. *Tanks and Other Armored Fighting Vehicles, 1900-1918*. (New York, 1970).

212. Wolcott, Edgar Francis. *Army Horses: Remount Systems Abroad, Improvements Suggested at Home*. (Washington, D.C., 1908).

213. Wood, Evelyn. *Achievements of Cavalry*. (London, 1897).

See also: Part 1: 96; Addendum: 89.

214. Buchan, Alastair. War in Modern Society: An Introduction. (New York, 1968).

215. *Finer, Samuel E. The Man on Horseback; the Role of the Military in Politics. (New York, 1962).

216. Harvie, Christopher T. War and Society in the 19th Century. (Bletchley, Bucks, England, 1973).

217. Howard, Michael, ed. Soldiers and Governments: Nine Studies in Civil Military Relations. (London, 1957).

218. *Huntington, Samuel P. The Soldier and the State: The Theory and Politics of Civil-Military Relations. (Cambridge, Massachusetts, 1957).

219. *Larson, Arthur D., compl. Civil-Military Relations and Militarism; A Classified Bibliography Covering the United States and Other Nations of the World. (Manhattan, Kansas, 1971).

220. Military Historic Symposium, 4th United States Air Force Academy, 1970, Soldiers and Statesmen: The Proceedings of the 4th Military History Symposium. Edited by Monte D. Wright and Lawrence J. Paszek. (Washington, D.C., 1973).

221. Military History Symposium, 5th, United States Air Force Academy, 1972. The Military and Society: The Proceedings of the Fifth Military History Symposium. Edited by David MacIssac. (Washington, D.C., 1975).

222. *Perlmutter, Amos. The Military and Politics in Modern Times: On Professionals, Praetorians, and Revolutionary Soldiers. (New Haven, Connecticut: Yale, 1977).

223. Vieth von Glossenau, Arnold F. (Ludwig Renn, pseudo). Warfare: the Relation of War to Society. Translated by Edward Fitzgerald. (New York, 1939).

224. War and Society: A Yearbook of Military History. Volume 1. Edited by Brian Bond and Ian Roy. (London, 1975).

225. War and Society: A Yearbook of Military History. Volume 2. Edited by Brain Bond and Ian Roy. (New York, 1977).

COMBINED SERVICES

226. Aston, George G. Sea, Land, and Air Strategy: A Comparison.
(London, 1914).

227. Callwell, Charles E. The Effect of Maritime Command on Land
Campaigns Since Waterloo. (London, 1897).

228. *Creswell, John. Generals and Admirals: The Story of Amphibious
Command. (London, 1952).

229. *Vagts, Alfred. Landing Operations: Strategy, Psychology, Tactics,
Politics, From Antiquity to 1945. (Harrisburg, Pennsylvania, 1946).

See also: Addendum: 5.

COMMAND AND COMMANDERS

230. *Blumenson, Martin and James L. Stokesbury. Masters of the Art of
Command. (Boston, 1975).

231. Fair, Charles. From the Jaws of Victory: A History of the Character,
Causes and Consequences of Military Stupidity from Crassus to
Johnston and Westmoreland. (New York, 1971).

232. Laffin, John. Links of Leadership: Thirty Centuries of Military
Command. (New York, 1970).

233. Military History Symposium, 2nd, United States Air Force Academy, 1968.
Command and Commanders in Modern Warfare: Proceedings of the Second
Military History Symposium. Edited by William Gefen. (Colorado Springs,
Colorado, 1969; Second Edition, Enlarged, Colorado Springs, Colorado, 1972).

234. Rundle, Wilfred C. The Baton, and Historical Study of the Marshalate.
(London, 1950).

235. Showalter, Dennis E. "Commander and Leader: Army Officer as Merito-
crat." MR 56 (November 1976), 80-89.

235A. Tuchman, Barbara W. "Generalship." P 2, No.2 (1972), 2-11.

236. Vagts, Alfred. "Generals--Old or Young." JP 4 (August 1942),
396-406.

See also: Part 1: 550; Addendum: 59.

237. The Armies of Today; A Description of the Armies of the Leading Nations at the Present Time. (New York, 1893).

238. Brackenbury, Charles B. Foreign Armies and Home Reserves. (London, 1871).

239. Jerram, Charles S. The Armies of the World. (London, 1899).

240. Kempster, Walter. "The Armies of Other Countries," in The Military Order of the Loyal Legion of the United States, Wisconsin Commandery, War Papers, Volume 2 (Milwaukee, Wisconsin, 1896), 399-429.

241. Koppen, Fedor von. The Armies of Europe Illustrated. Translated by Edward Gleichen. (London, 1890).

242. Low, T.A. (Marine Corps). "Notes of a Visit to Some Foreign Armies." JMSI 39 (November-December 1906), 388-97.

243. United States, Adjutant General's Office, Military Information Division. Colonial Army Systems of the Netherlands, Great Britain, France, Germany, Portugal, Italy, and Belgium. (Washington, D.C., 1901).

244. United States, Adjutant General's Office, Military Information Division. Notes and Statistics of Organization, Armament, and Military Progress in American and European Armies. (Washington, D.C., 1896).

245. United States, Adjutant General's Office, Military Information Division. Staffs of Various Armies. (Washington, D.C., 1899).

246. United States, General Staff, War College Division. Strength and Organization of the Armies of France, Germany, Austria, Russia, England, Italy, Mexico and Japan. (Washington, D.C., 1911).

247. United States, General Staff, War Plans Division. Strength and Organization of the Armies of France, Germany, Austria, Russia, England, Italy, Mexico and Japan. (Showing Conditions in July, 1914). (Washington, D.C. 1916).

248. Upton, Emory. The Armies of Asia and Europe. (New York, 1878).

249. Woodward, D. Armies of the World, 1854-1914. (London, 1978).

250. Wraxall, Lascelles. The Armies of the Great Powers. (London, 1859).

251. Zogbaum, Rufus F. Horse, Foot and Dragoons; Sketches of Army Life at Home and Abroad. (New York, 1888).

252. *Anderson, Martin, ed. Conscription: A Select and Annotated Bibliography. Compiled by Martin Anderson and Valerie Bloom. (Stanford, California, 1976).

253. Barnett, Correlli. "On the Raising of Armies." H 10 (Summer 1968), 40-47.

254. Cutler, Frederick M. "The History of Military Conscription with Special Reference to (the) United States." Ph.D. dissertation, Clark University. (Worcester, Massachusetts, 1922).

255. *Doty, Hiram, compl. Bibliography of Conscientious Objection to War: A Selected List of 173 Titles. (Philadelphia, 1954).

256. Hamilton, Ian. Compulsory Service: A Study of the Question in the Light of Experience. (London, 1910).

257. Maude, Frederic N. Voluntary Versus Compulsory Service. (London, 1897).

258. Paret, Peter. "Nationalism and the Sense of Military Obligation." MA 34 (February 1970), 2-6.

259. Rankin, Maj. Robert H. "A History of the Selective Service." USNIP 77 (October 1951), 1072-1081.

260. *Slonaker, John, compl. The Volunteer Army (Bibliography). (Carlisle Barracks, Pennsylvania, 1972).

261. Sullivan, A.E. "Conscription: An Historical Survey." AQ 101 (July 1971), 465-474.

262. United States, Selective Service System. Backgrounds of Selective Service: A Historical Review of the Principle of Citizen Compulsion in the Raising of Armies. Volume 1 (Washington, D.C., 1947).

263. United States, Selective Service System. Outline of Historical Background of Selective Service from Biblical Days to January 1, 1952. Prepared by Irving W. Hart. (Revised Edition, Washington, D.C., 1952).

DICTIONARIES

264. Beadnell, Charles M., compl. An Encyclopedic Dictionary of Science and War. (London, 1943).

265. *Craig, Hardin, Jr., compl. A Bibliography of Encyclopedias and Dictionaries Dealing with Military, Naval and Maritime Affairs, 1577-1971. (4th Edition, Houston, Texas, 1971).

266. Hayward, P.H., compl. Jane's Dictionary of Military Terms. (New York, 1976).

267. James, Charles, compl. A New and Enlarged Military Dictionary in French and English: In Which are Explained the Principal Terms, with Appropriate Illustrations of all the Sciences that are, More or Less, Necessary for an Officer and Engineer. (Third Edition, 2 vols., London, 1810).

268. Knollys, William W., compl. A Handy Dictionary of Military Terms. (London, 1873).

269. Luttwak, Edward, compl. Dictionary of Modern War. (New York, 1971).

270. Quick, John, compl. Dictionary of Weapons and Military Terms. (New York, 1973).

271. Scott, Henry L., compl. Military Dictionary: Comprising Technical Definitions; Information on Raising and Keeping Troops; Actual Service, Including Makeshifts and Improved Material; and Law, Government, Regulation, and Administration relating to Land Forces. (New York, 1861).

272. Voyle, George E., compl. A Military Dictionary Comprising Terms, Scientific and Otherwise, Connected with the Science of War. (Third Edition, London, 1876).

273. Wilhelm, Thomas, compl. A Military Dictionary and Gazetteer. (Revised Edition, Philadelphia, Pennsylvania, 1881).

274. Wisser, John P. and H.C. Gauss, compls. A Military and Naval Dictionary. (New York, 1905).

275. *Wrinkle, Barbara, compl. Language Dictionaries with an Emphasis on Military Dictionaries (Bibliography). (Carlisle Barracks, Pennsylvania, 1971).

DISARMAMENT

276. Dupuy, Trevor N. and Gay Hammerman, ed. Documentary History of Arms Control and Disarmament. (New York, 1973).

277. Tate, Merze. The Disarmament Illusion: The Movement for a Limitation of Armaments to 1907. (New York, 1942).

ECONOMICS AND WAR

278. Angell, Norman. The Great Illusion: A Study of the Relation of Military Power in Nations to Their Economic and Social Advantage. (London, 1910).

279. Lewinsohn, Richard. The Profits of War Through the Ages. Translated by Geoffrey Sainsbury. (New York, 1936).

280. Silberner, Edmund. The Problem of War in Nineteenth Century Economic Thought. Translated by Alexander H. Krappe. (Princeton, 1946).

281. Staley, Eugene. War and the Private Investor; A Study in the Relations of International Politics and International Private Investment. (Chicago, 1935).

See also: Part I: 169, 174.

ENCYCLOPEDIAS

282. Bidwell, Sheford, et. al., The Encyclopedia of Land Warfare in the 20th Century. (New York, 1977).

283. *Dupuy, Richard Ernest and Trevor N. Dupuy. Encyclopedia of Military History from 3500 B.C. to the Present. (Revised Edition, New York, 1977).

284. Farrow, Edward S. Farrow's Military Encyclopedia: A Dictionary of Military Knowledge; Illustrated with Maps and About Three Thousand Wood Engravings. (3 vols., New York, 1895).

285. Great Britain, Army Corps of Royal Engineers. Aide-Memoire to the Military Sciences. (3 vols., London, 1846-52).

286. Parkinson, Roger. Encyclopedia of Modern War. (London, 1977).

287. Siddons, Joachim H. (J.H. Stocqueler, pseudo.). The Military Encyclopedia, A Technical, Biographical and Historical Dictionary Referring Exclusively to the Military Sciences, the Memoirs of Distinguished Soldiers, and the Narratives of Remarkable Battles. (London, 1853).

See also: Part 1: 265.

EQUIPAGE AND EQUIPMENT

288. Brunker, Howard M.E. Notes on Organization and Equipment. (London, 1896).

289. Dean, Bashford. Helmets and Body Armor in Modern Warfare. (New Haven, Connecticut, 1920).

290. Lavisse, Emile Charles. Comparative Studies of the Field Equipment of the Foot Soldier of the French and Foreign Armies. Translated by Edward P. Lawton. (Washington, D.C., 1906).

290A. Munson, Edward L. The Soldier's Foot and the Military Shoe... (Fort Leavenworth, Kansas, 1912).

291. Reade, Philip Hildreth. History of the Military Canteen. (Chicago, Illinois, 1901).

292. Renbourn, E.T. "The Knapsack and Pack." MR 34 (July 1954), 87-97.

293. Rhodes, Godfrey. _Tents and Tent-Life, from the Earliest Ages to the Present Time to which is Added the Practice of Encamping an Army in Ancient and Modern Times_. (London, 1858).

294. Salquin, S. A. _The Military Shoe_. (Washington, D.C., 1883).

295. Wise, Terrence. _Military Flags of the World, 1618-1900_. (New York, 1978).

See also: Part 1, Uniforms

FORTIFICATION

296. Brackenbury, Charles B. _Field Works, Their Technical Construction and Tactical Application_. (London, 1888).

297. Brialmont, Alexis Henri. _Hasty Entrenchments_. Translated by Charles A. Empson. (London, 1872).

298. Chandler, David. "The Development of Fortifications" in Cyril Falls, ed., _Great Military Battles_. (London, 1964), 292-3.

299. Chesney, Charles C. _On the Value of Fortresses and Fortified Positions in Defensive Operations_. (London, 1864).

300. Chesney, Clement H.R. _The Art of Camouflage_. (London, 1941).

301. Codd, Lt. A. P. "The Artillery Defense of a Fortress." Ordnance Note No. 281, March 30, 1883 in United States, Ordnance Department _Ordnance Notes_. (12 vols., Washington, D.C., 1873-84).

302. De La Croix, Horst. _Military Considerations in City Planning: Fortifications._ (New York, 1972).

303. Douglas, Howard. _Observations on Modern Systems of Fortifications, Including that Proposed by M. Carnot, and a Comparison of the Polygonal with the Bastion System; To Which are Added, Some Reflections on Intrenched Positions, and a Tract on the Naval, Littoral, and Internal Defence of England_. (London, 1859).

304. *Duffy, Christopher. _Fire and Stone; The Science of Fortress Warfare, 1660-1860_. (London, 1975).

23

305. Eis, Egon. The Forts of Folly: The History of an Illusion. Translated by A.J. Pomerans. (London, 1959).

306. Gay de Vernon, Simon F. Treatise on the Science of War and Fortification. Translated by John M. O'Connor. (2 vols., New York, 1817).

307. Hogg, Ian V. Fortress: A History of Military Defense. (London, 1975).

308. *Hughes, James Quentin. Military Architecture. (London, 1974).

309. Lendy, Auguste F. Treatise on Fortification; or, Lectures Delivered to Officers Reading for the Staff. (London, 1862).

310. Lloyd, Ernest M. "Fortress Warfare: An Abstract of Muller's History of Fortress Warfare." Ordnance Note No. 226, October 10, 1882, in United States,Ordnance Department, Ordnance Notes. (12 vols., Washington, D.C., 1873-84).

311. Lloyd, Ernest M. "The Forts of To-Day." Ordnance Note No. 248, February 16, 1883, in United States,Ordnance Department, Ordnance Notes. (12 vols., Washington, D.C., 1873-84).

312. Mahan, Dennis H. A Complete Treatise on Field Fortification, with the General Outlines of the Principles Regulating the Arrangement, the Attack, and the Defence of Permanent Works. (New York, 1836).

313. Shadwell, Leonard Julius and William Ewbank. Fortification Applied to Schemes. (Calcutta, 1904).

314. Sutcliffe, Sheila. Martello Towers. (Newton Abbot, Devon, England, 1972).

315. Straith, Hector. A Treatise on Fortification. (Croydon, 1833).

316. Sydenham, George S. Clarke, Baron. Fortification: Its Past Achievements, Recent Developments, and Future Progress. (London, 1890).

317. Sydenham, George S. Clarke, Baron. "Provisional Fortification." Ordnance Note No. 327, November 24, 1883, in United States,Ordnance Department, Ordnance Notes. (12 vols., Washington, D.C., 1873-84).

318. Thuillier, Henry F., Capt. The Principles of Land Defence and Their Application to the Conditions of To-day. (London, 1902).

319. Vauban, Sebastien Le Prestre de. A Manual of Siegecraft and Fortification. Translated by George A. Rothrock. (Ann Arbor, Michigan, 1968).

320. Viollet-le-Duc, Eugene E. Annals of a Fortress. Translated by Benjamin Bucknall. (London, 1875).

321. Viollet-le-Duc, Eugene E. Military Architecture. Translated by Martin MacDermott. (Third Edition, London, 1907).

322. Ward, Bernard R. Notes on Fortifications. (London, 1902).

323. Yule, Henry. Fortification for Officers of the Army and Students of Military History. (London, 1851).

See also: Addendum: 172.

GUERILLA/PRIMITIVE WARFARE

324. *American University, Washington, D.C., Special Operations Research Office. Unconventional Warfare, an Interim Bibliography. (Washington, D.C., 1961).

325. *Asprey, Robert B. War in the Shadows:The Guerrilla in History. (2 vols., Garden City, New York, 1975).

326. Beals, Carleton. Great Guerrilla Warriors. (Englewood Cliffs, New Jersey, 1970).

327. Blacker, Irwin R., ed. Irregulars, Partisans, Guerrillas: Great Stories from Rogers' Rangers to the Haganah. (New York, 1954).

328. *Campbell, Arthur. Guerillas: A History and Analysis. (London, 1967).

329. *Divale, William T., compl. Warfare in Primitive Societies: A Bibliography. (Revised Edition, Santa Barbara, California, 1973).

330. Ellis, John. A Short History of Guerrilla Warfare. (New York, 1976).

331. Davie, Maurice R. The Evolution of War: A Study of Its Role in Early Society. (New Haven, Connecticut, 1929).

332. *Gann, Lewis. Guerrillas in History. (Stanford, California, 1971).

333. Laqueur, Walter, ed. The Guerrilla Reader: A Historical Anthology. (Bergenfield, New Jersey, 1977).

334. Maguire, Thomas Miller. Guerilla and Partisan Warfare. (London, 1904).

335. Standing, Percy Cross. Guerilla Leaders of the World from Charette to DeWet. (London, 1912).

336. Turney-High, Harry H. The Practice of Primitive War. (Missoula, Montana, 1942).

337. Turney-High, Harry H. Primitive War, Its Practice and Concepts. (Columbia, South Carolina, 1949).

338. United States, Military Academy, West Point, Department of History. History of Revolutionary Warfare. Edited by VeLoy J. Varner. (West Point, New York, 1970).

See also: Addendum: 103.

INFANTRY

339. Crawford, Charles. Infantry Weapons. (Fort Leavenworth, Kansas, 1907).

340. Graham, Lumley. The Tactics of Infantry in Battle. (Fort Monroe, Virginia, 1886).

341. Graham, Lumley. "The Tactics of Infantry in Battle." Ordnance Note No. 254, February 24, 1883 in United States, Ordnance Department, Ordnance Notes. (12 vols., Washington, D.C., 1873-84).

342. Hohenlohe-Ingelfingen, Karl A.E. Letters on Infantry. Translated by N.L. Walford. (London, 1889).

343. Lloyd, Ernest M. A Review of the History of Infantry. (London, 1908).

344. Maude, Frederic N. Notes on the Evolution of Infantry Tactics. (London, 1905).

345. Mayne, Charles B. The Infantry Weapon and Its Use in War. (London, 1903).

346. Stuart, Henry B. A History of Infantry from Earliest Times to the Present. (London, 1861).

347. Wagner, Arthur L. Modern Infantry. (Fort Leavenworth, Kansas, 1894).

348. Best, Geoffrey. "How Right is Might? Some Aspects of the International Debate About How to Fight Wars and How to Win Them, 1870-1918," in Geoffrey Best and Andrew Wheatcroft, eds., War, Economy and the Military Mind. (London, 1976), 120-35.

349. Bond, Brian. "The 'Just War' in Historical Perspective." HT 16 (February 1966), 111-19.

350. Gibson, Claud L. "The Hague Peace Conference of 1899." MR 56 (January 1976), 79-88.

351. Graber, Doris A. The Development of the Law of Belligerent Occupation, 1863-1914, a Historical Survey. (New York, 1949).

352. Greenspan, Morris. The Modern Law of Land Warfare. (Berkeley, California, 1959).

353. Holland, Thomas E., ed. The Law and Customs of War on Land, as Defined by the Hague Convention of 1899. (London, 1904).

354. Stowell, Ellery C. "Convention Relative to the Opening of Hostilities." AJIL 2 (January 1908), 50-62.

355. *Walzer, Michael. Just and Unjust Wars; A Moral Argument with Historical Illustrations. (New York, 1977).

See also: Addendum: 57.

LOGISTICS

356. Brett-James, Antony. "War and Logistics, 1861-1918." HT 14 (September 1964), 597-607.

357. *Creveld, Martin van. Supplying War; Logistics from Wallenstein to Patton. (New York, 1977).

358. Daniel, Hawthorn. For Want of a Nail: The Influence of Logistics on War. (New York, 1948).

359. Sharpe, Henry G. The Provisioning of the Modern Army in the Field. (Kansas City, 1905).

360. Shaw, George C. Supply in Modern War. (London, 1938).

LOSSES OF LIFE FROM WAR

361. Bodart, Gaston. *Losses of Life in Modern Wars, Austria-Hungary; France*. (Oxford, 1916).

362. Dumas, Samuel and Knud O. Vedel-Petersen. *Losses of Life Caused by War*. (Oxford, 1923).

363. Major, Ralph H. *Fatal Partners: War and Disease*. (Garden City, New York, 1941).

364. Prinzing, Friedrich. *Epidemics Resulting from Wars*. (Oxford, 1916).

MEDICINE AND WAR

365. Garrison, Fielding H. *Notes on the History of Military Medicine*. (Washington, D.C., 1922).

366. Great Britain, War Office. *Handbook of Medical Services of Foreign Armies*. (6 vols., London, 1908-11).

367. Howard, Francis (Frank). *Handbook of the Medical Organization (chiefly for war) of Foreign Armies*. (London, 1902).

368. Huidekoper, R.S. "Army Veterinary Service." *JCMVA* 11 (January 1890), 12-22.

369. *John Crerar Library, Chicago. *A Selected List of Books on Military Medicine and Surgery*. (Chicago, 1917).

370. Laffin, John. *Surgeons in the Field*. (London, 1970).

371. L'Etang, Hugh. "Some Fighting Doctors." *AQ* 84 (April 1962), 65-9.

372. Maisel, Albert Z. *Miracles of Military Medicine*. (New York, 1943).

373. Marshall, Henry. *Hints to Young Medical Officers of the Army on the Examination of Recruits, and Respecting the Feigned Disabilities of Soldiers; with Official Documents, and the Regulations for the Inspection of Conscripts for the French and Prussian Armies*. (London, 1828).

28

MILITARISM

374. Ferrero, Gugliemo. <u>Militarism.</u> (London, 1902).

375. Lauterbach, Albert T. "Militarism in the Western World, A Comparative Study." <u>JHI</u> 5 (October 1944), 446-78.

376. Liebknecht, Karl Paul A.I. <u>Militarism.</u> (New York, 1917).

377. Toynbee, Arnold J. <u>War and Civilization.</u> Edited by Albert V. Fowler. (New York, 1950).

378. Vagts, Alfred. <u>A History of Militarism; Romance and Realism of a Profession.</u> (New York, 1937).

MILITARY CUSTOMS

379. Farrer, James Ansom. <u>Military Manners and Customs: The Laws and Observances of Warfare in Ancient and Modern Times.</u> (London, 1885).

380. Moss, James A. <u>Origin and Significance of Military Customs Including Military Miscellany of Interst to Soldiers and Civilians.</u> (Menosha, Wisconsin, 1917).

MILITARY EDUCATION

381. Arthur, George. "The Soldier as Student." <u>FR</u> 88 (October 1907), 620- 9.

382. Barnard, Henry. <u>Military Schools and Courses of Instruction in the Science and Art of War.</u> (Revised Edition, New York, 1872).

383. Barnett, Corelli. "The Education of Military Elites." <u>JCONH</u> 2 (July 1967), 15-35.

384. Chesney, Charles C. "The Study of Military Science in Time of Peace." JRUSI 15, No. 63 (1871), 254-68.

385. Echols, Charles P. Report Upon Foreign (Military) Schools. (West Point, New York, 1907).

386. Hildyard, H. "The Training and Officering of Reserves in Foreign Armies." Ordnance Note No. 265, March 12, 1883, in United States, Ordnance Department, Ordnance Notes. (12 vols., Washington, D.C., 1873-84).

387. James, Walter H. Capt.,late R.E. "Military Education and Training." Ordnance Note No. 283, April 2, 1883, in United States, Ordnance Department, Ordnance Notes. (12 vols., Washington, D.C., 1873-84).

388. United States, Adjutant General's Office, Military Information Division. The Military Schools of Europe,.... (Washington, D.C., 1896).

389. Virginia Military Institute, Lexington. Special Report of the Superintendent of the Virginia Military Institute, on Scientific Education in Europe. (Richmond, Virginia, 1859).

MILITARY GEOGRAPHY

390. Maguire, Thomas M. Outline of Military Geography. (Cambridge, England, 1899).

391. May, Edward S. An Introduction to Military Geography. (London, 1909).

392. May, Edward S. Geography in Relation to War. (London, 1907).

393. *Peltier, Louis C., compl. Bibliography of Military Geography. (Washington, D.C., 1962).

MILITARY HISTORY--ITS PURPOSE

394. Conger, Arthur L. "The Function of Military History." <u>MVHR</u> 3 (September 1916), 161-71.

395. Craven, Wesley Frank. <u>Why Military History</u>. (United States Air Force Academy, Colorado, 1959).

396. Donaldson, John W.E. <u>The Application of Military History to Modern Warfare</u>. (Calcutta, 1905).

397. Howard, Michael. "The Demand for Military History." <u>MR</u> 51 (May 1971), 34-42.

398. Howard, Michael. "The Use and Abuse of Military History." <u>JRUSI</u> 107 (February 1962), 4-10.

399. <u>Remarks on the Scope and Uses of Military Literature and History</u>. Part I. (Calcutta, 1846).

MILITARY INTELLIGENCE AND ESPIONAGE

400. Haswell, Chetwynd J.D. (Jock). <u>Spies and Spymasters: A Concise History of Intelligence</u>. (New York, 1977).

401. Hoehling, Adolph A. <u>Women Who Spied</u>. (New York, 1967).

402. Ind, Allison. <u>A Short History of Espionage: From the Trojan Horse to Cuba</u>. (New York, 1963).

403. Kahn, David. <u>The Codebreakers: The Story of Secret Writing</u>. (New York, 1967).

404. Laffin, John. <u>Codes and Ciphers: Secret Writing Through the Ages</u>. (London, 1964).

405. Pratt, Fletcher. <u>Secret and Urgent: The Story of Codes and Ciphers</u>. (London, 1939).

406. Rowan, Richard Wilmer with Robert G. Deindorfer. <u>Secret Service: Thirty-three Centuries of Espionage</u>. (New York, 1967).

407. Rowan, Richard Wilmer. <u>Spy and Counter-Spy; The Development of Modern Espionage</u>. (London, n.d.).

408. Rowan, Richard Wilmer. _The Story of Secret Service_. (Garden City, New York, 1937).

409. Seth, Ronald. _Encyclopedia of Espionage_. (Garden City, New York, 1972).

410. *Shulman, David, compl. _An Annotated Bibliography of Cryptography_. (New York, 1976).

411. Sweeney, Walter. _Military Intelligence, a New Weapon in War_. (New York, 1924).

MILITARY MANUALS

412. Bernhardi, Friedrich A.J. von. _On War of Today_. Translated by Karl von Donat. (2 vols., London, 1912-13).

413. Bronsart von Schellendorf, Paul Leopold E.H.A. _The Duties of the General Staff_. Translated by William A.H. Hare. (2 vols., London, 1877-80).

414. Callwell, Charles E. _Small Wars, Their Principles and Practice_. (London, 1896).

415. Clausewitz, Carl von. _A Short Guide to Clausewitz On War_. Edited by Roger A. Leonard. (New York, 1968).

416. Clausewitz, Carl von. _On War_. Edited and translated by Michael Howard and Peter Paret. (Princeton, New Jersey, 1976).

417. Delabarre-Duparcq, Nicolas Edward. _Elements of Military Art and History, Comprising the History and Tactics of the Separate Arms, the Combinations of the Arms, and the Minor Operations of War_. Translated by George W. Cullum. (New York, 1863).

418. Goltz, Colmar F. von der. _The Nation in Arms_. Translated by Philip A. Ashworth. (London, 1887).

419. Goltz, Colmar F. von der. _The Conduct of War, a Short Treatise on Its Most Important Branches and Guiding Rules_. Translated by George F. Leverson. (London, 1899).

420. Graham, Lumley, ed. and trans. _The New Tactics of Infantry (Studies in)_. By Major Wilhelm von Scherff. (Leavenworth, Kansas, 1891).

421. Haking, Richard C.B. <u>Staff Rides and Regimental Tours</u>. (London, 1908).

422. Halleck, Henry W. <u>Elements of Military Art and Science</u>. (New York, 1846).

423. Hamley, Edward B. <u>The Operations of War, Explained and Illustrated</u>. (London, 1865).

424. Havelock-Allan, Henry M. <u>Three Main Military Questions of the Day</u>. (London, 1867).

425. Henderson, George F.R. <u>The Science of War</u>. Edited by Neill Malcolm. (New York, 1906).

426. Heneker, William C. <u>Bush Warfare</u>. (London, 1907).

427. Jomini, Henri. <u>The Art of War</u>. Translated by George H. Mendell and William P. Craighill. (Philadelphia, Pennsylvania, 1862).

428. Jomini, Henri. <u>Treatise on Grand Military Operations; or, a Critical and Military History of the Wars of Frederick the Great, as Contrasted with the Modern System, together with a few of the Most Important Principles of the Art of War</u>. Translated by Col. Samuel B. Holabird. (New York, 1865).

429. MacDougall, Patrick. <u>The Theory of War: Illustrated by Numerous Examples from Military History</u>. (London, 1856).

430. Marmont, Auguste Frederic L.V. <u>The Spirit of Military Institutions; or Essential Principles of the Art of War</u>. Translated by Henry Coppee. (Philadelphia, Pennsylvania, 1862).

431. Schalk, Emil. <u>Summary of the Art of War</u>. (Philadelphia, Pennsylvania, 1862).

432. Verdy du Vernois, Julius A.F.W. von. <u>Studies in Troop Leading</u>. Translated by Henry J.T. Hildyard. (2 vols., London, 1872- 7).

433. Wagner, Arthur L. <u>Elements of Military Science</u>. (Kansas City, 1898).

434. Wagner, Arthur L. <u>The Service of Security and Information</u>. (Kansas City, 1896).

435. Wolseley, Garnet J. <u>Soldier's Pocket-Book for Field Service</u>. (London, 1871).

MILITARY MEDALS

436. Dorling, Henry Tarpell with L.F. Guill. Ribbons and Medals; The
World's Military and Civil Awards. Edited by Francis K. Mason.
(Revised edition, Garden City, New York, 1974).

437. Rairden, P.W. "Campaign and Service Medals--Their History and
Traditions." USNIP 75 (May 1949), 515-21.

MILITARY MUSEUMS

438. International Association of Museums of Arms and Military History.
Directory of Museums of Arms and Military History. Compiled by Arne Hoff.
(Copenhagen, Denmark, 1970).

MILITARY MUSIC

439. *Denisoff, R. Serge, compl. Songs of Protest, War, and Peace: A
Bibliography and Discography. (Santa Barbara, California, 1973).

440. Farmer, Henry G. Military Music. (London, 1950).

441. Farmer, Henry G. Military Music and its Story; he Rise and Development of Military Music. (London, 1912).

442. Farmer, Henry G. The Rise and Development of Military Music.
(London, 1912).

443. Kappey, Jacob A. Military Music; A History of Wind Instrumental
Bands. (London, 1894).

444. Kobbe, Gustave. "The Trumpet in Camp and Battle." CIMM 56 (August
1898), 537-43.

445. Malcolm, Charles A. The Piper in Peace and War. (London, 1927).

MILITARY PHOTOGRAPHY

446. Baillie, J. "Photography Applied to Military Science." JRUSI 13, No. 56 (1869), 449-59.

447. Griffin, Eugene. Notes on Military Photography. (Willets Point, New York, 1882).

448. Pritchard, H. Baden. "The Application of Photography to Military Purposes." JRUSI 13, No. 55 (1869), 419-34.

449. Reber, Samuel. Manual of Photography for the Use of the U.S. Army. (Washington, D.C., 1896).

450. Wheeler, Owen E. Military Photography. (London, 1891).

MILITARY PROFESSIONALISM

451. Brabazon, Luke. Soldiers and Their Science. (London, 1860).

452. Field, Cyril. Old Times Under Arms: A Military Garner. (London, 1939).

453. Hackett, John W. The Profession of Arms. (London, 1963).

454. Janowitz, Morris. The Professional Soldier; A Social and Political Portrait. (New York, 1960).

455. Teitler, Gerke. The Genesis of the Professional Officers' Corps. (Beverly Hills, California, 1977).

456. Tulloch, A.B. "The Education, and Professional Instruction of Officers." JRUSI 17, No. 75 (1873), 759-85.

457. Van Doorn, Jacques. The Soldier and Social Change: Comparative Studies in the History and Sociology of the Military. (Beverly Hills, Californai, 1975).

MILITARY/GENERAL STAFF

458. Azan, P. "The Historical Section in a General Staff." MH&E 3 (April 1918), 87 91.

459. Bronsart von Schellendorff, Paul L.E.H.A. The Duties of the General Staff. Translated by William A.H. Hare. (2 vols., London, 1877-78).

460. *Hittle, James D. The Military Staff: Its History and Development. (Revised edition, Harrisburg, Pennsylvania, 1961).

461. Irvine, Dallas D. "The Origin of Capital Staffs." JMH 10 (June 1938), 161-79.

462. Magoffin, Ralph Van Deman. "Historical Work by Army General Staffs." AHR 24 (July 1919), 630- 6.

463. Murphy, Maj. Gen. James. "The Evolution of the General Staff Concept." DMJ 12 (July 1976), 34-39.

464. Perkins, E.J. "The Military Staff: Its History and Development." CAJ 7 (April 1953), 25-35.

465. Perry, E. Warren. "The General Staff System." CAJ 3 (August 1949), 13-15 and 30- 1; (September 1949), 27-30.

See also: Part 1: 245.

MILITARY ORGANIZATION

466. Alison, Archibald. On Army Organization. (Edinburgh, 1869).

467. Foster, Hubert J. Organization: How Armies are Formed for War. (London, 1913).

468. Maude, Frederic N. Letters on Tactics and Organisation. (Calcutta, 1888).

See also: Part I: 183, 184, 244, 246, 247, 288.

469. Beca, Colonel. A Study of the Development of Infantry Tactics. Translated by Alfred F. Custance. (London, 1911).

470. Becke, Archibald F. An Introduction to the History of Tactics, 1740-1905. (London, 1909).

471. Bird, Wilkinson D. A Precis of Strategy. (London, 1910).

472. Boatner, Mark M. "Surprise." ARMY 20 (January 1970), 33-38.

473. Bond, Paul S. and Michael J. McDonough. Technique of Modern Tactics. A Study of Troop Leading Methods in the Operations of Detachments of all Arms. (Third Edition, Menasha, Wisconsin, 1914).

474. Caemerer, Rudolf von. The Development of Strategical Science during the 19th Century. Translated by Karl von Donat. (London, 1905).

475. Callwell, Charles E. The Tactics of To-Day Written While Advancing With the Natal Field Force. (London, 1903).

476. Clery, Cornelius F. Minor Tactics. (London, 1877).

477. Clive, Col. Edward. "On the Influence of Breech-Loading Arms on Tactics, and On the Supply of Ammunition in the Field." Ordnance Note No. 91, November 26, 1878 in United States, Ordnance Department, Ordnance Notes. (12 vols., Washington, D.C., 1873-84).

478. Colin, Jean Lambert Alphonse. The Transformations of War. Translated by Ladislas H.R. Pope-Hennessey. (London, 1912).

479. Dufour, Guillaume H. Strategy and Tactics. Translated by William P. Craighill. (New York, 1864).

480. Friedrich Karl, Prince of Prussia. The Influence of Firearms Upon Tactics. Translated by Capt. Edmund H. Wickham. (London, 1876).

481. Gilbert, Gerald E.L. The Evolution of Tactics. (London, 1907).

482. Great Britain, War Office. Memorandum on Numbers of Troops to the Yard in the Principle Battles Since 1850. With the Opinions of Modern Authorities on the Limits of Extension at the Present Day. (London, 1884).

483. Hohenlohe-Ingelfingen, Karl A.E. Friedrich. Letters on Strategy. Edited by Walter H. James. (2 vols., London, 1898).

484. Home, Robert. A Precis of Modern Tactics: Compiled from the Works of Recent Continental Writers at the Topographical and Statistical Department of the War Office. (London, 1873).

485. Johnstone, Henry M. A History of Tactics. (London, 1906).

486. Laffin, John. *The Face of War: The Evolution of Weapons and Tactics and Their Use in Ten Famous Battles.* (New York, 1964).

487. Liddell Hart, Basil H. *The Ghost of Napoleon.* (London, 1933).

487A. Liddell Hart, Basil H. *Strategy.* (Second Revised Edition, New York, 1967).

488. Magrath, Richard N. *An Historical Sketch of the Progress of the Art of War.* (Dublin, 1838).

489. Maguire, Thomas Miller. *The Development of Tactics Since 1866.* (London, 1904).

490. Maguire, Thomas Miller. *Notes on the Outlines of Strategy. With Historical Illustrations and References to Authorities.* (London, 1902).

491. Maguire, Thomas Miller. *Strategy and Tactics in Mountain Ranges.* (London, 1904).

492. Maude, Frederic N. *Evolution of Modern Strategy from the XVIIIth Century to the Present Time.* (London, 1905).

493. Nickerson, Hoffman. "Nineteenth Century Military Techniques." JWH 4, No. 2 (1958), 348-58.

494. R.E.C. "Modern Tactics." SLM 26, New Series (January 1858), 1-20.

495. Terraine, John. "Big Battalions: The Napoleonic Legacy." HT 12 (June 1962), 416-25.

496. Wagner, Arthur L. *Modern Strategy.* (Fort Leavenworth, Kansas, 1894).

497. Wagner, Arthur L. *Organization and Tactics.* (New York, 1895).

498. Wagner, Arthur L. *Strategy.* (Kansas City, Missouri, 1904).

499. Weller, Jac. *Weapons and Tactics; Hastings to Berlin.* (London, 1966).

500. Wintringham, Thomas H. *The Story of Weapons and Tactics From Troy to Stalingrad.* (Boston, 1943).

See also: Part 1: 184, 188, 202, 224, 344, 420, 468.

OFFICIAL MILITARY HISTORY

501. *Higham, Robin, ed. Official Histories: Essays and Bibliographies from Around the World. (Manhattan, Kansas, 1970).

See also: Part 1: 458, 462.

PEACE STUDIES

502. Beales, Arthur C.F. The History of Peace. (London, 1931).

503. Bloch, Ivan S. The Future of War in Its Technical, Economic and Political Relations; Is War Now Impossible. (New York, 1899).

504. Caldwell, Robert G. The Peace Congresses of the Nineteenth Century. (Houston, Texas, 1918).

505. Clarke, Igantius F. Voices Prophesying War, 1763-1984. (New York, 1966).

506. *Cook, Blanche Wiesen, ed. Bibliography on Peace Research in History. (Santa Barbara, California, 1969).

507. Gallie, W.B. Philosophers of Peace and War: Kant, Clausewitz, Marx, Engels and Tolstoy. (New York, 1978).

508. Gibson, Maj. Cloud L. "The Hague Peace Conference of 1899." MR 56 (January 1976), 79-88.

509. Howard, Michael. Wars and the Liberal Conscience. (New Brunswick, New Jersey, 1978).

510. Israel, Fred L., ed. Major Peace Treaties of Modern History, 1648-1967. (4 vols., New York, 1967).

511. McCollester, Mary A. "Attitudes to Peace and War in the Eighteen-Forties and the Eighteen-Nineties: A Comparison of the Two Decades." M. Litt. Thesis, Cambridge (England), 1965.

See also: Part 1: 147, 278.

PERIODICALS

512. *Adolphus, Lalit and Eric H. Boehm, eds. <u>Historical Periodicals: An Annotated World List of Historical and Related Serial Publications</u>. (Santa Barbara, California, 1961).

513. Birkos, Alexander S. "A Bibliographical Introduction to Foreign Military Periodicals." <u>MA</u> 33 (December 1969), 393-6.

514. Spence, Paul H. and Helen Hopewell, eds. <u>Union List of Foreign Military Periodicals</u>. (Maxwell Air Force Base, Alabama, 1957).

515. United States, Air University Library, Maxwell Air Force Base, Alabama. <u>Air University Library Index to Military Periodicals</u>. (Maxwell Air Force Base, Alabama, 1949--).

See also: Part 1: 152 (pgs. 47-51).

COLLECTIONS OF GREAT QUOTATIONS AND WRITINGS ON WAR

516. Heinl, Robert D., ed. <u>Dictionary of Military and Naval Quotations</u>. (Annapolis, Maryland, 1966).

517. Liddell Hart, Basil H., ed. <u>The Sword and the Pen; Selections from the World's Greatest Military Writings</u>. Edited by Adrian Liddell Hart. (New York, 1976).

518. Singh, Rajendra, ed. <u>Words of Wisdom on War: A Collection of Military Statements of Great Philosophers, Writers and Masters of War</u>. (New Delhi, India, 1966).

REVOLUTIONS, COUP D'ETATS AND MUTINIES

519. Andrews, William G. and Uri Ra Anan, eds., with Martin C. Needler and others. <u>The Politics of the Coup d'Etat: Five Case Studies</u>. (New York, 1969).

520. Baechler, Jean. <u>Revolution</u>. Translated by Joan Vickers. (New York, 1975).

521. Beals, Carleton. _The Nature of Revolution_. (New York, 1970).

522. *Blackey, Robert. _Modern Revolutions and Revolutionists: A Bibliography_. (Santa Barbara, California, 1976).

523. Breunig, Charles. _The Age of Revolution and Reaction, 1789-1850_. (New York, 1970).

524. Charlesworth, Mary. _Revolution in Perspective: People Seeking Change, 1775 to the Present Day_. (London, 1972).

525. *Chorley, Katherine. _Armies and the Art of Revolution_. (London, 1943).

526. Ellis, John. _Armies in Revolution_. (New York, 1974).

527. Gooch, Herbert E., III. "Coup D'Etat: Historical and Ideological Dimensions of the Concept." Ph.D. Dissertation, University of California at Los Angeles, 1977.

528. Goodspeed, Donald J. _The Conspirators: A Study of the Coup D'Etat_. (London, 1962).

529. Hyams, Edward. _A Dictionary of Modern Revolution_. (New York, 1973).

530. Luttwak, Edward. _Coup D'Etat: A Practical Handbook_. (New York, 1969).

530A. McGuffie, Thomas H. _Stories of Famous Mutinies_. (London, 1966).

531. Possony, Stefan T. _A Century of Conflict; Communist Techniques of World Revolution_. (Chicago, 1953).

532. _Revolutions 1775-1930_. Edited by Merryn Williams. (Baltimore, Maryland, 1971).

533. Schneider, Irwin. "The Mindful Peasant: Sketches for a Study of Rebellion." _JASS_ 32 (August 1973), 579-89.

534. Thompson, William R. "Explanations of the Military Coup." Ph.D. Dissertation, University of Washington, 1972.

535. Wintringham, Thomas H. _Mutiny: Being a Survey of Mutinies from Spartacus to Invergordon_. (London, 1936).

536. Woodcock, George, ed. _A Hundred Years of Revolution, 1848 and After_. (New York, 1974).

See also: Part I: 134; Addendum: 32, 86.

SCIENCE, TECHNOLOGY, INDUSTRY AND WARFARE

537. Basiuk, Victor. "The Differential Impact of Technological Change on the Great Powers, 1870-1914: The Case of Steel." Ph.D. Dissertation, Columbia University, 1956.

538. Engelbrecht, Helmuth C. and Frank Hanighen. Merchants of Death; A Study of the International Armament Industry. (New York, 1934).

539. *Ferguson, Eugene S., compl. Bibliography of the History of Technology. (Cambridge, Massachusetts, 1968).

540. Military History Symposium, 3d, U.S. Air Force Academy, 1969. Science, Technology, and Warfare; Proceedings. Edited by Monte D. Wright and Lawrence J. Paszek. (Washington, D.C., 1971).

541. *Nef, John U. War and Human Progress: An Essay on the Rise of Industrial Civilization. (Cambridge, Massachusetts, 1952).

542. Perris, George H. The War Traders. (London, 1914).

543. Portway, Donald. Science and Mechanisation in Land Warfare. (Cambridge, England, 1938).

544. Wheeler, Hugh Grant. "The Effects of War on Industrial Growth, 1816-1970." Ph.D. Dissertation, University of Michigan, 1975.

SOCIO-PSYCHOLOGICAL STUDIES OF WARFARE AND THE MILITARY

545. American Anthropological Association. War: The Anthropology of Armed Conflict and Aggression. Edited by Morton Fried, Marvin Harris and Robert Murphy. (Garden City, New York, 1968).

546. Ardant du Picq, Charles P. Battle Studies: Ancient and Modern Battle. Translated by John N. Greely and Robert C. Cotton. (New York, 1921).

547. Bramson, Leon and G.W. Goethals, eds. War: Studies from Psychology, Sociology, and Anthropology. (New York, 1964).

548. Carthy, John D. and Francis J. Ebling, eds. The Natural History of Agression. (New York, 1964).

549. Coblentz, Stanton A. From Arrow to Atom Bomb: The Psychological History of War. (New York, 1953).

550. Dixon, Norman F. *On the Psychology of Military Incompetence*. (New York, 1976).

551. Keegan, John. *The Face of Battle*. (New York, 1976).

552. *Lang, Kurt, compl. *Military Institutions and the Sociology of War; A Review of the Literature with Annotated Bibliography*. (Beverly Hills, California, 1972).

553. McNeil, Elton B., ed. *The Nature of Human Conflict*. (Englewood Cliffs, New Jersey, 1965).

554. Richardson, Frank M. *Fighting Spirit: Psychological Factors in War*. (New York, 1978).

SOLDIERS AND THEIR LOT

555. Coggins, Jack. *The Fighting Man: An Illustrated History of the World's Greatest Fighting Forces Through the Ages*. (Garden City, 1966).

556. Ellacott, S.E. *Conscripts on the March: The Story of the Soldier from Napoleon to the Nuclear Age*. (New York, 1966).

557. *Fighting Men: The Western Military Heritage*. Edited by Archie P. McDonald and James C. Calahan. (N.P., 196-).

558. Hargreaves, Reginald. "What Sort of Recruit." *MR* 52 (January 1972), 58-67.

559. Leveson, Henry A. (The Old Shekary, pseudo.). *Camp Life and Its Requirements for Soldiers, Travellers and Sportsmen*. Part I. (London, 1872).

560. McGuffie, Thomas H., compl. *Rank and File: The Common Soldier at Peace and War, 1642-1914*. (London, 1964).

561. "Military Punishment in Foreign Armies." *JRUSI* 24, No. 107 (1880), 928-33.

562. Mockler, Anthony. *The Mercenaries*. (New York, 1970).

563. Powers, Harry H. *The Things Men Fight For, With Some Application to Present Conditions in Europe*. (Boston, 1916).

564. Russell, Bertrand. Why Men Fight: A Method of Abolishing the International Duel. (New York, 1917).

565. Windrow, Martin and Frederick Wilkinson, eds. The Universal Soldier: Fourteen Studies in Campaign Life A.D. 43-1944. (Garden City, New York, 1971).

SOLDIERS AND A NURSE OF FORTUNE

566. Davis, Richard Harding. Real Soldiers of Fortune. (New York, 1906).

567. Dufour, Charles L. Gentle Tiger: The Gallant Life of Roberdeau Wheat. (Baton Rouge, Louisiana, 1957).

568. Furley, John. In Peace and War: Autobiographical Sketches. (London, 1905).

569. Hyatt, Stanley P. The Diary of a Soldier of Fortune. (London, 1910).

570. McCormick, Donald. One Man's Wars: The Story of Charles Sweeney: Soldier of Fortune. (London, 1972).

571. McDonald, John W. A Soldier of Fortune, The Life and Adventures of General Henry Ronald Maciver. (New York, 1888).

572. Nogales y Mendez, Rafael de. Memoirs of a Soldier of Fortune. (London, 1931).

573. Oliphant, Laurence. Episodes in a Life of Adventure, or Moss from a Rolling Stone. (London, 1887).

574. Oliphant, Laurence. Patriots and Filibusters; or Incidents of Political and Exploratory Travel. (London, 1860).

575. Pipping, Ellen. Soldier of Fortune: The Story of a Nineteenth Century Adventurer. Translated by Naomi Walford. (Boston, 1971).

576. Starr, Stephen Z. Colonel Grenfell's Wars: The Life of a Soldier of Fortune. (Baton Rouge, Louisiana, 1971).

TRANSPORTATION AND COMMUNICATION

577. Bishop, Denis and Keith Davies. <u>Railways and War Before 1918</u>. (New York, 1972).

578. *Bureau of Railway Economics, Washington, D.C.,Library. <u>Railroads in Defense and War: A Bibliography</u>. Compiled by Helen Ruth Richardson. (Washington, D.C.,1953).

579. Caidin, Martin and Jay Barbree. <u>Bicycles in War</u>. (New York, 1974).

580. Carter, Ernest F. <u>Railways in Wartime</u>. (London, 1964).

581. Furse, George A. <u>Information in War: Its Acquisition and Transmission</u>. (London, 1895).

582. Furse, George A. <u>The Organization and Administration of the Lines of Communications in War</u>. (London, 1894).

583. Luard, C.E. "Field Railways and Their General Application in War." <u>JRUSI</u> 17, No. 74 (1873), 693-724.

584. Myer, Albert J. <u>A Manual of Signals for the Use of Signal Officers in the Field, and for Military and Naval Students, Military Schools, etc.</u> (New York, 1868).

585. Parsons, Clifford. "Military Transport." Ordnance Note No. 121, January 5, 1880 in United States, Ordnance Department, <u>Ordnance Notes</u>. (12 vols., Washington, D.C., 1873-84).

586. Pratt, Edwin A. <u>Rise of Rail Power in War and Conquest, 1833-1914</u>. (London, 1915).

587. Reichmann, Carl. <u>The Use of Railroads in War. A Lecture Delivered Before the Class of Officers at the U.S. Infantry and Cavalry School at Ft. Leavenworth, Kansas, December 17, 1894</u>. (Fort Leavenworth, Kansas, 1895).

See also: Part 1: 185, 189, 194, 196; Part II: 357.

UNIFORMS

588. Beaumont, Roger A. and Bernard J. James. "The Sukhomlinov Effect." <u>H</u> 13 (Winter 1971), 66- 9.

589. Blakeslee, Fred G. <u>Uniforms of the World</u>. (New York, 1929).

590. Carman, William Y. _A Dictionary of Military Uniform._ (New York, 1977).

591. Cassin-Scott, Jack and John Tabb. _Ceremonial Uniforms of the World._ (London, 1973).

592. D'Ami, Rinaldo D., ed. _World Uniforms in Color._ Translated by F. D. Fawcett. (2 vols., London, 1969).

593. Emilio, Luis Fenollosa. _The Emilio Collection of Military Buttons: American, British, French and Spanish, with Some of Other Countries, and Non-Military in the Museum of the Essex Institute, Salem, Massachusetts._ (Salem, Massachusetts, 1911).

594. Funcken, Fred and Liliane. _Arms and Uniforms: Late Eighteenth Century to the Present Day._ (New York, 1974).

595. Kannik, Preben. _Military Uniforms in Color._ Edited by William Y. Carman. Translated by John Hewish. (London, 1968).

596. *Mollo, John. _Military Fashion: A Comparative History of the Uniforms of the Great Armies from the 17th Century to the First World War._ (New York, 1972).

597. North, Rene. _Military Uniforms 1686-1918._ (New York, 1970).

598. Rankin, Robert H. _Military Headdress: A Pictorial History of Military Headgear from 1660-1914._ (New York, 1976).

599. Schick, I. T. _Battledress: The Uniforms of the World's Greatest Armies 1700 to the Present._ (Boston, 1978).

600. Toman, Karel. _A Book of Military Uniforms and Weapons: An Illustrated Survey of Military Dress, Arms, and Practice Through the Ages._ Translated by Alice Denesova. (London, 1964).

601. Wilkinson, Frederic J. _Battle Dress: A Gallery of Military Style and Ornament._ (Garden City, New York, 1970).

WAR AND FOREIGN AFFAIRS

602. Benjamin, Roger W. and Lewis J. Edinger. "Conditions for Military Control Over Foreign Policy Decisions in Major States: A Historical Exploration." _JCR_ 15 (March 1971), 5-31.

603. Benjamin, Roger W. "Military Influence in Foreign Policy-Making." Ph.D. Dissertation, Washington University, St. Louis, Missouri, 1967.

604. Schelling, Thomas C. _Arms and Influence. Modern War and Diplomacy_. (New Haven, Connecticut, 1966).

605. *Vagts, Alfred. _The Military Attache_. (Princeton, New Jersey, 1967).

606. *Vagts, Alfred. _Defense and Diplomacy: The Soldier and the Conduct of Foreign Relations_. (New York, 1956).

WAR CORRESPONDENTS, ARTISTS AND PHOTOGRAPHERS

607. Atkins, John B. _Incidents and Reflections_. (London, 1947).

608. Baynes, Ken. _War_. (London, 1970).

609. Bullard, Frederic Lauriston. _Famous War Correspondents_. (Boston, 1914).

610. Churchill, Winston L.S. _My Early Life: A Roving Commission_. (London, 1930).

611. Churchill, Winston L.S. _Young Winston's Wars: The Original Despatches of Winston S. Churchill, War Correspondent, 1897-1900_. Edited by Frederick Woods. (New York, 1972).

612. Crane, Stephen. _Reports of War: War Dispatches and Great Battles of the World_. Edited by Fredson Bowers. (Charlottesville, Virginia, 1971).

613. Crane, Stephen. _The War Dispatches of Stephen Crane_. Edited by R.W. Stallman and E.R. Hagemann. (London, 1964).

614. Davis, Charles B., ed. _Adventures and Letters of Richard Harding Davis_. (New York, 1917).

615. Davis, Richard Harding. _The Notes of a War Correspondent_. (New York, 1912).

616. Downey, Fairfax D. _Richard Harding Davis: His Day_. (New York, 1933).

617. Forbes, Archibald. _Memories and Studies of War and Peace_. (London, 1895).

618. Gould, Lewis L. and Richard Greffe. _Photojournalist: The Career of Jimmy Hare_. (Austin, Texas, 1977).

619. Furneaux, Rupert. The First War Correspondent, William Howard Russell of "The Times." (London, 1944).

620. *Furneaux, Rupert. News of War: Stories and Adventures of the Great War Correspondents. (London, 1964).

621. Hargreaves, Reginald. "The Link." MR 34 (February 1955), 3-13.

622. Hawkes, Charles P. Authors-at-Arms: The Soldiering of Six Great Writers. (London, 1935).

623. Hodgson, Pat. Early War Photographs. (Reading, Berkshire, England, 1974).

624. Hodgson, Pat. The War Illustrators. (New York, 1977).

625. Jakes, John W. Great War Correspondents. (New York, 1968).

626. James, Lionel. Times of Stress. (London, 1929).

627. James, Lionel. High Pressure: Being Some Record of Activities in the Service of "The Times" Newspaper. (London, 1929).

628. Knight, Edward F. Reminiscences: The Wanderings of a Yachtsman and War Correspondent. (London, 1923).

629. *Knightley, Phillip. The First Casualty: The War Correspondent as Hero, Propagandist and Myth Maker. (New York, 1975).

630. Longford, Gerald. The Richard Harding Davis Years: A Biography of a Mother and Son. (New York, 1961).

631. Lynch, George. Impressions of a War Correspondent. (London, 1903).

632. Lynch, George and Frederick Palmer, eds. In Many Wars, by Many War-correspondents. (Tokyo, 1904).

633. McCullagh, Francis. "The Question of the War Correspondent." CR 103 (February 1913), 203-13.

634. Mathews, Joseph J. "Heralds of the Imperialistic Wars." MA 19 (Fall 1955), 145-55.

635. *Mathews, Joseph J. Reporting the Wars. (Minneapolis, Minnesota, 1957).

636. Montagu, Irving. Camp and Studio. (London, 1890).

637. Montagu, Irving. Things I Have Seen in War. (London, 1899)

638. Montagu, Irving. Wanderings of a War Artist. (London, 1889).

639. Palmer, Frederick, With My Own Eyes: A Personal Story of Battle Years. (Indianapolis, Indiana, 1933).

640. Prior, Melton. _Campaigns of a War Correspondent._ (New York, 1912).

641. Sullivan, A.E. "Military Art and Artists." _AQ_ 77 (January 1959), 233-38.

642. Villiers, Frederic. _Villiers: His Five Decades of Adventure._ (New York, 1920).

643. _War: The Camera's Battlefield View of Man's Most Terrible Adventure, From the First Photographer in the Crimea to Vietnam._ Text by Albert R. Leventhal. Picture research by Del Byrne. (New York, 1973).

644. Zogbaum, Rufus. "War and the Artist." _S_ 57 (January 1915), 16-35.

WAR GAMES

645. *Featherstone, Donald F. _War Games Through the Ages, 1792-1859._ Volume 3. (London, 1975).

646. Hjalmarson, J.K. "The Development of War Games." _CAJ_ 15 (Winter 1961), 4-10.

647. Immanuel, Friedrich. _The Regimental War Games._ Translated by Walter Kueger. (Kansas City, 1907).

648. Matute, Edgardo B. "Birth and Evolution of War Games." _MR_ 50 (July 1970), 49-56.

649. *Riley, Vera and John P. Young. _Bibliography of War Gaming._ (Chevy Chase, Maryland, 1957).

650. Verdy Du Vernois, Julius A.F. von. _A Simplified War Game._ Translated by Capt. Eben Swift. (Kansas City, Missouri, 1897).

651. Wells, Herbert G. _Little Wars: A Game for Boys from Twelve Years of Age to One Hundred and Fifty and for that More Intelligent Sort of Girls Who Like Boys' Games and Books With an Appendix on Kriegspeil with Marginal Drawings._ (Boston, 1913).

652. Wilson, Andrew. _The Bomb and the Computer: A Crucial History of War Games._ (New York, 1968).

653. Young, Peter, ed. _The War Game._ (London, 1972).

654. Jordan, David S. and Harvey E. War's Aftermath: A Preliminary Study of the Eugenics of War as Illustrated by the Civil War of the United States and the Late War in the Balkans. (Boston, 1914).

655. Vieth von Glossenau, Arnold F. (Ludwig Renn, pseudo.). After War. (New York, 1931).

WEAPONS AND AMMUNITION

656. Adams, John M. "The Importance of the Bayonet." JMSI 44 (March-April 1909), 257-59.

657. Ashdown, Charles H. British and Foreign Arms and Armor. (London, 1909).

658. Bailey, De Witt. Percussion Guns and Rifles: An Illustrated Reference Guide. (Harrisburg, Pennsylvania, 1972).

659. Bartlett, Wallace A. and D.B. Gallatin, compls. A Digest of Cartridges for Small Arms, Patented in the United States, England, and France, So Far as Patents Have Been Published. (Washington, D.C., 1878).

660. Belote, Theodore T. American and European Swords in the Historical Collections of the United States Museums. (Washington, D.C., 1932).

661. Bennett, Charles A. Essay (giving) Historical Account of Development (since 1346) of Small Arms and Ammunition for same, and Effect of Same Upon (the) Science of War. (Fort Monroe, Virginia, 1886).

662. Blackmore, Howard L. Firearms. (New York, 1964).

663. Blair, Claude. European and American Arms 1100-1850. (New York, 1962).

664. Blanch, H. J. A Century of Guns; A Sketch of the Leading Types of Sporting and Military Small Arms. (London, 1909).

665. Boothroyd, Geoffrey. Guns Through the Ages. (New York, 1962).

666. Bormann, Charles G. The Shrapnel Shell in England and in Belgium with Some Reflections on the Use of this Projectile in the Late Crimean War. A Historico-Technical Sketch. (Second Edition, Brussels, 1862).

667. Bowen, Daniel, compl. <u>Encyclopedia of War Machines: An Historical Survey of the World's Great Weapons</u>. (London, 1977).

668. *Braun, Wernher von and Frederick I. Ordway, III. <u>The Rocket's Red Glare: An Illustrated History of Rocketry Through the Ages</u>. (Garden City, New York, 1976).

669. *Brodie, Bernard and Fawn. <u>From Crossbow to H-Bomb</u>. (Revised and Enlarged Edition, Bloomington, Indiana, 1973).

670. Canby, Courtland. <u>A History of Weaponry</u>. (New York, 1973).

671. Carman, William Y. <u>A History of Firearms From Earliest Times to 1914</u>. (London, 1955).

672. Carter, John A. with illustrations by John Walter. <u>The Bayonet: A History of Knife and Sword Bayonets, 1850-1973</u>. (New York, 1974).

673. Castle, B.F. "Some Interesting Features of Foreign Military Rifles." <u>IJ</u> 10 (September-October 1913), 198-206.

674. Chamberlain, R.H. <u>Early Loading Tools and Bullet Molds</u>. (Porterville, California, 1970).

675. Chant, Christopher, ed. <u>How Weapons Work</u>. (Chicago, Illinois, 1976).

676. *Chinn, George M. <u>The Machine Gun: History, Evolution and Development of Manual, Automatic and Airborne Repeating Weapons</u>. (4 vols., Washington, D.C., 1951- 5).

677. Cleator, Philip E. <u>Weapons of War</u>. (New York, 1968).

678. Cline, Walter M. <u>The Muzzle-loading Rifle, Then and Now</u>. (Huntington, West Virginia, 1942).

679. Demmin, Auguste Frederic. <u>Weapons of War: Being a History of Arms and Armour from the Earliest Period to the Present Time</u>. Translated by Charles C. Black. (London, 1870).

680. "The Development of Weapons: Proceedures and Doctrine." in Irving B. Holley, Jr., <u>Ideas and Weapons</u>. (New Haven, Connecticut, 1953), 3-22.

681. Eames, Henry E. <u>The Rifle in War</u>. (Fort Leavenworth, Kansas, 1908).

682. Ellacott, S.E. <u>Guns</u>. (New York, 1956).

683. *Ellis, John. <u>The Social History of the Machine Gun</u>. (London, 1973).

684. Faber, Henry B. <u>Military Pyrotechnics. With an Historical Introduction by Marvin Dana</u>. (3 vols., Washington, D.C., 1919).

685. Fuller, John F.C. <u>Armaments and History: A Study of the Influence of Armament on History from the Dawn of Classical Warfare to the Second World War</u>. (London, 1946).

686. Gardner, Robert E. Arms Fabricators, Ancient and Modern: A Compilation of the Names and Dates of Gunsmiths, Bladesmiths, Armourers, Bowyers and Cannoneers Offered with Such Pertinent Data Upon Their Lives and Activities as is Discoverable Together with Three Hundred Sixty-Eight Identified Poincons. (Columbus, Ohio, 1934).

687. Hargreaves, Reginald. "The Dominant Weapon." CAJ 6 (December 1952), 15-26.

688. Hargreaves, Reginald. "Victory to the Stronger." USNIP 95 (April 1969), 74-84.

689. Haven, Charles T. and Melvin M. Johnson, Jr. Ammunition: Its History, Development and Use, 1600-1943--.22BB Cap to 20 mm. Shell. (New York, 1943).

690. Haven, Charles T. and Melvin M. Johnson, Jr. Automatic Arms: Their History, Development and Use. (New York, 1941).

691. Hime, Henry W.L. Gunpowder and Ammunition: Their Origin and Progress. (London, 1904).

692. Historical Evaluation and Research Organization. Historical Trends Related to Weapons Lethality. (Washington, D.C., 1964).

693. Hobart, Frank W.A. Pictorial History of the Machine Gun. (London, 1971).

694. Hogg, Ian V. and John S. Weeks. Military Small Arms of the 20th Century. (Northfield, Illinois, 1973).

695. Howard, Robert A. "Black Powder Manufacture." IA 1 (Summer 1975), 13-28.

696. Hughes, Basil P. Firepower: Weapons Effectiveness on the Battlefield, 1630-1850. (London, 1974).

697. Hurley, Vic. Arrow Against Steel: The History of the Bow. (New York, 1975).

698. Hutchison, Graham S. Machine Guns, Their History and Tactical Employment. (London, 1938).

699. Ingalls, James M. Interior Ballistics. (New York, 1912).

700. Lewis, Berkeley R. Small Arms Ammunition at the International Exposition, Philadelphia, 1876. (Washington, D.C., 1972).

701. Ley, Willey. "War Rockets of the Past." CARJ 84 (May-June 1941), 226-233.

702. Longstaff, Frederick V. and Andrew H. Atteridge. The Book of the Machine Gun. (London, 1917).

703. Low, Archibarld M. Muskets to Machine Gun. (New York, 1942).

704. Lynall, Thomas. <u>Rifled Ordnance</u>. (New York, 1864).

705. McCullagh, Francis. <u>Syndicates for War; The Influence of the Makers of War Material and of Capital Invested in War Supplies</u>. (Boston, 1911).

706. MacDonald, George W. <u>Historical Papers on Modern Explosives</u>. (New York, 1912).

707. McFarland, Earl. "Trend in Weapon Types and Design." <u>JFI</u> 230 (October 1940), 413-432.

708. McGuffie, Thomas H. "The Bayonet: A Survey of the Weapon's Employment in Warfare Over the Last Three Centuries." <u>HT</u> 12 (August 1962), 588-93.

709. McGuffie, Thomas H. "The Lance in Battle." <u>HT</u> 8 (August 1958), 574-81.

710. McGuffie, Thomas H. "Musket and Rifle." <u>HT</u> 7 (April 1957), 257-63; (July 1957), 473- 9.

711. McGuffie, Thomas H. "The Puissant Pike." <u>HT</u> 9 (September 1961), 632- 6.

712. McGuffie, Thomas H. "The Sword in Warfare." <u>HT</u> 8 (July 1958), 443-52.

713. Maeurer, Herman A. <u>Military Edged Weapons of the World, 1800-1965; A Private Collection</u>. (College Point, New York, 1967).

714. Marshall, Arthur. <u>Explosives</u>. (2 vols., Philadelphia, Pennsylvania, 1917).

715. Maude, Fredric N. "Military Training and Modern Weapons." <u>CR</u> 77 (March 1900), 305-22.

716. Maxim, Hiram S. <u>My Life</u>. (London, 1915).

717. Mayne, Charles B. <u>The Infantry Weapon and Its Use in War</u>. (London, 1903).

718. Metschl, John. <u>The Rudolph J. Nunnemacher Collection of Projectile Arms</u>. (2 vols., Milwaukee, Wisconsin, 1928).

719. Montague, Leopold A.D. <u>Weapons and Implements of Savage Races (Australia, Asia, Oceania and Africa)</u>. (London, 1921).

720. *Munroe, Charles E. <u>Index to the Literature of Explosives</u>. (2 Parts, Baltimore, Maryland, 1883-93).

721. Newman, James R. <u>The Tools of War</u>. (Garden City, New York, 1942).

722. Nickel, Helmut. <u>Arms and Armour Through the Ages</u>. (Revised ed., London, 1971).

723. Norton, Charles B. and William T. Valentine. Report on the Munitions of War, Paris Universal Exposition, 1867. (Washington, D.C., 1868).

724. O'Callaghan, Desmond and George S. Clarke Sydenham. Report on the Exhibits at the Paris Exhibition of 1889. (London, 1890).

725. Parkerson, Codman. A Brief History of Bullet Moulds. (Nashville, Tennessee, 1974).

726. Peterson, Harold L., compl. Encyclopedia of Firearms. (New York, 1964).

727. Peterson, Harold L. A History of Firearms. (New York, 1961).

728. Pollard, Hugh B.C. A History of Firearms. (Boston, 1926).

729. Poole, J.B. "A Sword Undrawn; Chemical Warfare and the Victorian Age." AQ 106 (October 1976), 463- 9; 107 (January 1977), 87-92.

730. Pridham, Charles H.B. Superiority of Fire, a Short History of Rifles and Machine Guns. (London, 1945).

731. *Reid, William. Arms Through the Ages. (New York, 1976).

732. Reynolds, Edmund G.B. The Lee-Enfield Rifle. (New York, 1962).

733. Ricketts, Howard. Firearms. (London, 1965).

734. *Riling, Raymond L.J. Guns and Shooting, A Selected Chronological Bibliography. (New York, 1951).

735. Sargeaient, B.E. "The Bayonet: The History of the Bayonet." JMSI 44 (March-April 1909), 251- 6.

736. Scoffern, John. New Resources of Warfare, With Especial Reference to Rifled Ordnance. (London, 1859).

737. Scoffern, John. Projectile Weapons of War and Explosive Compounds. (London, 1845).

738. Scott, Sibbald David. "On the History of the Bayonet." JRUSI 7 (May 1863), 333-48.

739. Shepherd, E.H. "The Evolution of the Modern Rifle." AQ 65 (January 1953), 199-201.

740. Shepperd, Gilbert A. A History of War and Weapons 1660 to 1918. (New York, 1972).

741. Stephens, Frederick J. Bayonets: An Illustrated History and Reference Guide. (London, 1968).

742. Stockholm International Peace Research Institute (SIPRI). Incendiary Weapons by Malvern Lumsden. (Cambridge, Massachusetts, 1975).

743. Swenson, George W.P. _Pictorial History of the Rifle_. (New York, 1972).

744. Tarassuk, Leonid. _Antique European and American Firearms at the Hermitage Museum_. (Text in Russian and English.) (New York, 1972).

745. Thompson, A.L. "The Bayonet." _MR_ 49 (May 1969), 93- 7.

746. Trench, Charles Chenevix. "From Arquebus to Rifle: The Pursuit of Perfection." _HT_ 23 (June 1973), 407-17.

747. Tunis, Edwin. _Weapons: A Pictorial History_. (New York, 1954).

748. United States, General Staff, 2d (Military Information) Division. _Selected Translations Pertaining to the Tactical Use and Value of Machine Guns_. (Washington, D.C., 1906).

749. United States, Ordnance Department. _Reports of Experiments on the Strength and Other Properties of Metals for Cannon: Description of the Machines for Testing Metals, and of the Classification of Cannon in Service_. (Philadelphia, Pennsylvania, 1856).

750. Wahl, Paul F. and Donald R. Toppel. _The Gatling Gun_. (New York, 1965).

751. Weaver, Erasmus M. _Notes on Military Explosives_. (New York, 1906).

752. Wilcox, Cadmus M. _Rifles and Rifle Practice_. (New York, 1861).

753. Wilkinson, Henry. _Engines of War: or, Historical and Experimental Observations on Ancient and Modern Warlike Machines and Implements, Including the Manufacture of Guns, Gunpowder, and Swords, with Remarks on Bronze, Iron, Steel, etc_. (London, 1841).

754. Young, Peter. _The Machinery of War: An Illustrated History of Weapons_. (London, 1973).

See also: Part I, Artillery and 109, 155, 189, 192, 203, 211, 270, Disarmament, 339, 345, 477, 480, 486, 499, 594, 600; Addendum: 115.

WOMEN AND BOYS IN BATTLE

755. Clayton, Ellen C. _Female Warriors: Memorials of Female Valour and Heroism, from the Mythological Ages to the Present Era_. (2 vols., London, 1879).

756. Laffin, John. Boys in Battle. (London, 1967).

757. Laffin, John. Women in Battle. (New York, 1967).

758. Truby, David J. Women at War. (Boulder, Colorado, 1977).

MISCELLANEOUS STUDIES

759. Avis, Frederick C. Historical Bodyguards. (London, 1954).

760. Barringer, Richard E. with Robert K. Ramers. War: Patterns of Conflict. (Cambridge, Massachusetts, 1972).

761. Bauer, Eddy. "The Evolution of Armies Throughout the Ages." NATOL 14 (March 1966), 8-21.

762. Carter, Robert G. The Art and Science of War Versus the Art of Fighting. (Washington, D.C., 1922).

763. Chevers, Norman. Humanity in War. (Calcutta, 1869).

764. *Coats, Wendell J. Armed Force as Power: The Theory of War Reconsidered. (New York, 1966).

765. Colin, Jean L.A. The Transformations of War. Translated by L.H.R. Pope-Hennessey. (London, 1912).

766. Cowan, Andrew Reid. War in World History: Suggestions for Students. (New York, 1929).

767. Coudenhove-Kalergi, Richard. From War to Peace. Translated by Constantine Fitzgibbon. (London, 1959).

768. Crozier, Brian. A Theory of Conflict. (New York, 1974).

769. Cunliffe, Marcus. The Age of Expansion, 1848-1917. (Springfield, Massachusetts, 1974).

770. Custance, Reginald N. A Study of War. (London, 1924).

771. Denton, Frank H. and Warren Phillips. "Some Patterss in the History of Violence." JCR 12 (June 1968), 182-95.

772. Dupuy, Trevor N. _Numbers, Predictions and War_. (Indianapolis, Indiana, 1977).

773. Falls, Cyril. _The Place of War in History_. (Oxford, England, 1947).

774. *Fieldhouse, David K. _The Colonial Empires: A Comparative Survey from the Eighteenth Century_. (New York, 1965).

775. Fuller, John F.C. _The Reformation of War_. (London, 1923).

776. Gumpert, Martin. _Dunant, The Story of the Red Cross_. (New York, 1938).

777. Hargreaves, Major Reginald. "This Thing Called War." _USNIP_ 77 (August 1951), 861- 7.

778. Haswell, Chetwynd J.D. (Jock). _Citizen Armies_. (London, 1973).

779. Liddell Hart, Basil H. _Why Don't We Learn from History_. (London, 1944).

780. McCartney, Eugene S. _Warfare by Land and Sea_. (New York, 1923).

781. Maude, Frederic N. _Attack or Defence; Seven Military Essays_. (London, 1896).

782. Maude, Frederic N. _Military Letters and Essays_. (Kansas City, Missouri, 1895).

783. Maude, Frederic N. _War and the World's Life_. (London, 1907).

784. Maurice, John Frederick. _War_. (London, 1891).

785. Melegari, Vezio. _The World's Greatest Regiments_. Translated by Ronald Strom. (London, 1969).

786. Mrazek, James. _The Art of Winning Wars_. (London, 1968).

787. Naroll, Raoul, et.al. _Military Deterrence in History: A Pilot Cross-Historical Survey_. (New York, 1974).

788. *Ney, Virgil. _The Evolution of Military Unit Control, 500 B.C.-1965 A.D._ (Fort Belvoir, Virginia, 1965).

789. Nicolai, George F. _The Biology of War_. Translated by Constance A. Grande and Julian Grande. (New York, 1918).

790. Preston, Richard A. "History and the Multi-Cultural and Multi-National Problems of Armed Forces," in Russell F. Weigley, ed., _New Dimensions in Military History_. (San Rafael, California, 1975), 225-54.

791.*Richardson, Lewis F. _Deadly Quarrels_. (Pittsburgh, Pennsylvania, 1960).

792. Roberts, Adam. _Nations in Arms: The Theory and Practice of Territorial Defense_. (New York, 1976).

793. *Singer, Joel David and Melvin Small. _The Wages of War, 1816-1969. A Statistical Handbook_. (New York, 1972).

794. Small, Melvin and Joel David Singer. "Patterns in International Warfare, 1816-1965." _AAAPSS_ 391 (September 1970), 145-55.

795. Smoke, Richard. _War: Controlling Escalation_. (Cambridge, Massachusetts, 1977).

796. Sumner, Benedict H. _War and History_. (Edinburgh, 1945).

797. Sullivan, A.E. "The 1860's and the 1960's: A Parallel." _AQ_ 88 (July 1964), 188-94.

798. Tzabar, Shimon. _The White Flag Principle: How to Lose a War and Why_. (New York, 1972).

799. _War; A Historical, Political and Social Study_. Edited by Lancelot L. Farrar. (Santa Barbara, California, 1978).

800. Wells, Donald A. _The War Myth_. (New York, 1967).

801. "What is War?", in John W. Fortescue, _The Last Post_. (London, 1934), 53-76.

802. Wintringham, Thomas H. _Armies of Freemen_. (London, 1940).

803. *Wright, Quincy. _A Study of War_. (2 vols., Chicago, Illinois, 1942).

   See also: Addendum: 72.

EVENTS LEADING UP TO WORLD WAR I

804. Albertini, Luigi. _The Origins of the War of 1914_. Translated and Edited by Isabelle M. Massey. (3 vols., London, 1952- 7).

805. Churchill, Winston L.S. The World Crisis, 1911-1914. Volume 1. (London, 1923).

806. Davis, William S. The Roots of the War: A Non-Technical History of Europe, 1870-1914. (New York, 1918).

807. Dedijer, Vladimir. The Road to Sarajevo. (New York, 1966).

808. Fay, Sidney B. The Origins of the World War. (2 vols., New York, 1928).

809. Gooch, George P. Before the War. (2 vols., London, 1936- 8).

810. Haldane, Richard B. Before the War. (London, 1920).

811. *Hale, Oron J. The Great Illusion, 1900-1914. (New York, 1971).

812. Kautsky, Karl. Outbreak of the World War: German Documents. Collected by Karl Kautsky, Edited by Max Montgelas and Walter Schucking and Translated by Carnegie Endowment for International Peace. (New York, 1924).

813. *LaFore, Laurence. The Long Fuse: An Interpretation of the Origins of World War I. (Philadelphia, 1965).

814. Laqueur, Walter Ze'ev, ed. 1914: The Coming of the First World War. (New York, 1966).

815. Ludwig, Emil. July 1914. Translated by Carlile A. Macartney. (London, 1929).

816. Mansergh, Nicholas. The Coming of the First World War: A Study in the European Balance, 1878-1914. (New York, 1949).

817. Newbold, John T.W. How Europe Armed for War (1871-1914). (London, 1916).

818. Petrie, Charles A. The Drift to World War 1900-1914. (London, 1968).

819. Remak, Joachim. The Origins of World War I, 1871-1914. (New York, 1967).

820. Rumbold, Horace. The War Crisis in Berlin: July-August 1914.... (London, 1940).

821. Schmitt, Bernadotte E. The Coming of the War, 1914. (2 vols., New York, 1930).

822. Scott, Jonathan F. Five Weeks: The Surge of Public Opinion on the Eve of the Great War. (New York, 1927).

823. Seton-Watson, Robert W. German, Slav, and Magyar: A Study in the Origins of the Great War. (London, 1916).

824. Seton-Watson, Robert W. Sarajevo, A Study in the Origins of the Great War. (London, 1925).

825. Taylor, Alan J.P. War by Time Table: How the First World War Began. (New York, 1969).

826. Towle, P. "European Balance of Power in 1914." AQ 104 (April 1974), 332-42.

827. Trainor, Lake. "The European States System and the Origins of the First World War 1903-1915." NZJH 9 (October 1975), 171-78.

828. *Tuchman, Barbara W. The Guns of August. (New York, 1962).

829. Turner, L.C.F. "The Role of the General Staffs in July 1914." AJPH 11 (December 1965), 305-23.

830. Wilkinson, Spensor. August 1914, The Coming of the War. (New York, 1914).

PART II: CONTINENTS, SMALLER LAND AREAS AND COUNTRIES

Part II contains citations for publications pertaining to Nineteenth Century armed land conflict in the various continents, smaller land areas and countries. These include references to general publications on the military and armed conflict within the boundaries of the geographical and political areas of the world; however, those publications relating to specific armed conflicts will be found in Part III. Quite naturally, the sections for English-speaking areas are generally larger than those for others, but many pertinent publications on countries such as France and Germany have been written in English. Unfortunately, little interest in Nineteenth Century armed conflict in Africa had been expressed in the English language until recently except for certain battles and wars in which British troops were engaged.

AFRICA

The political boundaries in Africa have changed frequently throughout the centuries and, of course, they have not necessarily been respected by the native tribes. Thus, citations to pertinent publications will most likely be found under a section heading denoting a geographical area of Africa but a few long established country names have been used.

1. Alexander, Boyd. From the Niger to the Nile. (2 vols., London, 1907).

2. Axelson, Eric A. Portugal and the Scramble for Africa, 1875-91. (Johannesburg, 1967).

3. Bartlett, Vernon. Struggle for Africa. (New York, 1953).

4. *Bridgman, Jon and David E. Clarke, compls. German Africa: A Select Annotated Bibliography. (Stanford, California, 1965).

5. Britain and Germany in Africa: Imperial Rivalry and Colonial Rule. Edited by Prosser Gifford and William R. Louis. (New Haven, Connecticut, 1967).

6. Chamberlain, Muriel E. The Scramble for Africa. (New York, 1974).

7. Cohen, William B. Rulers of Empire: The French Colonial Service in Africa. (Stanford, California, 1971).

8. Cooke, James J. New French Imperialism, 1880-1910: The Third Republic and Colonial Expansion. (Hamden, Connecticut, 1973).

9. Duffy, James E. Portugal in Africa. (Cambridge, Massachusetts, 1962).

10. France and Britain in Africa: Imperial Rivalry and Colonial Rule. Edited by Prosser Gifford and William R. Louis. (New Haven, Connecticut, 1971).

11. Gann, Lewis H. and Peter Duignan. Burden of Empire; An Appraisal of Western Colonization in Africa South of the Sahara. (New York, 1967).

12. Gann, Lewis H. and Peter Duignan. The Rulers of German Africa, 1884-1914. (Stanford, California, 1977).

13.*Hess, Robert L. and Dalvan M. Coger. Semper ex Africa...A Bibliography of Primary Sources for 19th Century Tropical Africa: As Reported by Explorers, Missionaries, Traders, Travelers, Administrators, Military Men, Adventurers and Others. (Stanford, California, 1972).

14. Kiernan, V.G. "Colonial Africa and Its Armies," in War and Society: A Yearbook of Military History. Volume 1. Edited by Brian Bond and Ian Roy. (New York, 1977), 20-39.

15. Latimer, Elizabeth. Europe in Africa in the Nineteenth Century. (Chicago, Illinois, 1895).

16. Leadership in 19th Century Africa: Essays from Tarikh. Edited by Obara Ikime. (London, 1974).

17. Lemarchand, Rene. "African Armies in Historical Contemporary Perspectives: The Search for Connections." JPMS 4 (Fall 1976), 261-75.

18. Lewin, Percy Evans. The Germans in Africa. (New York, 1915).

19. Lloyd, Edwin. Three Great African Chiefs (Khame, Sebele and Bathoeng). (London, 1895).

20. Maxse, Frederick I. Seymour Vandeleur...A Plain Narrative of the Part Played by British Officers in the Acquisition of Colonies and Dependencies in Africa.... (London, 1906).

21. Middleton, Lamar. The Rape of Africa. (New York, 1936).

22. Moreira, Adriano. Portugal's Stand in Africa. (New York, 1962).

23. Robinson, Ronald and John Gallagher with Alice Denny. Africa and the Victorians: The Climax of Imperialism in the Dark Continent. (New York, 1961).

24. Sanderson, Edgar. Africa in the Nineteenth Century. (New York, 1898).

25. Scholefield, Alan. _The Dark Kingdoms: The Impact of White Civilization on Three Great African Monarchies_. (London, 1975).

26. Suret-Canale, Jean. _French Colonialism in Tropical Africa, 1900-1945_. Translated by Till Gottheiner. (New York, 1971).

27. Taylor, Alan J.P. _Germany's First Bid for Colonies, 1884-1885, A Move in Bismark's European Policy_. (London, 1938).

28. Thruston, Arthur B. _African Incidents; Personal Experiences in Egypt and Unyoro, with an Introduction by General Sir A. Hunter, A Memoir of the Author, and an Account of Major Thruston's Last Stay in 1897 in the Protectorate, his Death, and the Mutiny of the Uganda Rifles_. (London, 1900).

29. *Universities of East Africa Social Science Conference, 5th, Nairobi, 1969. _War and Society in Africa_. Edited by Bethwell A. Ogot. (London, 1972).

30. Vandeleur, Seymour (Cecil Foster Seymour). _Campaigning on the Upper Nile and Niger_. (London, 1898).

31. Wheeler, Douglas L. "African Elements in Portugal's Armies in Africa (1891-1974)." _AFS_ 2 (Winter 1976), 233-50.

32. White, Gavin. "Firearms in Africa: An Introduction." _JAH_ 12, No. 2 (1971), 173-84.

33. *Woolbert, Robert Gale. "Italian Colonial Expansion in Africa (Bibliographical Article)." _JMH_ 4 (September 1932), 430-45.

See also: Part I: 1, 5, 22, 719; Part II: 342, 1975; Addendum: 105, 148.

CENTRAL AFRICA

34. Baker, Samuel White. _Ismailia: A Narrative of the Expedition to Central Africa for the Suppression of the Slave Trade, Organized by Ismail, Khedive of Egypt_. (London, 1874).

35. Fisher, Humphrey J. and Virginia Rowland. "Firearms in Central Africa." _JAFH_ 12, No. 2 (1972), 215-39.

36. Gordon, Charles G. _Colonel Gordon in Central Africa, 1874-1879_. Edited by George B. Hill. (London, 1881).

37. Great Britain, War Office, Intelligence Division. <u>Precis of Information Concerning the British Central Africa Protectorate with Notes on Adjoining Territories</u> by Courtenay B. Vyvyan. (London, 1899).

38. Moyse-Bartlett, Hubert. "The King's African Rifles: A Study in the Military History of East and Central Africa, 1890-1914." Ph.D. Dissertation, University of London, 1954.

39. *Moyse-Bartlett, Hubert. <u>The King's African Rifles: A Study in the Military History of East and Central Africa, 1890-1945.</u> (Aldershot, England, 1956).

40. Tabler, Edward C., ed. <u>Trade and Travel in Early Barotseland; The Diaries of Sir George Westbeech, 1885-1888, and Captain Norman MacLeod, 1875-1876.</u> (Berkeley, California, 1963).

CONGO

41. Burrows, Guy. <u>The Curse of Central Africa, With Which is Incorporated a Campaign Amongst Cannibals</u> by Edgar Canisius. (London, 1903).

42. Collins, Robert O. <u>King Leopold, England, and the Upper Nile, 1899-1909.</u> (New Haven, Connecticut, 1968).

43. Morel, Edmund D. <u>King Leopold's Rule in Africa.</u> (London, 1904).

44. Slade, Ruth M. <u>King Leopold's Congo; Aspects of the Development of Race Relations in the Congo Independent State.</u> (New York, 1962).

45. Thomas, Mary Elizabeth. "Anglo-Belgian Military Relations and the Congo Question, 1911-1913." <u>JMH</u> 25 (June 1953), 157-65.

46. Wack, Henry W. <u>Story of the Congo Free State; Social, Political, and Economic Aspects of the Belgian System of Government in Central Africa.</u> (New York, 1905).

EAST AFRICA

47. Austen, Ralph A. Northwest Tanzania Under German and British Rule; Colonial Policy and Tribal Politics, 1889-1939. (New Haven, Connecticut, 1968).

48. Beachey, R.W. "The Arms Trade in East Africa in the Late Nineteenth Century." JAFH 3, No. 3 (1962), 451-67.

49. Bennett, Norman R. Mirambo of Tanzania, 1840-1884. (New York, 1971).

50. Coupland, Reginald. The Exploitation of East Africa, 1856-1890: The Slave Trade and the Scramble. (London, 1939).

51. Coupland, Reginald. East Africa and Its Invaders, from the Earliest Time to the Death of Seyyid Said in 1856. (Oxford, England, 1938).

52. Galbraith, John S. MacKinnon and East Africa, 1878-1895: A Study in the "New Imperialism." (Cambridge, England, 1972).

53. Great Britain, War Office, Intelligence Division. Handbook of British East Africa, Including Zanzibar, Uganda, and the Territory of the Imperial British East Africa Company. (London, 1893).

54. Great Britain, War Office, Intelligence Division. Precis of Information Concerning the British East Africa Protectorate and Zanzibar. (London, 1901).

55. Gregory, John W. The Foundation of British East Africa. (London, 1901).

56. Iliffe, John. Tanganyika Under German Rule, 1905-1912. (London, 1969).

57. Lord, John. Duty, Honor, Empire; The Life and Times of Colonel Richard Meinertzhagen. (New York, 1970).

58. Lugard, Frederick J.D. The Rise of Our East African Empire; Early Efforts in Nyassaland and Uganda. (2 vols., London, 1895).

59. MacDonald, James R.L. Soldiering and Surveying in British East Africa. (London, 1897).

60. Meinertzhagen, Richard. Army Diary 1899-1926. (Edinburgh, 1960).

61. Meinertzhagen, Richard. Kenya Diary, 1902-1906. (Edinburgh, 1957).

62. Moyse-Bartlett, Hubert. "Bugle with Strings." AQ 97 (January 1969), 223-34.

63. Perham, Margery, ed. The Diaries of Lord Lugard. (3 vols., Evanston, Illinois, 1959).

64. *Perham, Margery F. Lugard. (2 vols., London, 1956-60).

65. Redmayne, Alison. "Mkwawa and the Hehe Wars." JAFH 9, No. 3 (1968), 409-36.

66. Rigby, Christopher P. General Rigby, Zanzibar and the Slave Trade, with Journals, Dispatches, Etc. Edited by Lilian M. Russell.

    See also: Part II: 38, 39, 276; Addendum: 142.

ABYSSINIA (ETHIOPIA)

67. Darkwah, R.H.K. Shewa, Menilek and the Ethiopian Empire, 1813-1889. (London, 1975).

68. Marcus, Harold G. The Life and Times of Menelik II: Ethiopia, 1844-1913. (New York, 1975).

69. Parkhurst, Richard K.P. An Introduction to the History of the Ethiopian Army. (Addis Ababa, Ethiopia, 1967).

70. Rassam, Hormuzd. Narrative of the British Mission to Theodore, King of Abyssinia. (London, 1869).

71. Wylde, Augustus B. Modern Abyssinia. (London, 1901).

    See also: Part II: 157.

SOMALILAND

72. Battersby, Henry, F.P. Richard Corfield of Somaliland. (London, 1914).

73. Great Britain, War Office, General Staff. Military Report on Somaliland, 1907, Geographical, Descriptive, and Historical. Volume 1. (London, 1907).

74. Hamilton, Angus. _Somaliland_. (London, 1911).

75. Jardine, Douglas J. _The Mad Mullah of Somaliland_. (London, 1923).

76. Jennings, James W. _With the Abysinnians in Somaliland_. (London, 1905).

77. McNeill, Malcolm. _In Pursuit of the "Mad" Mullah: Service and Sport in the Somali Protectorate_. (London, 1902).

78. Silberman, Leo. "The 'Mad' Mullah: Hero of Somali Nationalism." _HT_ 10 (August 1960), 523-34.

UGANDA

79. Beattie, John H.M. _Bunyoro: An African Kingdom_. (New York, 1960).

80. Great Britain, War Office, Intelligence Division. _Precis of Information Concerning the Uganda Protectorate_, by E.M. Woodward. (London, 1902).

81. Ingham, Kenneth. _The Kingdom of Toro in Uganda_. (London, 1975).

82. Karugire, Samwiri R. _A History of the Kingdom of Nkore in Western Uganda to 1896_. (Oxford, England, 1971).

83. Low, D.A. "Warbands and Ground-Level Imperialism in Uganda, 1870-1900." _HSANZ_ 16 (October 1975), 584-97.

   See also: Part II: 53, 58.

NORTH AFRICA

84. Boahen, A.A. "British Penetration of the Sahara and Western Sudan, 1788-1861." Ph.D. Dissertation, University of London, 1959.

85. Cooke, George Wingrove. _Conquest and Colonization in North Africa_. (London, 1860).

86. *Perkins, Kenneth P. "Pressure and Persuasion in the Policies of the French Military in Colonial North Africa." <u>MA</u> 40 (April 1976), 74-78.

87. Perkins, Kenneth P. "Quids, Captains, and Colons: French Military Administration in the Colonial Maghrib, 1844-1934." Ph.D. Dissertation, Princeton University, 1973.

ALGERIA

88. Cowan, L. Gray. "The New Face of Algeria, Part I, Political and Administrative Development." <u>PSQ</u> 66 (September 1951), 340-65.

89. Crealock, J. North. "Algerian Warfare." <u>JRUSI</u> 21, No. 92 (1877), 1150-71.

90. Great Britain, War Office. <u>Report on the Causes of Reduced Mortality in the French Army Serving in Algeria</u>. (London, 1867).

91. Cave, Laurence T. <u>The French in Africa</u>. (London, 1859).

MOROCCO

92. Burke, Edmund III. <u>Prelude to Protectorate in Morocco: Precolonial Protest and Resistance, 1860-1912</u>. (Chicago, 1977).

93. Carrouges, Michel. <u>Soldier of the Spirit: The Life of Charles DeFoucauld</u>. Translated by Marie-Christine Hellin. (New York, 1956).

94. Confer, Carl V. "Lyautey and the Moroccan Problem, 1903 to 1907." Ph.D. Dissertation, University of Pennsylvania, 1939.

95. Cooke, James J. "Lyautey and Etienne: The Soldier and the Politician in the Penetration of Morocco, 1904-1906." <u>MA</u> 36 (February 1972), 14-18.

68

96. Dunn, Ross Edmunds. "The Colonial Offensive in Southeastern Morocco, 1881-1912:Patterns of Response." Ph.D. Dissertation, University of Wisconsin, 1969.

97. Herman, Fred J. "The Regular Army of Morocco." JMSI 45 (November-December 1909), 431-35.

98. Rankin, Reginald. In Morocco with General D'Amade. (London, 1908).

99. *Scham, Alan. Lyautey in Morocco: Protectorate Administration, 1912-1925. (Berkeley, California, 1970).

100. Usborne, Cecil V. The Conquest of Morocco. (London, 1936).

TUNISIA

101. Broadley, Alexander M. The Last Punic War; or Tunis, Past and Present, with a Narrative of the French Conquest of the Regency. (Edinburgh, 1882).

102. Brown, Leon C. The Tunisia of Ahmad Bey, 1837-1855. (Princeton, New Jersey, 1974).

103. Ling, Dwight Leroy. "The French Occupation and Administration of Tunisia, 1881-1892." Ph.D. Dissertation, Illinois, 1955.

104. McKay, Donald Vernon. "The French Acquisition of Tunis." Ph.D. Dissertation, Cornell University, 1939.

105. Macken, Richard Alan. "The Indigenous Reaction to the French Protectorate in Tunisia, 1881-1900." Ph.D. Dissertation, Princeton University, 1973.

106. O'Donnell, Joseph Dean. "Charles Cardinal Lavigerie and the Establishment of the 1881 French Protectorate in Tunisia." Ph.D. Dissertation, Rutgers University, 1970.

NORTHEAST AFRICA

107. Sanderson, George N. England, France, and the Upper Nile, 1882-1899; A Study in the Partition of Africa. (Edinburgh, 1965).

EGYPT

108. Berger, Morroe. Military Elite and Social Change; Egypt Since Napoleon. (Princeton, New Jersey, 1960).

109. Blaxland, Gregory. Egypt and Sinai: Eternal Battleground. (New York, 1968).

110. Blunt, Wilfred S. Secret History of the English Occupation of Egypt; Being a Personal Narrative of Events. (London, 1907).

111. Broadley, Alexander M. How We Defended Arabi and His Friends, A Story of Egypt and the Egyptians. (London, 1884).

112. Carman, William Y. The Military History of Egypt; The Story of the Egyptian Army, Its Battles, Organization and Uniforms from the Pharohs to the Present Day. (Cairo, 1945).

113. Challie-Long, Charles. My Life in Four Continents. (London, 1912).

114. Clementson, J. The Re-organization of the Egyptian Army and its Contribution to the Reconquest of the Egyptian Sudan, 1882-99. M.A. Thesis, Durham University, 1970.

115. Crabites, Pierre. Americans in the Egyptian Army. (London, 1938).

116. Crabites, Pierre. Ibrahim of Egypt. (London, 1935).

117. Crabites, Pierre. Ismail the Maligned. (New York, 1933).

118. Czeslaw, G. Jessman. "American Officers of Khedive Ismail." AFA 57 (October 1958), 302-7.

119. Dicey, Edward. The Story of the Khedivate. (New York, 1902).

120. Dodwell, Henry H. The Founder of Modern Egypt; A Study of Muhammed Ali. (Cambridge, England, 1931).

70

121. Dye, William McEntyre. _Moslem Egypt and Christian Abyssinia; or, Military Service Under the Khedive, in His Provinces and Beyond Their Borders, as Experienced by the American Staff._ (New York, 1880).

122. Gordon, John. _My Six Years with the Black Watch, 1881-1887; Egyptian Campaign, Eastern Soudan, Nile Expedition, Egyptian Frontier Field Force._ (Boston, Massachusetts, 1929).

123. Great Britain, War Office, General Staff. _Military Report on Egypt, 1906._ Compiled by A. Kenney-Herbert. (London, 1906).

124. Great Britain, War Office, Intelligence Division. _Report on Egypt._ (London, 1882).

125. Great Britain, War Office, Intelligence Division. _Report on the Egyptian Provinces of the Sudan, Red Sea and Equator._ (London, 1883).

126. *Hesseltine, William B. and Hazel C. Wolf. _The Blue and the Gray on the Nile._ (Chicago, 1961).

127. Hill, Richarld L. _Egypt in the Sudan, 1820-1881._ (New York, 1959).

128. Kopcsak, Arpad A., Jr. "Short Tour--1870." _A_ 34 (December 1975), 16-17, 37-39.

129. Loring, William W. _A Confederate Soldier in Egypt._ (New York, 1884).

130. MacMunn, George. "The Story of the British in Egypt and the Sudan." _AQ_ 63 (January 1952), 150-2.

131. Mansfield, Peter. _The British in Egypt._ (New York, 1972).

132. Milner, Alfred. _England in Egypt._ (London, 1892).

133. Nicolle, David. Nizam--Egypt's Army in the 19th Century." _AQ_ 108 (January 1978), 69-78.

134. Sandes, Edward W.C. _The Royal Engineers in Egypt and the Sudan._ (Chatham, England, 1937).

135. Stewart, Desmond. "Mohammed Ali, Pasha of Egypt." _HT_ 8 (May 1958), 321-27.

See also: Part II: 28.

136. Alford, Henry S. and William D. Sword. The Egyptian Soudan; Its Loss and Recovery. (London, 1898).

137. Allen, Bernard M. Gordon and the Sudan. (London, 1931).

138. Bedri, Babikr. The Memoirs of Babikr Bedri. Translated by Yousef Bedri and George Scott. (London, 1969).

139. Bermann, Richard A. The Mahdi of Allah; The Story of the Derivsh, Mohammed Ahmed. Translated by John Robin. (New York, 1931).

140. Brook-Shepherd, Gordon. Between Two Flags; The Life of Baron Sir Rudolf von Slatin Pasha. (New York, 1973).

141. Collins, Robert Oakley. "The Mahdist Invasions of the Southern Sudan, 1883-1898." Ph.D. Dissertation, Yale University, 1959.

142. Crabites, Pierre. The Winning of the Sudan. (London, 1934).

143. Crabites, Pierre. Gordon, the Sudan and Slavery. (London, 1933).

144. Farwell, Bryon. Prisoners of the Mahdi; The Story of the Mahdist Revolt which Frustrated Queen Victoria's Designs on the Sudan, Humbled Egypt, and Led to the Fall of Khartoum, the Death of Gordon, and Kitchener's Victory at Omdurman Fourteen Years Later. (New York, 1967).

145. Gessi, Romolo (Pasha). Seven Years in the Soudan; Being a Record of Explorations, Adventures, and Campaigns Against the Arab Slave Hunters (1874-1881). (London, 1892).

146. Great Britain, War Office, Intelligence Division. Handbook of the Sudan. Compiled by Edward Gleichen. (London, 1898); Supplement... (July 1899). (London, 1899).

147. Great Britain, War Office, Intelligence Division. Report on the Nile and Country between Dongola, Suakin, Kassala and Omdurman. Describing the Various Routes Bearing on this Country. Compiled by Edward Gleichen. (2nd Edition, London, 1898).

148. Hill, Richard L. Slatin Pasha. (London, 1965).

149. Holt, Peter M. The Mahdist State in the Sudan, 1881-1898; A Study of its Origins, Development and Overthrow. (London, 1958).

150. Holt, Peter M. "The Mahdia in the Sudan, 1881-1898." HT 8 (March 1958), 187-95.

151. Jackson, Henry C. Osman Digna. (London, 1926).

152. Neufeld, Charles. A Prisoner of the Khaleffa: Twelve Years Captivity at Omdurman. (3rd Edition, London, 1899).

153. Slatin, Rudolph C. Fire and Sword in the Sudan: A Personal Narrative of Fighting and Serving the Dervishes, 1879-1895. (London, 1896).

154. Warburg, Gabriel. The Sudan Under Wingate: Administration in the Anglo-Egyptian Sudan, 1899-1816. (London, 1971).

155. Warner, Philip. Dervish; The Rise and Fall of an African Empire. (New York, 1975).

156. Wingate, Francis R. Mahdism and the Egyptian Soudan; Being an Account of the Rise and Progress of Mahdism and Subsequent Events in the Soudan to the Present Time. (London, 1891).

157. Wylde, Augustus B. '83 to '87 in the Soudan, with an Account of Sir William Hewett's Mission to King John of Abyssinia. (2 vols., London, 1888).

See also: Part II: 114, 125, 127, 130, 134, 142, 143, 144, 149.

SOUTH AFRICA

158. Atmore, Anthony, J.M. Chirenje and S.I. Mudenge. "Firearms in South Central Africa." JAFH 12, No. 4 (1971), 545-56.

159. Atmore, Anthony and Peter Sanders. "Sotho Arms and Ammunition in the Nineteenth Century." JAFH 12, No. 4 (1971), 535-44.

160. Baines, Thomas. Journal of a Residence in Africa, 1842-1853. Edited by Reginald F. Kennedy. (2 vols., Cape Town, 1964).

161. Beach, D.N. "Ndebele Raiders and Shona Power." JAFH 15, No. 4 (1974), 633-51.

162. Binns, C.T. The Last Zulu King; The Life and Death of Cetshwayo. (London, 1963).

163. Bisset, John J. Sport and War; or, Recollections of Fighting and Hunting in South Africa from the Year 1834 to 1867.... (London,1875).

164. Bullock, Charles. The Mashona and the Matabele. (Cape Town, 1950).

165. Buxton, Earl. General Botha. (New York, 1924).

166. Caddell, William W. and Douglas Blackburn. Secret Service in South Africa. (London, 1911).

167. Cannon, Richard. History of the Mounted Rifleman with a Brief Account of the Colony of the Cape of Good Hope. (London, 1842).

168. Chanaiwa, David. "The Army and Politics in Pre-Industrial Africa: The Ndebele Nation, 1822-1893." AFSR 19 (September 1976), 49-67.

169. Colvin, Ian D. Cecil John Rhodes, 1853-1902. (London, 1902).

170. Cooper-Chadwick, J. Three Years with Lobengula, and Experiences in South Africa. (London, 1894).

171. Cork, Barry J. Rider on a Grey Horse: A Life of Hodson of Hodson's Horse. (London, 1958).

172. Crafford, Frederick S. Jan Smuts, A Biography. (Garden City, New York, 1943).

173. Cunynghame, Arthur T. My Command in South Africa, 1874-1878; Comprising Experiences of Travel in the Colonies of South Africa and the Independent States. (London, 1879); Index. Compiled by M. Balkind. (Johannesburg, 1964).

174. Curson, Herbert H. Colours and Honors in South Africa, 1783-1948. (Pretoria, 1948).

175. Curson, Herbert H. More Military and Police Devices from South Africa, 1790-1962. (Pretoria, 1962).

176. Curson, Herbert H. Regimental Devices in South Africa, 1783-1954. (Pretoria, 1954).

177. Devitt, Napier, ed. Galloping Jack: The Reminiscences of Brigadier General John Robinson Royston. (London, 1937).

178. Flint, John. Cecil Rhodes. (Boston, Massachusetts, 1974).

179. Fuller, Thomas E. The Right Honourable Cecil John Rhodes, A Monograph and a Reminiscence. (London, 1910).

180. Galbraith, John S. Reluctant Empire, British Policy on the South African Frontier, 1834-54. (Berkeley, California, 1963).

181. Gann, Lewis H. "The Development of Southern Rhodesia's Military System, 1890-1953." Occasional Papers of the National Archives of Rhodesia, No. 1 (1965), 60-79.

182. Gibbs, Peter. The True Book About Cecil Rhodes. (London, 1956).

183. Gibson, James Y. The Story of the Zulus. (New Revised Edition, New York, 1911).

184. Gordon-Brown, Alfred, ed. The Narrative of Private Buck Adams, 7th (Princess Royal's) Dragoon Guards, on the Eastern Frontier of the Cape of Good Hope, 1843-8. (Cape Town, 1941).

185. Great Britain, War Office, General Staff. The Native Tribes of the Transvaal. (London, 1905).

186. Great Britain, War Office, Intelligence Division. Precis of Information Concerning the Colony of Natal, with a Map, Corrected to July 1879. (London, 1879).

187. Great Britain, War Office, Intelligence Division. Precis of Information Concerning Southern Rhodesia. Compiled by Charles T. Dawkins. (London, 1899).

188. Great Britain, War Office, Intelligence Division. Precis of Information Concerning the Zulu Country with a Map. (London, 1879).

189. Great Britain, War Office, Intelligence Division. Precis of Information Concerning Zululand, with a Map. (Corrected to December 1892). By Capt. George Wemyss. (London, 1893).

190. Great Britain, War Office, Intelligence Division. Precis of Information Concerning Zululand, with a Map. (Corrected to December 1894). By Capt. George Wemyss. (London, 1895).

191. Griggs, T.S. "Fashoda South: The British Occupation of Mashonaland and Manica, 1890-91." JSAHR 51 (Spring 1973), 27-39.

192. Gross, Felix. Rhodes of Africa. (London, 1956).

193. Haggard, Henry R. Cetywayo and His White Neighbors; or, Remarks on Recent Events in Zululand, Natal, and the Transvaal. (London, 1890).

194. Harding, Colin. Frontier Patrols. (London, 1937).

195. Hensman, Howard. Cecil Rhodes; A Study of a Carreer. (London, 1901).

196. Hole, Hugh M. Lobengula. (London, 1929).

197. Hook, David B. With Sword and Statute on the Cape of Good Hope Frontier. (Cape Town, 1907).

198. *Johannesburg, Public Library. Catalogue of British Regimental Histories with Notes on Their Service in South Africa. (Johannesburg, 1953).

199. Kemp, Samuel. Black Frontiers; Pioneer Adventures with Cecil Rhodes' Mounted Police in Africa. (London, 1932).

200. Kruger, Stephanus J.P. The Memoirs of Paul Kruger, Four Times President of the South African Republic. (2 vols., New York, 1902).

201. LeMay, Godfrey H.L. British Supremacy in South Africa, 1899-1907. (New York, 1965).

202. Lockhart, John G. and Christopher M. Woodhouse. Cecil Rhodes; The Colossus of Southern Africa. (New York, 1963).

203. Lovell, Reginald I. The Struggle for South Africa, 1875-1899; A Study in Economic Imperialism. (New York, 1934).

204. Lucas, Thomas J. The Zulus and the British Frontiers. (New York, 1969).

205. McDonald, James G. Rhodes, A Life. (London, 1927).

206. Marks, Shula and Anthony Atmore. "Firearms in Southern Africa: A Survey." JAFH 12, No. 4 (1971), 517-30.

207. Martineau, John, ed. Life and Correspondence of Bartle Frere. (Second Edition, 2 vols., London, 1895).

208. Michell, Lewis. The Life of the Right Honorable Cecil John Rhodes. (2 vols., New York, 1910).

209. Millin, Sarah G. Rhodes, Biography of Cecil Rhodes. (London, 1933).

210. Molyneux, Maj. W.C.F. "Notes on Hasty Defenses as Practiced in South Africa." Ordnance Note No. 247, February 14, 1883 in United States, Ordnance Department, Ordnance Notes. (12 vols., Washington, D.C., 1873-84).

211. Moodie, Duncan C.F. The History of the Battles and Adventures of the British, the Boers, and the Zulus, &c. in Southern Africa, From the Time of Pharaoh Necho to 1880. (2 vols., Cape Town, 1888).

212. Murray, Henry. Memoir and Correspondence of the Late Captain Arthur Stormont Murray, of the 1st Battalion of the Rifle Brigade. (London, 1859).

213. Mutunhu, Tendai. "The Matebele Nation: The Dynamic Sociopolitical and Military Development of an African State, 1840-1893." JAFS 3, (Summer 1976), 165-182.

214. Napier, Edward D.H.E. Excursions in South Africa, Including a History of Cape Colony, An Account of the Native Tribes, Etc. (2 vols., London, 1849).

215. O'Callaghan, Desmond. Guns, Gunners, and Others. (London, 1925).

216. Orpen, Neil D. Gunners of the Cape; The Story of the Cape Artillery. (Cape Town, 1965).

217. Preller, Gustav S. Lobengula; The Tragedy of a Matabele King. (Johannesburg, 1963).

218. Ritter, Ernest A. Shaka Zulu; The Rise of the Zulu Empire. (New York, 1957).

219. Roberts, Brian. The Zulu Kings. (New York, 1974).

220. Ross, Robert. "The Kora Wars on the Orange River, 1830-1880." JAFH 16, No. 4 (1975), 561-76.

221. Sacks, Benjamin. South Africa: An Imperial Dilemma; Non-Europeans and the British Nation, 1902-1914. (Albuquerque, New Mexico, 1967).

222. Schreiner, Olive. Trooper Peter Halket of Mashonaland. (Boston, 1897).

223. Selby, John. Shaka's Heirs. (London, 1971).

224. Selby, John. "Rhodesia's Origin." AQ 107 (January 1977), 48-53.

225. Summers, Roger and C.W. Pagden. The Warriors. (Cape Town, 1970).

226. Tylden, Geoffrey. The Armed Forces of South Africa, With an Appendix on the Commandos. (Johannesburg, 1954).

227. Tylden, Geoffrey. "The British Army and the Transvaal, 1875 to 1885." JSAHR 30 (Winter 1952), 159-71.

228. Tylden, Geoffrey. The Rise of the Basuto. (Cape Town, 1950).

229. Uys, Ian S. For Valour; The History of Southern Africa's Victoria Cross Heroes. (Johannesburg, 1973).

230. Warren, Charles. On the Veldt in the Seventies. (London, 1902).

231. Williams, Basil. Cecil Rhodes. (London, 1921).

232. Wolseley, Garnet J. The South African Diaries of Sir Garnet Wolseley, 1875. Edited by Adrian Preston. (Cape Town, 1971).

233. Worsfold, William Basil. Sir Bartle Frere, a Footnote to the History of the British Empire. (London, 1923).

234. Young, P.J. Boot and Saddle, a Narrative Record of the Cape Regiment The British Cape Mounted Riflemen, The Frontier Armed Mounted Police, and the Colonial Cape Mounted Riflemen. (Cape Town, 1955).

See also: Part I: 13; Part II: 253, 1157, 1383; Addendum: 9, 12, 13, 24, 34, 49, 128.

SOUTHWEST AFRICA

235. Calvert, Albert F. South-West Africa, During the German Occupation, 1884-1914. (London, 1915).

236. Ajayi, J.F. Ade and Robert S. Smith. Yoruba Warfare in the Nineteenth Century. (Cambridge, England, 1964).

237. Akintoye, Stephen Adebanji. Revolution and Power Politics in Yorubaland, 1840-1893: Ibadan Expansion and the Rise of Kkitiparapo. (New York, 1971).

238. Asiwaju, A.I. Western Yorubaland Under European Rule, 1889-1945: A Comparative Analysis of French and British Colonialism. (Atlantic Highlands, New Jersey, 1976).

239. Atteridge, Andrew H. "Recent Expeditions in West Africa, 1894-1899." JRUSI 94 (February 1900), 111-36.

240. Awe, Bolanle. "Militarism and Economic Development in 19th Century Youuba Country: The Ibadan Example." JAFH 14, No. 1 (1973), 65-77.

241. Baden-Powell, Robert S.S. The Downfall of Prempeh; A Diary of Life with the Native Levy in Ashantee in 1895-96. (London, 1896).

242. Balesi, Charles J. "From Adversary to Comrades-in-Arms: West Africans and the French Military, 1895-1919." Ph.D. Dissertation, University of Illinois, Chicago Circle, 1976.

243. Brackenbury, Henry and George L. Huyshe. Fanti and Ashanti, Three Papers Read on Board the S.S. Ambriz on the Voyage to the Gold Coast. (London, 1873).

244. Crowder, Michael. Senegal; A Study of French Assimilation Policy. (London, 1967).

245. Crowder, Michael, ed. West African Resistance: The Military Response to Colonial Occupation. (New York, 1971).

246. Crowder, Michael. West Africa under Colonial Rule. (Evanston, Illinois, 1968).

247. Crozier, Brig. Gen. Frank P. Five Years Hard; Being an Account of the Fall of the Fulani Empire. (London, 1932).

248. Davis, Shelby C. Reservoirs of Men: A History of the Black Troops of French West Africa. (Chambery, 1934).

249. Echenberg, M.J. "Late 19th Century Military Technology in Upper Volta." JAFH 12, No. 2 (1971), 241-254.

250. Etheridge, N.H.R. "The Sierra Leone Frontier Police: A Study in the Functions and Employment of a Colonial Force." M.Litt., Aberdeen, England, 1967.

251. Forde, Cyril D. and Phyllis M. Kaberry, eds. West African Kingdoms in the Nineteenth Century. (London, 1967).

252. Gore, Albert A. A Contribution to the Medical History of Our West African Campaigns. (London, 1876).

253. Great Britain, War Office. Statistical Reports on the Sickness, Mortality, and Invaliding Among the Troops in Western Africa, St. Helena, the Cape of Good Hope, and the Mauritius. (London, 1840).

254. Great Britain, War Office, Intelligence Division. Report on the Northern Territories of the Gold Coast. Compiled by Henry P. North-cott. (London, 1899).

255. Hargreaves, John D. Prelude to the Partition of West Africa. (New York, 1963).

256. Haywood, Austin H.W. and Frederick A.S. Clarke. The History of the Royal West African Frontier Force. (Aldershot, England, 1964).

257. Kanya-Forstner, Alexander S. The Conquest of the Western Sudan: A Study in French Military Imperialism. (London, 1969).

258. Kanya-Forstner, Alexander S. "The Role of the Military in the Formulation of French Policy Towards the Western Sudan, 1879-99." Ph.D. Dissertation, Cambridge, England, 1965.

259. Kea, R.A. "Firearms and Warfare on the Gold and Slave Coast From 16th Century to 19th Century." JAFH 12, No. 2 (1971), 185-213.

260. Klein, Martin A. Islam and Imperialism in Senegal: Sine-Saloum, 1847-1914. (Stanford, California, 1968).

261. Law, Robin. "Horses, Firearms, and Political Power in Pre-Colonial West Africa." P&P 72 (August 1976), 112-32.

262. Lawrence, Arnold W. Trade Castles and Forts of West Africa. (London, 1963).

263. Legassick, Martin. "Firearms, Horses and Samorian Army Organization 1870-1898." JAFH 7, No. 1 (1966), 95-115.

264. Little, Kenneth L. The Mende of Sierra Leone; A West African People in Transition. (London, 1951).

265. Lystad, Robert A. The Ashanti: A Proud People. (New Brunswick, New Jersey, 1958).

266. Mbaeyi, P.M. "Military and Naval Factors in British West African History, 1823-74: Being an Examination of the Organization of British Naval and Military Forces in West Africa, and Their Role in the Struggle for the Coast and the Principal Rivers." Ph.D. Dissertation, Oxford University, England, 1966.

267. Mockler-Ferryman, Augustus F. British West Africa; Its Rise and Progress. (London, 1898).

268. Muffett, David J. Concerning Brave Captains: Being a History of the British Occupation of Kano and Sokoto and of the Last Stand of the Fulani Forces. (Ontario, Canada, 1964).

269. Obichere, Boniface I. West African States and European Expansion; The Dahomey-Niger Hinterland, 1885-1898. (New Haven, Connecticut, 1971).

270. Preston, G.N. "Perseus and Medusa in Africa: Military Art in Fanteland, 1834-1972." AFAR 8 (Spring 1975), 36-41, 68-71, 91-92.

271. Rattray, Robert Sutherland. Ashanti. (Oxford, England, 1923).

272. Rattray, Robert Sutherland. Tribes of the Ashanti Hinterland. (Oxford, England, 1932).

273. Rudin, Henry R. Germans in the Cameroons, 1884-1914; A Case Study in Modern Imperialism. (New Haven, Connecticut, 1938).

274. Smaldone, Joseph P. Warfare in the Sokoto Caliphate: Historical and Sociological Persepctives. (New York, 1977).

275. Teba, P.T. "Britain's Role in the Regulation of the Arms Traffic in West Africa, 1873-1919." M. Litt., Cambridge, England, 1967.

276. Thomson, Arthur A.M. and Dorothy Middleton. Lugard in Africa. (London, 1959).

277. Tordoff, William. Ashanti Under the Prempehs. (London, 1965).

278. Ukpabi, Samson C. "British Military Expeditions in West Africa Re-Examined." PAFJ 8 (Spring 1975), 31-43.

279. Ukpabi, Samson C. "Military Recruitment and Social Mobility in Nineteenth Century British West Africa." JAFS 2 (Spring 1975), 87-107.

280. Ukpabi, Samson C. "The West African Frontier Force, An Instrument of Imperial Policy, 1897-1914." M.A. Thesis, Birmingham, England, 1964.

281. Ukpabi, Samson C. "West African Troops and the Defence of British West Africa in the Nineteenth Century." AFSR 17 (April 1974), 133-50.

282. West African Chiefs: Their Changing Status under Colonial Rule and Independence. Edited by Michael Crowder and Obaro Ikime. Translated by Brenda Packman. (New York, 1970).

See also: Addendum: 2, 104.

NIGERIA

283. Anjorin, A.O. "The British Occupation and Development of Northern Nigeria, 1897-1914." Ph.D. Dissertation, University of London, 1966.

284. Bacon, Reginald H.S. Benin the City of Blood. (London, 1897).

285. Crowder, Michael. Revolt in Bussa; A Study of British "Native Administration" in Nigerian Borgu, 1902-1935. (Evanston, Illinois, 1973).

286. Flint, John E. Sir George Goldie and the Making of Nigeria. (London, 1960).

287. Hall, Herbert C. Barrack and Bush in North Nigeria. (London, 1923).

288. Orr, Capt. Charles W.J. The Making of Northern Nigeria. (London, 1911).

289. Wellesley, Dorothy. Sir George Goldie; Founder of Nigeria. (London, 1934).

MADAGASCAR

290. Maude, Francis C. Five Years in Madagascar with Notes on the Military Situation. (London, 1895).

291. Oliver, Samuel P. Examples of Military Operations in Madagascar by Foreign Powers and Native Campaigns, 1642-1881. (London, 1885).

292. Wastell, R.E.P. "British Imperial Policy in Relation to Madagascar, 1810-96." Ph.D. Dissertation, University of London, 1944.

ASIA

293. Cady, John F. The Roots of French Imperialism in Eastern Asia. (Ithaca, New York, 1954).

294. Edwardes, Michael. The West in Asia, 1850-1914. (London, 1967).

295. Knight, Edward F. Where Three Empires Meet; A Narrative of Recent Travel in Kashmir, Tibet, Gilgit and Adjoining Countries. (New York, 1900).

296. Lamb, Alastair. Britain and Chinese Central Asia; The Road to Lhasa, 1767-1905. (London, 1960).

297. Maki, John M. Conflict and Tension in the Far East: Key Documents, 1894-1960. (Seattle, Washington, 1961).

298. Mohl, Raymond A. "Confrontation in Central Asia, 1885." HT 19 (March 1969), 176-183.

299. Vambery, Armin. Central Asia and the Anglo-Russian Frontier Question: A Series of Political Papers. Translated by Tony E. Bunnett. (London, 1874).

300. Yate, Lt. Arthur C. England and Russia Face to Face in Asia; Travels with the Afghan Boundary Commission. (London, 1887).

See also: Part I: 248, 719; Part II: 392, 571, 1165, 1188, 1473, 1842, 1846, 1847, 1856, 1874, 1880, 1895, 1910, 1919, 1927, 1931, 1932, 1945, 1946, 1947, 1954, 1963, 1975, 2356, 3478; Addendum: 87, 125.

CHINA

301. Anderson, John. Mandalay to Momein: A Narrative of the Two Expeditions to Western China of 1868 and 1875 Under Colonel Edward B. Slader and Colonel Horace Browne. (London, 1876).

302. Beresford, Charles. The Break-Up of China: An Account of Its Present Commerce, Currency, Waterways, Armies, Railways, Politics and Future Prospects. (New York, 1899).

303. Bland, John O.P. Li Hung-chang. (London, 1917).

304. Bruce, Robert. Sun Yat-Sen. (London, 1969).

305. Cavendish, A.E.J. "The Armed Strength of China." JRUSI 42 (June 1898), 705-23.

306. Ch'en, Chi-t'ien (Gideon Chen). Lin Tse-hsu, Pioneer Promoter of the Adoption of Western Means of Maritime Defense in China. (Peiping, 1934).

307. Chesneaux, Jean. Peasant Revolts in China, 1840-1949. Translated by C.A. Curwen. (London, 1973).

308. Chesneaux, Jean, Marianne Bastid and Marie-Claire Bergere. China from the Opium Wars to the 1911 Revolution. Translated by Anne Destenay. (New York, 1976).

309. Chu, Wen-Chang. The Moslem Rebellion in Northwest China, 1862-1878; A Study of Government Minority Policy. (The Hague, 1966).

310. Collier, Harry H. and Paul Chin-Chih Lai. Organizational Changes in the Chinese Army, 1895-1950. (Taipei, Taiwan, 1969).(See Addendum: 171).

311. Conflict and Control in Late Imperial China. Edited by Frederic Wakeman, Jr. and Carolyn Grant. (Berkeley, California, 1976).

312. Cranston, Earl. "The Rise and Decline of Occidental Intervention in China." PHR 12 (March 1943), 23-32.

313. Deacon, Richard. The Chinese Secret Service. (New York, 1974).

314. Franke, Wolfgang. A Century of Chinese Revolution, 1851-1949. Translated by Stanley Rudman. (New York, 1971).

315. Gill, William. "The Chinese Army." JRUSI 24 (April 1880), 358-77.

316. Grimshaw, Mabel I. "The Great Powers and the Far East, from the Seizure of Kiao-chau to the Boxer Settlement, 1897-1901." M.A. Thesis, Birmingham, England, 1929.

317. *Hacker, Barton C. "The Weapons of the West: Military Technology and Modernization in 19th Century China and Japan." T&C 18 (January 1977), 43-55.

318. Harrison, James T. The Communists and Chinese Peasant Rebellion; A Study in the Re-Writing of Chinese History. (New York, 1969).

319. Hibbert, Christopher. The Dragon Wakes; China and the West, 1793-1911. (New York, 1970).

320. Hsiao, Kung-chuan. Rural China: Imperial Control in the Nineteenth Century. (Seattle, Washington, 1960).

321. Hsu, Imanuel C.Y. "Gordon in China, 1880." PHR 33 (May 1964), 147-66.

322. Hughes, Ernest R. The Invasion of China by the Western World. (London, 1937).

323. Hunt, Michael H. *Frontier Defense and the Open Door: Manchuria in Chinese-American Relations 1895-1911*. (New Haven, Connecticut, 1973).

324. India, Army, Intelligence Branch. *...Report on the Burma-China Boundary between the Taping and the Shweli* by Henry R. Davies. (Rangoon, 1894).

325. India, Quartermaster-General's Department, Intelligence Branch. *...China: Being a Military Report on the North-Eastern Portions of the Provinces of Chih-li and Shan-tung; Nanking and its Approaches; Canton and its Approaches; etc., etc., together with an Account of the Chinese Civil, Naval and Military Administration, etc., etc., and a Narrative of the Wars Between Great Britain and China* by Mark S. Bell. (3 vols., Simla, 1894).

326. India, Quartermaster-General's Department, Intelligence Branch. *Military Report on the Chin-Lushai Country*. (Simla, 1893).

327. *Kuhn, Philip A. *Rebellion and Its Enemies in Late Imperial China; Militarization and Social Structure, 1796-1864*. (Cambridge, Massachusetts, 1970).

328. Lamprey, J. "The Economy of the Chinese Army." *JRUSI* 11 (April 1867), 403-33.

329. Lattimore, Owen. *Manchuria; Cradle of Conflict*. (New York, 1932).

330. Lee, J.S. "The Periodic Recurrence of Internecine Wars in China." *CHJ* 14 (March 1931), 111-15, 159-62.

331. Lin, T.C. "The Amur Frontier Question between China and Russia, 1850-1860." *PHR* 3 (March 1934), 1-27.

332. Martin, Bernard and Shui Chien-Tung. *Makers of China: Confucius to Mao*. (New York, 1972).

333. Michael, Franz H. "The Chinese Military Tradition." *FES* 15 (1946), 65-69, 84-87.

334. Michael, Franz H. "Revolution and Renaissance in Nineteenth-Century China: The Age of Tseng Kuo-fan." *PHR* 16 (May 1947), 144-151.

335. Morton, Louis. "Army and Marines on the China Station: A Study in Military and Political Rivalry." *PHR* 29 (February 1960), 51-73.

336. Nye, Gideon. *The Rationale of the China Question: Comprising an Inquiry into the Repressive Policy of the Imperial Government with Considerations of the Duties of the Three Treaty Powers, England, France and America, in Regard to It; and a Glance at the Origins of the First and Second Wars with China, with Incidental Notices of the Rebellion by an American*. (Third Edition, Macao, 1857).

337. Powell, Ralph L. *The Modernization and Control of the Chinese Armies, 1895-1912*. Ph.D. Dissertation, Harvard University, 1953.

338. *Powell, Ralph L. The Rise of Chinese Military Power, 1895-1912.
(Princeton, New Jersey, 1955).

339. Preston, Adrian. "Chinese Military Policy in the Mid-Nineteenth
Century." AQ 101 (January 1971), 206-14.

340. Scarth, John. Twelve Years in China; The People, the Rebels, and
the Mandarins By a British Resident. (Edinburgh, 1860).

341. Schrecker, John E. Imperialism and Chinese Nationalism; Germany
in Shantung. (Cambridge, Massachusetts, 1971).

342. Schwabe, G. Salis. "Carrier Corps and Coolies on Active Service in
China, India and Africa, 1860-1879." JRUSI 24, No. 107 (1881),
815-46.

343. Schwartz, Harry. Tsars, Mandarins, and Commissars; A History of
Chinese-Russian Relations. (Philadelphia, 1964).

344. Siang-tseh, Chiang. The Nien Rebellion. (Seattle, Washington, 1954).

345. Skrine, Clarmont P. and Pamela Nightingale. MaCartney at Kashgar;
New Light on British, Chinese and Russian Activities in Sinkiang,
1890-1918. (London, 1973).

346. *Spector, Stanley. Li Hung-chang and the Huai Army; A Study in
Nineteenth Century Chinese Regionalism. (Seattle, Washington, 1964).

347. Spence, Jonathan. The China Helpers; Western Advisors in China,
1620-1910. (London, 1969).

348. Teng, Ssu-yu and John K. Fairbank. China's Response to the West:
A Documentary Survey, 1839-1923. (Cambridge, Massachusetts, 1954)
and Research Guide. (Cambridge, Massachusetts, 1954).

349. Teng, Ssu-yu. The Nien Army and Their Guerilla Warfare, 1851-1868.
(The Hague, 1961).

350. United States, Adjutant Generals' Office, Military Information
Division. Notes on China. August 1900. (Washington, D.C., 1900).

351. Wakeman, Frederic E. Strangers at the Gate; Social Disorder in South
China, 1839-1861. (Berkeley, California, 1966).

352. Warser, Marina. The Dragon Empress; Life and Times of Tz'u-Hsi,
Empress Dowager of China, 1835-1908. (New York, 1972).

353. Wehrle, Edmund S. Britain, China, and the Antimissionary Riots,
1891-1900. (Minneapolis, Minnesota, 1966).

354. *Whitson, William Wallace and Paul Chin-Chih Lai, compls. Chronology
of Military Campaigns in China, 1895-1950. (n.p., 1967).

See also: Part I: 7; Part II: 298, 447, 670, 1184, 1851, 2081;
         Addendum: 69, 171.

INDIA

355. Adye, John. _Indian Frontier Policy, an Historical Sketch_. (London, 1897).

356. Adye, John. _Sitana: A Mountain Campaign on the Borders of Afghanistan in 1863_. (London, 1867).

357. Andrew, William P. _The Bolan and Khyber Railways with a Memorandum by Sir Henry Green on Portable Railways in Military Operations_. (London, 1879).

358. Archer, Mildred. "The Two Worlds of Colonel Skinner." _HT_ 10 (September 1960), 608-615.

359. _The Army in India, 1850-1914: A Photographic Record_. (London, 1968).

360. _Army in India and Its Evolution Including an Account of the Establishment of the Royal Air Force in India_. (Calcutta, 1924).

361. Baden-Powell, Robert S.S. _Indian Memoires; Recollections of Soldiering, Sport, Etc_. (London, 1915).

362. Badenach, Walter. _Inquiry into the State of the Indian Army, with Suggestions for its Improvement, and the Establishment of a Military Policy for India_. (London, 1826).

363. Bajwa, Fauja S. _Military System of the Sikhs During the Period 1799-1849_. (Delhi, 1964).

364. Barat, Amiya. _The Bengal Native Infantry; Its Organization and Discipline, 1796-1852_. (Calcutta, 1962).

365. Beatson, Stuart. _A History of the Imperial Service Troops of the Native States_. (Calcutta, 1903).

366. *Beaumont, Roger. _Sword of the Raj; The Old Indian Army_. (Indianapolis, 1977).

367. Bell, Evans. _The Annexation of the Punjaub and the Maharajah Dulcep Singh_. (London, 1882).

368. Bernard, Edward H., compl. _A Text-book of Indian Military Law: Being a Collection of the Various Enactments and Regulations Relating to Indian Military Law_. (London, 1896).

369. Bevan, Henry. _Thirty Years in India; or, a Soldier's Reminiscences of Native and European Life in the Presidencies, from 1808 to 1838_. (2 vols., London, 1839).

370. Bonarjee, Pitt D. _A Handbook of the Fighting Races of India_. (Calcutta, 1899).

371. Bristow, Robert C. Memories of the British Raj: A Soldier in India. (London, 1974).

372. Broome, Arthur. History of the Rise and Progress of the Bengal Army. (Calcutta, 1850).

373. Browne, Samuel J. Journal of the Late General Sir Sam Browne from 1840-1878. (Edinburgh, 1937).

374, Buckle, E. Memoir of the Services of the Bengal Artillery, from the Formation of the Corps to the Present Time, with Some Account of its Internal Organization. Edited by John W. Kaye. (London, 1852).

375. Bullock, Humphrey. Indian Cavalry Standards. (London, 1930).

376. Bullock, Humphrey. Indian Infantry Colours. (Bombay, 1931).

377. Bullock, Humphrey. "John Company's Old Contonments." AQ 62 (January 1954), 229-32.

378. Bullock, Humphrey. List of Local Officers of the Nizam's Army, 1807-1853. (Second Edition, Rawalpindi, 1938).

379. Cadell, Patrick. History of the Bombay Army. (New York, 1938).

380. Caine, Caesar, ed. Barracks and Battlefields in India; or, the Experiences of a Soldier (Thomas Malcolm) of the 10th Foot in the Sikh Wars and Sepoy Mutiny. (York, England, 1891).

381. Campbell, Walter. My Indian Journal. (Edinburgh, 1864).

382. Candler, Edmund. Sepoy. (London, 1919).

383. Cardew, Francis G. A Sketch of the Services of the Bengal Army to the Year 1895. (Calcutta, 1903).

384. Caroe, Olaf K. The Pathans, 550 B.C.-A.D.1957. (London, 1958).

385. Caulfield, James. Observations on the Indian Administration, Civil and Military. (London, 1832).

386. Caulfield, James. The Punjaub and the Indian Army. (London, 1846).

387. Chakravorty, Birendra. British Relations with the Hill Tribes of Assam since 1858. (Calcutta, 1964).

388. Chandra, S. "The Development of Mountain Warfare in India in the 19th Century." M.Ph., University of London, 1968.

389.*Cockle, Maurice J.D., compl. A Catalogue of Books Relating to the Military History of India. (Simla, 1901).

390. *Cohen, Stephen P. The Indian Army: Its Contribution to the Development of a Nation. (Berkeley, California, 1971).

391. Collen, Edwin H.H. The Indian Army: A Sketch of Its History and Organization. (Oxford, England, 1907).

392. Colquhoun, Archibald R. Russia Against India; The Struggle for Asia. (New York, 1900).

393. Colvin, Ian D. The Life of General Dyer. (London, 1929).

394. Conran, Henry M. Autobiography of an Indian Soldier. (London, 1870).

395. Cooper, Leonard. Havelock. (London, 1957).

396. Cotton, Sydney J. Nine Years on the North-west Frontier of India from 1854-63. (London, 1868).

397. Creagh, O'Moore. The Autobiography of General Sir O'Moore Creagh. Edited by Charles E. Callwell. (London, 1924).

398. Crooke, W.M. "Indian Infantry Buttons, 1903-1922." JSAHR 55 (Spring 1977), 15-31.

399. Crozier, S.F. "The Indian Army Room at Sandhurst." AQ 67 (October 1953), 89-93.

400. Cumberland, R.B. Stray Leaves from the Diary of an Indian Officer... (London, 1865).

401. Cunningham, Joseph D. A History of the Sikhs, from the Origin of the Nation to the Battles of the Stulej. (London, 1849).

402. Dalhousie, James A.B.R. Private Letters of the Marquess of Dalhousie. Edited by John G.A. Baird. (London, 1910).

403. Daly, Hugh. Memoirs of General Sir Henry Dermot Daly Sometime Commander of Central India Horse, Political Assistant for Western Malwa, Etc. (London, 1905).

404. Danvers, Frederick C. The Portuguese in India. Being a History of the Rise and Decline of their Eastern Empire. (2 vols., London, 1894).

405. Das, Shiva T. Indian Military: Its History and Development. (New Delhi, 1969).

406. Davies, Cuthbert Collin. The Problem of the North-West Frontier, 1890-1908, With a Survey of Policy Since 1849. (Second Revised Edition, New York, 1975).

407. Dodwell, Henry H. Sepoy Recruitment in the Old Madras Army. (Calcutta, 1922).

408. Duff, James G. A History of the Mahrattas. (3 vols., London, 1826).

409. Edwardes, Herbert B. Memorials of the Life and Letters of Major-General Sir Herbert B. Edwardes...by his wife, Emma Edwardes. (London, 1886).

410. Edwardes, Maj. Herbert B. A Year on the Punjab Frontier, in 1848-1849. (2 vols., London, 1851).

411. Egerton, Wilbraham E. An Illustrated Handbook of Indian Arms; Being a Classified and Descriptive Catalogue of the Arms Exhibited at the India Museum, with an Introductory Sketch of the Military History of India. (London, 1880).

412. Elliot, James G. The Frontier 1839-1947; The Story of the North-West Frontier of India. (London, 1968).

413. Elphinstone, Mountstuart. An Account of the Kingdom of Caubul, and Its Dependencies in Persia, Tartary, and India, Comprising a View of the Afghaun Nation, and a History of the Dooraunee Monarchy. (London, 1815).

414. Elwin, Varrier, ed. India's North-east Frontier in the Nineteenth Century. (London, 1959).

415. Ewart, Joseph. A Digest of the Vital Statistics of the European and Native Armies in India; Interspersed with Suggestions for the Eradication and Mitigation of the Preventible and Avoidable Causes of Sickness and Mortality Amongst Imported and Indigenous Troops. (London, 1859).

416. Fforde, C.W. DeL. "The Memoirs of Captain Charles Wilbraham Ford; The Honourable East India Company's Service." JSAHR 55 (Summer 1977), 73-84.

417. Forbes, Archibald. Havelock. (London, 1890).

418. Forrest, George W. A History of the Indian Mutiny. (3 vols., London, 1904-12).

419. Forrest, George W. Life of Field Marshal Sir Neville Chamberlain. (London, 1909).

420. Forrest, George W. Sepoy Generals: Wellington to Roberts. (Edinburgh, 1901).

421. Foster, William. John Company. (London, 1926).

422. Fraser, Hastings. Memoir and Correspondence of General James Stuart Fraser of the Madras Army. (London, 1885).

423. Fraser, James B. Military Memoir of Lieut.-Colonel James Skinner... (2 vols., London, 1851).

424. Fraser, John. _Sixty Years in Uniform_. (London, 1939).

425. Fraser, Thomas G. _Records of Sport and Military Life in Western India_. (London, 1881).

426. Fredericks, Pierce S. _The Sepoy and the Cossacks_. (New York, 1971).

427. Gardner, Alexander H.C. _Soldier and Traveller: Memoirs of Alexander Gardner, Colonel of Artillery in the Service of Maharaja Ranjit Singh_. Edited by Hugh Pearse. (London, 1898).

428. Gleig, George R. _India and Its Army. An Essay_. (London, 1857).

429. Glover, Michael. _An Assemblage of Indian Army Soldiers and Uniforms from the Original Paintings of the Late Chater Paul Chater_. (London, 1973).

430. Goddard, E. "The Indian Army; Company and Raj." _ASA_ 63 (October 1976), 263-76.

431. Gordon, Charles A. _Experiences of an Army Surgeon in India_. (London, 1872).

432. Gordon, John J.H. _The Sikhs_. (Edinburgh, 1904).

433. Graham, Cuthbert A.L. _A History of the Indian Mountain Artillery_. (Aldershot, England, 1957).

434. Great Britain, Colonial Office. _East India Army Administration; Correspondence Regarding the Administration of the Army in India_. (London, 1905).

435. Great Britain, Colonial Office, East India (Northwest Frontier). _Papers Regarding I. Orakzais: Request of Certain Clans to be Taken Under British Administration. II. Zakka Khel Afridis: Operations. III. Mohmonds: Operations_. (London, 1908).

436. Great Britain, War Office. _Our Indian Empire. A Short Review and Some Hints for the Use of Soldiers Proceeding to India_. (London, 1912).

437. Grey, Charles. _European Adventurers of Northern India, 1785 to 1849_. Edited by Herbert O. Garrett. (Lahore, 1929).

438. Griffin, Lepal H. _Ranjit Singh_. (Oxford, England, 1892).

439. Gupta, S. "British Policy on the North-east Frontier of India, (1826-86)." Ph.D. Dissertation, Oxford, England, 1948.

440. Harden, F.G. "Sepoy Head-Dresses." _JUSII_ 82 (July-October 1952), 175-80.

441. Harden, F.G. "Uniforms of the Indian Soldier Plassy to Partition." _JUSII_ 96 (January-March 1966), 71-76.

442. *Heathcote, T.A. The Indian Army; The Garrison of British Imperial India 1822-1922. (Newton Abbot, Devon, England, 1974).

443. Hitsman, John Mackay. "The Army in India, 1665-1865." CAJ 12 (January 1958), 69-75.

444. Hodder, Reginald. Famous Fights of Indian Native Regiments. (London, 1914).

445. Hodgson, John S. Opinions on the Indian Army. (London, 1857).

446. Holdich, Thomas H. The Indian Borderland, 1880-1900. (London, 1901).

447. Hough, William. A History of British Military Exploits and Political Events in India, Afghanistan, and China, from the Capture of Calcutta in 1757, to the Battle of Chillianwalla in 1849. (2 vols., London, 1853).

448. Hughes, Basil P. The Bengal Horse Artillery, 1800-1861: The "Red Men," A Nineteenth Century Corps d'Elite. (London, 1971).

449. India, Army. The Army in India and its Evolution, Including an Account of the Establishment of the Royal Air Force in India. (Calcutta, 1924).

450. India, Army. Abstract of General Orders from 1817 to 1840 by David Thompson. (Delhi, 1840).

451. India, Army, Adjutant-General's Branch. Report on the Attack Man-oeuvres, February 1900. (Simla, 1900).

452. India, Army, Punjab Frontier Force. A Brief Account of the Punjab Frontier Force from its Organization in 1849 to Its Re-distribution on 31st March 1903. Compiled from various records by Boydo Nath Dey. (Abbottsbad, 1903).

453. India, Defence Department. Army Tables of Fort Armaments. (Revised Edition, Calcutta, 1913).

454. India, Defence Department. Army Tables of the Corps of Frontier Garrison Artillery, 1907. (Calcutta, 1907).

455. India, Defence Department. ...Reports on the Signalling Operations with the 1. Isazai Field Force, 1892, 2. Waziristan Field Force, 1894-95, 3. Chitral Relief Force, 1895, 4. Techi Field Force, 1897, 5. Mohamand Field Force, 1897, 6. Malakand and Buner Field Forces, 1897-98, 7. Tirsh Expeditionary Force, 1897-98. (7 vols., Simla, 1892).

456. India, Intelligence Branch. Frontier and Overseas Expeditions from India. (6 vols. in 8, Calcutta and Simla, 1907-11).

457. India, Quartermaster-General's Department. Photographs of Types of the Native Indian Arms, Views in Afghanistan, Taken During the War of 1879; North-West Frontier of Hindustan; Burmah, During the British Operations in that Country; Miscellaneous Indian Photographs. (n.p., 1895).

458. India, Quartermaster-General's Department, Intelligence Branch. A Dictionary of the Pathan Tribes on the North-West Frontier of India. Compiled by James Wolfe Murray. (Calcutta, 1899).

459. India, Quartermaster-General's Department, Intelligence Branch. A Dictionary of the Pathan Tribes on the North-West Frontier of India. (Calcutta, 1910).

460. India, Quartermaster-General's Department, Intelligence Branch. Gazetteer of Manipur by E.W. Dun. (Calcutta, 1886).

461. India, Quartermaster-General's Department, Intelligence Branch. Gazetteer of the Eastern Hindu Kush by E.C. Barrow. (4 pts. in one vol., Simla, 1888).

462. India, Quartermaster General's Department, Intelligence Branch. Military Report on the Chin-Lushai Country. (Simla, 1893).

463. Indian Army School of Cookery. Indian Manual of Military Cookery. (Calcutta, 1906).

464. Ingram, E. "The Rules of the Game; A Commentary on the Defence of British India, 1798-1829." JI&CH 3 (January 1975), 257-79.

465. Innes, James John McLeod. The Life and Times of General Sir James Browne... (Buster Browne). (London, 1905).

466. Jackson, Donovan. India's Army. (London, 1942).

467. Jacob, John. Tracts on the Native Army of India, Its Organization and Discipline. (Bombay, 1857).

468. James, Harold D. and Denis Sheil-Small. The Gurkhas. (London, 1965).

469. Jeffreys, Julius. The British Army in India: Its Preservation (Clothing, Housing, Locating, Recreative Employment and Hopeful Encouragement of the Troops with an Appendix on India). (London, 1858).

470. Kaye, John W. Lives of Indian Officers, Illustrative of the History of the Civil and Military Service of India. (3 vols., London, 1869-73).

471. Keene, Henry G. Hindustan under Free Lances, 1770-1820; Sketches of Military Adventure in Hindustand During the Period Immediately Preceeding British Occupation. (London, 1907).

472. Keppel, Arnold. Gun-Running and the Indian North-West Frontier. (London, 1911).

473. Krishna Sinha, Narendra K. Rise of the Sikh Power. (Calcutta, 1936).

474. Lala, Mohana. Life of the Amir Dost Mohammed Khan of Kabul. (With his Political Proceedings towards the English, Russian, and Persian Governments, including the Victory and Disasters of the British Army in Afghanistan). (London, 1846).

475. Lambrick, H.F. Sind; A General Introduction. (Hyderabad, 1960).

476. Lawford, James P. Britain's Army in India from its Origins to the Conquest of Bengal. (Winchester, Massachusetts, 1978).

477. Lawrence, George. Reminiscences of Forty-Three Years in India, including the Cabul Disasters, Captivities in Afghanistan and the Punjab, and a Narrative of the Mutinies in Rajputana. Edited by William Edwards. (London, 1874).

478. Lawrence, Henry M.L. Adventures of an Officer in the Service of Runjeet Singh. (2 vols., London, 1845).

479. Lawrence, Henry M.L. Essays, Military and Political, Written in India. (London, 1859).

480. Lee-Warner, William. The Life of the Marquis of Dalhousie. (London, 1904).

481.*Leslie, John H and David Smith, compls. A Bibliography of Works by Officers, Non Commissioned Officers and Men Who Ever Served in the Royal, Bengal, Madras, or Bombay Artillery. (Leicester, England, 1909).

482. Longer, V. Red Coats to Olive Green: A History of the Indian Army, 1600-1974. (Bombay, 1974).

483. Low, Ursula. Fifty Years with John Company from the Letters of General Sir John Low of Clatto, 1822-1858. (London, 1936).

484. Lunt, James. Bokhara Burnes. (New York, 1969).

485. Lydgate, J.E. "Curzon, Kitchener and the Problem of Indian Army Administration, 1899-1909." Ph.D. Dissertation, University of London, 1965.

486. McGregor, William Lewis. The History of the Sikhs; Containing the Lives of the Gooroos; the History of the Independent Sirdars, or Missuls, and the Life of the Great Founder of the Sikh Monarchy, Maharajah Runjeet Singh. (London, 1846).

487. MacGregor, Charles M. The Life and Opinions of Major General Sir Charles Metcalf MacGregor, Quartermaster General in India. Edited by Charlotte Mary MacGregor. (2 vols., London, 1888).

488. MacMunn, George F. The Armies of India. Painted by A.C. Lovett. (London, 1911).

489. MacMunn, George F. The Martial Races of India. (London, 1933).

490. MacMunn, George F. "Quartermaster-General's Department and the Administrative Services in India from the Mutiny to the Present Time." JRUSI 70 (February 1925), 101-34.

491. MacMunn, George F. Vignettes from Indian Wars. (London, 1932).

492. MacPherson, Maj. Samuel C. Memorial of Service in India from the Correspondence of the Late Major Samuel Charters MacPherson. Edited by William MacPherson. (London, 1865).

493. Majumdar, B.N. "Development of the Transport System in the Indian Army from 1760 to 1914." AQ 77 (January 1959), 250-60.

494. Majumdar, B.N. The Military System of the Sikhs. (New Delhi, 1965).

495. Majumdar, B.N. A Study of Indian Military History. (New Delhi, 1963).

496. Majumdar, Kanchanmoy. "Recruitment of the Gurkhas in the Indian Army, 1814-1877." JUSII 93 (April-June 1963), 143-57.

497. Malleson, George B. Decisive Battles of India from 1746 to 1849. (London, 1883).

498. Marshman, John C. Memoirs of Major General Sir Henry Havelock. (London, 1860).

499. *Mason, Philip. A Matter of Honor; An Account of the Indian Army, Its Officers and Men. (New York, 1974).

500. Mawbey, H.L. "Past and Future of the Royal Indian Marines." JRUSI 69 (August 1924), 465-487.

501. Mehra, Parshotam. The McMahon Line and After: A Study of the Triangular Contest on India's North-Eastern Frontier Between Britain, China and Tibet, 1904-1947. (Delhi, 1974).

502. Miller, Charles. Khyber: The Story of an Imperial Migraine. (New York, 1977).

503. Moore, Arthur T. Notes for Officers Proceeding to India. (Chatham, England, 1904).

504. Morison, John L. From Alexander Burnes to Frederick Roberts; A Survey of Imperial Frontier Policy. (London, 1936).

505. Mouat, F.J. "British Soldier in India." JRUSI 10, No. 40 (1866), 347-86.

506. Mouat, Frederic J. Death Tribute of England to India: Being an Examination of the Deaths and Invaliding of Officers of Her Majesty's British Forces Serving in India, from 1861 to 1870 Inclusive, Considered with Special Reference to the Question of the Present Value of European Life in India. (London, 1875).

507. Mountain, Armine S.H. Memoirs and Letters of the Late Colonel Armine S.H. Mountain, Adjutant-General of Her Majesty's Forces in India. Edited by Mrs. Armine Mountain. (London, 1858).

508. Murland, H.F. Records of the IV Madras Pioneers 1759-1903. (Bangalore, 1922).

509. Murray, Hugh. History of British India, With Continuation Comprising the Afghan War, the Conquest of Sinde and Gwalior, War in the Punjab, etc. (London, 1849).

510. Myers, Margaret A. Regimental Histories of the Indian Army. (London, 1957).

511. Nandan, Sri. "The Military Tradition." JUSII 100 (October-December 1970), 350-56.

512. Napier, Charles James. Records of the Indian Command of General Sir Charles James Napier, G.C.B., Comprising all his General Orders, Remarks on Courts Martial, etc., etc., with an Appendix, Containing Reports of Speeches, Copies of Letters, and Notices of his Public Proceedings, Extracted from Contemporaneous Prints. Compiled by John Mawson. (Calcutta, 1851).

513. Napier, Charles James. Defects Civil and Military, of the Indian Government. Edited by Sir William F.P. Napier. (Second Edition, London, 1853).

514. Napier, William F.P. History of General Sir Charles Napier's Administration of Scinde, and Campaign in the Cutchee Hills. (London, 1851).

515. Nevill, Hugh L. Campaigns on the North-west Frontier. (London, 1912).

516. Newall, D.J.F. "Military Colonization as a Reserve for India." JRUSI 25, No. 113 (1881), 719-44.

517. Nolan, Edward H. The Illustrated History of the British Empire in India and the East, from the Earliest Times to the Suppression of the Sepoy Mutiny in 1859. (2 vols., London, 1858-60).

518. North, R. The Punjab Frontier Force. A Brief Record of Their Services. 1846-1924. (Dera Ismail Khan, 1934).

519. Osborne, William G. The Court and Camp of Runjeet Sing, with Introductory Sketch on the Origin and Rise of the Sikh State. (London, 1840).

520. Paget, William H. A Record of the Expeditions Undertaken Against the North-west Frontier Tribes. (Calcutta, 1874).

521. Pal, Dharm. Traditions of the Indian Army. (Delhi, 1961).

522. Parlby, Samuel, ed. The British Indian Military Repository...
(5 vols., Calcutta, 1822-27).

523. Paul, Lt. Col. Ernest T. The Imperial Army of India. (Calcutta, 1902).

524. Pearman, John. Sergeant Pearman'sMemoirs: Being, Chiefly, His Account of Service With the Third (King's Own) Light Dragoons in India, from 1845 to 1853, Including the First, and Second Sikh Wars. Edited by the Marquis of Anglesey. (London, 1968).

525. Pitt, D.C. Dean. "Transport for Asiatic Warfare, with a Brief Account of the Transport Operations from Sukkur to Quetta in 1879." JRUSI 24,No. 106 (1880), 498-521.

526. *Prasad, S.N. A Survey of Work Done on the Military History of India. (Calcutta, 1976).

527. Preston, Adrian W. "British Military Policy and the Defence of India; A Study of British Military Policy, Plans and Preparations During the Russian Crisis, 1876-80." Ph.D. Dissertation, University of London, 1966.

528. Preston, Adrian W. "The Indian Army and Indo-British Political and Strategic Relations, 1745-1947." JUSII 100 (October-December 1970), 357-89.

529. Preston, Adrian W. "Sir Charles MacGregor and the Defence of India, 1857-1887." JUSII 97 (July-September 1967), 193-211.

530. Prinsep, Henry T. Origin of the Sikh Power in the Punjab, and Political Life of Muha-Raja Runjeet Singh, with an Account of the Present Condition, Religion, Laws and Customs of the Sikhs. (Calcutta, 1834).

531. Rafter, Capt. Michael. Our Indian Army: A Military History of the British Empire in the East. (London, 1855).

532. Rawson, Philip S. The Indian Sword. Edited by K.W. Petersen. (Copenhagen, 1967).

533. Razzell, P.E. "Social Origins of Officers in the Indian and British Home Army, 1758-1962." BJS 14, No. 3 (1963), 248-60.

534. Reid, Douglas M. The Story of Fort St. George. (Madras, 1945).

535. Rivett-Carnac, Edward S. The Presidential Armies of India. (London, 1890).

536. Rizvi, H.A. "The Military in Politics in India and Pakistan Since 1907." M.Phil. Thesis, University of Leeds, England, 1970.

537. Roberts, Frederick S. Forty-one Years in India from Subaltern to Commander-in-Chief. (2 vols., London, 1897).

538. Robertson, George S. The Kafirs of the Hindu-Kush. (London, 1896).

539. Rodenbough, Theodore F. Afghanistan and the Anglo-Russian Dispute; An Account of Russia's Advance toward India...with a Description of Afghanistan and of the Military Resources of the Powers Concerned. (New York, 1885).

540. Russia's March Towards India by an Indian Officer. (London, 1894).

541. Sandes, Edward W.C. The Military Engineer in India. (Chatham, 1933).

542. Sandes, Edward W.C. The Indian Sappers and Mines. (Chatham, 1948).

543. Sarkar, Jadunath. Military History of India. (Calcutta, 1960).

544. Sapena, Krishan M.L. The Military System of India, 1850-1900. (New Delhi, 1974).

545. Sharma, Gautam. Indian Army Through the Ages. (New Delhi, 1966).

546. Sheppard, E.W. "Little Known Soldiers of the Past, The Marquess of Hastings (1754-1826)." AQ 84 (April 1962), 70-79.

547. Shibly, A.H. "The Reorganisation of the Indian Armies, 1858-79." Ph.D. Dissertation, University of London, 1969.

548. Shipp, John. The Path of Glory: Being the Memoirs of the Extra-ordinary Military Career of John Shipp. Edited by Charles J. Stranks. (London, 1969).

549. Shipp, John. Memoirs of the Extraordinary Military Career of Lieut. John Shipp. (London, 1829).

550. Singh, Ganda. Maharajah Ranjit Singh; a Life Sketch. (Amritsar, 1939).

551. Singh, Ganda. The British Occupation of the Panjab. (Patiala, India, 1955).

552. Singh, Khushwant. A History of the Sikhs. (2 vols., Princeton, New Jersey, 1963-66).

553. Singh, Khushwant. Ranjit Singh, Maharajah of the Punjab. (London, 1962).

554. Singh, Khushwant. The Sikhs. (London, 1953).

555. *Singh, Madan P. Indian Army Under the East India Company. (New Delhi, 1976).

556. Singh, Nagendra. The Theorgy of Force and Organization of Defence in Indian Constitutional History; from Earliest Times to 1947. (New York, 1969).

557. Singh, Sant Nihal. India's Fighters: Their Mettle, History and Services to Britain. (London, 1914).

558. Singh, Brig. Rajendra. History of the Indian Army. (New Delhi, 1963).

559. Sinha, Narendra K. Ranjit Singh. (Calcutta, 1933).

560. Sita, Ram Pandey. From Sepoy to Subedar; Being the Life and Adventures of a Native Officer of the Bengal Army. (Lahore, India, 1880).

561. Steinbach, Henry. The Punjaub. (New York, 1976).

562. Stubbs, Francis W. History of the Organization, Equipment, and War Services of the Regiment of Bengal Artillery. (3 vols., London, 1877-95).

563. Sleeman, William H. Rambles and Recollections of an Indian Official. (2 vols., London, 1844).

564. Subrahmanyam, T.G. Famous Battles in Indian History. (Dehra Dun, 1969).

565. Swinson, Arthur. North-West Frontier: People and Events, 1839-1947. (London, 1967).

566. Terraine, John. "The Army in India: 1850-1915. A Photographic Record." HT 19 (February 1969), 130- 1.

567. Thorburn, Septimus S. The Punjab in Peace and War. (London, 1914).

568. Toy, Sidney. The Strongholds of India. (London, 1957).

569. Trotter, Lionel J. The Bayard of India; A Life of General Sir James Outram. (London, 1909).

570. Trotter, Lionel J. The Life of Hodson of Hodson's Horse. (London, 1910).

571. Vambery, Armin. The Coming Struggle for India, being an Account of the Encroachments of Russia in Central Asia, and of the Difficulties Sure to Arise Therefrom to England. (London, 1885).

572. Vibart, Henry M. Addiscombe, Its Heroes and Men of Note. (Westminster, England, 1894).

573. Vibart, Henry M. The Military History of the Madras Engineers and Pioneers, from 1743 up to the Present Time. (2 vols., London, 1881-83).

574. Wakefield, George E.C. Recollections, 50 Years in the Service of India. (Lahore, 1942).

575. Walker, Thomas N. Through the Mutiny, Reminiscences of Thirty Years' Active Service and Sport in India, 1854-83. (London, 1907).

576. Warburton, Robert. Eighteen Years in the Khyber 1879-1898. (London, 1900).

577. Waterfield, Robert. The Memoirs of Private Waterfield, Soldier in Her Majesty's 32nd Regiment of Foot, 1842-57. Edited by Arthur Swinson and Donald Scott. (London, 1968).

578. Western, John S.E. Reminiscences of an Indian Cavalry Officer. (London, 1922).

579. Wolpert, Stanley A. Tilak and Gokhale: Revolution and Reform in the Making of Modern India. (Bombay and London, 1962).

580. Woodcock, George. "The Army of the Pure (Sikhs)." HT 12, No. 9 (September 1962), 603-13.

581. Wylly, Col. Harold C. From the Black Mountain to Waziristan, being an Account of the Border Countries and the More Turbulent of the Tribes Controlled by the North West Frontier Province, and of Our Military Relations with Them in the Past. (London, 1912).

582. Yate, Charles E. Northern Afghanistan, or Letters from the Afghan Boundary Commission. (London, 1888).

583. Yeats-Brown, Francis C.C. The Lives of a Bengal Lancer. (New York, 1930).

584. Young, Henry A. The East India Company's Arsenals and Manufactories. (Oxford, England, 1937).

585. Younghusband, George J. Indian Frontier Warfare. (London, 1898).

586. Younghusband, George J. The Story of the Guides. (London, 1908).

See also: Part II: 342, 636, 1184, 1581, 1680, 1861, 1908, 1909, 1910, 1934, 1960; Addendum: 83, 108, 112, 152.

JAPAN

587. Anderson, L. John. Japanese Armour. (Harrisburg, Pennsylvania, 1968).

588. Arima, Seiho. "The Western Influence on Japanese Military Science, Shipbuilding, and Navigation." MN 19, Nos. 3-4 (1964), 118-45.

589. Balet, Jean C. Military Japan; The Japanese Army and Navy in 1910. Translated by C.A. Parry. (Yokohama, 1910).

590. Barrow, Col. E. "Military Japan After the War." USM 12, New Series, (October 1895), 13-20.

591. Borton, Hugh. Peasant Uprisings in Japan of the Tokugawa Period. (Tokyo, 1938).

592. Caruthers, Sandra Carol Taylor. "Charels LeGendre, American Diplomacy, and Expansion in Meiji Japan, 1868-1893." Ph.D. Dissertation, University of Colorado, 1966.

593. Ch'en, Hsien-t'ing. "The Japanese Government and the Creation of the Imperial Army, 1870-1873." Ph.D. Dissertation, Harvard University, 1963.

594. Conroy, Hilary. The Japanese Seizure of Korea; 1868-1910: A Study of Realism and Idealism in International Relations. (Philadelphia, Pennsylvania, 1974).

595. Coox, Alvin D. "National Security and Military Command; The Japanese Army Experience," in Russell F. Weigley, ed., New Dimensions in Military History. (San Rafael, California, 1975), 125-51.

596. Dobree, Alfred. Japanese Sword Blades. (Edgware, Middlesex, England, 1967).

597. Gordon, Leonard. "Japan's Abortive Colonial Venture in Taiwan, 1874." JMH 37 (June 1965), 171-85.

598. Great Britain, War Office, Intelligence Division. The Armed Strength of Japan by James M. Grierson. (London, 1886).

599. Hackett, Roger F. "The Military: Japan," in Robert E. Ward and Dankwart A. Rustow, eds., Political Modernization in Japan and Turkey. (Princeton, New Jersey, 1964), 328-51.

600. Hawley, Willis M. Japanese Swords. (Hollywood, California, 1945).

601. Honeycutt, Fred L., Jr. and F. Pratt Anthony. Military Rifles of Japan, 1897-1945. (Lake Park, Florida, 1977).

602. Kennedy, Malcolm D. The Military Side of Japanese Life. (Boston, 1923).

603. Kennedy, Malcolm D. Some Aspects of Japan and Her Defence Forces. (London, 1928).

604. Knutsen, Roland N. Japanese Polearms. (London, 1963).

605. Kobayashi, Ushisaburo. Military Industries of Japan. (New York, 1922).

606. Kobayashi, Ushisaburo. War and Armament Taxes of Japan. (New York, 1923).

607. Kublin, Hyman. "The 'Modern' Army of Early Meiji Japan." FEQ 9 (November 1949), 20-41.

608. Lynch, Charles. Medical Department of the Japanese Army. (Boston, 1906).

609. Medzini, Meron. "French Policy in Japan During the Closing Years of the Tokugawa Regime." Ph.D. Dissertation, Harvard University, 1964.

610. Morris, John. Makers of Japan. (London, 1906).

611. Moss, Michael E., ed. Japanese Samurai Swords 1100 to 1900 a.d. The David E.J. Pepin Collection; An Exhibition Sponsored by the West Point Museum. (West Point, New York, 1977).

612. Nam, C'ang-u, compl., under the direction of Peter A. Berton. Japanese Penetration of Korea: A Checklist of Japanese Archives in the Hoover Institution. (Stanford, California, 1959).

613. Nobutaka, Ike. "War and Modernization," in Robert E. Ward, ed., Political Development in Modern Japan. (Princeton, New Jersey, 1968), 189-211.

614. Norman, E. Herbert. Soldier and Peasant in Japan: The Origins of Conscription. (New York, 1943).

615. Piggott, Francis S.G. Broken Thread; An Autobiography. (Aldershot, England, 1950).

616. Pollard, Robert T. "Dynamics of Japanese Imperialism." PHR 8 (March 1939), 5-35.

617. *Presseisen, Ernst L. Before Aggression: Europeans Prepare the Japanese Army. (Tucson, Arizona, 1965).

618. Shingo, Fukushima. "The Building of a National Army." DE 3 (December 1965), 516-39.

619. Takata, Yasuma. Conscription System in Japan. by Ogawa Gotaro. (New York, 1921).

620. "Tokugawa Military Organization," in Conrad D. Totman, Politics in the Tokugawa Bakufu, 1600-1843. (Cambridge, Massachusetts, 1967), 43-63.

621. Vinicke, Harold M. "Review Article; Japanese Imperialism." JMH 5 (September 1933), 366-80.

622. Washburn, Stanley. Nogi, a Man Against the Background of a Great War. (New York, 1913).

623. Yumoto, John M. The Samurai Sword, a Handbook. (Rutland, Vermont, 1958).

624. Zhukov, Y.M., ed. The Rise and Fall of the Gumbatsu; A Study in Military History. Translated by David Skvirsky. (Moscow, 1975).

See also: Part II: 317, 626, 628, 1160, 1783.

KOREA

625. Choe, Ching Young. The Rule of the Taewon'gun, 1864-1873; Restoration in Yi Korea. (Cambridge, Massachusetts, 1972).

626. Conger, Dean. The Japanese Seizure of Korea, 1868-1910. (Philadelphia, Pennsylvania, 1960).

627. McKenzie, Frederick A. Korea's Fight for Freedom. (London, 1920).

628. Synn, Seung Kwon. "The Russo-Japanese Struggle for Control of Korea, 1894-1904." Ph.D. Dissertation, Harvard University, 1967.

See also: Part II: 594, 612; Addendum: 98.

MIDDLE EAST

629. Anderson, Matthew Smith. The Great Powers and the Near East, 1774-1923. (New York, 1970).

630. Benab, Younes P. "The Origin and Development of Imperialist Contention in Iran; 1884-1921: A Case Study in Semicolonialism." RIPEH 1 (June 1977), 5-77.

631. Creswell, Keppel A. Cameron, compl. A Bibliography of Arms and Armour in Islam. (London, 1956).

632. Graves, Robert W. Storm Centers of the Near East; Personal Memories 1879-1929. (London, 1933).

633. Haddad, George M. Revolutions and Military Rule in the Middle East: The Northern Tier. (New York, 1965).

634. Hunter, Frederick M. An Account of the British Settlement of Aden in Arabia. (London, 1877).

635. India, Quartermaster General's Department, Intelligence Branch. Routes in Persia. Compiled under the orders of Sir C.M. MacGregor. (Simld, 1887).

636. Kaye, John W. The Life and Correspondence of Major General Sir John Malcolm Late Envoy to Persia, and Governor of Bombay; from Unpublished Letters and Journals. (2 vols., London, 1856).

637. Kazemzadex, F. "The Origin and Early Development of the Persian Cossack Brigade." ASEER 15 (October 1956), 351-63.

638. Napier, George C. Collection of Journals and Reports Received from Captain the Honorable George C. Napier On Special Duty in Persia, 1874. (London, 1876).

639. Polk, William R. The Opening of South Lebanon, 1788-1840: A Study of the Impact of the West on the Middle East. (Cambridge, Massachusetts, 1963).

640. Schiff, Zeev. A History of the Israeli Army (1870-1974). Translated and Edited by Raphael Rothstein. (San Francisco, 1974).

641. Shorrock, William I. French Imperialism in the Middle East: The Failure of Policy in Syria and Lebanon 1900-1914. (Madison, Wisconsin, 1976).

642. Stuart, Donald. The Struggle for Persia. (London, 1902).

643. Waines, David. The Unholy War: Israel and Palestine 1897-1971. (Wilmette, Illinois, 1971).

644. War, Technology and Society in the Middle East. Edited by V.J. Parry and M.E. Yapp. (New York, 1975).

645. Waterfield, Gordon. Sultans of Aden. (London, 1968).

See also: Part II: 109, 413, 1946, 1956; Addendum: 77, 82, 136.

TURKEY

646. Cooke, William S. The Ottoman Empire and Its Tributary States (Excepting Egypt) with a Sketch of Greece. (London, 1876).

647. Eliot, Charles N.E.(Odysseus). Turkey in Europe. (Revised Edition, London, 1908).

648. Great Britain, War Office. Reports and Memoranda Relative to Defence of Constantinople and Other Positions in Turkey also on the Route in Roumelia. (London, 1877).

649. Great Britain, War Office, Intelligence Division. Handbook of the Turkish Army by Charles E. Callwell. (London, 1892).

650. Great Britain, War Office, Intelligence Division. Handbook of the Turkish Army. by Montague C.P. Ward. (London, 1900).

651. Great Britain, War Office, Intelligence Division. Handbook of the Turkish Army. (Fifth Edition, London, 1912).

652. Great Britain, War Office, Intelligence Division. The Ottoman Empire, by W.A.H. Ware. (London, 1885).

653. Great Britain, War Office, Intelligence Division. Turkish Infantry Regiments to September 30, 1917. (Cairo, Egypt, 1917).

654. Home, Robert. Report of the Defences of Constantinople and the Dardanelles. (London, 1878).

655. MacDonald, John. Turkey and the Eastern Question. (New York, 1913).

656. McGarity, J.M. "Foreign Influence on the Ottoman Turkish Army, 1800-1918." Ph.D. Dissertation, American University, 1968.

657. The Military Costume of Turkey. (London, 1818).

658. Rhodes, Capt. Godfrey. A Personal Narrative of a Tour of Military Inspection in Various Parts of European Turkey Performed from August to November 1853, n Company with the Military and Scientific Commission Under General Prim, Conte De Reuss. (London, 1854).

659. Rich, E.V. "The Military Career of Kemel Ataturk." AQ 91 (January 1966), 205-13.

660. Skelton, Gladys, (John Presland, pseudo.). Deedes Bey; A Study of Sir Wyndham Deedes, 1883-1923. (London, 1942).

661. Ubicini, Jean H.A. Letters on Turkey: An Account of the Religious, Political, Social, and Commercial Condition of the Ottoman Empire; the Reformed Institutions, Army, Navy, etc, etc. Translated by Lady Elizabeth Easthope. (London, 1856).

662. Urquhart, David. The Military Strength of Turkey (From Manuscript Entitied "The Ottoman Empire Under Abdul Medjid" written in 1852). (London, 1868).

See also: Part II: 864, 1837, 2010, 2014; Addendum: 127, 149, 155.

SOUTHEAST ASIA

663. Browne, Edmond C. The Coming of the Great Queen, a Narrative of the Acquisition of Burma. (London, 1888).

664. Crosthwaite, Charles H.T. The Pacification of Burma. (London, 1912).

665. Draeger, Donn F. The Weapons and Fighting Arts of the Indonesian Archipelago. (Rutland, Vermont, 1972).

666. Forman, Werner. Swords and Daggers of Indonesia. Photographs by Werner Forman, with Text by Vaclav Solc. Translated by Till Gottheiner. (London, 1958).

667. Gardner, G.B. Keris and Other Malay Weapons. Edited by B.Lumsden Milne. (Singapore, 1936).

668. Great Britain, War Office, Intelligence Division. Precis of Information Concerning the Straits Settlements and the Native States of the Malay Peninsula. Corrected up to 1891 by Capt. Hubert J. Foster. (London, 1891).

669. Lamb, Helen B. Vietnam's Will to Be; Resistance to Foreign Aggression from Early Times Through the Nineteenth Century. (New York, 1972).

670. McMahon, A.R. "Through Burma to China: And French Susceptibilities." USM 12, New Series (January 1896), 363-371.

671. Marks, Harry J. The First Contest for Singapore, 1819-1824. (Gravenhage, 1959).

672. Marr, David G. Vietnamese Anticolonialism, 1885-1925. (Berkeley, California, 1971).

673. Marshall, Henry. Ceylon, a General Description of the Island and its Inhabitants, with an Historical Sketch of the Conquest of the Colony by the English. (London, 1846).

674. Masselman, George. The Cradle of Colonialism. (New Haven, Connecticut, 1963).

675. Osborne, Milton E. The French Presence in Cochinchina and Cambodia; Rule and Response (1859-1905). (Ithaca, New York, 1969).

676. Parkinson, Cyril N. British Intervention in Malaya, 1867-1877. (Singapore, 1960).

677. Pringle, Robert. Rajahs and Rebels; The Ibans of Sarawak Under Brooke Rule, 1841-1941. (Ithaca, New York, 1970).

678. *Reid, Anthony. The Contest for North Sumatra; Atjeh, The Netherlands and Britain, 1858-1898. (New York, 1969).

679. Singhal, D.P. The Annexation of Upper Burma. (Singapore, 1960).

680. Skinner, Thomas. Fifty Years in Ceylon. An Autobiography. Edited by Annie Skinner. (London, 1891).

681. Tregonning, Kenneth G. The British in Malaya; The First Forty Years, 1786-1826. (Tucson, 1965).

682. Truong-Buu-Lam. Patterns of Vietnamese Response to Foreign Intervention: 1858-1900. (New Haven, Connecticut, 1968).

683. Watson, D.R. "The French in Indo-China." HT 20 (August 1970), 534-42.

684. Welsh, Col. James. Military Reminiscences; Extracted from a Journal of Nearly Forty Years Active Service in the East Indies. (2 vols., London, 1880).

        See also: Part II: 324, 670; Addendum: 38, 51, 66.

AUSTRALIA

685. Australia, Army, 1st Infantry Regiment (N.S.W.). Historical Record and Jubilee, 1854-1904 (of) the First Australian Infantry Regiment Militia (N.S.W.). (Sydney, 1905).

686. Australia, Department of Defence. Australian Military Forces. Physical Training Report by Col. C. Bjeke-Petersen. (Melbourne, 1914).

687. Australia, Department of Defence. Military Forces. Extracts from the Annual Report by Major-General George M. Kirkpatrick, Inspector-General, 30th May, 1911. (Melbourne, 1911).

688. Australia, Department of Defence. Regulations (provisional) and Instructions for Universal Training. (5 pts. in 1 vol., Melbourne, 1913-14).

689. Australia, Department of Defence. Standing Orders for the Mobilization of the Military Forces of the Commonwealth of Australia, 1911.(with Amendments to M.O. 382/1912). (Melbourne, 1912).

690. Australia, Department of Defence. Tables of Peace Organization and Establishments, 1913, 1914, 1915. (Melbourne, 1915?).

691. Australia, Department of Inspector-General of the Forces. Report on an Inspection of the Military Forces of the Commonwealth of Australia by General Sir Ian Hamilton...Inspector-General of the Overseas Forces. (Melbourne, 1914).

692. Australian War Memorial, Canberra. Guide to the Australian War Memorial. (New Revised Edition, Sydney, 1960).

693. Bartlett, Norman, ed. Australia at Arms. (Canberra, 1962).

694. Brook, D.N. "Artillery in South Australia, 1840-1960." AAJ 159 (August 1962), 39-45.

695. Browne, G.H. "The Australian Army Service Corps from Federation 1901 until the General Reorganization of the Commonwealth Forces 1912." AAJ 285 (February 1973), 41-57.

696. Corcoran, John. The Target Rifle in Australia, 1860-1900. (Hunters Hill, New South Wales, Australia, 1975).

697. Craig, George C. The Federal Defence of Australasia. (London, 1897).

698. Crawford, James Coutts. Australasian Federation; Federation of the Empire and Colonial Defence. (Wellington, 1885).

699* Dornbusch, Charles E., compl. Australian Military Bibliography. (Cornwallville, New York, 1963).

700. Downey, M. The Standard Catalogue of Orders, Decorations, and Medals Awarded to Australians, with Valuation. (Sydney, 1971).

701. Festberg, Alfred N. Australian Army Guidons and Colours. (Melbourne, 1972).

702. Festberg, Alfred N. Australian Army Insignia, 1903-1966. (Melbourne, 1967).

703. Festberg, Alfred N. The Lineage of the Australian Army. (Melbourne, 1972).

704. Festberg, Alfred N. and Barry J. Videon. Uniforms of the Australian Colonies. (Melbourne, 1972).

705. *Firkins, Peter. The Australians in Nine Wars: Waikato to Long Tan. (London, 1972).

706. Forward, Roy and Bob Reece, eds. Conscription in Australia. (St. Lucia, Brisbane, Australia, 1968).

707. Gray, Robert. "Regiments Raised in South Australia, 1840-1937." JSAHR 35 (December 1957), 165-9.

708. Halls, Christopher. Guns in Australia. (Sydney, 1974).

709. Isaacs, Keith. Military Aircarft of Australia, 1909-1918. (Canberra, 1971).

710. Jauncey, Leslie C. The Story of Conscription in Australia. (London, 1935).

711. Johnston, E.N. "The Australian System of Universal Training for Purposes of Military Defense." PAPS 6 (July 1916), 113-33.

712. Laffin, John. Anzacs at War; The Story of Australian and New Zealand Battles. (New York, 1965).

713. Laffin, John. Digger: The Story of the Australian Soldier. (London, 1959).

714. Lee, Joseph E. Duntroon, The Royal Military College of Australia, 1911-1946. (Canberra, 1952).

715. MacCallum, Duncan. "The Early Volunteer Corps--the Origins of the Modern Australian Army." ARTS 1 (September 1959), 142-66.

716. Millar, T.B. "The History of the Defence Forces of the Port Phillip District and Colony of Victoria, 1836-1900." M.A. Theses, University of Melbourne, 1957.

717. New South Wales Military Historical Society. Military Colours in New South Wales. (Ryde, New South Wales, 1968).

718. Perry, Warren. "The Commonwealth of Australia; Its Inauguration and Immediate Military Problems (1900)." AAJ 316 (September 1975), 28-38.

719. Perry, Warren. "The Military Life of Major General Sir John Charles Hood." VHM 29 (August 1959), 169-204.

720. Perry, Maj. Warren. "'1901-2-3-4': Australia's Immediate Post Federation Military Forces." AAJ 328 (September 1976), 29-43.

721. Perry, Warren. "Military Reforms of General Sir Edward Hutton in the Commonwealth of Australia, 1902-04." VHM 29 (February 1959), 1-26.

722. Perry, Warren. "Military Reforms of General Sir Edward Hutton in New South Wales, 1893-96." AUSQ 28 (December 1956), 1-11.

723. Scratchley, Peter H. Australian Defences and New Guinea. Compiled from the Papers of the Late Major-General Sir Peter Scratchley by Clements Kinloch-Cooke. (London, 1887).

724. Skennerton, Ian D. Australian Service Longarms. (Margate, Australia, 1975).

725. Skennerton, Ian D. Australian Service Bayonets. (Margate, Australia, 1977).

726. Tapp, E.J. "Australian and New Zealand Defence Relations, 1900-1950." AUSO 5 (September 1951), 165-75.

727. Trainor, Luke. "British Imperial Defence Policy and the Australian Colonies." HSANZ 14 (April 1970), 204-18.

728. Vader, John. Anzac: History of Australian and New Zealand Soldiers. (London, 1971).

729. Wilde, Richard H. "The Boxer Affair and Australian Responsibility for Imperial Defense." PHR 26 (February 1957), 51-65.

730. Winter, C. "Development of the Coastal Defences of Australia, 1840-50." AAJ 296 (January 1974), 40-56; 297 (February 1974), 30-42.

See also: Part I: 719; Part II: 1157, 1383, 2356; Addendum: 95, 99, 119.

NEW ZEALAND

731. Corbett, David A. The Regimental Badges of New Zealand; Being a Concise and Illustrated History of the Badges Worn by the Militia, Volunteer and Territorial Corps which Were the Proud Forerunners of the New Zealand Army. (Auckland, 1970).

732.*Dornbusch, Charles E., compl. The New Zealand Army; A Bibliography. (Cornwallville, New York, 1961).

733. Gascoyne, Frederick J.W. Soldiering in New Zealand; Being Reminiscences of a Veteran. (London, 1916).

734. Gudgeon, Thomas W. The Defenders of New Zealand, Being a Short Biography of Colonists who Distinguished Themselves in Upholding Her Majesty's Supremacy in These Islands. (Auckland, 1887).

735. Haigh, J.B. "The Royal New Zealand Army Service Corps; A Short History." BMHS 27 (February 1977), 77-82.

736. Hensley, Gerald C. "The Withdrawal of British Troops from New Zealand 1864-1870." M.A. Thesis, University of Canterbury, 1957.

737. "Introduction." New Zealand, National Archives. Preliminary Inventory No. 3, Archives of the Army Department. (Wellington, New Zealand, 1953), 2-6.

738. Kippenberger, Howard. "The New Zealand Army." JRUSI 102 (February 1957), 66-74.

739. Miller, Harold. Race Conflict in New Zealand, 1814-1865. (Auckland, 1966).

740. Miller, John O. Early Victorian New Zealand: A Study of Racial Tension and Social Attitudes, 1839-52. (London, 1958).

741. New Zealand, Army. Notes on the History of the New Zealand Military Forces 1840-1935. (Second Edition, Wellington, 1935).

742. New Zealand, Army, Royal Artillery, Band of the Northern Military District. Official History of the Band of the Royal Regiment of New Zealand Artillery, Northern Military District, 1864-1964. (Auckland, 1964).

743. New Zealand, Army Headquarters, Medical Section. The First Fifty Years; A Commentary on the Development of the Royal New Zealand Army Medical Corps, from Its Inception in 1908. (Wellington, 1958).

744. New Zealand, Defence Department. Dress Regulations, (1912) of the New Zealand Military Forces. (Wellington, 1912).

745. New Zealand, Defence Department. Regulations for the Military Forces of the Dominion of New Zealand, 1913. (Wellington, 1914).

746. Ross, W. Hugh. Te Kooti Rikirangi, General and Prophet. (Auckland, 1966).

747. Scholefield, Guy H. Captain William Holson, First Governor of New Zealand. (London, 1934).

748. Sewell, Henry. New Zealand Native Rebellions. (Wellington, 1975).

749. Vayda, Andrew P. Maori Warfare. (Wellington, 1960).

See also: Part II: 697, 698, 712, 726, 1383; Addendum: 14, 23, 64, 71, 79, 118, 140, 156, 174.

EUROPE

750. Abbot, Henry L. Hasty Notes Relating to Military Engineering in Europe, Made in the Autumn of 1883. (Washington, D.C., 1883).

751. Adams, Charles. Great Campaigns: A Succinct Account of the Principal Military Operations which have taken Place in Europe from 1796 to 1870. Edited by Charles Cooper King. (London, 1877).

752. Brackenbury, Charles B. European Armaments in 1867. (London, 1867).

753. Beukema, Herman. "Social and Political Aspects of Conscription: Europe's Experience." MA 5 (Spring 1941), 21-31.

754. Chandler, David, ed. Battlefields of Europe. (2 vols., London, 1965).

755. de Bohigas, Nuria Sales. "Some Opinions on Exemption from Military Service in Nineteenth-Century Europe." CSSH 10 (April 1968), 261-89.

756. Dehio, Ludwig. The Precarious Balance: The Politics of Power in Europe 1494-1945. Translated by Charles Fullman. (London, 1963).

757. Essays on Modern European Revolutionary History. Edited by Bede K. Lackner and Kenneth Roy Philp. (Austin, Texas, 1977).

758. Hall, Walter Phelps. World Wars and Revolutions: The Course of Europe Since 1900. (New York, 1943).

759.* Halstead, John P. and Serafino Porcari, compls. Modern European Imperialism: A Bibliography of Books and Articles, 1815-1972. (2 vols., Boston, 1974).

760. Horsetzky, Adolph von. A Short History of the Chief Campaigns in Europe Since 1792. Translated by Kenneth B. Ferguson. (London, 1909).

761. Howard, Michael. War in European History. (New York, 1976).

762. Hurst, Michael, compl. Key Treaties for the Great Powers, 1814-1914. (2 vols., New York, 1972).

763. Hutton, Alfred. The Sword and the Centuries; or, Old Sword Days and Old Sword Ways; Being a Description of the Various Swords Used in Civilized Europe during the Last Five Centuries. (London, 1901).

764. Langer, William L. European Alliances and Alignments, 1871-1890. (Revised Edition, New York, 1931).

765. McClellan, George B. The Armies of Europe. (Philadelphia, 1861).

766. McClellan, George B. European Cavalry, Including Details of the Organization of the Cavalry Service Among the Principal Nations of Europe. (Philadelphia, 1861).

767. Mallory, Keith and Arvid Ottar. The Architecture of War. (New York, 1973).

768. Martin, Paul. European Military Uniforms; A Short History. (London, 1967).

769. Maurice, John Frederick. The Balance of Military Power in Europe An Examination of the War Resources of Great Britain and the Continental States. (London, 1888).

111

770. Mayer, Arno J. "Internal Causes and Purposes of War in Europe, 1870-1956: A Research Assignment." JMH 41 (September 1969), 291-303.

771. Middleton, Oswald R. Outlines of Military History; or, A Concise Account of the Principal Campaigns in Europe Between the Years 1740 and 1870, Being Those Generally Referred to in Our Military Textbooks. (London, n.d.).

772. Miles, Nelson A. Military Europe; A Narrative of Personal Observation and Personal Experience. (New York, 1898).

773. Militarism, Politics and Working Class Attitudes in Late Nineteenth-Century Europe. Edited by Sandi E. Cooper. (New York, 1971).

774. The Military Costume of Europe. (2 vols., London, 1822).

775. Oakes, Sir Augustus H. and Robert B. Mowart, eds. The Great European Treaties of the Nineteenth Century. (Oxford, 1918).

776. Petrie, Martin. "The Military Forces of the Nations of Europe." JRUSI 5 (February 1861), 45-67.

777. Postgate, Raymond W., ed. Revolution from 1789-1906; Documents. (London, 1920).

778. Pratt, S.C. " Comparative Table of Austrian, English, French, German, Italian, and Russian Field Guns." Ordnance Note No. 350, May 29, 1884 in United States, Ordnance Department, Ordnance Notes. (12 vols., Washington, D.C., 1873-84).

779. *Ralston, David B., ed. Soldiers and States; Civil-Military Relations in Modern Europe. (Boston, 1966).

780. Revolt to Revolution: Studies in the 19th and 20th Century European Experience. By Michael Elliott-Bateman, John Ellis and Tom Bowden. (Totowa, New Jersey, 1974).

781. Schoen, Julius. Rifled Infantry; A Brief Description of the Modern System of Small Arms Adopted in the Various European Armies. Translated by Josiah Gorgas. (Second Edition, Dresden, 1855).

782. Thornton, A.P. "Overseas Empires: The Century of European World Power," in Asa Briggs, ed., The Nineteenth Century: The Contradictions of Progress. (London, 1970), 215-38.

783. Todd, Frederick P. "The Military Museum in Europe." MA 12 (Spring 1948), 36-45.

784. Townsend, Mary E. with Cyrus H. Peake. European Colonial Expansion Since 1871. (New York, 1941).

785. United States, Adjutant-General's Office, Military Information Division. Re-enlistments and Guarantees of Employment for Non-commissioned Officers and Ex-soldiers in European Armies. (Washington, D.C., 1896).

786. United States, Adjutant General's Office, Military Information Division. Subsistence and Messing in European Armies. (Washington, D.C., 1897).

787. United States, General Staff, War Plans Division. The Recruitment of Officers in Time of Peace in the Principal Armies of Europe. (Washington, D.C., 1916).

788. Woods, Frederick A. and Alexander Balitzly. Is War Diminishing? A Study of the Prevalence of War in Europe From 1450 to the Present Day. (Boston, 1915).

789. Wraxhall, Frederick C.L. Handbook to the Naval and Military Resources of the Principal European Nations. (London, 1856).

790. Westrate, J. Lee. European Military Museums; A Survey of Their Philosophy, Facilities, Programs, and Management. (Washington, D.C., 1961).

See also: Part I: 103, 243, 244, 248, 388, 389, 563, 817, 827; Part II: 15, 269, 617, 647, 1108, 1137, 1157, 1901, 1921, 2013, 2337, 3545; Addendum: 88, 165.

AUSTRIA-HUNGARY

791. *Alfoldi, Laszlow M., compl. The Armies of Austria-Hungary and Germany, 1740-1914.(Bibliography) (Carlisle Barracks, Pennsylvania, 1975).

792. Bagger, Eugene S. Francis Joseph: Emperor of Austria, King of Hungary. (New York, 1927).

793. Great Britain, War Office, Intelligence Division. The Armed Strength of Austria by William S. Cooke. (London, 1873-74).

794. Great Britain, War Office, Intelligence Division. Report on Horse Breeding in Hungary, 1894 by Douglas Dawson. (London, 1895).

795. Gribble, Francis. The Life of the Emperor Francis Joseph. (New York, 1914).

796. Hein, Otto L. "Report on Military Educttion in Austrai-Hungary," in United States, War Department, Annual Report of the Secretary of War for the Year 1891. Volume 5 (Washington, D.C., 18-- to 19--), 528-38.

797. James, Walter H. "Musketry Instruction and Long-Range Infantry Fire in Austria, France, and Prussia." Ordnance Note No. 111, August 15, 1879 in United States, Ordnance Department, Ordnance Notes. (12 vols., Washington, D.C., 1873-84).

798. Jelavich, Barbara. The Hapsburg Empire in European Affairs 1814-1918. (Chicago, 1969).

799. Kann, Robert A. The Multinational Empire; Nationalism and National Reform in the Hapsburg Monarchy, 1848-1914. (2 vols., New York, 1950).

800. Helmreich, E.C. "Documents--An Unpublished Report on Austro-German Military Conversations of November 1912." JMH 5 (June 1933), 197-207.

801. Jaszi, Oscar (Oszkar). The Dissolution of the Habsburg Monarchy. (Chicago, 1929).

802. Longard de Longgarde, Mme. Dorthea (Gerard). The Austrian Officer at Work and at Play. (London, 1913).

803. Marek, George R. The Eagles Die: Franz Joseph, Elisabeth, and Their Austria. (New York, 1974).

804. Margutti, Albert A.V. The Emperor Francis Joseph and His Times. (London, 1921).

805. May, Arthur J. The Hapsburg Monarchy, 1867-1914. (Cambridge, Massachusetts, 1951).

806. Murad, Anatol. Franz Joseph I of Austria and His Empire. (New York, 1968).

807. Neville, Donald G. Medals, Ribbons and Orders of Imperial Germany and Austria. (St. Ives, Cambs, England, 1974).

808. Pribram, Alfred F. The Secret Treaties of Austria-Hungary, 1879-1914. (2 vols., Cambridge, Massachusetts, 1920).

809. Protitch, Stojan. "The Secret Treaty Between Servia and Austria-Hungary." FR 85, New Series. (May 1909), 838-49.

810. Redlich, Joseph. Emperor Francis Joseph of Austria: A Biography. (New York, 1929).

811. Rock, Kenneth W. "Felix Schwarzenberg, Military Diplomat." AHY 11 (1975), 85-109.

812. Ross-of-Bladensburg, John. "The Austrain Army; More Especially with Reference to the Military Train, and the Organisation of the Lines of Communications in the Field." JRUSI 25, No. 113 (1881), 790-823.

813. Rothenberg, Gunther E. "The Army of Austria-Hungary, 1868-1918: A Case Study of a Multi-Ethnic Force," in Russell F. Weigley, ed., New Dimensions in Military History. (San Rafael, California, 1975), 242-54.

814. *Rothenberg, Gunther E. The Army of Francis Joseph. (West Lafayette, Indiana, 1976).

815. Rothenberg, Gunther E. "The Austrian Army in the Age of Metternich." JMH 40 (June 1968), 155-65.

816. Rothenberg, Gunther E. "The Hapsburg Army and the Nationality Problem in the Nineteenth Century, 1815-1914." AHY 3 (1967), 70-87.

817. Rothenberg, Gunther E. "Military Aviation in Austria-Hungary 1893-1918." AEH 19 (June 1972), 77-82.

818. *Rothenberg, Gunther E. The Military Border in Croatia, 1740-1881; The Study of an Imperial Institution. (Chicago, 1966).

819. Rothenberg, Gunther E. "Nobility and Military Careers: The Habsburg Officer Corps, 1740-1914." MA 40 (December 1976), 182- 6.

820. Rothenberg, Gunther E. "The Struggle Over the Dissolution of the Croatian Military Border, 1850-1871." SLR 23 (March 1964), 63-78.

821. Rothenberg, Gunther E. "Toward a National Hungarian Army: The Military Compromise of 1868 and its Consequences." SLR 31 (December 1972), 805-16.

822. Rumbold, Horace. Francis Joseph and His Times. (New York, 1909).

823. Sangar, J.P. "The Austrian Artillery." US 4 (May 1881), 555-60; (June 1881), 685-704.

824. Seton-Watson, Robert W. The Future of Austria-Hungary and the Attitude of the Great Powers. (London, 1907).

825. Seton-Watson, Robert W. Racial Problems in Hungary. (London, 1908).

826. Sheppard, E.W. "Little Known Soldiers of the Past, Field-Marshal von Benedek (1804-1881)." AQ 82 (July 1961), 207-17.

827. Sked, A. "The Austrian Army, 1830-50, with Special Emphasis on the Revolutions of 1848." Ph.D. Dissertation, Oxford, England, 1975.

828. Skelton, Gladys (John Presland, pseudo.). Vae Victis: The Life of Ludwig von Benedek, 1804-1881. (London, 1934).

829. Stone, Norman. "Army and Society in the Habsburg Monarchy, 1900-1914." P&P No. 33 (April 1966), 95-111.

830. Stone, Norman. "Moltke-Conrad: Relations Between the Austro-Hungarian and German General Staffs, 1909-14." HJ 9, No. 2 (1966), 201-28.

831. Taylor, Alan J.P. The Hapsburg Monarchy, 1809-1918; A History of the Austrian Empire and Austria-Hungary. (London, 1941).

832. Vincent, C.E.H. "The Austrian Army." JRUSI 17 (May 1873), 527-42.

833. Wank, Solomon. "Some Reflections on Conrad von Hotzendorf and his Memoirs Based on Old and New Sources." AHY 1 (1965), 75-89.

834. Wickham-Steed, Henry. The Hapsburg Monarchy. (London, 1914).

835. Wilcox, Cadmus M. Evolutions of the Line as Practiced by the Austrain Infantry. (New York, 1860).

See also: Part I: 666; Part II: 45, 46, 778, 992, 1180, 1412, 1878;
Addendum: 22, 65, 88, 176.

THE BALKANS

836. Booth, J.L.D. Trouble in the Balkans. (London, 1905).

837. Great Britain, War Office, Intelligence Division. The Armed Strength of Roumania by Charles E. Callwell. (London, 1888).

838. Great Britain, War Office, Intelligence Division. Handbook of the Armies of the Balkan States by Montague C.P. Ward. (London, 1900).

839. Great Britain, War Office, Intelligence Division. Handbook of the Armies of Bulgaria, Greece, Montenegro, Roumania, and Servia by W.E. Fairholme and Edward Gleichen. (London, 1895).

840. Great Britain, War Office, Intelligence Division. Handbook of the Armies of the Minor Balkan States by Charles E. Callwell. (London, 1891).

841. Helmreich, E.C. and C.E. Black. "The Russo-Bulgarian Military Convention of 1902." JMH 9 (December 1937), 471-82.

842. Idris, Col. Cejvan. "Belgrade Military Museum, New Permanent Exposition." JUSII 95 (July-September 1965), 159-78.

843. MacDermott, Mercia. The Apostle of Freedom: A Portrait of Vasil Levsky Against a Background of Nineteenth Century Bulgraia. (London, 1967).

844. Palmer, A.W. "Shadow over Serbia: The Black Hand." HT 8 (December 1958), 837-46.

845. Riker, Thad W. The Making of Roumania; A Study of an International Problem, 1856-1866. (London, 1931).

846. Romania, The Center for Military History and Theory Studies and Research. Pages from the History of the Romanian Army. (Bucharest, 1975).

847. Seton-Watson, Robert W. The Rise of Nationality in the Balkans. (London, 1917).

848. Seton-Watson, Robert W. The Role of Bosnia in International Politics (1875-1914). (London, 1932).

849. Sforza, Carlo. Fifty Years of War and Diplomacy in the Balkans; Pashich and the Union of the Yugoslavs. Translated by Jacques G. Clemenceau Le Clercq. (New York, 1940).

850. Sonnichsen, Albert. Confessions of a Macedonian Bandit. (New York, 1909).

851. Stavrianos, Leften S. Balkan Federation. A History of the Movement Towards Balkan Unity in Modern Times. (Northampton, Massachusetts, 1944).

852. Stickney, Edith Pierpont. Southern Albania or Northern Epirus in European International Affairs, 1912-1923. (Stanford, California, 1926).

853. Vucinich, Wayne S. Serbia Between East and West; The Events of 1903-1908. (Stanford, California, 1954).

    See also: Part II: 1881; Addendum: 155, 167.

GREECE

854. Beauchamp, Alphonse de. The Life of Ali Pacha of Jannina, Late Vizier of Eprius, Surnamed Aslan, or the Lion. (London, 1822).

855. Christopher, Prince of Greece. Memoirs of H.R.H. Prince Christopher of Greece. (London, 1938).

856. Dakin, Douglas. "British Sources Concerning the Greek Struggle in Macedonia, 1901-1909." BKS 2, No. 1 (1961), 71-84.

857. *Dakin, Douglas. The Greek Struggle in Macedonia, 1897-1913. (Thessaloniki, 1966).

858. Dontas, Domma N. Greece and the Great Powers: 1863-1875. (Thessaloniki, 1966).

859. Heron, Audrey H. "The Administration of Colonel James Napier in the Island of Cefalonia, 1822-30." M.A. Thesis, University of London, 1952.

860. Kofos, Evangelos. Greece and the Eastern Crisis 1875-1878. (Thessaloniki, 1975).

861. Makrygiannes, Ioannes. Makriyannis: The Memoirs of General Makriyannis, 1797-1864. Edited by H.A. Lidderdale. (London, 1966).

862. The Movement for Greek Independence, 1770-1821: A Collection of Documents. Edited and Translated by Richard Clogg. (London, 1976).

863. Repington, Charles A'Court (Charles Martel, pseudo.). "The Greek Army." A&N 82 (August 1887), 331-43.

864. United States, Adjutant General's Office, Military Information Division. The Military Systems of Greece and Turkey, Including Description of Greco-Turkish Frontier. (Washington, D.C., 1897).

865. Veremis, T. "The Officer Corps in Greece, 1912-1936." BZMGS 2 (1976), 113-33.

See also: Part II: 647, 839.

BELGIUM

866. A Belgian Officer. "The Defence of Belgium." Translated by Captain Salusbury. USM 12, New Series (March 1896), 583-96.

867. Cammaerts, Emile. "The Belgian Military Conversations of 1912." CR 144 (July 1933), 47-55.

868. Great Britain, War Office, Intelligence Division. The Armed Strength of Belgium. (London, 1882).

869. Great Britain, War Office, Intelligence Division. Handbook of the Belgian Army by Nathaniel Walter. (London, 1899).

870. Great Britain, War Office, Intelligence Division. Handbook of the Belgian Army. (London, 1906).

871. Reynolds, H.C., transl. "Belgium: Army and Defensive System." JRUSI 24, No. 107 (1880), 760-78.

See also: Addendum: 126.

FRANCE

872. Allan, William. "Marshal Soult." HT 19 (October 1969), 665-71.

873. Ambler, John S. Soldiers Against the State: The French Army in Politics. (New York, 1968).

874. Arnold, Joseph C. "French Tactical Doctrine, 1870-1914." MA 42 (April 1978), 61- 7.

875. Artz, Frederick B. The Development of Technical Education in France, 1500-1850. (Cambridge, Massachusetts, 1966).

876. Aston, George G. The Biography of the Late Marshal Foch. (New York, 1929).

877. Bankwitz, Philip C.F. Maxime Weygand and Civil-Military Relations in Modern France. (Cambridge, Massachusetts, 1967).

878. Barthelemey, H. "The French Army." Ordnance Note No. 300, June 14, 1883 in United States, Ordnance Department, Ordnance Notes. (12 vols., 1873-84).

879. Bolton, Glorney. Petain. (London, 1957).

880. Brunschwig, Henri. French Colonialism, 1870-1914: Myths and Realities. Translated by William G. Brown. (New York, 1966).

881. Bury, John P.T. Napoleon III and the Second Empire. (New York, 1968).

882. Cairns, John C. "International Politics and the Military Mind: The Case of the French Republic, 1911-1914." JMH 25 (September 1953), 273-85.

883. *Case, Lynn M. French Opinion on War and Diplomacy in the Second Empire. (Philadelphia, 1954).

884. Challener, Richard D. "French National Security Policies, 1871-1939," in Russell F. Weigley, ed., New Dimensions in Military History. (San Rafael, California, 1975), 92-121.

885. *Challener, Richard D. The French Theory of the Nation in Arms, 1866-1939. (New York, 1955).

886. Chapman, Guy. The Dreyfus Case, A Reassessment. (New York, 1956).

887. Charpentier, Armand. The Dreyfus Case. Translated by James L. May. (London, 1935).

888. Coblentz, Paul. The Silence of Surrail. Translated by Arthur Chambers. (London, 1929).

889. Cole, Ronald H. "'Forward with the Bayonet.' The French Army Prepares for Offensive Warfare, 1911-1914." M.A. Thesis, University of Maryland, 1975.

890. Confer, Carl Vincent. "The Social Influence of the Officer in the Third French Republic." MA 111 (Fall 1939), 157-65.

891. Conybeare, Frederick. The Dreyfus Case. (New York, 1898).

892. Cooke, James Jerome. "Eugene Etienne and New French Imperialism, 1880-1910." Ph.D. Dissertation, University of Georgia, 1969.

893. Corley, Thomas A.B. Democratic Despot; A Life of Napoleon III. (New York, 1961).

894. *Cornelius, John, compl. Military Forces of France (Bibliography). (Carlisle Barracks, Pennsylvania, 1977).

895. D'Auvergne, Edmund B.F. Napoleon The Third: A Biography. (London, 1929).

896. Decle, Lionel. Trooper 3809; A Private Soldier of the Third Republic. (New York, 1899).

897. de la Gorce, Paul-Marie. The French Army, A Military-Political History. (New York, 1963).

898. Dennery, Etienne. "Democracy and the French Army." MA 5 (Winter 1941), 233-40.

899. Dredge, James. Modern French Artillery (The St. Chamond, De Bange, Canet and Hotchkiss Systems) with Illustrations of French Warships. (New York, 1892).

900. Dreyfus, Alfred and Pierre. The Dreyfus Case. Edited and Translated by Donald C. McKay. (New Haven, Connecticut, 1937).

901. Dreyfus, Alfred. Five Years of My Life, 1894-1899. Translated by James Mortimer. (New York, 1901).

902. Dumas, Mathieu. Memoirs of His Own Time, Including the Revolution, the Empire, and the Restoration. (2 vols., London, 1839).

903. Falls, Cyril B. Marshal Foch. (London, 1939).

904. Filon, Pierre M.A. Memoirs of the Prince Imperial, 1856-1879 from the French of Augustin Filon. (Boston, 1913).

905. Forbes, Archibald. The Life of Napoleon the Third. (New York, 1897).

906. Forbes-Leith, William. The Scots Men-at-Arms and Life-Guards in France from Their Formation Until Their Final Dissolution, A.D. 1418-1830. (2 vols., Edinburgh, 1882).

907. Fossati, William Joseph. "Educational Influences in the Career of Marshal Ferdinand Foch of France." Ph.D. Dissertation, University of Kansas, 1976.

908. The French Army from Within by Ex-trooper (pseudo.). (New York, 1914).

909. Gaulle, Charles de. France and Her Army. Translated by Frank L. Dash. (New York, 1945).

910. Gooch, Brison D. "A Commentary on the Napoleonic Legend." MA 30 (Winter 1966-67), 199-206.

911. Gourgaud, Gaspard. Talks of Napoleon at St. Helena with General Baron Gourgaud, Together with the Journal Kept by Gourgaud on their Journey from Waterloo to St. Helena. Translated by Elizabeth Latimer. (Chicago, 1903).

912. Great Britain, War Office, Intelligence Division. Armed Strength of France by Cecil J. Ernest. (London, 1877).

913. Great Britain, War Office, Intelligence Division. Handbook of the French Army by Nathaniel W. Barnardiston. (London, 1901).

914. Griffiths, Richard M. Petain; A Biography of Marshal Philippe Petain of Vichy. (Garden City, New York, 1970).

915. Guedella, Philip. The Two Marshals: Bazaine, Petain. (New York, 1943).

916. Guillemard, Charles O.B. (Robert). The Adventures of a French Sergeant during his Campaigns in Italy, Spain, Germany, Russia, etc., from 1805 to 1823 written by Himself. (London, 1898).

917. Holasz, Nicholas. Captain Dreyfus: The Story of a Mass Hysteria. (New York, 1955).

918. Hale, Richard W. The Dreyfus Story. (Boston, 1899).

919. Harding, James. The Astonishing Adventures of General Boulanger. (New York, 1971).

920. Harding, William, ed. Dreyfus; The Prisoner of Devil's Island: A Full Story of the Most Remarkable Military Trial and Scandal of the Age. (New York, 1899).

921. Hicks, James E. Notes on French Ordnance, 1717 to 1936. (Mt. Vernon, New York, 1938).

922. Holmes, E.D. "The French Army of the Second Empire." Ph.D. Dissertation, University of Reading, England, 1975.

923. Holroyd, Richard. "Bourbon Army, 1815-1830." HJ 14 (September 1971), 529-52.

924. Holt, Edgar. Plon-Plon, The Life of Prince Napoleon. (London, 1973).

925. House, Jonathan M. "The Decisive Attack: A New Look at French Infantry Tactics on the Eve of World War I." MA 40 (December 1976), 164-69.

926. Hunter, Thomas M. Marshal Foch; A Study in Leadership. (Ottowa, Canada, 1961).

927. Ideville, Henri A. le Lorgne. Memoirs of Marshal Bugeaud From His Private Correspondence and Original Documents, 1784-1849. Edited by Charlotte M. Yonge. (2 vols., London, 1884).

928. Irvine, Dallas D. "The French and Prussian Staff Systems before 1870." MA 2 (Winter 1938), 192-203.

929. Irvine, Dallas D. "The French Discovery of Clausewitz and Napoleon." MA 4 (Fall 1940), 143-61.

930. Irvine, Dallas D. "French Military Policy and the Russian Alliance of 1891." Ph.D. Dissertation, University of Pennsylvania, 1934.

931. Jerrold, Blanchard. The French Under Arms, Being Essays on Military Matters in France. (London, 1860).

932. Johnston-Jones, D.R. "The Tale of a French Lancer." AQ 102 (October 1971), 108-111.

933. Joinville, Francois Ferdinand P.L.M. d'Orleans, Prince de. Memoirs of the Prince de Joinville. Translated by Mary S. Loyd. (New York, 1895).

934. Joseph, Marguerite (Maginot). The Biography of Andre Maginot; He Might Have Saved France. (New York, 1941).

935. Kayser, Jacques. The Dreyfus Affair. Translated by Nora Bickley. (New York, 1931).

936. Kearny, Thomas. "Philip Kearny,Soldier of America; Soldier of France." JASFLH 7 (October 1936), 115-23.

937. Kovacs, Arpad. "French Military Institutions Before the Franco-Prussian War." AHR 51 (January 1946), 217-35.

938. Kovacs, Arpad. "French Military Legislation in the Third Republic, 1871-1940." MA 13 (Spring 1949), 1-13.

939. Langer, William L. The Franco-Russian Alliance, 1890-1894. (Cambridge, Massachusetts, 1929).

940. Lewis, David L. Prisoner of Honor; The Dreyfus Affair. (New York, 1973).

941. Liddell Hart, Basil H. Foch, The Man of Orleans. (London, 1931).

942. Liddell Hart, Basil H. "French Military Ideas before the First World War" in Martin Gilbert, ed., A Century of Conflict, 1850-1950: Essays for Alan J.P. Taylor. (New York, 1967), 133-48.

943. Laloy, Emile. "French Military Theory 1871-1914." MH&E 2 (July 1917), 267-86.

944. Paleologue, George M. My Secret Diary of the Dreyfus Case. Translated by Eric Mosbacher. (London, 1957).

945. Plomer, W. "The French Army Manoeuvres, 1895." USM 12, New Series (November 1895), 125-36.

946. *Porch, Douglas. Army and Revolution; France, 1815-1848. (London, 1974).

947. Porch, Douglas. "French Army Law of 1832." HJ 14 (December 1971), 751-69.

948. Priestley, Herbert I. France Overseas; A Study of Modern Imperialism. (New York, 1938).

949. *Ralston, David B. The Army of the Republic; The Place of the Military in the Political Evolution of France, 1871-1914. (Cambridge, Massachusetts, 1967).

950. Ridley, Jack B. "Marshal Bugeaud, the July Monarchy, and the Question of Algeria, 1841-1847; A Study in Civil-Military Relations." Ph.D. Dissertation, University of Oklahoma, 1970.

951. Roberts, John. "The Dreyfus Case, 1894-1906." HT 4 (June 1954), 374-384.

952. Rude, George F.E. The Crowd in History: A Study of Popular Disturbances in France and England, 1730-1848. (New York, 1964).

953. Ryan, Stephen. Petain the Soldier. (New York, 1969).

954. Schachter, Betty. The Dreyfus Affair; A National Scandal. (Boston, 1965).

955. Schuman, Frederick L. War and Diplomacy in the French Republic; An Inquiry into Political Motivations and the Control of Foreign Policy. (New York, 1931).

956. Seager, Frederic H. The Boulanger Affair; Political Crossroad of France, 1886-1889. (Ithaca, New York, 1969).

957. Setzen, Joel A. "Background to the French Failures of August 1914: Civilian and Military Dimensions." MA 42 (April 1978), 87-90.

958. Smith, William H.C. Napoleon III. (New York, 1972).

959. Snyder, Louis L. The Dreyfus Case: A Documentary History. (New Brunswick, New Jersey, 1973).

960. Snynder, David and Charles Tilly. "Hardship and Collective Violence in France, 1830 to 1960." ASR 37 (October 1972), 520-32.

961. "The State of the French Army." BLM 118 (August 1875), 125-41.

962. Steevens, George W. The Tragedy of Dreyfus. (New York, 1899).

963. Stewart, George. "The Great Military Schools of France 1. Saint-Cyr." JASFLH 27 (Summer 1956), 170-82.

964. Stewart, Col. George. "The Great Military Schools of France 2. L'Ecole Polytechnique." JASFLH 27 (Autumn 1956), 265-78.

965. *Tannenbaum, Jan Karl. General Maurice Sarrail, 1856-1929: The French Army and Left-Wing Politics. (Chapel Hill, North Carolina, 1974).

966. Terraine, John. "The Army in Modern France." HT 11 (November 1961), 733-42.

967. Thackeray, Thomas J. The Military Organization and Administration of France. (2 vols., London, 1856).

968. Thorburn, William A. "The French Army and Its Uniforms, 1815-1870." HT 10 (June 1960), 424- 9.

969. Thorburn, William A. French Army Regiments and Uniforms from the Revolution to 1870. (London, 1969).

970. Van Haute, Andre. The Pictorial History of the French Air Force. (1909-1940) Volume I. (London, 1974).

971. Vigny, Alfred V., Compte de. The Military Necessity. Translated by Humphrey Hare. (London, 1953).

972. Whitridge, Arnold. Alfred de Vigny. (New York, 1933).

973. Wilcox, Cadmus M. A Tabular Statement of the Composition of the French Army on a War Footing. (New York, 1860).

974. Williamson, Samuel R. The Politics of Grand Strategy; Britain and France Prepare for War, 1904-1914. (Cambridge, Massachusetts, 1969).

975. Woodward, Ernest L. French Revolutions. (London, 1934).

976. Wright, Gordon. "Public Opinion and Conscription in France, 1866-70 JMH 14 (March 1942), 26-45.

See also: Part II: 7, 8, 10, 26, 86, 87, 90, 91, 92, 93, 94, 95, 96, 98, 99, 100, 101, 103, 104, 105, 106, 107, 238, 242, 244, 248, 257, 258, 293, 336, 609, 641, 670, 675, 683, 778, 797, French Foreign Legion, 998, 1034, 1180, 1186, 1522, 1558, 1725, 1798, 3554; Addendum: 6, 35, 51, 61, 62, 63, 65, 77, 82, 88, 114, 135, 136, 143, 161, 162.

THE FRENCH FOREIGN LEGION

977. Bocca, Geoffrey. La Legion! The French Foreign Legion and the Men Who Made It Famous. (New York, 1964).

978. Carle, Erwin (Erwin Rosen, pseudo.). In the Foreign Legion. (London, 1910).

979. Kanitz, Walter. The White Kepi; A Casual History of the French Foreign Legion. (Chicago, 1956).

980. Kinross, James. "The Foreign Legion." HT (August 1952), 558-63.

981. *McLeave, Hugh. The Damned Die Hard; The Colorful True Story of the French Foreign Legion. (New York, 1973).

982. Manington, George. A Soldier of the Legion; An Englishman's Adventures Under the French Flag in Algeria and Tonquin. Edited by William B. Slater and Arthur J. Sarl. (London, 1907).

983. Martyn, Frederic. Life in the Legion From a Soldier's Point of View. (London, 1911).

984. *Mercer, Charles. Legion of Strangers; The Vivid History of a Unique Military Tradition--The Foreign Legion. (New York, 1964).

985. O'Ballance, Edgar. The Story of the French Foreign Legion. (London, 1961).

986. Price, George Ward. In Morocco With the Legion. (London, 1934).

987. Swiggert, Howard. March or Die; The Story of the French Foreign Legion. (New York, 1953).

988. Wellard, James. The French Foreign Legion. (Boston, 1974).

GERMANY

989. *Addington, Larry H. The Blitzkrieg Era and the German General Staff, 1865-1941. (New Brunswick, New Jersey, 1971).

990. Alfoldi, Laszlo M. "The Prussian General Staff, 1804-1919" in Essays in Some Dimensions of Military History. Volume 4. (Carlisle Barracks, Pennsylvania, 1976), 28-47.

991. Angress, Werner T. "Prussia's Army and the Jewish Reserve Officer Controversy before World War I." LBIYB 17 (1972), 19-42.

992. Billinger, Robert D. "The War Scare of 1831 and Prussian-South German Plans for the End of Austrian Dominance in Germany." CEH 9 (September 1976), 203-19.

993. Bingham, T.A. "The Prussian Great General Staff and What it Contains that is Practical from an American Standpoint." JMSI 13 (September 1892), 666-76.

994. Brewer, Carey. "The General Staff of the German Army." MR 36 (September 1956), 28-38.

995. Burrows, William E. Richthofen; A True History of the Red Baron. (New York, 1969).

996. Campbell, Frederick Francis. "The Bavarian Army, 1870-1918; The Constitutional and Structural Relations with the Prussian Military Establishment." Ph.D. Dissertation, Ohio State University, 1973.

997. Campion, Loren K. As Bismarck Fell: The Restive Mind of the German Military. (Greenville, North Carolina, 1976).

998. Chesney, Charles C. and Henry Reeve. The Military Resources of Prussia and France, and Recent Changes in the Art of War. (London, 1870).

999. Chickering, Roger. Imperial Germany and a World Without War: The Peace Movement in German Society, 1892-1914. (Princeton, New Jersey, 1975).

1000. Childers, Erskine. German Influence on British Cavalry. (London, 1911).

1001. Cole, Hugh M. "The Organization of the Prussian Army Under Frederick William I." Ph.D. Dissertation, University of Minnesota, 1937.

1002. Coombes, J.E. and J.L. Anly, compls. German Mauser Rifle, Model of 1898. (New York, 1921).

1003. *Craig, Gordon. The Politics of the Prussian Army, 1640-1945. (New York, 1955).

1004. Craig, Gordon. "Military Diplomats in the Prussian and German Service: The Attaches, 1816-1914." PSQ 64 (March 1949), 65-94.

1005. Craig, Gordon. "Portrait of a Political General: Edwin Von Manteuffel and the Constitutional Conflict in Prussia." PSQ 46 (March 1951), 1-36.

1006. Cuneo, John R. Winged Mars. Volume 1 (The German Air Weapon, 1870-1914). (Harrisburg, Pennsylvania, 1942).

1007. Davis, John Francis. Army and Navy German Examination Papers, Compiled From Papers Recently Set at Public Examinations and Edited with a Complete English Vocabulary. (Boston, 1893).

1008. Degen, O.W. "German Barracks and Barrack Life." INFQ 10 (September-October 1913), 189-97.

1009. Demeter, Karl. The German Officer Corps in Society and State, 1650-1945. Translated by Angus Malcolm. (New York, 1965).

1010. Dickman, Josept T. Notes on the German Army. (Ft. Leavenworth, Kansas, 1897).

1011. Dupuy, Trevor N. A Genius for War: The German Army and General Staff, 1807-1945. (Englewood Cliffs, New Jersey, 1977).

1012. Dupuy, Trevor N. The Military Lives of Hindenburg and Ludendorff of Imperial Germany. (New York, 1970).

1013. Engels, Freidrich. The Role of Force in History; A Study of Bismarck's Policy of Blood and Iron. Translated by Jack Cohen. (New York, 1968).

1014. Ford, Guy Stanton. "Boyen's Military Law." AHR 20 (April 1915), 528-38.

1015. Friedjung, Heinrich. The Struggle for Supremacy in Germany, 1859-1866. Translated by Alan J.P. Taylor and William L. McElwee. (London, 1935).

1016. The German Army From Within by a British Officer Who Served in It. (London, 1914).

1017. Geyr, Leo von. "The German General Staff. Part 1: The Imperial Period." MR 42 (November 1962), 19-32.

1018. Gilman, Roda R. "Count Zeppelin and the American Atmosphere." SMJH 3 (Spring 1968), 29-40.

1019. Goerlitz, Walter. History of the German General Staff, 1657-1945. Translated by Brian Battershaw. (New York, 1953).

1020. Goldsmith, Margaret. Zeppelin, A Biography. (New York, 1931).

1021. Goodspeed, Donald J. Ludendorf; Soldier, Dictator, Revolutionary. (London, 1966).

1022. Graves, Armgaard R.(pseudo.). The German War Machine; An Account of the Inside Workings of the Most Stupendous and Efficient System Ever Devised by Man for War-fare and Secret Diplomatic Intelligence. (New York, 1914).

1023. Guttery, Thomas E. Zeppelin, an Illustrated Life of Count Ferdinand Von Zeppelin, 1838-1917. (Aylesburg, England, 1973).

1024. Great Britain, War Office, Intelligence Division. The Armed Strength of the German Empire by James M. Grierson and Edited by Cyril W.B. Bell. (London, 1888).

1025. Great Britain, War Office, Intelligence Division. Field Service Regulations of the German Army, 1908. (London, 1909).

1026. Great Britain, War Office, Intelligence Division. Handbook of the German Army. (London, 1897).

1027. Great Britain, War Office, Intelligence Division. Handbook of the German Army. Revised by James E. Edmonds. (Second Edition, London, 1900).

1028. Great Britain, War Office, Intelligence Division. Notes on the German Cavalry Regulations of 1886 by Cyril W.B. Bell. (London, 1887).

1029. Hacklander, Friedrich W. Ritter von. Military Life in Prussia: The Soldier in Time of Peace. (London, 1873).

1030. Hicks, James E. Notes on German Ordnance for the Collector, 1841-1918. (New York, 1937).

1031. Hindenburg, Gert von. Hindenburg, 1847-1934; Soldier and Statesman. Translated by Gerald Griffin. (London, 1935).

1032. Hogg, Ian V. German Pistols and Revolvers, 1871-1945. (Harrisburg, Pennsylvania, 1971).

1033. Holborn, Hajo. "Moltke's Strategical Concepts." MA 6 (Fall 1942), 153-168.

1034. Holland, P. "The German, French, and Russian Systems of Infantry Attack and Defense." JMSI 19 (September 1896), 359-69.

1035. Howard, Michael. "William I and the Reform of the Prussian Army" in Martin Gilbert, ed., A Century of Conflict, 1850-1950; Essays for Alan J.P. Taylor. (New York, 1967), 91-103.

1036. Hudson, Edmund. "Krupp's Works." Ordnance Note No. 328, December 3, 1883 in United States, Ordnance Department, Ordnance Notes. (12 vols., Washington, D.C., 1873-84).

1037. Humfrey, Lt. Col. John H. An Essay on the Modern System of Fortification Adopted for the Defence of the Rhine Frontier and Followed in a Greater or Less Degree in All the Principal Works of the Kind Now Constructed on the Continent Exemplified in a Copious Memoir on the Fortress of Coblenz and Illustrated by Plans and Sections of the Work at the Place. (London, 1838).

1038. Kent, Daniel. German 7.9 mm. Military Ammunition, 1888-1945. (Ann Arbor, Michigan, 1973).

1039. Kitchen, Martin. "Army and Society in the Wilhelmine Era." LUR 5 (June 1973), 49-65.

1040. *Kitchen, Martin. German Officer Corps, 1890-1914. (New York, 1968).

1041. *Kitchen, Martin. A Military History of Germany from the 18th Century to the Present Day. (Bloomington, Indiana, 1975).

1042. Kurenberg, Jaochim von. The Kaiser: A Life of William II, Last Emperor of Germany. Translated by H.T. Russell and Herta Hagen. (New York, 1955).

1043. Laffin, John. Jackboot; The Story of the German Soldier. (London, 1965).

1044. Laqueur, Walter. Russia and Germany; A Century of Conflict. (London 1965).

1045. Lauterbach, Albert T. "Roots and Implications of the German Idea of Military Society." MA 5 (Spring 1941), 1-20.

1046. Lumley, Capt. J.R. "The Training of Prussian Officers, Their Promotion, and How Their Capabilities are Tested." Ordnance Note No. 278, March 27, 1883 in United States, Ordnance Department, Ordnance Notes (12 vols., Washington, D.C., 1873-84).

1047. Lumley, J.R. "On the Interior Economy of a Prussian Regiment." Ordnance Note No. 218, September 20, 1882 in United States, Ordnance Department, Ordnance Notes (12 vols., Washington, D.C., 1873-84).

1048. Maehl, William H. German Militarism and Socialism. (Lincoln, Nebraska, 1968).

1049. Maguire, Thomas Miller. "Our Art of War as 'Made in Germany.'" JMSI 19 (July 1896), 151- 9; (October 1896), 312-21.

1050. Manchester, William. The Arms of Krupp, 1587-1968. (Boston, 1964).

1051. Maurice, John F. The System of Field Manoeuvres Best Adapted for Enabling Our Troops to Meet a Continental Army. (Edinburgh, 1872).

1052. Menne, Bernhard. Blood and Steel: The Rise of the House of Krupp. Translated by G.H. Smith. (New York, 1938).

1053. Meulder, Wilhelm. Field-marshal Count Moltke, 1870-1878. Translated by P.S. Pinkerton. Edited by Henry M. Hozier. (London, 1878).

1054. Moltke, Helmuth K.B. von. Essays, Speeches, and Memoirs of Field-Marshal Count Helmuth von Moltke. Translated by Charles Flint McClumpha, C. Barter and Mary Herms. (2 vols., New York, 1893).

1055. Moltke, Helmuth K.B. von. Field-Marshal Count Helmuth von Moltke as a Correspondent. Translated by Mary Herms. (London, 1893).

1056. Moltke, Helmuth K.B. von. Moltke: His Life and Character Sketched in Journals, Letters, Memoirs, A Novel and Autobiographical Notes. Translated by Mary Herms. (London, 1892).

1057. Moltke, Helmuth K.B. von. Moltke's Military Correspondence, 1870-71. Precis by Spencer Wilkinson. (Oxford, England, 1923).

1058. Moltke, Helmuth K.B. von. Moltke's Tactical Problems from 1858 to 1882.
    Translated by Karl von Donat. (London, 1894).

1059. Morris, William O'Conner. Moltke; A Biography and Critical Study.
    (London, 1893).

1060. Morrow, John Howard, Jr. Building German Airpower, 1909-1914.
    (Knoxville, Tennessee, 1976).

1061. Muhlen, Norbert. The Incredible Krupps: The Rise, Fall and Comeback
    of Germany's Industrial Family. (New York, 1959).

1062. Pandieu, Marie Felix de. A Critical Study of German Tactics and of
    the New German Regulations. Translated by Charles F. Martin. (Ft.
    Leavenworth, Kansas, 1912).

1063. Peterson, Harold L. "Famous Firearms: Dreyse Needle Gun." ARF 112
    (February 1964), 13.

1064. "Prussian Breech-Loading Field Gun." Ordnance Note No. 17, October
    27, 1873 in United States, Ordnance Department, Ordnance Notes (12
    vols., Washington, D.C., 1873-84).

1065. Rankin, Robert H. Helmets and Headdress of the Imperial German Army,
    1870-1918. (New Milford, Connecticut, 1965).

1066. "Relations Between Civilian and Military Authorities in the Second
    German Empire: Chancellor and Chief of Staff, 1871-1918," in Gordon
    A. Craig, War, Politics, and Diplomacy: Selected Essays. (New York,
    1966).

1067. Ritter, Gerhard. The Schlieffen Plan; Critique of a Myth. Trans-
    lated by Andrew and Eva Wilson. (London, 1958).

1068. Ritter, Gerhard. The Sword and the Scepter; The Problem of Militarism
    in Germany. Translated by Heinz Norden. Volumes 1 and 2. (Coral
    Gables, Florida, 1969-70).

1069. Rosinski, Herbert. The German Army. (London, 1939).

1070. Rothwell, J.S. "The German Army in 1886." JRUSI 30, No. 133 (1886),
    303-63.

1071. Sangar, J.P. "The Organization and Employment of the German Artillery."
    US 4 (January 1881), 92-125; (February 1881), 166-87; (April 1881),
    444-60.

1072. Seaton, Albert. The Army of the German Empire, 1870-1888. (Reading,
    Berkshire, England, 1973).

1073. Seeckt, Hans von. Thoughts of a Soldier. Translated by Gilbert
    Waterhouse. (London, 1930).

1074. Shanahan, William O. Prussian Military Reforms, 1786-1813. (New York, 1945).

1075. Showalter, Dennis E. "Diplomacy in France and Prussia, 1870." CEH 4 (December 1971), 346-353.

1076. Showalter, Dennis E. "Infantry Weapons, Infantry Tactics, and the Armies of Germany, 1849-64." EUSR 4 (April 1974), 119-40.

1077. Showalter, Dennis E. Railroads and Rifles; Soldiers, Technology, and the Unification of Germany. (Hamden, Connecticut, 1976).

1078. Showalter, Dennis E. "Soldiers and Steam: Railways and the Military in Prussia, 1832-1848." HST 32 (February 1972), 242-59.

1079. Showalter, Dennis E. "Soldiers into Postmasters? The Electric Telegraph as an Instrument of Command in the Prussian Army." MA 37 (April 1973), 48-52.

1080. Siegel, Gustov A. and Major General Von Specht, compls. Germany's Army and Navy by Pen and Picture. (Akron, Ohio, 1900).

1081. Stoffel, Eugene G.H.C. Military Reports, Addressed to the French War Minister, 1866-70. Translated by Capt. Robert Home. (London, 1872).

1082. Sullivan, A.E. "The Kaiser's Army." AQ 83 (January 1962), 221- 8.

1083. Talbot, Gerald F. Analysis of the Organization of the Prussian Army. (London, 1871).

1084. Tantum, William H., IV and E.J. Hoffschmidt, eds. German Army, Navy Uniforms and Insignia, 1871-1818. (Old Greenwich, Connecticut, 1968).

1085. Tschuppik, Karl. Ludendorff; The Tragedy of a Military Mind. Translated by Walter H. Johnston. (Boston, 1932).

1086. United States, Adjutant General's Office, Military Information Division. Report on the Organization of the German Army by Theodore Schwan. (Washington, D.C., 1894).

1087. Vagts, Alfred. "Hopes and Fears of an American-German War, 1870-1915." PSQ 54 (December 1939), 514-35; 55 (March 1940), 53-76.

1088. Vagts, Alfred. "Land and Sea Power in the Second German Reich." MA 3 (Winter 1939), 210-21.

1089. Waldersee, Alfred K.L., Graf von. A Field-Marshal's Memoirs: From the Diary, Correspondence and Reminiscences of Alfred, Count von Waldersee. Condensed and Translated by Frederic Whyte. (London, 1924).

1091. Walter, John. The Sword and Bayonet Makers of Imperial Germany, 1871-1918. (London, 1973).

1092. Whitton, Frederick E. Moltke. (New York, 1921).

1093. Whitman, Sidney. "Field Marshal Count Moltke." CH 20 (January 1895), 413- 7.

1094. Wilkinson, Spenser. The Brain of an Army; A Popular Account of the German General Staff. (London, 1890).

1095. Wilkinson, Spenser. The Early Life of Moltke. (Oxford, England, 1913).

1096. Wyatt, Capt. Walter James. The History of Prussia: From the Earliest Times to the Present Day. Tracing the Origins and Development of her Military Organization. (London, 1876).

1097. Ybarra, Thomas R. Hindenburg, the Man with Three Lives. (New York, 1932).

See also: Part I: 823; Part II: 4, 5, 12, 18, 27, 47, 56, 235, 273, 341, 778, 791, 797, 800, 830, 928, 1568, 1727, 1844, 2207, 3562, 3582; Addendum: 11, 44, 65, 88, 105, 130, 145, 154.

GREAT BRITAIN

GENERAL

1098. Beckett, Ian F.W. Victoria's Wars. (Aylesbury, England, 1974).

1099. Bond, Brian, ed. Victorian Military Campaigns. (New York, 1967).

1100. Bourne, Kenneth. Britain and the Balance of Power in North America, 1815-1908. (London, 1967).

1101. Bourne, Kenneth. "British Preparations for War With the North, 1861-1862." EHR 76 (October, 1961), 600- 32.

1102. Bowle, John. The Imperial Achievement; The Rise and Transformation of the British Empire. (Boston, 1974).

1103. Bulloch, John. M.I.5; The Origin and History of the British Counter-Espionage Service. (London, 1963).

1104. Carey, Arthur M. English, Irish and Scottish Firearms: When, Where, and What They Made from the Middle of the Sixteenth Century to the End of the Nineteenth Century. (New York, 1954).

1105. Carrington, Charles E. The British Overseas: Exploits of a Nation of Shopkeepers. (Cambridge, England, 1950).

1106. Carter, Thomas. Curiosities of War and Military Studies: Anecdotal, Descriptive, and Statistical. (Second Edition, London, 1871).

1107. Clinch, George. English Coast Defences from Roman Times to the Early Years of the Nineteenth Century. (London, 1915).

1108. Collier, Basil. The Lion and the Eagle; British and Anglo-American Strategy, 1900-1950. (New York, 1972).

1109. Colomb, John C.R. The Defence of Great and Greater Britain. Sketches of its Naval, Military, and Political Aspects, Annotated with Extracts from Discussions They Have Called Forth in the Press of Greater Britain. (London, 1880).

1110.*Craven, Wesley Frank. "Historical Study of the British Empire (Bibliographical Essay)." JMH 6 (March 1934), 40-69.

1111. Deacon, Richard. A History of the British Secret Service. (New York, 1970).

1112. Dilke, Charles and Spenser Wilkinson. Imperial Defence. (London, 1892).

1113. D'Ombrain, Nicholas J. "The Imperial General Staff and the Military Policy of a 'Continental Strategy' During the 1911 International Crisis." MA 34 (October 1970), 88-93.

1114. D'Ombrain, Nicholas J. "The Military Departments and the Committee of Imperial Defence, 1902-14: A Study in the Structural Problems of Defence Organisation." Ph.D. Dissertation, Oxford, England, 1969.

1115. D'Ombrain, Nicholas J. War Machinery and High Policy; Defence Administration in Peacetime Britain, 1902-1914. (London, 1974).

1116. Dupin, Pierre C.F. A Tour Through the Naval and Military Establishments of Great Britain, in the Years 1816-17-18-19 and 1820. (London, 1822).

1117. Ehrman, John. Cabinet Government and War, 1890-1940. (Cambridge, England, 1958).

1118. Eltringham, G.J. Nottingham University Officer's Training Corps, 1909-1964. (Nottingham, 1964).

1119. *Farwell, Byron. Queen Victoria's Small Wars. (New York, 1972).

1120. Featherstone, Donald. Colonial Small Wars, 1837-1901. (Newton Abbot, Devon, England, 1973).

1121. Ffoulkes, Charles J. The Gun-Founders of England, With a List of English and Continental Gun-Founders from the XIV to the XIX Centuries. (Cambridge, England, 1937).

1122. Fitzpatrick, William J. Secret Service Under Pitt. (New York, 1892).

1123. *Flint, John E. Books on the British Empire and Commonwealth: A Guide for Students. (London, 1968).

1124. Flournoy, Francis R. Parliament and War; The Relation of the British Parliament to the Administration of Foreign Policy in Connection with the Initiation of War. (London, 1927).

1125. Fuller, John F.C. Imperial Defence, 1588-1914. (London, 1926).

1126. Gammage, Robert G. History of the Chartist Movement, 1837-1854. (Newcastle-on-Tyne, 1894).

1127. Gibbs, Norman H. The Origins of Imperial Defence. (Oxford, England, 1955).

1128. *Gooch, Brison D. "Recent Literature on Queen Victoria's Little Wars." VS 17, No. 2 (1973), 217-24.

1129. Gooch, John. "Sir George Clarke's Career at the Committee of Imperial Defence, 1904-1907." HJ 18 (September 1975), 555-570.

1130. Gordon, Donald C. "The Colonial Defence Committee and Imperial Collaboration: 1885-1904." PSQ 77 (December 1962), 526-545.

1131. Gordon, Donald C. The Dominion Partnership in Imperial Defence, 1870-1914. (Baltimore, Maryland, 1965).

1132. Great Britain, Patent Office. Illustrated British Firearms Patents, 1714-1853. Compiled and Edited by Stephen V. Grancsay and Merrill Lindsay. (London, 1969).

1133. Great Britain, War Office. Report with Reference to the Progress Made in the Construction of the Fortifications for the Defence of the Dockyards and Naval Arsenals &c., of the United Kingdom by William F.D. Jervois. (London, 1867).

1134. *Greener, William O., compl. (Wirt Gerrare, pseudo.). A Bibliography of Guns and Shooting. Being a List of Ancient and Modern English and Foreign Books Relating to Firearms and Their Use, and to the Composition and Manufacture of Explosives; With an Introductory Chapter on Technical Books and the Writers of Them, Firearms Inventions, and the History of Gunmaking and the Development of the Art of Wing Shooting. (Westminster, England, 1896).

1135. Hankey, Maurice P.A. "Origin and Development of the Committee of Imperial Defence." AQ 14 (July 1927), 254-73.

1136. Hardinge, Fenella Fitz (Berkeley). Wars of Queen Victoria's Reign, 1837-1887. (London, 1886).

1137. Hargreaves, Reginald. "The Abiding Flaw." AQ 97 (January 1969), 203-17.

1138. Hayes, Denis. Conscription Conflict; The Conflict of Ideas in the Struggle for and Against Military Conscription in Britain Between 1901 and 1939. (London, 1949).

1139. Higham, Robin. The British Rigid Airship, 1908-1931; A Study in Weapons Policy. (London, 1961).

1140. *Higham, Robin, ed. A Guide to the Sources of British Military History. (Berkeley, California, 1971).

1141. Hogg, Ian V. Coast Defences of England and Wales, 1856-1956. (Newton Abbot, Devon, England, 1974).

1142. Howard, Michael. The British Way in Warfare: A Reappraisal. (Atlantic Highlands, New Jersey, 1975).

1143. Hyam, Ronald. Britain's Imperial Century, 1815-1914: A Study of Empire and Expansion. (New York, 1976).

1144. Huddleston, Francis J. Warriors in Undress. (Boston, 1926).

1145. Johnson, Stanley C. Chats on Military Curios. (London, 1915).

1146. Judd, Dennis. The Victorian Empire; A Pictorial History, 1837-1901. (New York, 1970).

1147. Kenyon, Edward R. Notes on Land and Coast Fortification. (Chatham, England, 1894).

1148. Keyes, Roger J.B. Amphibious Warfare and Combined Operations. (Cambridge, England, 1943).

1149. Knaplund, Paul. "Intra-Imperial Aspects of Britain's Defence Question, 1870-1900." CHR 3 (June 1922), 120-42.

1150. Lea, Homer. The Day of the Saxon. (New York, 1912).

1151. Lewis, Peter. British Aircraft, 1809-1914. With General Arrangement Drawings by Author. (London, 1962).

1152. Liddell Hart, Basil H. The British Way in Warfare. (London, 1932).

1153. Liddell Hart, Basil H. When Britain Goes to War; Adaptability and Mobility. (London, 1935).

1154. Lucas, Charles P. The Empire at War. (5 vols., New York, 1921-26).

1155. Mackie, William Ernest. "The Conscription Controversy and the End of Liberal Power in England, 1905-1916." Ph.D. Dissertation, University of North Carolina, 1966.

1156. Mackintosh, John P. "The Role of the Committee of Imperial Defence Before 1914." EHR (July 1962), 490-503.

1157. MacKirdy, K.A. "The Fear of American Intervention as a Factor in British Expansion: Western Australia and Natal." PHR 35 (May 1966), 123-39.

1158. Maurice, John Frederick. National Defences. (London, 1897).

1159. Moon, H.R. "The Invasion of the United Kingdom: Public Controversy and Official Planning, 1888-1918." Ph.D. Dissertation, University of London, 1968.

1160. Murray, Arthur M. Imperial Outposts, from a Strategical and Commercial Aspect, with Special Reference to the Japanese Alliance. (London, 1907).

1161. "The National Defenses of England: An Address Delivered by Sir W. Armstrong Before the Institution of Civil Engineers, January 10, 1882." Ordnance Note No. 186, April 10, 1882 in United States, Ordnance Department, Ordnance Notes. (12 vols., Washington, D.C., 1873-84).

1162. Patterson, Alfred T. "Palmerston's Folly;" The Portsdown and Spithead Forts. (Portsmouth, England, 1967).

1163. Penrose, Harold. British Aviation: The Pioneer Years, 1903-1914. (London, 1967).

1164. Preston, Richard A. "The Military Structure of the Old Commonwealth." INTJ 17 (Spring 1962), 98-121.

1165. Rawlinson, Henry C. England and Russia in the East. (London, 1875).

1166. Richmond, Herbert W. The Invasion of Britain: An Account of Plans, Attempts and Counter-measures from 1586 to 1918. (London, 1941).

1167. Richings, Mildred G. Espionage; the Story of the Secret Service of the English Crown. (London, 1935).

1168. Rooney, Meredith J. "Aspects of Imperial Defence: The Relevance of the 1879 Royal Commission on the Defence of British Possessions and Commerce Abroad." B.Ph. Thesis, Oxford University, 1963.

1169. Ropp, Theodore. "Conscription in Great Britain, 1900-1914." MA 20 (Summer 1956), 71-6.

1170. Roskill, S.W. "Lord Hankey--the Creation of the Machinery of Government." JRUSI 120 (September 1978), 110- 8.

1171. Saunders, A.D. "'Palmerston's Follies'--A Centenary." JRA 87 (Winter 1960), 138-44.

1172. Schurman, Donald M. "Imperial Defence, 1868-1887." Ph.D. Dissertation, Cambridge University, 1955.

1173. Schuyler, Robert L. "The Recall of the Legions: A Phase of the De-
centralization of the British Empire." AHR 26 (October 1920), 18-36.

1174. Strachan, Hew. History of the Cambridge Officers Training Corps, 1803-
1973. (Kent, England, 1976).

1175. Sydenham, George S. Clarke. Imperial Defence. (London, 1897).

1176. Trebilcock, Clive. "The British Armament Industry 1890-1914: False
Legend and True Utility," in Geoffrey Best and Andrew Wheatcroft,
eds., War, Economy and the Military Mind. (London, 1976), 89-107.

1177. Trebilcock, Clive. "'Spin-off' in British Economic History: Armaments
and Industry, 1760-1914." ECHR 22, New Series (December 1969), 474-
90.

1178. Trainor, Luke. "The Liberals and the Formation of Imperial Defence
Policy 1892-5." BIHR 42 (November 1969), 188-200.

1179. Travers, T.H.E. "Future Warfare: H.G. Wells and British Military
Theory, 1895-1916," in War and Society: A Yearbook of Military History.
Volume 1. Edited by Brian Bond and Ian Roy. (London, 1975), 67-87.

1180. Wadman, D.C. "The Anglo-French and Anglo-Belgian Military and Naval
Conversations from the 'Entente' to the Great War." M.A. Thesis,
University of Wales, 1939.

1181. Wellington, Duke of. "The Great Duke's Funeral." HT 2 (November 1952),
778-84.

1182. West, Julius. A History of the Chartist Movement. (London, 1920).

1183. Wilkinson, Spenser. War and Policy; Essays. (New York, 1900).

1184. Willcock, B.G. "British Policy and the Defence of Asia, 1903-5,
with Sepcial References to China and India." M.A. Thesis, University
of Nottingham, England, 1964.

1185. Williamson, James A. A Short History of British Expansion. (2 vols.,
Sixth Edition, London, 1967).

1186. Williamson, Samuel R., Jr. The Politics of Grand Strategy: Britain
and France Prepare for War, 1904-1914. (Cambridge, Massachusetts, 1969).

1187.*Winks, Robin, ed. The Historiography of the British Empire--Common-
wealth; Trends, Interpretations, and Resources. (Durham, North
Carolina, 1966).

1188. Wint, Guy. The British in Asia. (London, 1947).

1189. Zegger, Robert E. "Victorians in Arms: The Invasion Scare of 1859."
HT 23 (October 1973), 705-14.

     See also: Part I: 303, 606; Part II: 5, 10, 23, 42, 45, 47, 53, 54, 55, 58,
               70, 84, 107, 130, 131, 132, 180, 201, 204, 221, 238, 267, 283, 285,
               292, 296, 298, 299, 336, 345, 353, 387, 439, 527, 528, 539, 571,
               634, 673, 676, 678, 681, 727, 859, 952, 974, 1049, 1805, 1846,
               1855, 1947, 1986, 1991, 2035, 2052, 2117, 3542, 3554; Addendum: 43,
               61, 82, 131, 163.

1190. Adye, John. Recollections of a Military Life. (New York, 1895).

1191. Adye, John. Soldiers and Others I Have Known. (London, 1925).

1192. Alexander, Michael. The True Blue; The Life and Adventures of Colonel Fred Burnaby, 1842-1885. (New York, 1958).

1193. Arbuthnot, Alexander J. Major General Sir Thomas Munro, With Selections from His Minutes and Other Official Writings. (2 vols., London, 1881).

1194. Archer, Mildred. "The Two Worlds of Colonel Skinner." HT 10 (September 1960), 608-15.

1195. Arthur, George, ed. The Letters of Lord and Lady Wolseley 1870-1911. (London, 1922).

1196. Baden-Powell, Robert S.S. Adventures and Accidents. (London, 1934).

1197. Ballard, Colin R. Smith-Dorrien. (London, 1931).

1198. Bell, George. Rough Notes by an Old Soldier During Fifty Years Service, from Ensign to Major-General. (2 vols., London, 1867).

1199. Birdwood, William R. In My Time; Recollections and Anecdotes. (London, 1946).

1200. Birdwood, William R. Khaki and Gown; An Autobiography. (London, 1941).

1201. Blackburne, Haidee F. Trooper to Dean (H.W. Blackburne). (Bristol, England, 1955).

1202. Blood, Bindon. Four Score Years and Ten; Sir Bindon Blood's Reminiscences. (London, 1933).

1203. Biddulph, Robert. Lord Cardwell at the War Office. (London, 1904).

1204. Bonham-Carter, Victor. Soldier True; The Life and Times of Field-Marshal Sir William Robertson, 1860-1933. (London, 1963).

1205. Brackenbury, Henry. Some Memories of My Spare Time. (Edinburgh, 1909).

1206. Broadfoot, William. The Career of Major George Braodfoot...Compiled from his Personal Papers. (London, 1888).

1207. Brown, David. Diary of a Soldier 1805-1827. (Ardossan, 1934).

1208. Bruce, A.P.C. "The Military Services of Field Marshal Viscount Hardinge." AQ 106 (January 1976), 72- 8.

1209. Bruce, William Napier. Life of General Sir Charles Napier, G.C.B. (London, 1885).

1210. Butler, William F. Sir William Butler, An Autobiography. Edited by Eileen Butler. (London, 1911).

1211. Butler, William F. Charles George Gordon. (New York, 1889).

1212. Butler, William F. The Life of Sir George Pomeroy Colley, 1835-1881; Including Services in Kaffraria, in China, in Ashanti, in India and in Natal. (London, 1899).

1213. Butler, William F. Sir Charles Napier. (London, 1890).

1214. Calladine, George. The Diary of Colour-Sargeant George Calladine, 19th Foot, 1793-1837. Edited by Michael L. Ferrar. (London, 1922).

1215. Callwell, Charles E. Field-Marshal Sir Henry Wilson; His Life and Diaries. (2 vols., London, 1927).

1216. Callwell, Charles E. The Life of Sir Stanley Maude, Lieutenant-General. (Boston, 1920).

1217. Callwell, Charles E., ed. The Memoirs of Major-General Sir Hugh McCaimont. (London, 1924).

1218. Callwell, Charles E. Stray Recollections. (2 vols., London, 1923).

1219. Callwell, Charles E. Service Yarns and Memories. (London, 1912).

1220. Carton deWiart, Adrian. Happy Odyssey; Memoirs of Lieutenant-General Sir Adrian Carton deWiart. (London, 1950).

1221. Chesney, Louisa. The Life of the Late General F.R. Chesney, Colonel Commandant, Royal Artillery by his wife. Edited by Stanley Lane-Poole. (London, 1885).

1222. Childs, Wyndham. Episodes and Reflections; Being Some Records from the Life of Major-General Sir Wyndham Childs. (London, 1930).

1223. Clarke, John. Adventures of a Leicestershire Veteran. (Leicestershire, England, 1893).

1224. Coates, Thomas F.G. Hector MacDonald; or, the Private Who Became a General; A Highland Laddie's Life and Laurels. (London, 1900).

1225. Collins, Basil. Brasshat; A Biography of Field-Marshal Sir Henry Wilson. (London, 1961).

1226. Compton, Herbert E. King's Hussar; Being the Military Memoirs for Twenty-Five Years of a Troop-Sergeant-Major of the 14th (King's) Hussars. (London, 1893).

1227. Connolly, Thomas W.J. The Romance of the Ranks: or, Anecdotes, Episodes, and Social Incidents of Military Life. (London, 1859).

1228. Cooper, Duff. Haig. (2 vols., Garden City, New York, 1936).

1229. Cotton, James S. Mountstuart Elphinstone. (Oxford, 1892).

1230. Crozier, Frank P. Impressions and Recollections. (London, 1930).

1231. Dawson, Douglas. A Soldier Diplomat. (London, 1927).

1232. Dawson, Capt. Lionel. Sport in War. (London, 1936).

1233. DeLisle, Beauvoir. Reminiscences of Sport and War. (London, 1939).

1234. Denison, George T. The Struggle for Imperial Unity; Recollections and Experiences. (London, 1909).

1235. Dyott, William. Dyott's Diary 1781-1845; A Selection from the Journal of William Dyott, Sometime General in the British Army and Aide-de-Camp to his Majesty King George III. Edited by R.W. Jeffery. (2 vols., London, 1907).

1236. Dundonald, Douglas M.B.H.C. My Army Life. (London, 1926).

1237. Esher, Reginald B.B. Journals and Letters of Reginald, Viscount Esher. Edited by Maurice V.B. Brett. (4 vols., London, 1934- 8).

1238. Falls, Cyril. "Lieutenant General Sir Stanley Maude." HT 17 (October 1967), 701-7.

1239. Findlay, James L.O.B. Fighting Padre (Memoirs of an Army Chaplain) (1901-1925). (London, 1941).

1240. Forbes, Archibald. Barracks, Bivouacs and Battles. (London, 1891).

1241. Forbes, Archibald. Camps, Quarters and Casual Places. (London, 1890).

1242. Forbes, Archibald. Colin Campbell, Lord Clyde. (London, 1895).

1243. Fortescue, John W. Wellington. (London, 1925).

1244. Fraser, Pamela and Leslie H. Thornton. The Congreaves, Father and Son; General Sir William Norris Congreave, V.C., Bt.-Major William La Touche Congreave, V.C. (London, 1930).

1245. Fraser, Thomas. Recollections and Reflections. (London, 1914).

1246. French, Gerald. The Life of Field-Marshal Sir John French, First Earl of Ypres. (London, 1931).

1247. Fuller, John F.C. The Army in My Time. (London, 1935).

1248. Fuller, John F.C. Memoirs of an Unconventional Soldier. (London, 1936).

1249. Gambier-Pary, Ernest. Reynell Taylor, C.B., C.S.I.; A Biography. (London, 1888).

1250. Gatacre, Beatrix W. General Gatacre; The Story of the Life and Services of Sir William Forbes Gatacre..., 1843-1906. (London, 1910).

1251. George, Second Duke of Cambridge. George, Duke of Cambridge; A Memoir of His Private Life based on the Journals and Correspondence of his Royal Highness. Edited by Edgar Sheppard. (2 vols., New York, 1906).

1252. Gleichen, Edward. A Guardsman's Memories; A Book of Recollections. (London, 1932).

1253. Gordon, Charles A. Recollections of Thirty-Nine Years in the Army... (London, 1898).

1254. Gordon, Joseph M. The Chronicles of a Gay Gordon. (London, 1921).

1255. Gough, Hugh H. Old Memories. (London, 1897).

1256. Gough, Hubert. Soldiering On; Being the Memoirs of General Sir Hubert Gough. (London, 1954).

1257. Gowing, Timothy. A Soldier's Experiences, or a Voice from the Ranks... (Nottingham, England, 1886).

1258. Greaves, George Richard. Memoirs of General Sir George Richard Greaves Written by Himself. (London, 1924).

1259. Grenfell, Francis Wallace. Memoirs of Field Marshal Lord Grenfell. (London, 1925).

1260. Gronow, Rees H. The Reminiscences and Recollections of Captain Gronow, 1810-1860. (4 vols., London, 1889).

1261. Haldane, Richard B. Richard Burton Haldane: An Autobiography. (London, 1929).

1262. Hamilton, Ian B.M. The Happy Warrior: A Life of General Sir Ian Hamilton. (London, 1966).

1263. Hamilton, Ian S.B. Listening for the Drums. (London, 1944).

1264. Hannah, W.H. Bobs; Kiplings General. (London, 1972).

1265. Bengough, Harcourt M. Memories of a Soldier's Life. (London, 1913).

1266. Harrison, Richard. Recollections of a Life in the British Army During the Latter Half of the Nineteenth Century. (London, 1908).

1267. Hart-Synnot, Arthur F. Letters of Major-General Fitzroy Hart-Synnot. (London, 1912).

1268. Hawker, Peter. The Diary of Colonel Peter Hawker, 1802-1853. (2 vols., London, 1893).

1269. Henry, Walter. Trifles from My Port-folio, or Recollections of
      Scenes and Small Adventures during Twenty-nine Years' Military Service
      in the Peninsular War and Invasion of France, the East Indies, Campaign
      in Nepaul, St. Helena during the Detention and Until the Death of
      Napoleon, and Upper and Lower Canada. (Quebec, 1839).

1270. Higginson, George W.A. Seventy-One Years of a Guradsman's Life.
      (London, 1916).

1271. Holt, Edgar. "Sir Garnet Wolseley." HT 8 (October 1958), 706-13.

1272. Jacob, John. The Views and Opinions of Brigadier-General John Jacob.
      Collected and Edited by Lewis Pelly. (Second Edition, London, 1858).

1273. Jarvis, Weston. Jottings from an Active Live. (London, 1928).

1274. Koss, Stephen E. Lord Haldane; Scapegoat for Liberalism. (New York,
      1969).

1275. Latham, H.B. "Major-General Sir John May, 1779-1847." JRA 82
      (January 1955), 25-30.

1276. LeCaron, Henri, pseudo. (Thomas Miller Beach). Twenty Five Years
      in the Secret Service; The Recollections of a Spy. (London, 1892).

1277. Lee-Warner, William. Memoirs of Field Marshal Sir Henry Wylie
      Norman. (London, 1908).

1278. Lehmann, Joseph H. The Model Major General; A Biography of Field-
      Marshal Lord Wolseley. (Boston, 1964).

1279. Lloyd, Robert A. A Trooper in the "Tins;" The Autobiography of a
      Life Guardsman. (London, 1938).

1280. Longford, Elizabeth. Wellington; Pillar of State. (New York, 1972).

1281. Low, Charles R. Life and Correspondence of Field Marshal Sir George
      Pollack... (London, 1873).

1282. Lyttelton, Neville G. Eighty Years Soldiering, Politics, Games.
      (London, 1927).

1283. McCourt, Edward. Remember Butler; The Story of Sir William Butler.
      (London, 1967).

1284. MacDonald, John. Autobiographical Journal of John MacDonald,
      Schoolmaster and Soldier, 1770-1830. (Edinburgh, 1906).

1285. MacDonald, John H.A. Fifty Years of It; The Experiences and Struggles
      of a Volunteer of 1859. (London, 1909).

1286. Mackenzie, Colin. Storms and Sunshine of a Soldier's Life. (2 vols.,
      Edinburgh, 1884).

1287. McKiernan, Thomas. Experiences of a British Veteran Soldier. (Aber-avon, Port Talbot, South Wales, 1892).

1288. MacMullen, John M. Camp and Barrack Room; or, the British Army as It Is; By a Late Staff Sergeant of the 13th Light Infantry. (London, 1846).

1289. MacMunn, George F. Always Into Battle; Some Forgotten Army Sagas. (Aldershot, England, 1952).

1290. MacMunn, George F. Behind the Scenes of Many Wars; Being the Military Reminiscences of Lieutenant-General Sir George MacMunn. (London, 1930).

1291. Macready, Nevil. Annals of an Active Life. (2 vols., London, 1924).

1292. Magnus, Philip M. Kitchener; Portrait of an Imperialist. (London, 1958).

1293. Mansfield, H.O. Charles Ashe Windham; A Norfolk Soldier (1810-1870). (Lavenham, Suffolk, England, 1973).

1294. Maurice, Frederick B. Haldane, 1856-1915; The Life of Viscount Haldane of Choan... (2 vols., London, 1937- 9).

1295. Maurice, Frederick B., ed. Soldier, Artist, Sportsman: The Life of General Lord Rawlinson of Trent from his Journals and Letters. (Boston, 1928).

1296. Maxwell, Francis K. Frank Maxwell, Brigadier General..., A Memoir and Some Letters. (London, 1921).

1297. May, Edward S. Changes and Chances of a Soldier's Life. (London, 1925).

1298. Melville, Charles H. Life of General, The Right Honourable Sir Redvers Buller. (2 vols., London, 1923).

1299. Miller, David S. A Captain of the Gordons. Service Experiences, 1900-1909. Edited by Margaret and Helen R. Miller. (London, 1913).

1300. Miller, John. Recollections of a Military Life. (London, 1895).

1301. Mockler-Ferryman, Augustus Ferryman. Regimental War Tales,1741-1914, Told for the Soldiers of the Oxfordshire and Buckinghamshire Light Infantry(the old 43rd and 52nd). (Oxford, England, 1915).

1302. Montgomery, John. Toll for the Brave; the Tragedy of Major-General Sir Hector Macdonald. (London, 1963).

1303. Mott, Lt. Edward S. A Mingled Yarn, the Autobiography of Edward Spenser Mott, "Nathaniel Cubbins." (London, 1898).

1304. Moyse-Bartlett, Hubert. Louis Edward Nolan and his Influence on the British Cavalry. (London, 1971).

1305. Munro, William. Records of Service and Campaigning in Many Lands. (2 vols., London, 1887).

1306. Napier, Edward D.H.E. The Linesman; or, Service in the Guards and the Line during England's Long Peace and Little Wars. (London, 1856).

1307. Napier, Henry D. Field-Marshal Lord Napier of Magdala..., a Memoir, by his son. (London, 1927).

1308. Napier, William F.P. The Life and Opinions of General Sir Charles James Napier. (4 vols., London, 1857).

1309. Nott, William. Memoirs and Correspondence of Major-General Sir William Nott. Edited by Joachim H. Siddons. (London, 1854).

1310. Percival, Victor. The Duke of Wellington: A Pictorial Survey of His Life (1769-1852). (London, 1969).

1311. Pollock, John C. The Way to Glory: The Life of Havelock of Lucknow. (London, 1957).

1312. Poole, Stanley Lane. Watson Pasha, A Record of the Life-work of Sir Charles Moore Watson..., Colonel in the Royal Engineers. (London, 1919).

1313. Prinsep, E.S. MacLeod. "The Experiences of an Edwardian Subaltern." AQ 83 (October 1961), 110- 7.

1314. Rait, Robert S. The Life and Campaigns of Hugh, First Viscount Gough. (Westminster, England, 1903).

1315. Rait, Robert S. The Life of Field-Marshal Sir Frederick Paul Haines. (London, 1911).

1316. Ranken, George. Canada and the Crimea; or, Sketches of a Soldier's Life from the Journals and Correspondence of the Late Major Ranken, R.E. Edited by W. Bayne Ranken. (London, 1862).

1317. Ramsay, Balcarres D.W. Rough Recollections of Military Service and Society. (2 vols., Edinburgh, 1882).

1318. Robertson, William. From Private to Field-Marshall. (London, 1921).

1319. Robertson, Col. James P. Personal Adventures and Anecdotes of an Old Officer. (London, 1906).

1320. Robertson, John H. (John Connell, pseudo.). Wavell; Scholar and Soldier to June 1941. (New York, 1965).

1321. St. Aubyn, Giles. The Royal George, 1819-1904; The Life of H.R.H. Prince George, Duke of Cambridge. (New York, 1964).

1322. Seaton, Thomas. From Cadet to Colonel. The Record of a Life of Active Service. (2 vols., London, 1866).

1323. Seymour, William. "Lieutenant-General Sir Harry Smith: Fifty-Four Years as a Rifleman, with Service at Buenos Aires, Badajos, and in India and South Africa." HT 26 (August 1976), 339-45.

1324. Shadwell, Lawrence. The Life of Colin Campbell, Lord Clyde. Illustrated by Extracts from His Diary and Correspondence. (London, 1881).

1325. Sherson, Erroll H.S. Townshend of Chitral and Kut; Based on the Diaries and Private Papers of Major-General Sir Charles Vere Townshend. (London, 1928).

1326. Shervinton, Kathleen. The Shervintons, Soldiers of Fortune. Shervinton of Madagascar, Shervinton of Salvador and Tom Shervinton. (London, 1899).

1327. Shipp, John. The Military Bijou; or the Contents of a Soldier's Knapsack: Being the Gleanings of Thirty-Three Years' Active Service. (2 vols., London, 1831).

1328. Small, E. Milton, ed. and compl. Told from the Ranks: Recollections of Service During the Queen's Reign by Privates and Non-Commissioned Officers of the British Army. (London, 1897).

1329. Smith-Dorien, Horace L. Memories of Forty-Eight Years' Service. (New York, 1925).

1330. Smithers, A.J. The Men Who Disobeyed; Sir Horace Smith-Dorrien and His Enemies. (London, 1970).

1331. Stapleton, L. "Lieut.-Colonel Charles A.Court Repington, 1858-1925." AQ 105 (April 1975), 159-67.

1332. Stephenson, Frederick C.A. At Home and on the Battlefield; Letters from the Crimea, China and Egypt, 1854-1888... Collected and Arranged by Frank Pownall. (London, 1915).

1333. Stewart, Norman R. My Service Days; India, Afghanistan, Suakim '85, and China. (London, 1908).

1334. Strange, Thomas B. Gunner Jingo's Jubilee; An Autobiography. (London, 1893).

1335. Swinton, Ernest D. Over My Shoulder; The Autobiography of Sir Ernest D. Swinton. (Oxford, England, 1951).

1336. Surtees, G. "Roddy Owen." AQ 82 (April 1961), 48-50.

1337. Sylvester, John Henry. Cavalry Surgeon; The Recollections of John Henry Sylvester. Edited by A. McKenzie Annand. (London, 1971).

1338. Taylor, Philip Meadows. The Story of My Life. Edited by his daughter. (Second Edition, London, 1878).

1339. Thomas, Donald S. Charge! Hurrah! Hurrah! A Life of Cardigan of Balaclava. (London, 1974).

1340. Terraine, John. Douglas Haig, the Educated Soldier. (London, 1963).

1341. Trythall, Anthony J. "Boney" Fuller: Soldier, Strategist, and Writer, 1878-1966. (New Brunswick, New Jersey, 1977).

1342. Tulloch, Major-General Alexander B. Recollections of Forty Years' Service. (Edinburgh, 1903).

1343. Verner, William W.C., Assisted by Erasmus D. Parker. The Military Life of H.R.H. George, Duke of Cambridge. (2 vols., London, 1905).

1344. Vetch, Robert H. Life of Lieutenant General The Honorable Sir Andrew Clarke... (London, 1905).

1345. Vetch, Robert H. Life, Letters and Diaries of Lieutenant-General Sir Gerald Graham. (London, 1901).

1346. Waters, Wallscourt H.H. "Secret and Confidential;" The Experiences of a Military Attache. (New York, 1926).

1347. Watson, Charles M. The Life of Major-General Sir Charles William Wilson, Royal Engineers. (London, 1909).

1348. Wheeler, William. The Letters of Private Wheeler. Edited by Basil H. Liddell Hart. (Boston, 1952).

1349. Wilkinson, Spencer. Thirty-Five Years, 1874-1909. (London, 1933).

1350. Wilkinson-Latham, Robert. Kitchener; An Illustrated Life of Field Marshal Lord Kitchener, 1850-1916. (Aylesbury, England, 1973).

1351. Willcocks, James. From Kabul to Kumasi, Twenty-Four Years of Soldiering and Sport. (London, 1904).

1352. Wilson, John. "C.B." The Life of Sir Henry Campbell-Bannerman. (London, 1973).

1353. Wolseley, Garnet J. The Story of a Soldier's Life. (2 vols., Westminster, England, 1903).

1354. Wood, Elliott. Life and Adventures in Peace and War. (London, 1924).

1355. Wood, Evelyn. From Midshipman to Field Marshal. (London, 1906).

1356. Wood, Evelyn. Winnowed Memories. (New York, 1918).

1357. Woodford, L.W. "War and Peace--the Experiences of an Army Surgeon, 1810-27." JSAHR 49 (Spring 1971), 43-58.

1358. Wrottesley, George. The Life and Correspondence of Field Marshal Sir John Burgoyne. (2 vols., London, 1873).

1359. Wynne, F.C. "Extracts from 'Four Pence a Day and All Found.'" AQ
106 (January 1976), 37-43; (April 1976), 176-82.

1360. Younghusband, George J. Forty Years a Soldier. (London, 1923).

1361. Younghusband, George J. A Soldier's Memories in Peace and War. (New
York, 1917).

    See also: Addendum: 78, 160.

MILITARY FORCES

1362. Abbott, Peter E. and J.M.A. Tamplin. British Gallantry Awards.
(New York, 1972).

1363. Adams, William H.D. Famous Regiments of the British Army; Their Origin
and Services. (London, 1864).

1364. Allen, Frederick Stetson. "The British Army, 1860-1900: A Study of the
Cardwell Manpower Reforms." Ph.D. Dissertation, Harvard University,
1960.

1365. Ames, Edward and Nathan Rosenberg. "The Enfield Arsenal in Theory and
History." ECJ 78 (December 1968), 827-42.

1366. Archibald, James F.J. Blue Shirt and Khaki: A Comparison. (New York,
1901).

1367. Army Life in the 90's. Compiled by Philip Warner. (London, 1975).

1368. Army Museum's Ogilly Trust. Index to British Military Costume Prints,
1500-1914. (London, 1972).

1369. Arnold-Forster, Hugh O. The Army in 1906: A Policy and a Vindication.
(New York, 1906).

1370. Arnold-Forster, Hugh O. The War Office, The Army and the Empire.
(London, 1900).

1371. Arthur, George Compton. From Wellington to Wavell. (London, 1942).

1372. Ascoli, David. A Village in Chelsea: An Informed Account of the Royal
Hospital. (London, 1974).

1373. Atkinson, John C. A.B.C. of the Army; An Illustrated Guide to Military Knowledge for Those Who Seek a General Acquaintance with Elementary Matters Pertaining to the British Army. (London, 1910).

1374. Atkinson, John C. Sidelights on the History of the British Army. (London, 1913).

1375. Bailey, DeWitt. British Military Longarms, 1815-1865. (London, 1972).

1376. Baker, Bernard G. Old Cavalry Stations. (London, 1934).

1377. Baldry, W.Y. "Notes on the Early History of Billeting." JSAHR 13 (Summer 1934), 71- 3.

1378. Bamfield, Veronica. On the Strength. The Story of the British Army Wife. (London, 1974).

1379. Barclay, Glen St. J. The Empire is Marching; A Study of the Military Effort of the British Empire, 1800-1945. (London, 1976).

1380. Barnes, Robert M. The British Army of 1914; Its History, Uniforms, and Contemporary Continental Armies. (London, 1968).

1381. Barnes, Robert M. A History of the Regiments and Uniforms of the British Army. (London, 1950).

1382. Barnes, Robert M. Military Uniforms of Britain and the Empire, 1742 to the Present Time. (London, 1960).

1383. Barnes, Robert M. The Uniforms and History of the Scottish Regiments; Britain, Canada, Australia, New Zealand, South Africa, 1625 to the Present Day. (London, 1956).

1384. Barnett, Correlli. Britain and Her Army. (New York, 1970).

1385. Bassett, John Harvey. "The Purchase System in the British Army, 1660-1871." Ph.D. Dissertation, Boston University, 1969.

1386. Beadon, Roger. The Royal Army Service Corps: A History of Transport and Supply in the British Army. (2 vols., Cambridge, England, 1930-31).

1387. Beaver, William C. "The Intelligence Division Library, 1854-1902." JLIBH 11 (July 1976), 206-17.

1388. Beckett, Ian F.W. "The Problem of Military Discipline in the Volunteer Force, 1859-1899." JSAHR 56 (Summer 1978), 66-78.

1389. Beith, John Hay. (Ian Hay, pseudo.). The British Infantryman: An Informed History. (New York, 1942).

1390. Beith, John Hay. (Ian Hay, pseudo.). The Kings Service; Informal History of the British Infantry Soldier. (London, 1938).

1391. Beith, John Hay. (Ian Hay, pseudo.). One Hundred Years of Army Nursing; The Story of British Army Nursing Service from the Time of Florence Nightingale to the Present Day. (London, 1953).

1392. Bellairs, William. The Military Career; A Guide to Young Officers, Army Candidates, and Parents. (London, 1889).

1393. Bennett, R.W. "Military Law in 1839." JSAHR 48 (Winter 1970), 225-241.

1394. Benson, Francis R. and Algernon T. Craig, eds. The Book of the Army Pageant Held at Fulham Palace, 20th June to 2nd July, 1910. (London, 1910).

1395. Benson, R.H.R. "Military College of Science." JRA 61 (April 1934), 1-11.

1396. Biddulph, Robert. Lord Cardwell at the War Office; A History of His Administration, 1868-1874. (London, 1904).

1397. Binns, Percy L. A Hundred Years of Military Music, Being the Story of the Royal Military School of Music, Kneller Hall. (Gillingham, Dorest, England, 1959).

1398. Blackmore, Howard L. British Military Firearms, 1650-1850. (London, 1961).

1399. Blanco, Richard L. "Army Recruiting Reforms, 1861-1867." JSAHR 46 (Winter 1968), 217-224.

1400. Blanco, Richard L. "Attempts to Abolish Branding and Flogging in the Army of Victorian England Before 1881." JSAHR 46 (Autumn 1968), 137-45.

1401. Blanco, Richard L. "The Enlisted Man--Social Aspects of British Army Reforms, 1854-1867." Ph.D. Dissertation, Case Western Reserve University, 1960.

1402. Blanco, Richard L. "Reform and Wellington's Post-Waterloo Army, 1815-1854." MA 29 (Fall 1965), 123-31.

1403. Bond, Brian. "Edward Cardwell's Army Reforms, 1868-74." AQ 84 (April 1962), 108-17.

1404. Bond, Brian. "The Effect of the Cardwell Reforms on Army Organization, 1878-1904." JRUSI 105 (November 1960), 515-24.

1405. Bond, Brian. "Henry Wilson and the Staff College, 1906-1910." AQ 102 (January 1972), 173-80.

1406. Bond, Brian. "The Introduction and Operation of Short Service and Localisation in the British Army, 1868-92." M.A. Thesis, University of London, 1962.

1407. Bond, Brian. "The Late Victorian Army." HT 11 (September 1961), 616-24.

1408. Bond, Brian. "Prelude to the Cardwell Reforms, 1856-1868." JRUSI 106 (May 1961), 229-36.

1409. Bond, Brian. "Recruiting the Victorian Army, 1870-92." VS 5 (June 1962), 331-8.

1410. Bond, Brian. "The Territorial Army in Peace and War." HT 16 (March 1966), 157-66.

1411. Bond, Brian. The Victorian Army and the Staff College, 1854-1914. (London, 1972).

1412. Borman, Charles G. The Shrapnel Shell in England and in Belgium, with Some Reflections on the Use of this Projectile in the Late Crimean War; A Historico-Technical Sketch. (Second Edition Revised, Brussels, 1862).

1413. Bowling, Albert H. British Infantry Regiments, 1660-1914. (London, 1972).

1414. The British Army. (London, 1899).

1415. A British Soldier's Life in the Army. (London, 1886).

1416. Broke-Smith, P.W.L. History of Early British Military Aeronautics. (London, 1952).

1417. Brook, R. "The Barracks Act of 1890; Its Motives and Consequences, with Sepcial Reference to Shorncliffe Camp." M.A. Thesis, University of Wales, 1962.

1418. Brookes, Kenneth. Battle Thunder; The Story of Britain's Artillery. (Reading, 1973).

1419. Browne, James A. England's Artillerymen; An Historical Narrative of the Services of the Royal Artillery, from the Formation of the Regiment to the Amalgamation of the Royal and Indian Artilleries in 1862. (London, 1865).

1420. Browne, Douglas G. Private Thomas Atkins; A History of the British Soldier from 1840 to 1940. (London, 1940).

1421. *Bruce, Anthony P.C. An Annotated Bibliography of the British Army, 1660-1914. (New York, 1975).

1422. Bruce, Anthony P.C. "The System of Purchase and Sale of Officer's Commissions in the British Army and the Campaign for its Abolition, 1660-1871." Ph. D. Dissertation, University of Manchester, 1974.

1423. Brunker, Howard M.E. Notes on Organisation and Equipment. (London, 1896).

1424. Bryant, Arthur. Jackets of Green: A Study of the History, Philosophy and Character of the Rifle Brigade. (London, 1972).

1425. Bullock, H. "The Judge Advocate." AQ 18 (July 1929), 369-73.

1426. Burgoyne, John F. The Military Opinions of General Sir John Fox Burgoyne. Collected and Edited by George Wrottesley. (London, 1859).

1427. Burne, Alfred H. The Royal Artillery Mess, Woolwich, and Its Surroundings. (Portsmouth, England, 1935).

1428. Bush, Eric W. Salute and the Soldier; An Anthology of Quotations, Poems and Prose. (London, 1966).

1429. Cadell, Patrick. "The Beginnings of Khaki." JSAHR 31 (Autumn 1953), 132-3.

1430. Caillard, Maurice. "The War Office Fifty Years Ago." AQ 71 (October 1955), 56-63.

1431. Cairnes, William Elliot. Social Life in the British Army by a "British Officer." (New York, 1899).

1432. Callwell, Charles E. and John Headlam. The History of the Royal Artillery from the Indian Mutiny to the Great War. (3 vols., London, 1931-40).

1433. Callwell, Charles E. "War Office Reminiscences." BLM 190 (August 1911), 154-70.

1434. Camberley, England, Staff College. The Story of the Staff College, 1858-1958. Edited and Compiled by F.W. Young. (Camberley, Surrey, England, 1958).

1435. Campbell, Duncan A. The Dress of the Royal Artillery from 1898-1956. (London, 1960).

1436. Campbell, E.S. Norman. A Dictionary of the Military Science: Containing an Explanation of the Principal Terms used in Mathematics, Artillery and Fortification, and Comprising the Substance of the Latest Regulations on Courts Martial, Pay Pensions, Allowances, etc.; A Comparative Table of Ancient and Modern Geography; Achievements of the British Army; With an Address to Gentlemen Entering the Army. (New Edition, London, 1844).

1437. Cannon, Richard. Historical Records of the British Army, Comprising the History of Every Regiment in Her Majesty's Service. (63 vols., London, 1837-83).

1438. Cantlie, Neil. A History of the Army Medical Department. (2 vols., Edinburgh, 1974).

1439. Carew, Tim. How the Regiments Got Their Nicknames. (London, 1974).

1440. Carman, William Y. British Military Uniforms From Contemporary Pictures. (London, 1957).

1441. Carman, William Y. Head Dresses of the British Army; Cavalry.
(Sutton, Surrey, England, 1968).

1442. Carman, William Y. Headdresses of the British Army: Yeomanry.
(Sutton, Surrey, England, 1970).

1443. Carter, Thomas. War Medals of the British Army, and How They Were
Won. Revised, Englarged and Continued to the Present Time by William
H. Long. (London, 1893).

1444. Cassin-Scott, Jack and John Fabb. Military Bands and Their Uniforms.
(Dorset, England, 1968).

1445. Castle Museum, York. The Military Collections. (York, England, n.d.).

1446. Chandler, David. "The National Army Museum." HT 22 (September
1972), 664- 8.

1447. Chevers, Norman. A Historical Review of the Moral and Social Condition of the British Soldier. (Calcutta, 1865).

1448. Chichester, Henry M. and George Burges-Short. The Records and Badges
of Every Regiment and Corps in the British Army. (Third Edition,
London, 1902).

1449. Clammer, David. The Victorian Army in Photographs. (Newton Abbot,
Devon, England, 1975).

1450. Claver, Scott. Under the Lash; A History of Corporal Punishment in
the British Armed Forces, Including a Digest of the Report of the
Royal Commission, 1835-36... (London, 1954).

1451. Clode, Charles M. The Military Forces of the Crown; Their Administration and Government. (2 vols., London, 1869).

1452. Cole, David H. and Edgar C. Priestley. An Outline of British Military
History, 1660-1936. (London, 1937).

1453. Cole, Howard N., compl. The Origins of Military Aldershot; A Series
of Fifteen Engravings with Explanatory Notes. (Aldershot, 1972).

1454. Cole, Howard N. The Story of Aldershot; A History and Guide to
Town and Camp. (Aldershot, 1951).

1455. Collen, Edwin H.H. Report on the Intelligence Branch, Quartermaster
General's Department, Horse Guards. (London, 1878).

1456. Collinson, T.B. "Barracks." JRUSI 6 (April 1862), 539-58.

1457. Connolly, Thomas W.J. The History of the Corps of Royal Sappers and
Miners. (2 vols., London, 1855).

1458. Cooper, Leonard. British Regular Cavalry 1644-1914. (London, 1965).

1459. Cousins, Geoffrey. The Defenders; A History of the British Volunteers. (London, 1968).

1460. Cowper, J.M. "The Lure of the Red Coat." JRUSI 100 (May 1955), 272- 6.

1461. Creagh, O'Moore and Edith M. Humphris, eds. The V.C. and D.S.O. a Complete Record of all Those Officers, Non-commissioned Officers and Men of His Majesty's Naval, Military and Air Forces Who Have Been Awarded These Decorations from the Time of Their Institution... (3 vols., London, 1924).

1462. Cunliffe, Marcus. "The Army, 1815-54, as an Institution to be Considered as Regards the Administration, Organization, Composition, and its Relations to the Political and Social Conditons of the Country." B.Litt. Thesis, Oxford University, 1947.

1463. Cunningham, Hugh St. Claire. The Volunteer Force; A Social and Political History, 1859-1908. (London, 1975).

1464. Danby, Paul and Cyril Field. The British Army Book. (London, 1915).

1465. Daniel, William H. The Military Forces of the Crown. Their Organization and Equipment. Edited by Thomas M. Maguire. (London, 1901).

1466. Davies, F.J. The Sergeant-Major; The Origin and History of His Rank, with Notes on Military Customs and Habits of Former Times. (London, 1886).

1467. Dawnay, Nicolas P. The Badges of Warrant and Non-commissioned Rank in the British Army. (London, 1948).

1468. Dawnay, Nicolas P. The Distinction of Rank of Regimental Officers, 1684-1855. (London, 1960).

1469. Dawson, R. MacGregor. "The Cabinet Ministers and Administration: The British War Office, 1903-1916." CJEPS 5 (November 1939), 451-78.

1470. Dean, Charles G.F. The Royal Hospital,Chelsea. (London, 1950).

1471. DeFoublanque, Edward B. Treatise on the Administration and Organization of the British Army, with Especial Reference to Firearms and Supply. (London, 1858).

1472. Denholm, Anthony. "Lord DeGray and Army Reform, 1859-1866." AQ 102 (October 1971), 57-64.

1473. Devore, Ronald Marvin. "British Military Consuls in Asia Minor, 1878-1882." Ph.D. Dissertation, Indiana University, 1973.

1474. Dickinson, Richard J., compl. Officers Mess; Being a History of Mess Origins and Customs from a Wealth of Military Records; Enlivened Anecdotes of Mess Times Remembered from a Host of One-Time Mess Members; and the Progress of Charles Oswald Littlewart from 2nd Lieutenant to Major-General. (Turnbridge, England, 1973).

1475. Dow, Alexander C. Ministers to the Soldiers of Scotland; A History of the Chaplains of Scotland Prior to the War in the Crimea. (Edinburgh, 1962).

1476. Douglas, William. Dueling Days in the Army. (London, 1887).

1477. Dunlop, John K. The Development of the British Army, 1899-1914. (London, 1938).

1478. Dupin, (Pierre) Charles F. View of the History and Actual State of the Military Forces of Great Britain. (2 vols., London, 1822).

1479. Eady, Harold G. Historical Illustrations to Field Service Regulations. Volume 2. (London, 1927).

1480. Eady, Harold G. Historical Illustrations to Field Service Regulations, Operations, 1929. (London, 1930).

1481. Edmonds, James E. "The Abolition of the Sale and Purchase of Army Commissions." JRUSI 99 (November 1954), 588-93.

1482. Edmonds, James E. "Four Generations of Staff College Students--1896 to 1952." AQ 64 (April 1952), 42-55.

1483. Edmonds, James E. "The Army and Military Training in the Eighties." AQ 46 (July 1953), 224- 7.

1484. Edwards, Thomas J. Badges of H.M. Services. (Manchester, England, 1943).

1485. Edwards, Thomas J. "British Field Marshals." AQ 3 (July 1946), 244-47.

1486. Edwards, Thomas J. "The Field Marshal's Baton." AQ 53 (October 1946), 100-4.

1487. Edwards, Thomas J. Military Customs. Revised Edition by Arthur L. Kipling.(Fifth Edition, Aldershot, England, 1961).

1488. Edwards, Thomas J. Regimental Badges. (Aldershot, England, 1951).

1489. Edwards, Thomas J. "The Sergeant-Major." JRUSI 74 (August 1929), 594-6.

1490. Edwards, Thomas J. Standards, Guidons and Colours of the Commonwealth Forces. (Aldershot, England, 1953).

1491. Eldred, Margaret. "A Cadet of 1835." JRA 82 (October 1955), 309-11.

1492. Ellison, Gerald. "Lord Roberts and the General Staff." NC 112 (December 1932), 722-32.

1493. Erickson, Arvel B. "Abolition of Purchase in the British Army." MA 23 (Summer 1959), 65-76.

1494. Esson, D.M.R. "Cardwell and the Military Reformation." AQ 102 ((July 1972), 496-509.

1495. Fabb, John. The Victorian and Edwardian Army from Old Photographs. (London, 1975).

1496. Falls, Cyril. "The Army" in Simon H. Nowell-Smith, ed., Edwardian England, 1901-1914. (New York, 1964), 519-44.

1497. Farmer, Henry G. British Bands in Battle. (London, n.d.).

1498. Farmer, Henry G. History of the Royal Artillery Band, 1762-1953. (London, 1954).

1499. Farmer, Henry G. Memoirs of the Royal Artillery Band, its Origins, History and Progress. An Account of the Rise of Military Music in England. (New York, 1904).

1500. Farmer, John S. The Regimantal Records of the British Army; A Historical Resume, Chronologically Arranged, of Titles, Campaigns, Honours, Uniforms, Facings, Badges, Nicknames, &c. (London, 1901).

1501. Ffoulkes, Charles. Arms and Armament: An Historical Survey of the Weapons of the British Army. (London, 1945).

1502. Ffoulkes, Charles. The Gunfounders of England with a List of English and Continental Gun-Founders from the XIV to the XIX Centuries. (Cambridge, England, 1937).

1503. Ffoulkes, Charles and E.C. Hopkinson. Sword, Lance and Bayonet: A Record of the Arms of the British Army and Navy. (Cambridge, England, 1938).

1504. Field, Cyril. Britain's Sea-Soldiers, A History of the Royal Marines and Their Predecessors and of Their Service in Action, Ashore and Afloat, and Upon Sundry Other Occasions of Momment. (Liverpool, England, 1924).

1505. Field, Cyril. Echoes of Old Wars; Personal and Unofficial Letters, and Accounts of Bygone Battles, both by Land and or Sea by Those that were there 1513 to 1854; A Martial Anthology. (London, 1934).

1506. Firebrace, Cordell W. The Army and Navy Club, 1837-1933. (London, 1934).

1507. Forbes, Arthur. A History of the Army Ordnance Services. (3 vols., London, 1929).

1508. Fortescue, John W. British Regiments. (London, 1934).

1509. Fortescue, John W. The Empire and the Army. (London, 1928).

1510. Fortescue, John W. A History of the British Army. (13 vols. in 14, New York, 1899-1930).

1511. Fortescue, John W. A Gallant Company or Deeds of Duty and Discipline from the Story of the British Army. (London, 1927).

1512. Fortescue, John W. and Roger H. Beadon. The Royal Army Service Corps; A History of Supply and Transport in the British Army. (2 vols. Cambridge, England, 1930- 1).

1513. Fortescue, John W. A Short Account of Canteens in the British Army. (Cambridge, England, 1928).

1514. Franklyn, Harold E., C.N. Barclay, D.M.A. Wedderburn and James E. Edmonds. "Four Generations of Staff College Students, 1896 to 1952." AQ 65 (October 1952), 42-55.

1515. Fraser, Maj. T. "Personal Equipment of Officers on Active Service." Ordnance Note No. 107, June 20, 1879 in United States, Ordnance Department, Ordnance Notes. (12 vols., Washington, D.C., 1873-84).

1516. Frederick, John B.M. Lineage Book of the British Army; Mounted Corps and Infantry, 1660-1968. (Cornwallville, New York, 1969).

1517. French, Gerald. Good-bye to Boot and Saddle; or, the Tragic Passing of British Cavalry. (London, 1951).

1518. Furse, George A. Military Expeditions Beyond the Seas. (2 vols., London, 1897).

1519. Gallagher, Thomas F. "British Military Thinking and the Coming of the Franco-Prussian War." MA 39 (February 1975), 19-22.

1520. Gallagher, Thomas F. "'Cardwellian Mysteries': The Fate of the British Army Regulation Bill, 1871." HJ 18 (June 1975), 327-48.

1521. Gardiner, Robert W. Considerations on the Military Organization of the British Army. (London, 1858).

1522. Gareston, J. "Armies of Occupation I: The British in France 1815-1818." HT 11 (June 1961), 396-404.

1523. Gilbert, K.R. "The Ames Recessing Machine: A Survivor of the Original Enfield Rifle Machinery." T&C 4 (Spring 1963), 207-11.

1524. Gilby, Thomas. Britain at Arms; A Scrapbook from Queen Anne to the Present Day. (London, 1953).

1525. Gleig, George R. Chelsea Hospital and its Traditions. (3 vols., London, 1838).

1526. Goodenough, William H. and James C. Dalton. The Army Book for the British Empire. (London, 1893).

1527. Goodwin-Austen, Alfred R. The Staff and the Staff College. (London, 1927).

1528. Gooch, John. "The Origin and Development of the British and Imperial General Staffs to 1916." Ph.D. Dissertation, University of London, 1970.

1529.*Gooch, John. The Plans of War; The General Staff and British Military Strategy c. 1900-1916. (New York, 1974).

1530. Gordon, Hampden. The War Office. (London, 1935).

1531. Gordon, Lawrence L. Military Origins. Edited by J.B.R. Nicholson. (New York, 1971).

1532. Gordon, Lawrence L. British Battles and Medals; A Description of Every Campaign Medal and Bar Awarded Since the Armada, with the Historical Reasons for their Award and the Names of All the Ships, Regiments and Squadrons of the Royal Air Force whose Personnel are Entitled to Them. (Third Revised and Enlarged Edition, Aldershot, England, 1962).

1533. Gordon, Lawrence L. British Battles and Medals. Revised by Edward C. Joslin. (Fourth Edition, London, 1971).

1534. Gordon, Lawrence L. British Orders and Awards; A Description of All Orders, Decorations, Long Service, Coronation, Jubilee, and Commoration (sic) Meadals, together with Historical Details Concerning Knighthood, Service Ranks and Similar Information. (Stafford, England, 1959).

1535. Gordon, William J. Bands of the British Army. (London, 1921).

1536. Gore, Albert A. The Story of Our Services Under the Crown. A Historical Sketch of the Army Medical Staff. (London, 1879).

1537. Gorman, James T. The British Army. (London, 1940).

1538. Gould, Robert W. Campaign Medals of the British Army, 1815-1972. (London, 1972).

1539. Graham, Gerald S. A Concise History of the British Army. (New York, 1971).

1540. Great Britain, War Office. Army: State of the Military Forces in the United Kingdom, 1st June 1910. (London, 1911).

1541. Great Britain, War Office. Handbook on Military Bicycles, 1911. (London, 1911).

1542. Great Britain, War Office. Infantry Bugle Sounds. (London, 1860).

1543. Great Britain, War Office, Intelligence Division. The Military Forces of the British Colonies and Protectorates. (London, 1902).

1544. Great Britain, War Office. Report on the Regimental and Garrison Schools of the Army, and on Military Libraries and Reading Rooms. By John H. Lefroy. (London, 1859).

1545. Great Britain, War Office. <u>Statistical Reports on the Sickness,
Mortality, and Invaliding Among the Troops in the United Kingdom,
the Mediterranean and British America</u>. (London, 1839).

1546. Great Britain, War Office. <u>Statistical Reports on the Sickness,
Mortality, and Invaliding Among the Troops in the United Kingdom,
the Mediterranean and British America</u>. (London, 1853).

1547. Great Britain, War Office. <u>The Statutory Powers of Her Majesty's
Principal Secretary of State for the War Department. Ordnance Depart-
ment</u>. By Charles M. Clode. (London, 1879).

1548. Great Britain, War Office. <u>Trumpets and Bugle Sounds for the Army,
with Instructions for the Training of Trumpeters and Buglers</u>.
(London, 1895).

1549. Grierson, James M. <u>Records of the Scottish Volunteer Force, 1859-
1908</u>. (London, 1909).

1550. Griffiths, Arthur G.F. <u>The English Army; Its Past History, Present
Condition, and Future Prospects</u>. (London, 1878).

1551. Griffiths, Arthur G.F. <u>Famous British Regiments</u>. (London, 1900).

1552. Griffiths, Frederick A. <u>Artillerists Manual and British Soldiers
Compendium...of Infantry Exercise, Sword Exercise, Artillery Exercise...
Gunnery...</u> (Woolwich, England, 1840).

1553. Guggisberg, Frederick G. <u>"The Shop"; The Story of the Royal Military
Academy</u>. (New York, 1900).

1554. Haldane, Richard B. <u>Army Reform and Other Addresses</u>. (London, c. 1907).

1555. Harner, W.S. <u>The British Army; Civil-Military Relations 1885-1905</u>.
(New York, 1970).

1556. Hardy, Edward J. <u>Mr. Thomas Atkins</u>. (London, 1900).

1557. Hardy, Edward J. "Tommy Atkins at Play." <u>USM</u> 12, New Series (February
1896), 521-4.

1558. Hargreaves, J.D. "The Origins of the Anglo-French Military Conversations in 1905." <u>HIS</u> 36, New Series (October 1951), 244- 8.

1559. Hargreaves, Reginald. "Promotion from the Ranks." <u>AQ</u> 84 (July 1963),
200-10.

1560. Harries-Jenkins, Gwyn. <u>The Army in Victorian Society</u>. (London, 1977).

1561. Harries-Jenkins, Gwyn. "The Development of Professionalism in the
Victorian Army." <u>AFS</u> 1 (Summer 1975), 472-89.

1562. Harries-Jenkins, Gwyn. "The Victorian Military and the Political Order.'
<u>JPMS</u> 1 (Fall 1973), 279-89.

1563. Harvey, A.J.W. "Army Schools, III. The School of Artillery." AQ 68 (July 1954), 198-208.

1564. Haswell, Chetwynd J.D. (Jock). British Military Intelligence. (London, 1973).

1565. Hay, George J., compl. An Epitomized History of the Militia ("The Constitutional Force") Together with the Origin, Periods of Embodied Service, and Special Services (Including South Africa, 1899-1902) of Militia Units Existing October 31, 1905. (London, 1906).

1566. Haydon, Arthur L. The Book of the V.C.; A Record of the Deeds of Heroism for Which the Victoria Cross Has Been Bestowed. (Second Edition, London, 1906).

1567. Hilbert, Lothar W. "The Early Years of the Military Attache Service in British Diplomacy." JSAHR 37 (December 1959), 164-71.

1568. Hilbert, Lothar W. "The Role of Military and Naval Attaches in the British and German Service, with Particular Reference to Those in Berlin and London and Their Effect on Anglo-German Relations, 1871-1914." Ph.D. Dissertation, Cambridge University, 1954.

1569. Hobday, E.A.P. "The History and Traditions of the Royal Artillery." JRA 68 (April 1941), 179-208.

1570. Hogg, Ian V. Coast Defences of England and Wales, 1856-1956. (Newton Abbot, Devon, England, 1974).

1571. Hogg, Oliver F.G. "Forerunners of the Army Council." JSAHR 11 (July 1932), 101-48.

1572. Hogg, Oliver F.G. The Royal Arsenal: Its Background, Origin and Subsequent History. (2 vols., London, 1963).

1573. Holding, Thomas H. Uniforms of the British Army, Navy, and Court. (London, 1894).

1574. Hort, Richard. The Guards and the Line. (London, 1851).

1575. Hudleston, Francis J. "The War Office Library." AQ 1 (January 1920), 366-75.

1576. Hughes, Basil P. British Smooth-Bore Artillery; The Muzzle Loading Artillery of the 18th and 19th Centuries. (Harrisburg, Pennsylvania, 1969).

1577. Hutchison, Graham S. The British Army: A Brief History. (London, 1945).

1578. Illustrated London News. Uniforms of the British Army, and Regimental History. (London, 1936).

1579. Irwin, D. Hastings. War Medals and Decorations Issued to the British Military and Naval Forces and Allies from 1588 to 1910. (London, 1910).

1580. Jackson, Louis C. History of the United Service Club. (Aldershot, England, 1937).

1581. Jeffreys, Julius. "On Improvements in Helmets and Other Headdress for British Troops in the Tropics, More Especially in India." JRUSI 5, No. 20 (1862), 612-32.

1582. Jocelyn, Julian R.J. The History of the Royal Artillery. (London, 1911).

1583. Johnson, Franklyn A. Defence by Committee: The British Committee of Imperial Defence, 1885-1959. (New York, 1960).

1584. Johnson, J.D. "The Thinking Soldier." AQ 105 (July 1975), 290-303.

1585. Jones, Alfred S. "On the Education of Staff Officers." JRUSI 14, No. 59 (1870), 271-86.

1586. Jones, Philip Dwight. "The British Army in the Age of Reform, 1830-1854." Ph.D. Dissertation, Duke University, 1968.

1587. Judd, Dennis. Someone Has Blundered; Calamities of the British Army in the Victorian Age. (London, 1973).

1588. Kennedy, Alistar and George Crabb. The Postal History of the British Army in World War I--Before and After--1903-1929. (Epsom, England, 1977).

1589. King, Charles C. The Story of the British Army. (London, 1897).

1590. King, G.J.S. "Britain's War Secretaries." AQ 54 (April 1947), 42- 8; (July 1947), 199-205.

1591. Kingsland, P.W. and Susan Keable. British Military Uniforms and Equipment, 1788-1830. (London, 1971).

1592. Kipling, Arthur L. and Hugh L. King. Headdress Badges of the British Army. (London, 1973).

1593. Knaplund, Paul. "E.G. Wakefield on the Colonial Garrisons, 1851." CHR 5 (Spring 1924), 228-36.

1594. Koenig, Duane. "The National Army Museum, Chelsea." MA 36 (April 1972), 66-67.

1595. Laffin, John. British Campaign Medals. (New York, 1965).

1596. Laffin, John. Scotland The Brave; The Story of the Scottish Soldier. (London, 1963).

1597. Laffin, John. Tommy Atkins; The Story of the English Soldier. (London, 1966).

1598. Lambert, J.M. "Army Schools II: Past and Present at the School of Military Engineering, Chatam." AQ 68 (April 1954), 66-74.

1599. Langdon, Loomis L. "The Royal United Service Museum." _JMSI_ 44
(May-June 1909), 424-33.

1600. Langlois, Hippolyte. _The British Army in a European War..._
Translated by Captain C.F. Atkinson. (London, 1910).

1601. Lankford, Nelson D. "Status, Professionalism and Bureaucracy: The
Surgeon in the British Army, 1860-1914." Ph.D. Dissertation, Indiana
University, 1976.

1602. Laver, James. _British Military Uniforms_. (London, 1948).

1603. Lawrence-Archer, James H. _The British Army: Its Regimental Records,
Badges, Devices, &c._ (London, 1888).

1604. Laws, M.S.S., ed. _Battery Records of the Royal Artillery, 1716-1859_.
(London, 1952).

1605. Lawson, Cecil C.P. _The Uniforms of the British Army_. (3 vols.,
London, 1940).

1606. Lemonofides, Dino. _British Cavalry Standards_. (New Halden, Surrey,
England, 1971).

1607. Lemonofides, Dino. _British Infantry Colours_. (London, 1971).

1608. Lenney, John Joseph. _Rankers; the Odyssey of the Enlisted Regular
Soldier of America and Britain. A Study of the Ups and Downs of the
Enlisted Regular Soldier of America and Britain and his Promotion
Unaided and Unsung to Commissioned Grade, Particularly in the Regular
Army of the United States of America._ (New York, 1950).

1609. Leslie, John H. "Militia Regiments of Great Britain. A Calendar
of their Records and Histories." _JSAHR_ 12 (Spring 1933), 45-9;
(Summer 1933), 96-9.

1610. Leslie, John H. "The Honourable the Board of Ordnance 1299-1855."
JSAHR 4 (July-September 1925), 100-4.

1611. Leslie, N.B. _Battle Honours of the British and Indian Armies, 1695-
1914_. (London, 1970).

1612. Leslie, N.B. _The Succession of Colonels of the British Army from
1660 to the Present Day_. (London, 1974).

1613. Lewis, Peter M.H. _The British Fighter Since 1912: Fifty Years of
Design and Development_. (London, 1965).

1614. Lewis, Peter M.H. _Squadron Histories--R.F.C., R.N.A.S., and R.A.F.,
1912-59_. (London, 1959).

1615. London, Imperial War Museum. _The Victoria Cross and George Cross_.
(London, 1970).

1616. Lovegrove, Peter. Not Least in the Crusade. A Short History of the Royal Army Medical Corps. (Aldershot, England, 1951).

1617. Low, Charles R. Soldiers of the Victorian Age. (2 vols., London, 1880).

1618. Luard, John. A History of the Dress of the British Soldier From the Earliest Period to the Present Time. (London, 1852).

1619. Lunt, James. "The Passing of L'Arme Blanche: The Last Cavalry Charge in British Military History." HT 9 (January 1959), 40-7.

1620.*Luvaas, Jay. The Education of an Army; British Military Thought, 1815-1940. (Chicago, Illinois, 1964).

1621. Luvaas, Jay. "The First British Official Historians." MA 26 (Summer 1962), 49-58.

1622. McDermott, John. "The Revolution in British Military Thinking from the Boer War to the Moroccan Crisis." CJH 9, No. 2 (1974), 159-78.

1623. MacDonald, Reginald J. The History of the Dress of the Royal Regiment of Artillery, 1625-1897. (London, 1899).

1624. McGuffie, Thomas H. "Early Barrack Life." AQ 54 (April 1947), 65-8.

1625. McGuffie, Thomas H. "Life in the British Army, 1793-1820, in Relation to Social Conditions." M.A. Thesis, University of London, 1940.

1626. McGuffie, Thomas H. "Recruiting the British Army." AQ 72 (April 1956), 63-70.

1627. Mackenzie-Rogan, John. Fifty Years of Army Music. (London, 1926).

1628. MacMullen, John. Camp and Barrack Room: or, the British Army as it is. (London, 1846).

1629. MacMunn, George F. The Army. (London, 1929).

1630. Maguire, Thomas Miller. The British Army on the Continent of Europe, 1701-1855. (London, 1897).

1631. Majendie, Vivian D. The Arms and Ammunition of the British Service. (London, 1872).

1632. Marshall, Henry. A Historical Sketch of Military Punishments, in as Far as Regards Non-Commissioned Officers and Private Soldiers. (London, n.d.).

1633. Marshall, Henry. Military Miscellany: Comprehending a History of the Recruiting of the Army, Military Punishments, &c, &c. (London, 1846).

1634. Marshall, Henry. On the Enlisting, the Discharging, and the Pensioning of Soldiers: With the Official Documents on These Branches of Military Duty. (London, 1832).

1635. Masse, Charles H. The Predecessors of the Royal Army Service Corps (1757-1888). (Aldershot, England, 1948).

1636. Maude, Frederic N. Cavalry: Its Past and Future. (London, 1903).

1637. Maude, Frederic N. Letters on Tactics and Organization, or English Military Institutions and the Continental Systems. (Leavenworth, Kansas, 1891).

1638. Maurice-Jones, Kenneth W. The History of the Coast Artillery of the British Army. (London, 1959).

1639. Maurice-Jones, Kenneth W. The Shop Story, 1900-1939. (Woolwich, England, 1954).

1640. May, William E., William Y. Carman and John Tanner. Badges and Insignia of the British Armed Services. (New York, 1974).

1641. Mayo, John H. Medals and Decorations of the British Army and Navy. (2 vols., Westminster, England, 1897).

1642. Miles, W. "When Promotion was Slower Still. The Commission of Enquiry in 1838." JSAHR 12 (Winter 1933), 213-221.

1643. Miller, Archibald E. Howell and Nicolas P. Dawnay. Military Drawings and Paintings in the Collection of Her Majesty the Queen. (2 vols., London, 1966-70).

1644. Miller, W.S. The School of Musketry at Hythe. (London, 1892).

1645. Milne, Samuel M. The Standards and Colours of the Army from the Restoration 1661, to the Introduction of the Territorial System, 1881. (Leeds, England, 1893).

1646. Mockler-Ferryman, Augustus F. Annals of Sandhurst, A Chronicle of the Royal Military College with a Sketch of the History of the Staff College. (London, 1900).

1647. Mollo, Boris. The British Army from Old Photographs. (London, 1975).

1648. Montefiore, Cecil Seabag. A History of the Volunteer Forces from the Earliest Times to the Year 1860, Being a Recital of the Citizen Duty. (London, 1908).

1649. Moses, N.H. "Edward Cardwell's Abolition of the Purchase System in the British Army, 1868-1874: A Study of Administrative and Legislative Processes." Ph.D. Dissertation, University of London, 1969.

1650. Moyse-Bartlett, Hubert. "British Army in 1850." JSAHR 52 (Winter 1974), 221-37.

1651. *Moyse-Bartlett, Hubert. "Military Historiography, 1850-1860." JSAHR 45 (Winter 1967), 199-213.

1652. Myatt, Frederick. The Soldier's Trade; British Military Developments, 1660-1914. (London, 1974).

1653. Nalder, R.H.F. The Royal Corps of Signals; Its Antecedents and Development, circa 1800-1955. (London, 1958).

1654. Napier, Charles J. Remarks on Military Law and the Punishment of Flogging. (London, 1837).

1655. National Army Museum. The British Army from Photographs. Compiled by Boris Mollo. (London, 1975).

1656. National Army Museum. Sabretaches of the British Army: A Selection of Photographs of Sabretaches in the National Army Museum; With a Short History of the Development of the Sabretache Until it was Abolished. By William Y. Carman. (Camberley, England, 1969).

1657. National Book League. The British Soldier; An Exhibition of Books, Manuscripts and Prints Covering the Last 250 Years. By G.A. Sheppard. (London, 1956).

1658. Neave-Hill, W.B.R. "Brevet Rank." JSAHR 48 (Summer 1970), 85-104.

1659. Neave-Hill, W.B.R. "The Rank Titles of Brigadier and Brigadier General." JSAHR 47 (Summer 1969), 96-116.

1660. Nevill, Ralph H. British Military Prints. (London, 1909).

1661. Norman, Charles B. Battle Honours of the British Army, from Tangier, 1662, to the Commencement of the Reign of King Edward VII. (London, 1911).

1662. Omond, John S. Parliament and the Army, 1642-1904. (Cambridge, England, 1933).

1663. Otley, C.B. "The Origins and Recruitment of the British Army Elite, 1870-1959." Ph.D. Dissertation, Hull University, 1965.

1664. Owen, John F. Treatise on the Construction of Ordnance in the British Service. (London, 1877).

1665.*Paine, J. "A Bibliography of British Military Music." JRUSI 73 (May 1928), 334-341.

1666.*Paine, J. "A Bibliography of Regimental Colours." AQ 67 (October 1953), 123-8.

1667. Paine, J. "The Records of the Victoria Cross." JRUSI 77 (August 1932), 602-6.

1668. Pargiter, Robert B. and Harold G. Eady. The Army and Sea Power; A Historical Outline. (London, 1927).

1669. Parkyn, Harry G. Shoulder-Belt Plates and Buttons. (Aldershot, 1956).

1670. Parr, Henry H. The Dress, Horses and Equipment of Infantry and Staff Officers. (London, 1881).

1671. Parry, D.H. The V.C. Its Heroes and their Valour, from Personal Accounts, Official Records and Regimental Tradition. (New and Enlarged Edition, New York, 1913).

1672. Pendergast, Harris. The Law Relating to Officers in the Army. (London, 1855).

1673. Perry, Ottley L. Rank and Badges, Dates of Formation, Naval and Military Distinctions, Precedence, Salutes, Colours, and Small Arms, in Her Majesty's Army and Navy and Auxiliary Forces, Including a Record of the Naval and Military Forces in the Different Countries of Great Britain and Ireland.(Second Edition, Revised and Enlarged, London, 1888).

1674. Piggott, Francis S.G. "Promotion by Brevet." AQ 59 (October 1949), 97-104.

1675. Poe, Bryce, III. "British Army Reforms: 1902-1914." MA 31 (Fall 1967), 131- 8.

1676. Porter, Whitworth and Charles M. Watson. History of the Corps of Royal Engineers. (3 vols., London, 1889-1915).

1677. Preston, Adrian W. "British Military Thought, 1856-90." AQ 89 (October 1964), 57-74.

1678. Reynolds, Edmund G.B. The Lee-Enfield Rifle. (London, 1960).

1679. Rhodes, Godfrey. "Tents from Their Earliest Period to the Present Time." JRUSI 3 (March 1859), 238-55.

1680. Richards, Walter. Her Majesty's Army. Descriptive Account of the Various Regiments now Comprising the Queen's Forces, in India and the Colonies. (3 vols., London, 1888-91).

1681. Rimington, Michael F. Our Cavalry. (London, 1912).

1682. Ripley, Howard. Buttons of the British Army, 1855-1970; An Illustrated Guide for Collectors. (London, 1971).

1683. Ripley, Howard. "Buttons of the Officers Training Corps." BMHS 27 (August 1976), 1-15.

1684. Rizzi, R.A. "The British Army as a Riot-Control Force in Great Britain During the Years 1811-48 Inclusive." B. Litt, Oxford University, 1975.

1685. Roads, Christopher H. The British Soldier's Firearms, 1850-1864. (London, 1964).

1686. Roads, Christopher H. "The History of the Introduction of the Percussion Breech-Loading Rifle into British Military Service, 1850-70." Ph.D. Dissertation, Cambridge University, 1961.

1687. Roberts, Adam. "The British Armed Forces and Politics: A Historical Perspective." AFS 3 (Summer 1977), 531-56.

1688. Roberts, Frederick S. A Nation in Arms; Speeches on the Requirements of the British Army. (New York, 1907).

1689. Robertson, Bruce. British Military Aircraft Serials, 1911-1971. (Fourth Revised Edition, London, 1971).

1690. Robson, Brian. Swords of the British Army; The Regulation Patterns, 1788-1914. (London, 1975).

1691. Roe, Frederick P. The Soldier and the Empire. (Aldershot, England, 1932).

1692. Rogers, Hugh C.B. The Mounted Troops of the British Army, 1066-1945. (London, 1959).

1693. Rogers, Hugh C.B. Troopships and Their History. (London, 1963).

1694. Rogers, Hugh C.B. Weapons of the British Soldier. (London, 1960).

1695. Rose, Barrie. "The Volunteers of 1859." JSAHR 37 (September 1959), 97-110.

1696. Rosen, G. "Edmund A. Parkes in the Development of Hygiene." JRAMC 122 (October 1976), 187-91.

1697. Rowan-Robinson, Henry. The Infantry Experiment. (London, 1934).

1698. Royal United Service Institution, London, Museum. Official Catalogue of the Royal United Service Institution Museum, Whitehall, S.W. Compiled by Arthur Leetham and Bertram E. Sargeaunt. (3rd Edition, London, 1908).

1699. Ryan, Ernest. "Army Horse Transport: General Service, Ambulance, and Other Vehicles from the Crimean War to Mechanization." JSAHR 42 (September 1964), 121-131.

1700. Satre, Lowell J. "St. John Broderick and Army Reform, 1901-1903." JBS 15 (Spring 1976), 117-39.

1701. Saunders, Hilary A. St. George. Per Ardna; The Rise of British Air Power, 1911-1939. (London, 1944).

1702. Scott, James Sibbald D. The British Army: Its Origins, Progress, and Equipment. (3 vols., London, 1868-80).

1703. Sellwood, Arthur V. The Saturday Night Soldiers: The Stirring Story of the Territorial Army. (London, 1966).

1704. Seymour, William W. On Active Service. (London, 1939).

1705. Shakow, Zara. "The Defence Committee: A Forerunner of the Committee of Imperial Defence." CHR 36 (March 1955), 36-44.

1706. Sheppard, Eric W. "The Prince Consort's Library, Aldershot." AQ 81 (October 1960), 52-3.

1707. Sheppard, Eric W., ed. Red Coat; An Anthology of the British Soldier During the Last Three Hundred Years. (London, 1952).

1708. Sheppard, Eric W. A Short History of the British Army. (Fourth Edition, Revised, London, 1850).

1709. Siddons, Joachim H. (J.H. Stocqueler, pseudo.). The British Officer: His Position, Duties, Emoulments and Privileges. (London, 1851).

1710. *Silverthorne, L.C. and W.D. Gaskin. The British Foot Guards; A Bibliography. (Cornwallville, New York, 1960).

1711. Simkin, Richard. Our Armies, Illustrated and Described, with One Hundred and One Facsimile Water Colour Drawings. (London, 1891).

1712. Simmons, Linton. "The Critical Condition of the (British) Army." Ordnance Note No. 316, August 14, 1883 in United States, Ordnance Department, Ordnance Notes. (12 vols., Washington, D.C., 1873-84).

1713. Skelley, Alan R. "The Terms and Conditions of Service and Recruitment of the Rank and File of the British Regular Home Army, 1856-99." Ph.D. Dissertation, Edinburgh University, 1975.

1714. *Skelley, Alan R. The Victorian Army at Home: The Recruitment and Terms and Conditions of the British Regular, 1859-1899. (London, 1977).

1715. Smitherman, P.H. Uniforms of the British Army: A Selection. (London, 1970).

1716. Smyth, John G. In This Sign Conquer: The Story of the Army Chaplains. (London, 1968).

1717. *Smyth, John G. Sandhurst. (London, 1961).

1718. Smyth, John G. The Story of the George Cross. (London, 1968).

1719. Smyth, John G. The Story of the Victoria Cross, 1856-1963. (London, 1963).

1720. Spalding, Henry S. Epochs of the British Army. Illustrated by Richard Simkin. (London, 1891).

1721. Spearman, James M. Notes on Military Education. (London, 1853).

1722. Spiers, E.M. "The Use of Dum Dum Bullets in Colonial Warfare." JI&CH 3 (October 1975), 3-14.

1723. Strachan, Hew. "The Origins of the 1855 Uniform Changes--An Example of Pre-Crimean Reform." JSAHR 55 (Summer 1977), 85-117; (Autumn 1977), 165-74.

1724. Sullivan, A.E. "Fortescue's History of the Army." AQ 70 (April 1955), 53-59.

1725. Sullivan, A.E. "A French View of the Post-Waterloo British Army." AQ 85 (January 1963), 188-97.

1726. Sullivan, A.E. "Married Quarters--A Retrospect." AQ 63 (October 1951), 113-19.

1727. Summerton, N.W. "The Development of British Military Planning for a War Against Germany, 1904-14." Ph.D. Dissertation, University of London, 1970.

1728. Sunseri, Alvin R. "Reform in the British Army, 1850-1920." ARMOR 67 (November-December 1958), 54- 7.

1729. Swinson, Arthur. A Register of the Regiments and Corps of the British Army; The Ancestry of the Regiments and Corps of the Regular Establishment. (London, 1972).

1730. Taillefer, Nugent. The British Cavalry Songs. (Second Edition, London, 1866).

1731. Talbot-Booth, Eric C. The British Army; Its History, Customs, Traditions and Uniforms. (London, 1940).

1732. Teagarden Ernest M. Haldane at the War Office: A Study in Organization and Management. (New York, 1976).

1733. Teagarden, Ernest M. "Lord Haldane and the Origins of the Officer Training Corps." JSAHR 45 (Summer 1967), 91- 6.

1734. Thomas, Hugh. The Story of Sandhurst. (London, 1961).

1735. Thomson, Beverley. The Military Forces and Institutions of Great Britain and Ireland. (London, 1855).

1736. Thomson, Henry. "Punishments in the Army." BLM 15 (April 1824), 399-406.

1737. Thorburn, William A. Uniforms of the Scottish Infantry, 1740-1900. (Edinburgh, 1970).

1738. Towle, Philip. "The British Armed Forces and Japan Before 1914." JRUSI 119 (June 1974), 67-71.

1739. Townsend, Charles E.C. All Rank and No File: A History of the Engineer and Railway Staff Corps R.E., 1865-1965. (London, 1969).

1740. Trevelyan, Charles E. The British Army in 1868. (London, 1868).

1741. Trotter, J.K. "Military Operations in the United Kingdom Considered, Particularly as Influenced by the Inclosed Nature of the Country." Ordnance Note No. 279, March 28, 1883 in United States, Ordnance Department, Ordnance Notes. (12 vols., Washington, D.C., 1973-84).

1742. Tucker, Albert. "Army and Society in England 1870-1900: A Reassessment of the Cardwell Reforms." JBS 2 (May 1963), 110-41.

1743. Turner, Ernest S. Gallant Gentleman; A Portrait of the British Officer, 1600-1956. (London, 1956).

1744. Tylden, Geoffrey. Horses and Saddlery: An Account of the Animals Used by the British and Commonwealth Armies from the Seventeenth Century to the Present Day with a Description of Their Equipment. (London, 1965).

1745. Tylden, Geoffrey. "The Accoutrements of the British Infantryman, 1640 to 1940." JSAHR 47 (Spring 1969), 4-22.

1746. *Tyler, John E. The British Army and the Continent, 1904-1914. (London, 1938).

1747. United Services and Defence Review. Military Types of the British Army. (London, 1888-94).

1748. Vivian, Evelyn C.H. The British Army from Within. (New York, 1914).

1749. Walker, Arthur. "The Dress and Equipment of the Army." JRUSI 11 (June 1867), 375-401.

1750. Walters, John. Aldershot Review. (London, 1970).

1751. Wheaton, J. "The Effect and Impact of the Administrative Reform Movement Upon the Army in the mid-Victorian Period." Ph.D. Dissertation, University of Manchester, 1968.

1752. Wheeler, Owen. The War Office, Past and Present. (London, 1914).

1753. White, Archie C.F. The Story of Army Education, 1643-1963. (London, 1963).

1754. *White, Arthur S., compl. A Bibliography of Regimental Histories of the British Army. (London, 1965).

1755. Wiener, Frederick B. Civilians Under Military Justice; The British Practice Since 1689, Especially in North America. (Chicago, 1967).

1756. Wilkinson, Frederick J. Badges of the British Army, 1820-1960; An Illustrated Reference Guide for Collectors. (London, 1969).

1757. Wilkinson-Latham, John. British Military Swords; From 1800 to the Present Day. (London, 1966).

1758. Wilkinson-Latham, Robert. British Artillery on Land and Sea, 1790-1820. (Newton Abbot, Devon, England, 1973).

1759. Wilkinson-Latham, Robert and Christopher. Cavalry Uniforms; Including Other Mounted Troops of Britain and the Commonwealth. (New York, 1972).

1760. Williams, Gerald. Citizen Soldiers of the Royal Engineers Transportation and Movements and the Royal Army Service Corps, 1859 to 1965. (Aldershot, England, 1969).

1761. *Williams, N.T. St. John. Tommy Atkin's Children; The Story of the Education of the Army's Children, 1675-1970. (London, 1971).

1762. Wilson, Arnold. "Awards for Military Gallantry." QR 274 (January 1940), 18-26.

1763. Wilson, H.S. "The Army and Public Opinion from 1854 to the End of 1873." B. Litt. Thesis, Oxford University, 1955.

1764. *Winstock, Lewis. Songs and Music of the Redcoats: A History of the War Music of the British Army, 1642-1902. (Harrisburg, Pennsylvania, 1970).

1765. Wise, Terrence, compl. A Guide to Military Museums. (Bracknell, England, 1969).

1766. Wolseley, Garnet J. "The Army," in Thomas H. Ward, ed., The Reign of Queen Victoria, A Survey of Fifty Years of Progress. Volume 1. (London, 1887), 155-225.

1767. Wood, Evelyn. Our Fighting Services and How They Made the Empire. (London, 1916).

1768. Wood, Evelyn, ed. British Battles on Land and Sea...With a History of the Fighting Services. (2 vols., London, 1915).

1769. Wood, G.N. "More About Mercenaries." AQ 107 (January 1977), 75-80.

1770. Wood, Walter. The Romance of Regimental Marches. (London, 1932).

1771. Woolwich, England, Royal Artillery Institution, Museum. Official Catalogue of the Museum of Artillery in the Rotunda, Woolwich. (London, 1882).

1772. Woolwich, England, Royal Military Academy. Records of the Royal Military Academy. (London, 1851).

1773. Worthington, Ian. "Antecedent Education and Officer Recruitment: The Origins and Early Development of the Public School-Army Relationship." MA 41 (December 1977), 183- 9.

1774. Wraxall, Frederick C.L. Military Sketches. (London, 1864).

1775. Wyatt, Robert J. Collecting Volunteer Militaria. (Newton Abbot, Devon, England, 1974).

1776. Wyndham, Horace. Following the Drum.(Third Edition, London, 1914).

1777. Wyndham, Horace. The Queen's Service or, the Real "Tommy Atkins", Being the Experiences of a Private Soldier in the British Infantry at Home and Abroad. (Boston, 1899).

1778. Wyndham, Horace. Soldiers of the Queen. (London, 1899).

1779. Yarham, E.R. "The End of the Trooping Era." AQ 89 (January 1965), 176- 9.

1780. Yeates, E.P. "Edwardian Gentleman-Cadet." AQ 83 (April 1961), 115- 8.

1781. Young, F.W. "A Hundred Years at the Staff College." AQ 76 (July 1978), 173-80.

1782. Young, Peter. The British Army, 1642-1970. (London, 1967).

1783. Young, Peter and James P. Lawford. History of the British Army. (London, 1970).

    See also: Part II: 110, 111, 134, 198, 211, 253, 266, 278, 280, 281,
              415, 442, 447, 469, 505, 506, 531, 533, 736, 778, 1000, 1994,
              2054, 2099, 2112, 2113, 2118, 2131, 2992; Addendum: 45, 46,
              69, 129, 134.

HOLLAND (NETHERLANDS)

1784. Cats, B.C. and C.P. Coenders. A Survey of the Beret-, Shoulder- and Collarbadges as They Were And Are Worn by the Netherlands Army. (Kedichem, Holland, 1969).

1785. Clarke, Francis C.H. The Armed Strength of the Netherlands. (London, 1876).

1786. Great Britain, War Office, Intelligence Division. The Armed Strength of the Netherlands and Their Colonies. By James K. Trotter. (London, 1887).

1787. Great Britain, War Office, Intelligence Division. Handbook of the Dutch Army (Home and Colonial). By William L. White and Edward Agar. (London, 1896).

1788. Jones, Harry D., ed. Reports Relating to the Re-establishment of the Fortresses in the Netherlands from 1814 to 1830. (London, 1861).

1789. O'Ballance, Edgar. "In Defence of Holland." AQ 82 (July 1961), 182-91.

1790. Walford, N.L. "Holland and the Dutch (Military Resources)." JRUSI 26 (June 1882), 695-755.

See also: Part II: 678, 850; Addendum: 163.

IRELAND

1791. Hayes-McCoy, Gerald A. Irish Battles: A Military History of Ireland. (London, 1969).

1792. Hennessey, Maurice N. The Wild Geese; The Irish Soldier in Exile. (Old Greenwich, Connecticut, 1973).

1793. Phillips, Walter A. The Revolution in Ireland, 1906-1923. (New York, 1923).

1794. Tansill, Charles C. America and the Fight for Irish Freedom, 1866-1922; An Old Story Based Upon New Data. (New York, 1957).

See also:

ITALY

1795. Amicis, Edmondo De. Military Life in Italy; Sketches. Translated by Wilhelmina W. Cady. (New York, 1882).

1796. Ardagh, Maj. "The Military Position of Italy." JRUSI 24, No. 104 (1880), 123- 9.

1797. Barclay, Glen St. John. The Rise and Fall of the New Roman Empire; Italy's Bid for World Power, 1890-1943. (New York, 1973).

1798. Case, Lynn M. Franco-Italian Relations, 1860-1865: The Roman Question and the Convention of September. (Philadelphia, Pennsylvania, 1932).

1799. Cesare, Raffaele de. The Last Days of Papal Rome, 1850-1870. Translated by Helen Zimmern. (Boston, 1909).

1800. Chambers, Osborne W.S. Garibaldi and Italian Unity. (London, 1864).

1801. Cormier, Moise. The Journal of Moise Cormier Zouaves Pontificaux, 1868-1870. Edited by David Ross. (Winnipeg, Manitoba, Canada, 1975).

1802. Crispi, Francesco. The Memoirs of Francesco Crispi. Translated by Mary Prichard-Agnetti. (3 vols., London, 1912-14).

1803. Durkin, Joseph T. "A Re-Examination of Italian Unification" (from Materials in the Archives of the United States). Ph.D. Dissertation, Fordham University, 1942.

1804. Forester, Cecil S. Victor Emanuel II and the Union of Italy. (New York, 1927).

1805. Fries, F.T. "Anglo-Italian Relations, 1884-5, and the Italian Occupation of Massawah." Ph.D. Dissertation, Cambridge University, 1939.

1806. Garibaldi, Giuseppe. Autobiography of Guiseppe Garibaldi. Translated by Alice Werner with a Supplement by Jessie W. Mario. (3 vols., London, 1889).

1807. Garibaldi, Guiseppe. The Life of General Garibaldi, Translated from His Private Papers, with the History of His Splendid Exploits in Rome, Lombardy, Sicily and Naples, by Theodore Dwight; to which is Added the Life of Garibaldi from 1860 to His Death. By Henry Ketcham, (New York, 1903).

1808. Garibaldi, Guiseppe. The Memoirs of Garibaldi. Edited by Alexandre Dumas; Translated by Robert S. Garnett. (New York, 1931).

1809. Great Britain, War Office, Intelligence Division. Armed Strength of Italy. Translated by W.A.H. Hare. (London, 1875).

1810. Great Britain, War Office, Intelligence Division. Handbook of the Italian Army. By John R. Slade. (London, 1891).

1811. Great Britain, War Office, Intelligence Division. Handbook of the Italian Army. (London, 1913).

1812. Great Britain, War Office. Italian Cavalry Training Regulations, 1911. Training for Marches, Tactics of Minor Units, and Training of Patrols. (London, 1912).

1813. Hibbert, Christopher. Garibaldi and His Enemies; The Clash of Arms and Personalities in the Making of Italy. (New York, 1970).

1814. Holt, Edgar. The Making of Italy 1815-1870. (New York, 1971).

1815. Katz, Robert. The Fall of the House of Savoy; A Study in the Relevance of the Commonplace or the Vulgarity of History. (New York, 1971).

1816. King, Bolton. A History of Italian Unity, Being a Political History of Italy, From 1814 to 1871. (2 vols., London, 1899).

1817. Larg, David. Guiseppe Garibaldi, A Biography. (London, 1934).

1818. Mack Smith, Denis. Garibaldi. (Englewood Cliffs, New Jersey, 1969).

1819. Mack Smith, Denis, compl. "Garibaldi," HT 6 (March 1956), 188-96.

1820. Martinengo-Cesaresco, Evelyn L.H. The Liberation of Italy, 1815-70. (London, 1895).

1821. Morozzo della Rocco, Enrico. The Autobiography of a Veteran, 1807-1893. Translated by Janet Ross. (New York, 1898).

1822. Nolan, Edward H. The Liberators of Italy; or, The Lives of General Garibaldi; Victor Emmanual, King of Italy; Count Cavour; and Napoleon III, Emperor of the French. (5 Pts., London, 1864-65).

1823. Parris, John. The Lion of Caprera; A Biography of Giuseppe Garibaldi. (New York, 1962).

1824. Pepe, Guglielmo. Memoirs of General Pepe. Comprising the Principal Military and Political Events of Modern Italy. (London, 1846).

1825. Repington, Charles a'Court.(Charles Martel, pseudo.). Military Italy. (London, 1884).

1826. Ridley, Jasper. Garibaldi. (New York, 1976).

1827. Royal Engineers' Institute, Chatham. Fortress of Alessandria in Italy. (Chatham, England, 1823).

1828. Stillman, William J. Francesco Crispi, Insurgent, Exile, Revolutionist and Statesman. (London, 1899).

1829. Stillman, William J. The Union of Italy, 1815-1895. (Cambridge, England, 1898).

1830. *Whittam, John R. The Politics of the Italian Army, 1861-1918. (Hamden, Connecticut, 1976).

See also: Part II: 33, 778, 2086.

POLAND

1831. Cynk, Jerzy B. *Polish Aircraft, 1893-1939.* (London, 1971).

1832. Dziewanowski, Wladyslaw. *Polish Armed Forces Through the Ages; Thousand Years of the Polish Army.* (London, 1944).

1833. Nadolski, Andreze. *Polish Arms; Sidearms.* Translated by Maria Abramouiczowa. (Wroclaw, 1974).

1834. Wojtasik, Janusz. "The Infleence of Armament on the Art of War in Polish National Risings in the 18th and 19th Century," in Poland, Ministry of National Defence, Military Historical Institute, *Military Technique, Policy and Strategy in History.* (Warsaw, 1976), 95-196.

PORTUGAL

1835. Boxer, Charles R. *Four Centuries of Portuguese Expansion, 1415-1823; A Succinct Survey.* (Berkeley, California, 1969).

1836. Great Britain, War Office, Intelligence Division. *The Armed Strength of Portugal.* By Edward Gleichen. (London, 1887).

See also: Part II: 2, 9, 22, 32.

RUSSIA

1837. *Allen, William E.D. and Paul Muratoff. *Caucasian Battlefields; A History of the Wars on the Turco-Caucasian Border, 1828-1921.* (Cambridge, England, 1953).

1838. Allworth, Edward, ed. *Central Asia: A Century of Russian Rule.* (New York, 1967).

1839. Andolenko, Serge. Badges of Imperial Russia. Military, Civil and Religious. Translated and Enlarged by Robert Werlich. (Washington, D.C., 1972).

1840. Askew, W.C. "Russian Military Strength on the Eve of the Franco-Prussian War." SEER 30 (December 1951), 185-205.

1841. Baddeley, John F. The Russian Conquest of the Caucasus. (New York, 1908).

1842. Becker, Seymour. Russia's Protectorates in Central Asia: Bukhara and Khiva, 1865-1924. (Cambridge, Massachusetts, 1969).

1843. Beresford, Maj. C.E. de la Poer. "The Defensive Strength of Russia." JRUSI 42 (March 1898), 299-308.

1844. Bigelow, Poultney. The Borderland of Czar and Kaiser. Notes from Both Sides of the Russian Frontier. (New York, 1895).

1845. *Blanch, Lesley. The Sabres of Paradise. (New York, 1960).

1846. Boulger, Demetrius Charles de Kavanagh. England and Russia in Central Asia. (London, 1879).

1847. Burnaby, Capt. Fred. A Ride to Khiva. Travels and Adventures in Central Asia. (New York, 1876).

1848. Charques, Richard D. The Twilight of Imperial Russia. (London, 1958).

1849. Cowles, Virginia S. The Russian Dagger: Cold War in the Days of the Czars. (London, 1969).

1850. Crist, David S. "Russia's Far Eastern Policy in the Making." JMH 14 (September 1942), 317-41.

1851. Crist, David S. "Russia's Manchurian Policy, 1895-1905." Ph.D. Dissertation, University of Michigan, 1941.

1852. Curtiss, John Skelton. "The Army of Nicholas I: Its Role and Character." AHR 63 (July 1958), 880- 9.

1853. Curtiss, John Skelton. "The Peasant and the Army," in The Peasant in Nineteenth Century Russia. Edited by Wayne S. Vucinich. (Stanford, California, 1968), 108-32.

1854. *Curtiss, John Skelton. The Russian Army Under Nicholas I, 1825-1855. (Durham, North Carolina, 1965).

1855. Curzon, George N. Russia in Central Asia in 1889, and the Anglo-Russian Question. (New York, 1889).

1856. Dallin, David J. The Rise of Russia in Asia. (New Haven, Connecticut, 1949).

1857. Daly, R.W. "Russian Combat Landings." MCG 53 (June 1969), 39-42.

1858. Deacon, Richard. A History of the Russian Secret Service. (New York, 1972).

1859. Demko, George J. The Russian Colonization of Kazakhstan: 1896-1916. (Bloomington, Indiana, 1969).

1860. Denikin, Anton I. The Career of a Tsarist Officer: Memoirs, 1872-1916. Translated by Margaret Patoski. (Minneapolis, Minnesota, 1975).

1861. Edwards, Henry S. Russian Projects Against India from the Czar Peter to General Skobeleff. (London, 1855).

1862. Florinsky, Michael T. The End of the Russian Empire; A Study in the Economics and Social History of the War. (New Haven, Connecticut, 1931).

1863. Florinsky, Michael T. "The Russian Mobilization of 1914." PSQ 42 (June 1927), 203-227.

1864. Garthoff, Raymond L. "The Military in Russia, 1861-1965," in Jacques van Doorn, ed., Armed Forces and Society; Sociological Essays. (The Hague, 1968), 240-56.

1865. Glaskow, V.G. History of the Cossacks. (New York, 1972).

1866. Graham, Lumley. "The Russian Army in 1882." JRUSI 27, No. 119 (1883), 206-47; No. 120 (1883), 487-530; No. 121 (1883), 631-79.

1867. Great Britain, War Office, Intelligence Division. The Armed Strength of Russia. (London, 1873).

1868. Great Britain, War Office, Intelligence Division. The Armed Strength of Russia. (London, 1882).

1869. Great Britain, War Office, Intelligence Division. The Armed Strength of Russia. By James M. Grierson. (London, 1886).

1870. Great Britain, War Office, Intelligence Division. Handbook of the Military Forces of Russia. By James M. Grierson. (London, 1894).

1871. Great Britain, War Office, Intelligence Division. Handbook of the Military Forces of Russia. Revised by William A. MacBean. (Second Edition, London, 1898).

1872. Great Britain, War Office, Intelligence Division. Handbook of the Russian Army. By James W. Murray. (London, 1889).

1873. Great Britain, War Office, Intelligence Division. Handbook of the Russian Army... By William A. MacBean. (London, 1905).

1874. Great Britain, War Office, Intelligence Division. Handbook of the Russian Troops in Asia. By James W. Murray. (London, 1890).

1875. Great Britain, War Office, Intelligence Division. The Shores of the North-West Pacific, With an Account of the Russian Advances in that Region. (London, 1878).

1876. Greene, Francis V. Memoranda Concerning Russian Fortifications, Including Iron Shields and Turrets, and Torpedoes. (Washington, D.C., 1879).

1877. Greene, Francis V. Sketches of Army Life in Russia. (London, 1881).

1878. Hamley, Edward B. "The Armies of Russia and Austria." NC 3 (May 1878), 844-62.

1879. Hazelton, Alan W. The Russian Imperial Orders. (New York, 1932).

1880. Hellwald, Friedrich A.H. von. The Russians in Central Asia. Translated by Theodore Wirgman. (London, 1874).

1881. Helmreich, E.C. and C.E. Black. "The Russo-Bulgarian Military Convention of 1902." JMH 9 (December 1937), 471-82.

1882. Higham, Robin and Jacob W. Kipp, eds. Soviet Aviation and Air Power: A Historical View. (Boulder, Colordao, 1977).

1883. Hindus, Maurice. The Cossacks; The Story of a Warrior People. (Garden City, New York, 1945).

1884. Hunczak, Taras, ed. Russian Imperialism from Ivan the Great to the Revolution. (New Brunswick, New Jersey, 1974).

1885. Hutton, James. Central Asia: From the Aryan to the Cossack. (London, 1875).

1886. Ignat'ev, Aleksei A. A Subaltern in Old Russia. Translated by Ivor Montagu. (New York, 1944).

1887. Jelavich, Charles. "The Diary of D.A. Miliutin, 1878-1882: A Review Article." JMH 26 (September 1954), 255- 9.

1888. Jenkins, Michael. "Arakcheev and the Military Colonies." HT 19 (September 1969), 600-7.

1889. Jewsbury, George F. The Russian Annexation of Bessarabia, 1774-1828: A Study of Imperial Expansion. (Boulder, Colorado, 1976).

1890. Jones, David R. "The Imperial Russian Life Guards Grenadier Regiment, 1906-1917: The Disintegration of an Elite Unit." MA 33 (October 1949) 289-302.

1891. Kelly, Laurence. Lermontov; Tragedy in the Caucasus. (New York, 1978).

1892. Kerner, Robert J. "Russian Eastward Movement: Some Observations on Its Historical Significance." PHR 17 (May 1948), 135-48.

1893. Khiva and Turkestan. Translated by Henry Spalding. (London, 1874).

1894. Kochan, Lionel. _Russia in Revolution, 1890-1918._ (New York,1967).

1895. Krausse, Alexis S. _Russia in Asia; A Record and a Study 1558-1899._ (New York, 1899).

1896. Kropotkin, Peter A. _Memoirs of a Revolutionist._ (Boston, 1899).

1897. Kuropatkin, Aleksei N. _Kashgaria: (Eastern or Chinese Turkestan) Historical and Geographical Sketch of the Country; Its Military Strength, Industries and Trade._ Translated by Walter E. Gowan. (Calcutta, 1882).

1898. Lehovich, Dimitry V. _White Against Red: A Biography of General Anton Deniken._ (New York, 1974).

1899. Lensen, George A., ed. _Russia's Eastward Expansion._ (Englewood Cliffs, New Jersey, 1964).

1900. Lincoln, W. Bruce. "General Dimitri Milyutin and the Russian Army." _HT_ 26 (January 1976), 40- 7.

1901. Lobanov-Rostovsky, Andrei. _Russia and Europe, 1825-1878._ (Ann Arbor, Michigan, 1954).

1902. Longworth, Philip. _The Cossacks: Five Centuries of Turbulent Life on the Russian Steppes._ (New York, 1969).

1903. Luckett, Richard. "Pre-revolutionary Army Life in Russian Literature," in Geoffrey Best and Andrew Wheatcroft, eds., _War Economy and the Military Mind._ (London, 1976), 19-31.

1904. *Lyons, M., compl. _The Russian Imperial Army; A Bibliography of Regimental and Related Works._ (Stanford, California, 1968).

1905. MacKenzie, David. "Panslavism in Practice: Cherniaev in Serbia (1876)." _JMH_ 36 (September 1964), 279-97.

1906. *MacKenzie, David. _The Lion of Tashkent; The Career of General M.G. Cherniaev._ (Athens, Georgia, 1974).

1907. Maguire, Thomas Miller. _The Military History of Russia._ (Dublin, 1905).

1908. Marvin, Charles T. _The Russians at Merv and Herat and Their Power of Invading India._ (London, 1883).

1909. Marvin, Charles T. _The Russian Advance Towards India. Conversations with Skobeleff, Ignatieff and Other Distinguished Russian Generals and Statesmen, on the Central Asian Question._ (London, 1882).

1910. Marvin, Charles T. _Reconnoitring Central Asia: Pioneering Adventures in the Region Lying Between Russia and India._ (London, 1884).

1911. Mazour, Anatole G. "The Prelude to Russia's Departure from America." _PHR_ 10 (September 1941), 311- 9.

1912. Miller, Forrest A. Dimitri Miliutin and the Reform Era in Russia. (Nashville, Tennessee, 1968).

1913. Milsom, John. Russian Tanks, 1900-1970; The Complete Illustrated History of Soviet Armoured Theory and Design. (Harrisburg, Pennsylvania, 1971).

1914. Mitchell, Donald W. "Russian Mine Warfare: The Historical Record." JRUSI 109 (February 1964), 32- 9.

1915. Mitchell, John. Thoughts on Tactics and Military Organization: Together with an Enquiry into the Power and Position of Russia. (London, 1838).

1916. Mollo, Eugene. Russian Military Swords, 1801-1917. (London, 1969).

1917. Morgan, Gerald. "'A Clever Wily Fellow': General Count Ignatyev, 1832-1908." HT 27 (December 1977), 805-11.

1918. Morris, Peter. "The Russians in Central Asia, 1870-1887." SEER 53 (October 1975), 521-38.

1919. Murray, James W. Russia's Power to Concentrate Troops in Central Asia. (London, 1888).

1920. Nemirovich-Danchenko, Vasilii I. Personal Reminiscences of General Skobeleff. Translated by Edward A.B. Hodgetts. (London, 1884).

1921. Nikolaieff, A.M. "Universal Military Service in Russia and Western Europe." RR 8 (April 1949), 117-26.

1922. Novikova, Olga A. (O.K., pseudo). Skobeleff and the Slavonic Cause. (London, 1883).

1923. Nowarra, Heinz J. and Godfred R. Duval. Russian Civil and Military Aircraft, 1884-1969. Translated by Alan Myers. (London, 1971).

1924. Pahlen, Konstantin K. Mission to Turkestan: Being the Memoirs of Count K.K. Pahlen, 1908-1909. Edited by Richard A. Pierce. (London, 1964).

1925. Pares, Bernard. The Fall of the Russian Monarchy. (New York, 1939).

1926. Parry, Albert. Russian Cavalcade, A Military Record. (New York, 1944).

1927. *Pierce, Richard A., ed. Russian Central Asia, 1867-1917: A Select Bibliography. (Berkeley, California, 1953).

1928. Pierce, Richard A. Russian Central Aisa, 1867-1917; A Study in Colonial Rule. (Berkeley, California, 1960).

1929. Pipes, Richard E. "The Russian Military Colonies, 1810-1831." JMH 22 (September 1950), 205-19.

1930. Potto, Vasilii A. *Steppe Campaigns*. Translated by Francis C.H. Clarke. (London, 1874).

1931. Quested, R.K.I. *The Expansion of Russia in East Asia, 1857-1860*. (London, 1968).

1932. Ravenstein, Ernest G. *The Russians on the Amur: Its Discovery, Conquest, and Colonization; with a Description of the Country, Its Inhabitants, Productions, and Commercial Capabilities; and Personal Accounts of Russian Travellers*. (London, 1861).

1933. Ray, Oliver A. "The Imperial Russian Army Officer." *PSQ* 76 (December 1961), 576-92.

1934. Rodenbough, Theophilus T. *Afghanistan and the Anglo-Russian Dispute; An Account of Russia's Advance Toward India...with a Description of Afghanistan and of the Military Resources of the Powers Concerned*. (New York, 1885).

1935. Rodzianko, Paul. *Tattered Banners; An Autobiography*. (London, 1939).

1936. Romanov, Boris A. *Russia in Manchuria, 1892-1906*. Translated by Susan W. Jones. (Ann Arbor, Michigan, 1952).

1937. Semenov, Evgenii P. *The Russian Government and the Massacres, A Page of the Russian Counter-Revolution*. Translated by Lucien Wolf. (London, 1907).

1938. Seton-Watson, Hugh. *The Decline of Imperial Russia, 1855-1914*. (London, 1952).

1939. Seton-Watson, Hugh. *The Russian Empire, 1801-1917*. (Oxford, 1967).

1940. Simmons, E.J. "L.N. Tolstoi: A Cadet in the Caucasus." *SEER* 20 (December 1941), 1-27.

1941. Skrine, Francis H.B. *The Expansion of Russia, 1815-1900*. (Cambridge, England, 1903).

1942. *Sloan, John F. *Military History of Russia: A Preliminary Survey of the Sources*. (Garmisch, Germany, 1971).

1943. Steveni, William Barnes. *The Russian Army From Within*. (New York, 1914).

1944. Strakhovsky, Leonid I. "General Count N.P. Ignatiev and the Pan-Slav Movement." *JCEA* 17 (October 1957), 223-35.

1945. Stumm, Hugo. *Russia in Central Asia. Historical Sketch of Russia's Progress in the East to 1873; And of the Incidents which Led to the Campaign Against Khiva; With a Description of the Military Districts of the Caucasus, Orenburg, and Turkestan*. Translated by J.W. Ozanne and H. Sachs. (London, 1885).

1946. Sumner, Benedict H. Tsardom and Imperialism in the Far East and Middle East, 1880-1914. (London, 1942).

1947. Swartz, Willis G. "Anglo-Russian Rivalry in the Far East, 1895-1905." Ph.D. Dissertation, University of Iowa, 1929.

1948. Tagieev, Boris L. (Roustam Bek, pseudo.). Russia in Arms: A Story of the Czar's Troops. (London, 1916?).

1949. Treviranus, Gottfried R. Revolutions in Russia; Their Lessons for the Western World. (New York, 1944).

1950. Union of Soviet Socialist Republics, Order of Lenin State History Museum. Russian and Soviet Orders. (Moscow, n.d.)

1951. Union of Soviet Socialist Republics, Order of Lenin State History Museum. Russian Weaponry (17th-20th Centuries). (Moscow, n.d.).

1952. Vereshchagin, Aleksandr V. At Home and in War, 1853-1881. Reminiscences and Anecdotes. Translated by Isabel F. Hapgood. (New York, 1888).

1953. Vincent, Charles E.H. "The Russian Army." JRUSI 16, No. 67 (1872), 285-308.

1954. Volpicelli, Zenone.(Vladimir, pseudo.). Russia on the Pacific and the Siberian Railway. (London, 1899).

1955. Vrangel, Petr N. (Wrangel). The Memoirs of General Wrangel, The Last Commander-in-Chief of the Russian National Army. Translated by Sophie Goulston. (New York, 1930).

1956. Wagner, Moritz. Travels in Persia, Georgia and Koordistan; With Sketches of the Cossacks and the Caucasus. (3 vols., London, 1856).

1957. *Wahlde, Peter von. "Military Thought in Imperial Russia." Ph. D. Dissertation, Indiana University, 1966.

1958. Wahlde, Peter von. "A Pioneer of Russian Strategic Thought: G. A. Leer, 1829-1904." MA 35 (December 1971), 148-53.

1959. Wahlde, Peter von. "Russian Military Reform, 1862-74." MR 39 (January 1960), 60- 9.

1960. Walsh, Warren B. "The Imperial Russian General Staff and India." RR 16 (April 1957), 53- 8.

1961. *War and Society in Nineteenth Century Russian Empire; Selected Papers Presented in a Seminar Held at McGill University, 1967-1971. Edited by J.G. Purves and D.A. West. (Toronto, Canada, 1972).

1962. Wellesley, Frederick A. With the Russians in Peace and War; Recollections of a Military Attache. (London, 1905).

1963. Wheeler, Geoffrey. "The Russians in Central Asia." HT 6 (March 1956), 172-80.

1964. Whittock, Michael. "Ermolov, Proconsul of the Caucasus." RR 18 (January 1959), 53-60.

1965. Wilson, Robert T. A Sketch of the Military and Political Power of Russia in the Year 1817. (New York, 1817).

1966. Wincelberg, Shimon and Anita. The Samuri of Vishograd; The Notebooks of Jacob Marteck. (Philadelphia, Pennsylvania, 1976).

1967. Wright, Patricia. "Louis Melikov: Russia, 1880-1." HT 24 (June 1974), 413- 9.

1968. Zilliacus, Konni. The Russian Revolutionary Movement. (New York, 1905).

See also: Part II: 298, 299, 300, 331, 336, 343, 345, 392, 426, 539, 540, 571, 778, 841, 930, 939, 1034, 1044, 1165, 2099; Addendum: 26, 177.

SCANDINAVIA

1969. Aberg, Alf. "Recent Literature on Swedish Regimental History." RIHM 7:1, No. 26 (1967), 102-18.

1970. Cooke, William S. The Armed Strength of Sweden and Norway. (London, 1875).

1971. Cooke, William S. The Armed Strength of Denmark. (London, 1874).

1972. Fedorov, Evgenili. The Finnish Revolution in Preparation, 1889-1905 as Disclosed by Secret Documents. Translated by G. Dobson. (St. Petersburg, 1911).

1973. Great Britain, War Office, Intelligence Division. Handbook of the Armies of Sweden and Norway. By John H.V. Crowe. (London, 1901).

1974. Hoff, Arne. "The Danish Royal Museum of Arms and Armor." MA 3 (Summer 1939), 132- 6.

1975. Palmstierna, Nils. "Swedish Army Officers as Instructors in African and Asian Countries." RIHM 7:1, No. 26 (1967), 45-73.

1976. Seitz, Heribert. Svardt Ach Varjan Som Armevapen. (The History of the Swedish Army Sword, 1500-1860 . (Captions and Summary in English.) (Stockholm, 1955)

1977. "Swedish Army and Navy." Ordnance Note No. 73, November 1, 1877 in United States, Ordnance Department, Ordnance Notes. (12 vols., Washington, D.C., 1873-84).

1978. Thorson, Playford V., II. "The Defense Question in Sweden, 1911-1914." Ph.D. Dissertation, University of Minnesota, 1972.

1979. United States, Adjutant General's Office, Military Information Division. The Military System of Sweden. By Henry T. Allen. (Washington, D.C., 1896).

SPAIN

1980. Baker, Thomas H. "Imperial Finale: Crisis, Decolonization, and War in Spain, 1890-1898." Ph.D. Dissertation, Princeton University, 1977.

1981. *Brenan, Gerald. The Spanish Labyrinth; An Account of the Social and Political Background to the Spanish Civil War, 1873-1936. (New York, 1943).

1982. Bushnell, Lt. Col. G.E. "The Spanish Army." JMSI 44 (May-June 1909), 394- 8.

1983. Calvert, Albert F. Spanish Arms and Armour, Being a Historical and Descriptive Account of the Royal Armoury of Madrid. (New York, 1907).

1984. *Christiansen, Eric. The Origin of Military Power in Spain, 1800-1854. (London, 1967).

1985. Great Britain, War Office, Intelligence Division. The Armed Strength of Spain. (London, 1883).

1986. Harrison, R.J. "British Armament and European Industrialization, 1890-1914: The Spanish Case Re-examined." ECHR 27, 2nd Series (November 1974), 620- 4.

1987. Lavin, James D. A History of Spanish Firearms. (New York, 1965).

1988. McCabe, Joseph. Spain in Revolt, 1814-1931. (New York, 1932).

1989. Ostendi, Martinez, compl. Army Museum Visitor's Guide-Book. Translated by Juan Sancho-Sopranis Tavraud. (Third Edition, Madrid, 1964).

1990. *Payne, Stanley G. Politics and the Military in Modern Spain. (Stanford, California, 1967).

1991. Trebilcock, Clive. "British Armaments and European Industrialization, 1890-1914: The Spanish Case Re-affirmed." ECHR 27, 2nd Series (November 1974), 625-31.

1992. United States, Adjutant General's Office, Military Intelligence Division. Notes and Tables of Organization and Establishment of the Spanish Army in the Peninsula and Colonies. (Washington, D.C., 1894).

1993. United States, Adjutant General's Office, Military Information Division. Notes and Tables of Organization and Establishment of the Spanish Army in the Peninsula and Colonies. (Second Edition, Washington, D.C., 1896).

See also: Part II: 2009, 2013, 2154, 2192, 3495, 3514, 3531; Addendum: 123.

SWITZERLAND

1994. Cox, Harold. "The Swiss Army and England's Needs." NC 62 (October 1907), 524-37.

1995. Great Britain, War Office, Intelligence Division. The Armed Strength of Switzerland. By Cyril W. Bowdler. (London, 1889).

1996. Great Britain, War Office, Intelligence Division. Handbook of the Swiss Army. By Henry D. Laffan. (London, 1898).

1997. Hotze and Martini. "The Swiss Military System," JRUSI 15 (May 1871), 508-36.

1998. Radcliffe, Charles Delme-. A Territorial Army in Being; A Practical Study of the Swiss Militia; and The Norwegian Militia. By James W. Lewis. (London, 1908).

1999. Walford, N.L. "The Neutrality of Switzerland and Her Defences." JRUSI 25, No. 113 (1881), 843-73.

See also: Part II: 2352.

MEDITERRANEAN

2000. Bickford-Smith, Roandeu A.H. Cretan Sketches. (London, 1898).

2001. Bradford, Ernle. Gibralter; The History of a Fortress. (New York, 1971).

2002. Gamut-Tagliaferro, A. "The Royal Malta Artillery, 1800-1970." JRA 98 (March 1971), 15-25.

2003. Gardiner, Robert W. Report on Gibralter Considered as a Fortress and a Colony. (n.p. , 1856).

2004. Garratt, Geoffrey T. Gibralter and the Mediterranean. (New York, 1939).

2005. Great Britain, War Office, Intelligence Division. Cyprus. By A.R. Saville. (London, 1878).

2006. Harfield, A.G. "British Military Presence in Cyprus in the 19th Century." JSAHR 56 (Autumn 1978), 160-70.

2007. Harfield, A.G. "The Cyprus Pioneer Corps and the Cyprus Military Police During 1879-1882." BMHS 26 (August 1975), 1-8.

2008. Hughes, James Quentin. Fortress; Architecture and Military History in Malta. (London, 1969).

2009. Kenyon, Edward R. Gibralter Under Moor, Spaniard and Briton. Edited by Herbert A. Sansom. (London, 1938).

2010. Luke, Harry C.J. Cyprus Under the Turks 1571-1878... (London, 1921).

2011. Orr, Charles W.J. Cyprus Under British Rule. (London, 1918).

2012. Porter, Major. "The History of the Fortress of Malta." JRUSI 5 (January 1861), 19-30.

2013. Sayer, Frederick. The History of Gibralter and of its Political Relation to Events in Europe; From the Commencement of the Moorish Dynasty in Spain to the Last Morocco War. (London, 1862).

2014. Skinner, John E.H. Turkish Rule in Crete. (New York, 1877).

2015. Spain, Ministerio de Asuntos Exteriories. (Ministry of Foreign Affairs). Documents on Gibralter Presented to the Spanish Cortes. Non-official Translation. (Madrid, 1965).

2016. Stephens, Frederic G. History of Gibralter and Its Sieges. (London, 1873).

See also: Part II: 1545, 1546.

NORTH AMERICA

2017. War and Society in North America. Edited by J.L. Granatstein and
Robert D. Cuff. (Toronto, 1971).

2018. Windrow, Martin and Gerry Embleton. Military Dress of North America
1665-1970. (New York, 1973).

See also: Part II: 1100, 1911, 2196, 3534.

BERMUDA

2019. Whittingham, Ferdinand. Bermuda, A Colony, A Fortress, and A Prison;
or, Eighteen Months in the Somers' Islands... By a Field Officer.
(London, 1857).

2020. Willock, Roger. Bulwark of Empire; Bermuda's Fortified Naval Base,
1860-1920. (Princeton, New Jersey, 1962).

CANADA

2021. Armstrong, W.B. "Customs, Practices and Dress of the Canadian Army."
CAJ 17, No. 3 (1963), 72- 7.

2022. Atkin, Ronald. Maintain the Right; The Early History of the North
West Mounted Police, 1873-1900. (New York, 1973).

2023. Beach, Thomas M. (Henri LeCaron, pseudo.). Twenty-Five Years in the
Secret Service; The Recollections of a Spy. (London, 1892).

2024. The Bombardier (pseudo.). "The Father of the Canadian Artillery."
CDQ 2 (October 1924), 5-9.

2025. Canada, Army Historical Section. The Regiments and Corps of the Canadian Army. Volume 1. (Ottawa, 1964).

2026. Canada, Army, Royal Canadian Corps of Signals. History of the Royal Canadian Corps of Signals, 1903-1961. Edited by John S. Moir. (Ottawa, 1962).

2027. Canada, Arsenal, Quebec. The Dominion Arsenal at Quebec, 1880-1945. (Quebec, 1947).

2028. Canada, Department of Militia and Defence, General Staff. A History of the Organization, Development and Services of the Military and Naval Forces of Canada from the Peace of Paris in 1763 to the Present Time. (3 vols., Ottawa, 1919-20).

2029. Canada, Department of National Defence. Military Inspection Services in Canada, 1855-1950. By John Mackay Hitsman. (Ottawa, 1962).

2030. *Canada, Department of National Defence, Library. Canadian Service History; Thirty-Five Titles for the Large Library. (Ottawa, 1957).

2031. Cartwright, Richard J. Remarks on the Militia of Canada. (Kingston, 1864).

2032. Chambers, Ernest J. The Canadian Militia: A History of the Origin and Development of the Force. (Montreal, 1907).

2033. Classen, H. George. Thrust and Counterthrust: The Genesis of the Canada-United States Boundary. (Toronto, 1965).

2034. Coke, Edward T. A Subaltern's Furlough; Descriptive of Scenes in the United States, Upper and Lower Canada, New Brunswick, and Nova Scotia During the Summer and Autumn of 1832. (London, 1833).

2035. Cook, G.L. "Canada's Relations with Britain, 1911-19: Problems of Imperial Defence and Foreign Policy." Ph.D. Dissertation, Oxford (England) University, 1965.

2036. Crook, N.J.A. "Canadian Militia Sword, Pattern 1853." CJAC 13 (November 1975), 123- 9.

2037. Deane, Richard B. Mounted Police Life in Canada; A Record of Thirty-One Years' Service. (New York, 1916).

2038. Dempsey, Hugh A., ed. Men in Scarlet. (Calgary, 1974).

2039. Denison, George T. Canada; Is She Prepared for War? A Few Remarks on the State of Her Defences, by a Native Canadian. (Toronto, 1861).

2040. Denison, George T. The National Defences; Or, Observations on the Best Defensive Force for Canada. (Toronto, 1861).

2041. Denison, George T. (Junius, Jr., pseudo.). A Review of the Militia Policy of the Present Administration. (Hamilton, Ontario, 1863).

2042. Denison, George T. Soldiering in Canada: Recollections and Experiences. (London, 1900).

2043. *Dornbusch, Charles E. The Canadian Army, 1855-1965; Lineages, Regimental Histories. (Cornwallville, New York, 1966).

2044. *Dornbusch, Charles E. The Lineages of the Canadian Army, 1855-1961; Armour, Cavalry, Infantry. (Cornwallville, New York, 1961).

2045. *Dornbusch, Charles E. Preliminary List of Canadian Regimental Histories. (Cornwallville, New York, 1955).

2046. Duncan, Francis. Our Garrisons in the West; Or, Sketches in North America. (London, 1864).

2047. England, Robert. "Disbanded and Discharged Soldiers in Canada Prior to 1914." CHR 27 (March 1946), 1-18.

2048. Eyre, K.C. "Staff and Command in the Canadian Corps: The Canadian Militia, 1896-1914, as a Source of Senior Officers." M.A. Thesis, Duke University, 1967.

2049. Fetherstonhaugh, Robert C. The Royal Canadian Mounted Police. (Garden City, New York, 1940).

2050. Gagan, David P. "The Queens Champion: The Life of Sir George Taylor Denison, III, Soldier, Author, Magistrate, and Canadian Tory Patriot." Ph.D. Dissertation, Duke University, 1968.

2051. Gagan, David P. "Prophet Without Honour: George Taylor Denison III." MA 34 (April 1970), 56-9.

2052. Gooch, John. "Great Britain and the Defence of Canada, 1896-1914." JI&CH 3 (May 1975), 396-407.

2053. Gooding, Sidney J. The Canadian Gunsmiths, 1608-1900. (West Hill, Ontario, 1962).

2054. Gooding, Sidney J. An Introduction to British Artillery in North America. (Ottawa, 1965).

2055. Goodspeed, Donald J. The Armed Forces of Canada, 1867-1967, A Century of Achievement. (Ottawa, 1967).

2056. Gordon, Charles W. (Ralph Connor, pseudo.). Corporal Cameron of the North West Mounted Police: A Tale of the Macleod Trail. (New York, 1912).

2057. Halifax, Nova Scotia, Army Museum. Army Museum, Halifax Citadel, Halifax, Nova Scotia. By William B. Armit. (Halifax, 1957).

2058. Hamilton, C.F. "The Canadian Militia: From 1816 to the Crimean War." CDQ 5 (July 1928), 462-73.

2059. *Hannon, Leslie F. Forts of Canada; The Conflicts, Sieges and Battles That Forged a Great Nation. (Toronto, 1969).

2060. Hazelton, Alan W., compl. Uniform and Dress of the North West Mounted Police, the Royal North West Mounted Police, the Royal Canadian Mounted Police, from 1874 to the Present Day. (Hollywood, 1932).

2061. Hill, Douglas A. The Opening of the Canadian West. (New York, 1967).

2062. Hind, Henry Youle. Narrative of the Canadian Red River Exploring Expedition of 1857 and of the Assiniboine and Saskatchewan Exploring Expedition of 1858. (2 vols, London, 1860).

2063. Hitsman, John Mackay. Military Defenders of Prince Edward Island, 1775-1864. (Ottawa, 1965).

2064. Hitsman, John Mackay. Safeguarding Canada, 1763-1871. (Toronto, 1968).

2065. Hitsman, John Mackay. "Winter Troop Movements to Canada, 1862." CHR 43 (June 1962), 127-35.

2066. Horrall, S.W. The Pictorial History of the Royal Canadian Mounted Police. (New York, 1973).

2067. Hutchison, Bruce. The Struggle for the Border. (New York, 1955).

2068. Irwin, Ross W., compl. A Guide to the War Medals and Decorations of Canada. (Geulph, Ontario, Canada, 1969).

2069. Jackson, Harold M. The Roll of the Regiments. (2 vols, Ottawa, 1959-60).

2070. Jackson, Harold M. The Royal Regiment of Artillery, Ottawa, 1855-1952; A History... (Montreal, 1952).

2071. Jackson, Harold M. The Story of the Royal Canadian Dental Corps. (n.p., 1956).

2072. Jarvis, E. "Military Land Granting in Upper Canada Following the War of 1812." OH 67 (September 1975), 121-34.

2073. Jervois, William F.D. Report on the Defence of Canada. (London, 1864).

2074. Jones, F.L. "Soldiering in the Sixties." CAJ 6 (June 1952), 48-52.

2075. Kerry, Armine J. and W.A. McDill. The History of the Corps of Royal Canadian Engineers. Volume 1. (Ottawa, 1962).

2076. King, Walter D., compl. A Brief History of Militia Units Established at Various Periods at Yarmouth, Nova Scotia, 1812-1947. (Yarmouth, 1947).

2077. Lysons, Daniel. Early Reminiscences. (London, 1896).

2078. Machun, George C. Canada's V.C.'s; The Story of the Canadians Who Have Been Awarded the Victoria Cross, A Centenary Memorial. (Toronto, 1956).

2079. McInnis, Edgar W. The Unguarded Frontier: A History of American-Canadian Relations. (Garden City, New York, 1942).

2080. MacKinnon, Clarence S. "The Imperial Fortresses in Canada: Halifax and Esquimalt, 1871-1906." Ph.D. Dissertation, University of Toronto, 1965.

2081. MacLean, Guy R. "The Canadian Offer of Troops for Hong Kong." CHR 38 (December 1957), 275-83.

2082. MacLean, Guy R. "The Imperial Federalism Movement in Canada, 1884-1902." Ph.D. Dissertation, Duke University, 1958.

2083. MacLeod, R.C. The North-West Mounted Police and Law Enforcement, 1873-1905. (Toronto, 1976).

2084. Manarey, R. Barrie. The Canadian Bayonet. (Alberta, Canada, 1971).

2085. Manning, Helen T. The Revolt of French Canada, 1800-1835: A Chapter in the History of the British Commonwealth. (New York, 1962).

2086. Marraro, Howard R. Canadian and American Zouaves in the Papal Army, 1868-1870. (Toronto, 1945).

2087. Massey, Hector J., ed. The Canadian Military: A Profile. (Toronto, 1972).

2088. Moir, John S., ed. History of the Royal Canadian Corps of Signals, 1903-1961. (Ottawa, 1962).

2089. Moogk, Peter N. Vancouver Defended; A History of the Men and Guns of the Lower Mainland Defences, 1859-1949. (Surrey, British Columbia, Canada, 1978).

2090. Morton, Desmond. "Aid to the Civil Power: The Canadian Militia in Support of Social Order." CHR 51 (December 1970), 407-25.

2091. Morton, Desmond. "Authority and Policy in the Canadian Militia, 1874-1904." Ph.D. Dissertation, University of London, 1968.

2092. Morton, Desmond. The Canadian General: Sir William Otter. (Toronto, 1974).

2093. Morton, Desmond. "Comparison of U.S./Canadian Military Experience on the Frontier," in Military History Symposium, 7th, United States Air Force Academy, 1976, The American Military on the Frontier. (Washington, D.C., 1978), 17-35.

2094. Morton, Desmond. Ministers and Generals; Politics and the Canadian Militia, 1868-1904. (Toronto, 1970).

2095. Nicholson, Gerald W. L. The Gunners of Canada; The History of the Royal Regiment of Canadian Artillery. Volume 1. (Montreal, 1967).

2096. Penlington, Norman. Canada and Imperialism, 1896-1899. (Toronto, 1965).

2097. Penlington, Norman. "General Hutton and the Problem of Military Imperialism in Canada, 1898-1900." CHR 24 (June 1943), 156-71.

2098. Preston, Adrian W. "The Founding of the Royal Military College: Gleanings from the Royal Archives." QQ 74 (Autumn 1967), 398-412.

2099. Preston, Adrian W. "The Russian Crisis and the British Army Origins of Military Professionalism in Canada, 1874-1880." AQ 96 (April 1968), 88-97; (July 1968), 241-51.

2100. *Preston, Richard A. Canada and "Imperial Defense": A Study of the Origins of the British Commonwealth's Defence Organization, 1867-1919. (Durham, North Carolina, 1967).

2101. *Preston, Richard A. Canada's R.M.C.; A History of the Royal Military College. (Toronto, 1969).

2102. Preston, Richard A. Canadian Defence Policy and the Development of the Canadian Nation, 1867-1917. (Ottowa, 1970).

2103. Preston, Richard A. The Defence of the Undefended Border: Planning for War in North America, 1867-1939. (Toronto, 1977).

2104. Price, Karen. "Glimpses of Soldiering at Coteau-Du-Lac, Quebec-- 1780-1856," in Canada, National and Historic Parks Branch, History and Archaeology, No. 15 (Ottawa, Canada, 1977), 3-63.

2105. Purdon, Charles J. The Snider-Enfield. (Ottawa, Canada, 1973).

2106. Raudzens, George K. "The Military Impact on Canadian Canals, 1815-25." CHR 54 (September 1973), 273-86.

2107. Raudzens, George K. "A Successful Military Settlement: Earl Grey's Enrolled Pensioners of 1846 in Canada." CHR 52 (December 1971), 389-403.

2108. Robertson, Peter. Relentless Verity: Canadian Military Photographers Since 1885. (Toronto, 1973).

2109. Russell, William Howard. Canada: Its Defences, Condition, and Resources. (Boston, 1865).

2110. Sage, Walter N. "The Historical Peculiarities of Canada with Regard to Hemisphere Defense." PHR 10 (March 1941), 15-27.

2111. Saunders, Ivan J. "A History of Martello Towers in the Defence of British North America, 1796-1871," in Canada, National and Historic Parks Branch, Occasional Papers in Archaeology and History, No. 15 (Ottawa, Canada, 1976), 5-169.

2112. Senior, Elinor L. "The British Garrison in Montreal in the 1840's." JSAHR 52 (Summer 1974), 111-27.

2113. Senior, Elinor L. "An Imperial Garrison in Its Colonial Setting: British Regulars in Montreal, 1832-54." Ph.D. Dissertation, McGill University, 1976.

2114. Senior, Elinor L. "The Provincial Cavalry in Lower Canada 1837-50." CHR 57 (March 1976), 1-24.

2115. Siddons, Joachim H. The Canadian Volunteer's Hand-Book: A Compendium on Military Facts and Suggestions Adapted to Field Service. (Toronto, 1863).

2116. Slater, James. Three Years Under the Canadian Flag as a Cavalry Officer... (n.p., 1893).

2117. Stacey, Charles P. "Britain's Withdrawal from North America 1864-1871." CHR 36 (September 1955), 185-98.

2118. *Stacey, Charles P. Canada and the British Army, 1846-71; A Study in the Practice of Responsible Government. (Toronto, 1963).

2119. Stacey, Charles P. "The Development of the Canadian Army." CAJ 6 (April 1952), 1-10; (May 1952), 1-11; (June 1952), 1-9; (July 1952), 11-22.

2120. Stacey, Charles P. "A Hundred Years of Regimental Organizations: The Centenary of the Militia Act of 1855." CAJ 9 (April 1955), 2-9.

2121. *Stacey, Charles P. "The Military Aspect of Canada's Winning of the West, 1870-1885." CHR 21 (March 1940), 1-24.

2122. Stacey, Charles P. The Military Problems of Canada: A Survey of Defence Policies and Strategic Conditions Past and Present. (Toronto, 1940).

2123. Stacey, Charles P. "The Myth of the Unguarded Frontier, 1815-1871." AHR 56 (October 1950), 1-18.

2124. Stacey, Charles P. The Undefended Border; The Myth and the Reality. (Ottawa, 1953).

2125. Stacey, Charles P. "The Withdrawal of the Imperial Garrison from Newfoundland." CHR 16 (June 1936), 147-58.

2126. *Stanley, George F.G. Canada's Soldiers, 1604-1954: The Military History of an Unmilitary People. (Revised Edition, Toronto, 1960).

2127. Stanley, George F.G. A Short History of Kingston as a Military and Naval Centre. (Kingston, Ontario, Canada, 1950).

2128. Steele, Samuel B. Forty Years in Canada. Reminiscences of the Great Northwest. (Toronto, 1918).

2129. Stewart, Alice R. "Sir John A. Macdonald and the Imperial Defence Commission of 1879." CHR 35 (June 1954), 119-39.

2130. Stewart, Charles H. The Concise Lineages of the Canadian Army, 1855 to Date. (Toronto, 1968).

2131. Stewart, Charles H. The Service of British Regiments in Canada and North America; A Resume with a Chronological List of Uniforms Portrayed in Sources Consulted. (Ottawa, 1962); Addenda and Errata. (2 Parts, Ottawa, 1962- 4).

2132. Steele, Samuel B. Forty Years in Canada; Reminiscences of the Great North-west, with Some Account of His Service in South Africa. (London, 1915).

2133. Strange, Thomas B. Gunner Jingo's Jubilee; An Autobiography. (London, 1896).

2134. Strange, Thomas B. "The Military Aspect of Canada." Ordnance Note No. 120, December 5, 1879 in United States, Ordnance Department, Ordnance Notes. (12 vols., Washington, D.C., 1873-84).

2135. Swettenham, John A. "The Canadian War Museum." CDQ 4 (Spring 1975), 40- 5.

2136. Swettenham, John A., ed. Valiant Men; Canada's Victoria Cross and George Cross Winners. (Toronto, 1973).

2137. Thompson, Roy J.C. Wings of the Canadian Armed Forces, 1913-1972. (Dartmouth, Nova Scotia, Canada, 1973).

2138. Turner, C. Frank. Across the Medicine Line. (Toronto, 1973).

2139. Turner, John P. The North West Mounted Police, 1873-1893. (2 vols., Ottawa, 1950).

2140. The Upper Canada Historical Arms Society. The Military Arms of Canada. (Bloomfield, Ontario, Canada, 1963).

2141. Warren, Arnold. Wait for the Wagon; The Story of the Royal Canadian Army Service Corps. (Toronto, 1961).

2142. Way, Ronald L. "The Topographical Aspect of Canadian Defence, 1783-1871." CDQ 14 (April 1937), 275-87.

2143. Webster, Donald B., Jr. American Socket Bayonets, 1717-1873. (Ottawa, 1964).

2144. Wrong, Geroge M. "Canada and the Imperial War Cabinet." CHR 1 (March 1920), 3-25.

See also:Part II: 1383, 1545, 1546, 2333, 2484; Addendum: 153.

CARRIBEAN

2145. Fronde, James A. The English in the West Indies; or, The Bow of Ulysses. (London, 1888).

2146. Great Britain, War Office. Statistical Report on the Sickness, Mortality, and Invaliding Among the Troops in the West Indies. (London, 1838).

2147. Greely, Adolphus W. Report on Military Telegraph Lines in Porto Rico. (Washington, D.C., 1900).

2148. McGracklin, James H. Garde d'Haiti, 1915-1934; Twenty Years of Organization and Training by the United States Marines. (Annapolis, Maryland, 1956).

2149. *Manucy, Albert C. and Ricardo Torres-Reyes. Puerto Rico and the Forts of Old San Juan. (Riverside, Connecticut, 1973).

2150. *May, Robert E. The Southern Dream of a Caribbean Empire, 1854-1861. (Baton Rouge, 1973).

2151. Millett, Allan R. "'Cleansing the Augean Stables': The American Armed Forces in the Caribbean, 1898-1934," in Essays in Some Dimensions of Military History Volume 4. (Carlisle, Pennsylvania, 1976), 123-141.

2152. Munro, Dana G. Intervention and Dollar Diplomacy in the Carribean, 1900-1921. (Princeton, New Jersey, 1964).

2153. United States, Adjutant General's Office, Military Information Division. Military Notes on Puerto Rico. (Washington, D.C., 1898).

2154. United States, Army, Puerto Rico Coast Artillery Command. A History of the Harbor Defenses of San Juan, Puerto Rico, Under Spain, 1509-1898, Including a Brief History of Artillery and a Guide to the Ancient Fortifications by Edward A. Hoyt. (San Juan, 1943).

See also: Part II: 2475; Addendum: 10, 168.

CUBA

2155. Corbitt, Duvon C. "Cuban Revisionist Interpretations of Cuba's Struggle for Independence." HAHR 43 (August 1963), 395-404.

2156. Cosmas, Graham A. "Securing the Fruits of Victory: The U.S. Army Occupies Cuba, 1898-1899." MA 38 (October 1974), 85-91.

2157. Healy, David F. The United States in Cuba, 1898-1902: Generals, Politicians, and the Search for Policy. (Madison, Wisconsin, 1963).

2158. Hitchman, James H. "The American Touch in Imperial Administration: Leonard Wood in Cuba, 1898-1902." AMERS 24 (April 1968), 394-403.

2159. Millett, Allan R. "The Rise and Fall of the Cuban Rural Guard, 1898-1912." AMER 29 (October 1972), 191-213.

2160. Perez, Louis A., Jr. "Supervision of a Protectorate: The United States and the Cuban Army, 1898-1908." HAHR 52 (May 1972), 250-71.

2161. *Perez, Louis A., Jr. Army Politics in Cuba, 1898-1958. (Pittsburgh, Pennsylvania, 1976).

2162. *Thomas, Hugh. Cuba: The Pursuit of Freedom. (New York, 1971).

2163. United States, Adjutant General's Office, Military Information Division. Military Notes on Cuba. (Washington, D.C., 1898).

2164. United States, Adjutant General's Office, Military Information Division. Military Notes on Cuba. (Revised Edition, Washington, D.C., 1898).

2165. United States, General Staff. Military Notes on Cuba. (Washington, D.C., 1909).

2166. *United States, Library of Congress. List of Books Relating to Cuba (Including References to Collected Works and Periodicals) by A.P.C. Griffin With Bibliography of Maps by P. Lee Phillips. (Washington, D.C., 1898).

See also: Part II: 2475; Addendum: 85, 137.

MEXICO

2167. Acuna, Rodolfo F. Sonoran Strongman: Ignacio Pesqueira and His Times. (Tucson, Arizona, 1979).

2168. *Alexius, Robert M. "The Army and Politics in Porfirian Mexico." Ph.D. Dissertation, University of Texas at Austin, 1976.

2169. Beals, Carleton. *Porfirio Diaz, Dictator of Mexico*. (Philadelphia, 1932).

2170. Brady, Austin C. "Mexico's Fighting Equipment." *JMSI* 40 (January-February 1907), 114-21.

2171. *Brown, Robert B. "Guns over the Border." Ph.D. Dissertation, University of Michigan, Ann Arbor, 1951.

2172. Bryan, Anthony T. "Mexican Politics in Transition, 1900-1913: The Role of General Bernardo Reyes." Ph.D. Dissertation, The University of Nebraska at Lincoln, 1970.

2173. Bushnell, Clyde G. "The Military and Political Career of Juan Alvarez, 1790-1867." Ph.D. Dissertation, University of Texas at Austin, 1958.

2174. Callcott, Wilfrid H. *Santa Anna; The Story of an Enigma Who Once Was Mexico*. (Norman, Oklahoma, 1936).

2175. Church, George E. *Mexico, Its Revolutions: Are They Evidences of Retrogression or of Progress? A Historical and Political Review*. (New York, 1866).

2176. Cotner, Thomas E. *The Military and Political Career of Jose Joaquin de Herrera, 1792-1854*. (Austin, Texas, 1949).

2177. Creelman, James. *Diaz, Master of Mexico*. (New York, 1911).

2178. Cumberland, Charles C. *Francisco I. Madero, Revolutionary*. (Austin, Texas, 1949).

2179. Dyer, George B. and Charlotte L. "A Century of Strategic Intelligence Reporting: Mexico, 1822-1919." *GEOR* 44 (June 1954), 49-69.

2180. Fornaro, Carlo de. *Diaz, Czar of Mexico; An Arraignment*. (New York, 1909).

2181. Frost, John. *The History of Mexico and Its Wars*. (New Orleans, Louisiana, 1882).

2182. Godoy, Jose F. *Porfirio Diaz, President of Mexico. The Master Builder of a Great Commonwealth*. (New York, 1910).

2183. Gregg, Robert D. *The Influence of Border Troubles on Relations Between the United States and Mexico, 1876-1910*. (Baltimore, Maryland, 1937).

2184. Hanighen, Frank C. *Santa Anna; The Napoleon of the West*. (New York, 1934).

2185. Hannay, David. *Diaz*. (New York, 1917).

2186. Hindman, James and James Secrest. "Memoirs of a Revolutionary Soldier, General of Division Jesus Jaime Quinones." *MHT&SW* 11, No. 1 (1973), 51-62.

2187. Hughes, James B., Jr. Mexican Military Arms, The Cartridge Period 1866-1967. (Houston, Texas, 1968).

2188. Hutchinson, C. Alan. "General Jose Figueroa's Career in Mexico, 1792-1832." NMHR 48 (October 1973), 277-98.

2189. Jones, Oakah L. Santa Anna. (New York, 1968).

2190. Kelley, James R. "The Education and Training of Porfirian Officers: Success or Failure." MA 39 (October 1975), 124- 8.

2191. *Kelley, James R. "Professionalism in the Porfirian Army Officer Corps." Ph.D. Dissertation, Tulane University, 1970.

2192. Macaulay, Neill. "The Army of New Spain and the Mexican Delegation to the Spanish Cortes," in Nettre Lee Benson, ed., Mexico and the Spanish Cortes 1810-1822: Eight Essays. (Austin, Texas, 1966), 134-52.

2193. Meyer, Michael C. Huerta: A Political Portrait. (Lincoln, Nebraska, 1972).

2194. Meyer, Michael C. "The Militarization of Mexico." AMERS 27 (January 1971), 293-306.

2195. *Miller, David L. "Porfirio Diaz and the Army of the East." Ph.D. Dissertation, University of Michigan, Ann Arbor, 1960.

2196. Moorhead, Max L. The Presidio: Bastion of the Spanish Borderlands. (Norman, Oklahoma, 1975).

2197. Niemeyer, Richard V., Jr. "The Public Career of General Bernardo Reyes." Ph.D. Dissertation, University of Texas at Austin, 1958.

2198. Nieto, Angelina, Anne S.K. Brown and Joseph Hefter. The Mexican Soldier, 1837-1847. (Mexico City, 1958).

2199. Parkinson, Roger. Zapata. (New York, 1975).

2200. Robinson, Fayette. Mexico and Her Military Chieftains, from the Revolution of Hidalgo to the Present Time. Comprising Sketches of the Lives of Hidalgo, Morelos, Iturbide, Santa Anna, Gomez, Forias, Bustamente, Paredes, Almonte, Arista, Alaman, Ampudia, Herrera, and De la Vega. (Philadelphia, 1847).

2201. Roeder, Ralph. Juarez and His Mexico; A Biographical History. (2 vols., New York, 1947).

2202. Rolle, Andrew F. The Lost Cause: The Confederate Exocus to Mexico. (Norman, Oklahoma, 1965).

2203. Rosenblum, Morris. Heroes of Mexico. (New York, 1969).

2204. Ross, Stanley R. Francisco I. Madero, Apostle of Mexican Democracy. (New York, 1955).

2205. *Samponaro, Frank N. "The Political Role of the Army in Mexico, 1821-1848." Ph.D. Dissertation, State University of New York at Stony Brook, 1974.

2206. Santa Anna, Antonio Lopez de. The Eagle; The Autobiography of Santa Anna. Edited by Ann Fears Crawford. (Austin, Texas, 1967).

2207. Schiff, Warren. "German Military Penetration into Mexico During the Late Diaz Period." HAHR 39 (November 1959), 568-79.

2208. Smart, Charles A. Viva Juarez! A Biography. (London, 1963).

2209. Smith, Cornelius C., Jr. Emilio Kosterlitzky, Eagle of Sonora and the Southwest Border. (Glendale, California, 1970).

2210. Spicer, Edward H. "The Military History of the Yaquis from 1867-1910: Three Points of View," in Military History of the Spanish-American Southwest: A Seminar. Edited by Bruno J. Rolak. (Fort Huachuca, Arizona, 1976), 47-64.

2211. Stout, Joseph A., Jr. The Liberators: Filibustering Expeditions into Mexico 1848-1862 and the Last Thrust of Manifest Destiny. (Los Angeles, California, 1973).

2212. Tiveedie, Ethel (Mrs. Alec) B. Porforio Diaz, Seven Times President of Mexico. (London, 1906).

2213. United States, General Staff, War Plans Division. Monograph on Mexico. (Washington, D.C., 1914).

2214. *United States, War Department, Library. Index of Publications, Articles and Maps Relating to Mexico, in the War Department Library. (Washington, D.C., 1896).

See also: Part II: 2233, 2418, 2475, 2900, 3466, 3488, 3489, 3491, 3493, 3496, 3499, 3500, 3504, 3509, 3514, 3531; Addendum: 41.

GENERAL

2215. Aitkin, Hugh G.J. Taylorism at Watertown Arsenal. (Cambridge, Massachusetts, 1960).

2216. Allen, Jon. Aviation and Space Museums of America. (New York, 1975).

2217. Allen, Richard S. "American Coastal Forts: The Golden Years." CAMP 5 (Summer 1973), 2-7.

2218. Alstetter, Mabel and Gladys Watson. "Western Military Institute, 1847-1861." FCHQ 10 (April 1936), 100-15.

2219. Altmayer, Jay P. American Presentation Swords; A Study of the Design and Development of Presentation Swords in the U.S. from Post Revolutionary Times Until After the Close of the Spanish American War. (Mobile, Alabama, 1958).

2220. Ambrose, Stephen E. Duty, Honor, Country; A History of West Point. (Baltimore, Maryland, 1966).

2221. Andrist, Ralph K. The Long Death; The Last Days of the Plains Indians. (New York, 1964).

2222. Ansell, S.T. "Legal and Historical Aspects of the Militia." YLJ 26 (April 1917), 471-80.

2223. Aptheker, Herbert. American Negro Slave Revolts. (New York, 1943).

2224. Aquila, Richard. "Plains Indian War Medicine." JWEST 13 (April 1974), 19-43.

2225. Armstrong, Orland K. Fifteen Decisive Battles of the United States. (New York, 1961).

2226. Athearn, Robert G. "The Firewagon Road." MMWH 20 (April 1970), 2-19.

2227. Bailey, Lynn R. The Long Walk; A History of the Navajo Wars, 1848-68. (Los Angeles, California, 1964).

2228. Barnard, John G. Notes on Sea-Coast Defense. (New York, 1861).

2229. Bartlett, Richard A. Great Surveys of the American West. (Norman, Oklahoma, 1962).

2230. Bartlett, Wallace A. Some Weapons of War as Improved by Recent American Inventors. (Washington, D.C., 1883).

2231. Basso, Keith H., ed. Western Apache Raiding and Warfare, from the Notes of Grenville Goodwin. (Tucson, Arizona, 1971).

2232. Bearse, Ray. Centerfire American Rifle Cartridge, 1892-1963. (South Brunswick, New Jersey, 1966).

2233. Beers, Henry P. "Military Protection of the Santa Fe Trail to 1843." NMHR 12 (April 1937), 113-33.

2234. Beers, Henry P. The Western Military Frontier, 1815-1846. (Philadelphia, Pennsylvania, 1935).

2235. Bender, Averam B. The March of Empire: Frontier Defense in the Southwest, 1848-1860. (Lawrence, Kansas, 1952).

2236. Bender, Averam B. "Military Posts in the Southwest, 1848-1860." NMHR 16 (April 1941), 125-47.

2237. Berdahl, Clarence A. War Powers of the Executive in the United States. (Urbana, Illinois, 1921).

2238. Bigelow, Donald N. William Conant Church and the Army and Navy Journal. (New York, 1952).

2239. Birnie, Rogers, Jr. Gun Making in the United States. (Washington, D.C., 1914).

2240. Bledsoe, Anthony J. The Indian Wars of the Northwest. A California Sketch. (San Francisco, California, 1885).

2241. Bond, Oliver J. The Story of the Citadel. (Richmond, Virginia, 1936).

2242. Bond, Paul S. and Enoch B. Garey. Wars of the American Nation; The Military History of the United States, from Early Colonial Times to the End of the World War. (Annapolis, Maryland, 1923).

2243. Booth, Ken and Moorhead Wright, eds. American Thinking About Peace and War. (New York, 1978).

2244. Bowers, Claude G. The Tragic Era; The Revolution After Lincoln. (Cambridge, Massachusetts, 1929).

2245. Boylan, Bernard L. "The Forty-Fifth Congress and Army Reform." MID-A 41 (July 1959), 173-86.

2246. Brady, Cyrus T. Indian Fights and Fighters: The Soldier and the Sioux. (New York, 1904).

2247. Brady, Cyrus T. Northwestern Fights and Fighters. (New York, 1907).

2248. Brandes, Raymond, ed. Troopers West: Military and Indian Affairs on the American Frontier. (San Diego, California, 1970).

2249. Brininstool, Earl A. Chief Crazy Horse, His Career and Death. (Lincoln, Nebraska, 1929).

2250. Brininstool, Earl A., ed. Crazy Horse; The Invincible Ogalalla Sioux Chief; The "Inside Stories," by Actual Observers of a Most Treacherous Deed Against a Great Indian Leader. (Los Angeles, California, 1949).

2251. Brininstool, Earl A. Fighting Indian Warriors; True Tales of the Wild Frontiers. (Harrisburg, Pennsylvania, 1953).

2252. Brock, Peter. Pacifism in the United States; from the Colonial Era to the First World War. (Princeton, New Jersey, 1968).

2253. Brooks, Edward H. "The National Defense Policy of the Wilson Administration, 1913-1917." Ph.D. Dissertation, Stanford University, 1950.

2254. Brown, Dee A. and Martin F. Schmitt. Fighting Indians of the West. (New York, 1948).

2255. Brown, Richard M. Strain of Violence: Historical Studies of American Violence and Vigilantism. (New York, 1975).

2256. Brown, Rodney H. American Polearms, 1526-1865; The Lance, Halberd, Spontoon, Pike, and Naval Boarding Weapons. (New Milford, Connecticut, 1967).

2257. Brown, William C. The Indian Side of the Story; Being a Concourse of Presentations Historical and Biographical in Character Relating to the Indian Wars, and to the Treatment Accorded the Indians, in Washington Territory East of the Cascade Mountains During the Period from 1853 to 1889.... (Spokane, Washington, 1961).

2258. Bruce, Robert V. 1877: Year of Violence. (Indianapolis, Indiana, 1959).

2259. Brundage, Lyle D. "The Organization, Administration, and Training of the United States Ordinary and Volunteer Militia 1792-1861." Ed.D. Dissertation, University of Michigan, 1959.

2260. Bryan, George S. The Spy in America. (Philadelphia, Pennsylvania, 1943)

2261. Burns, Robert I. The Jesuits and the Indian Wars of the Northwest. (New Haven, Connecticut, 1966).

2262. Butler, David F. United States Firearms; The First Century, 1776-1875. (New York, 1975).

2263. Butt, Archibald W. Taft and Roosevelt; The Intimate Letters of Archie Butt, Military Aide. (2 vols., Garden City, New York, 1930).

2264. Byrne, Patrick E. Soldiers of the Plains. (New York, 1926).

2265. Calhoun, John C. The Papers of John C. Calhoun. Edited by Robert L. Meriweather, et.al. (Columbia, South Carolina, 1959.)

2266. Collan, John F., compl. The Military Laws of the United States, Relating to the Army, Marine Corps, Volunteers, Militia, and to Bounty Lands and Pensions, from the Foundation of the Government to the Year 1858. (Baltimore, Maryland, 1858).

2267. Campbell, Edward G. "Railroads in National Defense, 1829-1848." MVHR 27 (December 1940), 361-378.

2268. Carey, Arthur M. <u>American Firearms Makers: When, Where, and What They Made from the Colonial Period to the End of the Nineteenth Century</u>. (New York, 1953).

2269. Carrington, Henry B. <u>Military Education in American Colleges</u>. (Indianapolis, Indiana, 1870).

2270. Carroll, Charles C. "The Government's Importation of Camels: A Historical Sketch," in United States, Bureau of Animal Husbandry, <u>Annual Report of the Bureau of Animal Industry for the Year 1903</u>. (Washington, D.C., 1904), 391-409.

2271. Carroll, Joseph. <u>Slave Insurrections in the United States, 1800-1865</u>. (Boston, Massachusetts, 1938).

2272. Carter, William G.H. <u>Horses, Saddles and Bridles</u>. (Leavenworth, Kansas, 1895).

2273. Carter, William G.H. <u>Our Coast Defenses</u>. (Washington, D.C., 1903).

2274. Caughey, John W. "Their Majesties the Mob." <u>PHR</u> 26 (August 1957), 217-234.

2275. Cavaioli, Frank J. <u>West Point and the Presidency; The American Voter's Attitude Toward the Military Elite</u>. (New York, 1962).

2276. Cesari, Gene S. "American Arms-Making Machine Tool Development, 1798-1855." Ph.D. Dissertation, University of Pennsylvania, 1970.

2277. Challener, Richard D. <u>Admirals, Generals, and American Foreign Policy, 1898-1914</u>. (Princeton, New Jersey, 1972).

2278. Chambers, John Whiteclay II, ed. <u>Draftees or Volunteers: A Documentary History of the Debate over Military Conscription in the United States, 1787-1973</u>. (New York, 1975).

2279. Chinn, George M. and Bayless E. Hardin. <u>Encyclopedia of American Hand-Arms; A Book of Facts About American Short Arms, Detailing Their Birth and Development, and Describing in Minute Details Models from the Early Eighteenth Century Through to the Present Time</u>. (Huntington, West Virginia, 1942).

2280. Clifford, John G. <u>The Citizen Soldier: The Plattsburg Training Camp Movement, 1913-1920</u>. (Lexington, Kentucky, 1972).

2281. Cohen, Norman S., compl. <u>Civil Strife in America: A Historical Approach to the Study of Riots in America</u>. (Hinsdale, Illinois, 1972).

2282. Colvin, Fred H. and Ethan Viall. <u>United States Rifles and Machine Guns.....</u> (New York, 1917).

2283. Corson, William. <u>The Armies of Ignorance: The Rise of the American Intelligence Community</u>. (New York, 1977).

2284. Cress, Lawrence D. "The Standing Army, the Militia and the New Republic: Changing Attitudes toward the Military in American Society, 1768 to 1820." Ph.D. Dissertation, University of Virginia, 1976.

2285. Couper, William. One Hundred Years at V.M.I. (4 vols., Richmond, Virginia, 1939).

2286. Cromwell, Giles. The Virginia Manufactory of Arms. (Charlottesville, Virginia, 1975).

2287. Curti, Merle. Peace or War: The American Struggle, 1636-1936. (New York, 1936).

2288. Curtis, John O. and William H. Guthman. New England Militia Uniforms and Accoutrements. (Old Sturbridge Village, Sturbridge, Massachusetts, 1971).

2289. Curtis, Roy E. "The Law of Hostile Military Expeditions as Applied by the United States." AJIL 8 (April 1914), 224-55.

2290. Cutler, Frederick M. "The History of Military Conscription with Especial Reference to the United States." Ph.D. Dissertation, Clark University, 1922.

2291. Davies, Wallace E. Patriotism on Parade; the Story of Veterans' and Hereditary Organizations in America, 1783-1900. (Cambridge, Massachusetts, 1955).

2292. Davis, Roger G. "Conscientious Cooperators: The Seventh-Day Adventists and Military Service 1860-1945." Ph.D. Dissertation, George Washington University, 1970.

2293. Dawson, Henry B. Battles of the United States. (2 vols., New York, 1858).

2294. Dearing, Mary R. Veterans in Politics: The Story of the GAR. (Baton Rouge, Louisiana, 1952).

2295. D'Elia, Donald J. "The Argument Over Civilian or Military Indian Control, 1865-1880." HST 24 (February 1962), 207-25.

2296. De Rosier, Arthur H., Jr. The Removal of the Choctaw Indians. (Knoxville, Tennessee, 1970).

2297. Derthick, Martha. The National Guard in Politics. (Cambridge, Massachusetts, 1965).

2298. Duggan, Joseph C. The Legislative and Statutory Development of the Federal Concept of Conscription for Military Service. Washington, D.C., 1946).

2299. Dunn, Jacob P., Jr. Massacres of the Mountains; A History of the Indian Wars of the Far West 1815-1875. (New York, 1886).

2300. *Dupuy, Richard Ernest and William H. Baumer. The Little Wars of the United States; A Compact History from 1798 to 1920. (New York, 1968).

2301. *Dupuy, Richard Ernest and Trevor N. Dupuy. The Military Heritage of America. (New York, 1956).

2302. *Ekirch, Arthur A. The Civilian and the Military. (New York, 1956).

2303. Ellis, Edward S. The Indian Wars of the United States; From the First Settlement of Jamestown, in 1607 to the Great Uprising of 1890-91. (New York, 1892).

2304. Ellis, William A., ed. Norwich University, 1819-1911; Her History, Her Graduates, Her Roll of Honor by Maj. Gen. Grenville M. Dodge. (3 vols., Montpelier, Vermont, 1911).

2305. Evans, William McKee. To Die Game: The Story of the Lowry Band, Indian Guerrillas of Reconstruction. (Baton Rouge, Louisiana, 1971).

2306. Farrow, Edward S. American Small Arms: A Veritable Encyclopedia of Knowledge for Sportsmen and Military Men. (New York, 1904).

2307. Faulk, Odie B. Crimsoned Desert; Indian Wars of the American Southwest. (New York, 1974).

2308. Finnegan, John P. Against the Specter of a Dragon: The Campaign for American Military Preparedness, 1914-1917. (Westport, Connecticut, 1974).

2309. Fish, Carl R. "Back to Peace in 1865." AHR 24 (April 1919), 435-43.

2310. Fitzgerald, Edward A. "The Volunteer and the Conscript in American Military History." CUH 38 (April 1960), 205-13.

2311. Fitzpatrick, Edward A. Conscription and America: A Study of Conscription in a Democracy. (Milwaukee, Wisconsin, 1940).

2312. Foreman, Grant. Advancing the Frontier, 1830-1860. (Norman, Oklahoma, 1933).

2313. Fornell, Earl W. "Texans and Filibusters in the 1850's." SWHQ 59 (April 1956), 411-28.

2314. Franklin, John H. The Militant South, 1800-1861. (Cambridge, Massachusetts, 1956).

2315. *Frazer, Robert W. Forts of the West: Military Forts and Presidios and Posts Commonly Called Forts West of the Mississippi River to 1898. (Norman, Oklahoma, 1965).

2316. French, Marion O. America and War; The Military, Political and Economic Record. (Harrisburg, Pennsylvania, 1947).

2317. Fuller, John F.C. The Decisive Battles of the United States. (New York, 1942).

2318. Gardner, Robert E. Small Arms Makers: A Directory of Fabricators of Fire Arms, Edged Weapons, Crossbows and Polearms. (New York, 1963).

2319. Gignilliat, Leigh R. Arms and the Boy. (Indianapolis, Indiana, 1916).

2320. Glasson, William H. History of Military Pension Legislation in the United States. (New York, 1900).

2321. Gluckman, Arcadi and Leroy D. Satterlee. American Gun Makers. (Harrisburg, Pennsylvania, 1953).

2322. Goebel, Dorothy B. and Julius Goebel, Jr. Generals in the White House. (Garden City, New York, 1945).

2323. Graber, Doris A. Crisis Diplomacy; A History of U.S. Intervention Policies and Practices. (Washington, D.C., 1959).

2324. *Graham, Hugh D. and Ted R. Gurr, eds. The History of Violence in America: Historical and Comparative Perspectives. (New York, 1969).

2325. Greene, Francis V. The Present Military Situation in the United States. (New York, 1915).

2326. Gregg, Robert D. The Influence of Border Troubles on Relations Between the United States and Mexico, 1876-1910. (Baltimore, Maryland, 1937).

2327. Griffin, Eugene. Our Seacoast Defenses. (New York, 1885).

2328. Grinnell, George B. The Fighting Cheyennes. (New York, 1915).

2329. Gronert, Theodore G. "The First National Pastime in the Middle West (Volunteer Units)." INHM 29 (September 1933), 171-86.

2330. Hackley, F.W., W.H. Woodin and E.L. Scranton. History of Modern U.S. Military Small Arms Ammunition, 1880-1939. (New York, 1967).

2331. Halasz, Nicholas. The Rattling Chains--Slave Unrest and Revolt in the Antebellum South. (New York, 1966).

2332. Hamlin, Charles H. The War Myth in United States History. (New York, 1927).

2333. Hammond, John M. Quaint and Historic Forts of North America. (Philadelphia, Pennsylvania, 1915).

2334. Hans, Fred M. The Great Sioux Nation: A Complete History of Indian Life and Warfare in America, the Indians as Nature Made Them. (Chicago, Illinois, 1907).

2335. Harmon, Ernest N. Norwich University; Its Founder and His Ideals. (New York, 1951).

2336. Hassrick, Royal B. The Sioux: Life and Customs of a Warrior Society. (Norman, Oklahoma, 1964).

2337. Haury, Clifford W. "America and the European Balance of Power, 1866-1894." Ph.D. Dissertation, University of Virginia, 1976.

2338. Headley, Joel T. Pen and Pencil Sketches of the Great Riots. An
Illustrated History of the Railroad and Other Great American Riots
Including All Riots in the Early History of the Country. (New York,
1877).

2339. Hebard, Grace R. and Earl A. Brininstool. The Bozeman Trail; Historical Accounts of the Blazing of the Overland Routes into the Northwest,
and the Fights with Red Cloud's Warriors. (2 vols., Cleveland,
1922).

2340. Henry, Robert S. The Story of Reconstruction. (Indianapolis,
Indiana, 1938).

2341. Herman, Sondra R. Eleven Against War; Studies in American Inter-
nationalist Thought, 1898-1921. (Stanford, California, 1969).

2342. Hinds, James R. and Edmund Fitzgerald. "Fortifications in the Field
and on the Frontier." CAMP 9 (Spring 1977), 41- 9.

2343. Hinman, Eleanor H., ed. "Ogala Sources on the Life of Crazy Horse."
NEBH 57 (Spring 1976), 1-51.

2344. Hinckley, Ted C. The Americanization of Alaska, 1867-1897. (Palo
Alto, California, 1972).

2345. *Hofstadter, Richard and Michael Wallace, eds. American Violence: A
Documentary History. (New York, 1970).

2346. Holland, Lynwood M. "Georgia Military Institute, The West Point of
Georgia, 1851-1864." GAHQ 43 (September 1959), 225-47.

2347. Hood, Jennings and Charles J. Young, compls. American Orders and
Societies and Their Decorations; The Objects of the Military and Naval
Orders, Commemorative and Patriotic Societies of the United States
and the Requirements for Membership Therein. (Philadelphia, Pennsylvania, 1917).

2348. Horn, Stanley F. Invisible Empire; The Story of the Ku Klux Klan,
1866-1871. (Boston, Massachusetts, 1939).

2349. Horton, William T. "Peekskill Military Academy, 1833-1954." WECHH 31
(April 1955), 38-41.

2350. Howard, Oliver O. How Indians Fight. (Seattle, Washington, 1891).

2351. Howard, Oliver O. My Life and Experiences Among our Hostile Indians;
A Record of Personal Observations, Adventures, and Campaigns Among
the Indians of the Great West, with Somce Account of their Life,
Habits, Traits, Religion, Ceremonies, Dress, Savage Instincts, and
Customs in Peace and War. (Hartford, Connecticut, 1907).

2352. Howe, Lucien. Universal Military Education and Service; The Swiss
System for the United States. (New York, 1916).

2353. *Huntington, Samuel P. "Equilibrium and Disequilibrium in American Military Policy." PSQ 74 (December 1961), 481-502.

2354. Hyde, George E. Rangers and Regulars. (Columbus, Ohio, 1952).

2355. Jackson, Helen M.F.H. A Century of Dishonour; A Sketch of the United States Government's Dealings with Some of the North American Tribes. (London, 1881).

2356. Jacobs, Wilbur R. "The Fatal Confrontation: Early Native-White Relations on the Frontiers of Australia, New Guinea, and America-- A Comparative Study." PHR 40 (August 1971), 283-309.

2357. Jeffreys-Jones, Rhodri. American Espionage; From Secret Service to CIA. (New York, 1977).

2358. *Josephy, Alvin M. The Nez Perce Indians and the Opening of the Northwest. (New Haven, Connecticut, 1965).

2359. Josephy, Alvin M. The Patriot Chiefs; A Chronicle of American Indian Leadership. (New York, 1961).

2360. Kennett, Lee B. and James LaVerne Anderson. The Gun in America: The Origins of a National Dilemma. (Westport, Connecticut, 1975).

2361. Kirchner, David P. "American Harbor Defense Forts (Pictorial)." USNIP 84 (August 1958), 92-101.

2362. Knight, Oliver. Following the Indian Wars: The Story of the Newspaper Correspondents Among the Indian Campaigners. (Norman, Oklahoma, 1960).

2363. LaFeber, Walter. The New Empire; An Interpretation of American Expansion, 1860-1898. (Ithaca, New York, 1963).

2364. *Lane, Jack, ed. United States Wars and Military History: A Guide to Information Sources. (Detroit, Michigan, 1978).

2365. Lane, Roger and John J. Turner, eds. Riot, Rout, and Tumult: Readings in American Social and Political Violence. (Westport, Connecticut, 1978).

2366. Law, Thomas H. Citadel Cadets, the Journal of Cadet Tom Law, 1858-59. Edited by John A. Law. (Clinton, South Carolina, 1941).

2367. Lea, Homer. The Valour of Ignorance. (London, 1909).

2368. *Leach, Jack F. Conscription in the United States: Historical Background. (Rutland, Vermont, 1952).

2369. Leckie, Robert. The Wars of America. (2 vols., New York, 1968).

2370. Lens, Sidney. The Labor Wars: From the Molly Maguires to the Sit-downs. (Garden City, New York, 1973).

2371. *Lewis, Emanuel Raymond. Seacoast Fortifications of the United States; An Introductory History. (Washington, D.C., 1970).

2372. Limpus, Lowell M. Disarm. (New York, 1960).

2373. Little, Roger W., ed. Selective Service and American Society. (New York, 1969).

2374. Longstreet, Stephen. War Cries On Horseback; The Story of the Indian Wars of the Great Plains. (Garden City, New York, 1970).

2375. McCaleb, Walter F. The Conquest of the West. (New York, 1947).

2376. McCall, George A. New Mexico in 1850: A Military View. Edited by Robert W. Frazer. (Norman, Oklahoma, 1968).

2377. McFarling, Lloyd, ed. Exploring the Northern Plains, 1800-1876. (Caldwell, Idaho, 1955).

2378. McNitt, Frank. Navajo Wars; Military Campaigns, Slave Raids, and Reprisals. (Albuquerque, New Mexico, 1972).

2379. Mansfield, Joseph K.F. Mansfield on the Condition of Western Forts, 1853-1854. Edited by Robert W. Frazer. (Norman, Oklahoma, 1963).

2380. Marshall, Max L. "The Journal's First Half Century." CFJ 5 (October 1954), 17-20.

2381. *Marshall, Max L. "A Survey of Military Periodicals." M.A. Thesis, University of Missouri, 1953.

2382. May, Ernest R., ed. The Ultimate Decision: The President as Commander in Chief. (New York, 1960).

2383. Meade, Robert D. "The Military Spirit of the South." CUH 30 (April 1929), 55-60.

2384. Merrill, James M., ed. Uncommon Valor; The Exciting Story of the Army. (Chicago, 1964).

2385. Middleton, Lamar. Revolt, U.S.A. (New York, 1938).

2386. *"Military Relations," in Francis Paul Prucha, compl., A Bibliographical Guide to the History of Indian-White Relations in the United States. (Chicago, 1977), 130-90.

2387. Miller, Wayne C. An Armed America--Its Face in Fiction: A History of the American Military Novel. (New York, 1976).

2388. *Millett, Allan R. "American Military History: Over the Top," in The State of American History. Edited by Herbert J. Bass. (Chicago, 1970), 157-82.

2389. *Millett, Allan R. "American Military History: Struggling Through the Wire, " in Commission Internationale D'Histoire Militarie, ACTA No. 2 , Washington, D.C., August 13-19, 1975. (Manhattan, Kansas, 1977), 173-80.

2390. Millis, Walter. The Road to War; America 1914-1917. (Boston, 1935).

2391. Mishkin, Bernard. Rank and Warfare Among the Plains Indians. (New York, 1940).

2392. Monaghan, James. "Opposition to Involuntary Military Service in the United States." M.A. Thesis, University of Pennsylvania, 1918.

2393. Mullin, John R. "Fortifications in America: Invention and Reality." CAMP 6 (Fall 1974), 23- 6.

2394. Norton, Charles B., compl. American Breech-Loading Small Arms: A Description of the Inventions, Including the Gatling Gun, and a Chapter on Cartridges. (New York, 1872).

2395. Norton, Charles B., compl. American Inventions and Improvements in Breech-Loading Small Arms, Heavy Ordnance, Machine Guns, Magazine Arms, Fixed Ammunition, Pistols, Projectiles, Explosives, and Other Munitions of War, Including a Chapter on Sporting Arms. (Springfield, Massachusetts, 1880).

2396. Nye, Wilbur S. Bad Medicine and Good; Tales of the Kiowa. (Norman, Oklahoma, 1962).

2397. Nye, Wilbur S. Carbine and Lance; The Story of Old Fort Sill. (Norman, Oklahoma, 1937).

2398. Nye, Wilbur S. Plains Indian Raiders: The Final Phases of Warfare from the Arkansas to the Red River. (Norman, Oklahoma, 1968).

2399. Ober, Warren U. "Noise in the Guard Room,(V.M.I.)." VCAV 9 (Winter 1959), 38-47.

2400. O'Connor, Raymond G. American Defense Policy in Perspective: From Colonial Times to the Present. (New York, 1965).

2401. Ogle, Ralph H. Federal Control of the Western Apaches, 1848-1886. (Albuquerque, New Mexico, 1940).

2402. Olson, James C. Red Cloud and the Sioux Problem. (Lincoln,Nebraska 1965).

2403. "Origin of the State Military Academies." RUSM 4 (December 1858), 219-26.

2404. O'Sullivan, John and Alan M. Meckler, eds. The Draft and Its Enemies: A Documentary History. (Urbana, Illinois, 1974).

2405. Palmer, Williston B. The Evolution of Military Policy in the United States. (Carlisle Barracks, Pennsylvania, 1946).

2406. The Papers of the Order of Indian Wars. Compiled and edited by John M. Carroll. (Fort Collins, Colorado, 1975).

2407. Parker, James. The Old Army: Memories, 1872-1918. (Philadelphia, Pennsylvania, 1929).

2408. Parkhill, Forbes. The Last of the Indian Wars. (New York, 1961).

2409. Peters, Joseph P., ed. Indian Battles and Skirmishes on the American Frontier, 1790-1898. (Ann Arbor, Michigan, 1966).

2410. Peterson, Harold L. American Knives, the First History and Collectors' Guide. (New York, 1958).

2411. Proctor, Samuel. "The South Florida Military Institute." FLHQ 32 (July 1953), 28-40.

2412. *Prucha, Francis Paul. A Guide to the Military Posts of the United States, 1789-1895. (Madison, Wisconsin, 1964).

2413. Russell, Carl P. Guns on the Early Frontier; A History of Firearms from Colonial Times through the Years of the Western Fur Trade. (Berkeley, California, 1957).

2414. Reinhardt, George C. and William R. Kintner. The Haphazard Years; How America Has Gone to War. (Garden City, New York, 1960).

2415. Richards, Leonard L. Gentlemen of Property and Standing; Antiabolition Mobs in Jacksonian America. (New York, 1970).

2416. Richardson, Rupert N. The Commanche Barrier to South Plains Settlement; a Century and a Half of Savage Resistance to the Advancing White Frontier. (Glendale, California, 1933).

2417. Rippy, James Fred and Angie Debo. The Historical Background of the American Policy of Isolation. (Northampton, Massachusetts, 1924).

2418. Rippy, James Fred. "Border Trouble Along the Rio Grande, 1848-1860." SWHQ 23 (October 1919), 91-111.

2419. Rippy, James Fred. "Some Precedents of the Pershing Expedition into Mexico." SWHQ 24 (April 1921), 292-316.

2420. Rister, Carl C. The Southwestern Frontier 1865-1881. A History of the Coming of the Settlers, Indian Depredations and Massacres, Ranching Activities...&c. (Cleveland, Ohio, 1928).

2421. *Robinson, Willard B. American Forts: Architectural From and Function. (Urbana, Illinois, 1977).

2422. Robinson, Willard B. "North American Martello Towers." JSAH 33 (May 1974), 158-64.

2423. Roe, Frank Gilbert. The Indian and the Horse. (Norman, Oklahoma, 1955).

2424. Rohan, Jack. Yankee Arms Maker; The Incredible Career of Samuel Colt. (New York, 1935).

2425. Ruth, Kent. Great Day in the West: Forts, Posts, and Rendezvous Beyond the Mississippi. (Norman, Oklahoma, 1963).

2426. Rudd, Augustin G. Histories of Army Posts. (Governors Island, New York, 1924).

2427. Sandoz, Mari. Cheyenne Autumn. (New York, 1953).

2428. Satterlee, Leroy D. and Arcadi Gluckman. American Gun Makers. (Harrisburg, Pennsylvania, 1953).

2429. Sawyer, Charles W. Firearms in American History. (3 vols., Boston, 1910-20).

2430. Sawyer, Charles W. United States Single Shot Martial Pistols. (Boston, 1913).

2431. Schemmer, Benjamin F. Almanac of Liberty: A Chronology of American Military Anniversaries from 1775 to the Present. (New York, 1974).

2432. Schlissel, Lillian, compl. Conscience in America: A Documentary History of Conscientious Objection in America, 1757-1967. (New York, 1968).

2433. Schmitt, Martin F. and Dee A. Brown. Fighting Indians of the West. (New York, 1948).

2434. Schreier, Konrad F., Jr. Guide to United States Machine Guns. (Wiskenburg, Arizona, 1971).

2435. Secoy, Frank R. Changing Military Patterns on the Great Plains. (Locust Valley, New York, 1953).

2436. Sharpe, Phillip B. The Rifle in America. (New York, 1938).

2437. *Sherman, Morris, compl. Amnesty in America; An Annotated Bibliography. (Passaic, New Jersey, 1974).

2438. *Shy, John. "The American Military Experience: History and Learning." JIDH 1 (Winter 1971), 205-28.

2439. Singletary, Otis A. Negro Militia and Reconstruction. (Austin, Texas, 1957).

2440. Sloan, Irving J. Our Violent Past; An American Chronicle. (New York, 1970).

2441. Smith, Dale O. U.S. Military Doctrine; A Study and Appraisal. (New York, 1955).

2442. Smith, Francis Henney. The Virginia Military Institute, Its Building and Rebuilding. (Lynchburg, Virginia, 1912).

2443. Smith, Louis. American Democracy and Military Power; A Study of Civil Control of the Military Power in the United States. (Chicago, 1951).

2444. Smith, Marian W. "American Indian Warfare," in Transactions of the New York Academy of Sciences, 2nd Series, 13 (1951), 348-65.

2445. Smith, Merritt R. "John Hall, Simeon North, and the Milling Machine; The Nature of Innovation Among Antebellum Arms Makers." T&C 14 (Fall 1973), 573-91.

2446. Smith, Paul T. "Militia of the United States from 1846 to 1860." INHM 15 (March 1919), 20-47.

2447. Sofaer, Abraham D. War, Foreign Affairs and Constitutional Power; The Origins. (Cambridge, Massachusetts, 1976-).

2448. Somit, Albert. "The Military Hero as Presidential Candidate." POQ 12 (Summer 1948), 192-200.

2449. Stein, Meyer L. Under Fire; The Story of American War Correspondents. (New York, 1968).

2450. Stevens, William A. Pistols at Ten Paces: The Story of the Code of Honor in America. (Boston, 1940)

2451. Stroud, Virgil C. "Congressional Investigations of the Conduct of War." Ph.D. Dissertation, New York University, 1955.

2452. Stone, Irving. Men to Match My Mountains. The Opening of the Far West, 1840-1900. (Garden City, New York, 1956).

2453. Suydam, Charles R. The American Cartridge; An Illustrated Study of the Rimfire Cartridge in the United States. (Santa Ana, California, 1960).

2454. Tansill, Charles C. America Goes to War. (Boston, 1938).

2455. Taylor, Colin. The Warriors of the Plains. (New York, 1975).

2456. Tebbel, John and Keith Jennison. The American Indian Wars. (New York, 1960).

2457. Thomas, David Y. A History of Military Government in Newly Acquired Territory of the United States. (New York, 1904).

2458. Thomas, John P. The History of the South Carolina Military Academy. (Charleston, South Carolina, 1893).

2459. Thompson, Robert L. Wiring a Continent; A History of the Telegraphy Industry in the United States, 1832-1866. (Princeton, New Jersey, 1947).

2460. Tinsley, William W. "The American Preparedness Movement 1913-1916." Ph.D. Dissertation, Stanford, University, 1939.

2461. Todd, Frederick P. "The Huddy and Duval Prints: An Adventure in Military Lithography." MA 3 (Fall 1939), 166-76.

2462. Todd, Frederick P. "Our National Guard: An Introduction to Its History." MA 5 (Summer 1941), 73-86; (Fall 1941), 152-170.

2463. Tolosky, Edward A. Description of U.S. Military Rifle Sights. (Washington, D.C., 1971).

2464. Tompkins, E. Berkeley. Anti-Imperialism in the United States: The Great Debate, 1890-1920. (Philadelphia, Pennsylvania, 1970).

2465. Tousey, Thomas G. The Military History of Carlisle and Carlisle Barracks. (Richmond, Virginia, 1933).

2466. *Trussell, John B.B., Jr., compl. Pennsylvania Military History, (Bibliography). (Carlisle Barracks, Pennsylvania, 1974).

2467. Tuttle, Charles R. History of the Border Wars of Two Centuries, Embracing a Narrative of the Wars with the Indians from 1750 to 1874. (Chicago, 1874).

2468. Ulbrich, Otto. Catalogue of United States Martial Short Arms. (Buffalo, New York, 1939).

2469. United States, Library of Congress. American Battle Art, 1755-1918. (Washington, D.C., 1947).

2470. Van Gelder, Arthur P. and Hugo Schlatter. History of the Explosive Industry in America. (New York, 1927).

2471. Vaughn, Jesse W. Indian Fights; New Facts on Seven Encounters. (Norman, Oklahoma, 1966).

2472. Vestal, Stanley. Warpath and Council Fire: The Plains Indian's Struggle for Survival in War and In Diplomacy, 1851-1891. (New York, 1948).

2473. Victor, Frances A. The Early Indian Wars of Oregon. (Salem, Oregon, 1894).

2474. Vigness, D.M. "Indian Raids on the Lower Rio Grande, 1836-1837." SWHQ 59 (July 1955), 14-23.

2475. Wallace, Edward S. Destiny and Glory. Forgotten Chapters in American History of Hostile Expeditions Between Mexican and Civil Wars. (New York, 1957).

2476.* War, Business, and American Society. Edited by B(enjamin) Franklin Cooling. (Port Washington, New York, 1977).

2477. Watertown, Massachusetts. Watertown's Military History. (Boston, Massachusetts, 1907).

2478. Watson, Albert. Those Other Colts: or, Colt Conversions: A Study of Factory Alterations to Holster Revolvers from Percussion Cap to the Self-contained Metallic Cartridge. (Rapid City, South Dakota, 1975).

2479. Watson, Elmo Scott. "The Indian Wars and the Press." JOUQ 17 (December 1940), 301-12.

2480. Watson, Richard R., Jr. "Congressional Attitudes toward Military Preparedness, 1829-35." MVHR 34 (March 1948), 611-36.

2481. Weams, John E. Death Song; The Last of the Indian Wars. (Garden City, New York, 1976).

2482. Webb, Lester A. "The Origin of the Military School Movement in the United States." Ph. D. Dissertation, University of North Carolina, 1958.

2483. Webb, Walter P. The Texas Rangers; A Century of Frontier Defense. (Boston, Massachusetts, 1935).

2484. Webster, Donald B. American Socket Bayonets, 1717-1873. (Ottawa, Ontario, Canada, 1964).

2485. Weigley, Russell F. The American Way of War; A History of United States Strategy and Policy. (New York, 1973).

2486. Wellman, Paul I. Death on Horseback; Seventy Years of War for the American West. (Philadelphia, Pennsylvania, 1947).

2487. Wesley, Edgar B. Guarding the Frontier; A Study of Frontier Defense from 1815 to 1825. (Minneapolis, Minnesota, 1935).

2488. Western Apache Raiding and Warfare, from the Notes of Grenville Goodwin. Edited by Keith H. Basso with the assistance of E.W. Jernigan and W.B. Kessell. (Tucson, Arizona, 1971).

2489. White, Howard. Executive Influence in Determining Military Policy in the United States. (Urbana, Illinois, 1925).

2490. White, Lonnie J., ed. Hostiles and Horse Soldiers: Indian Battles and Campaigns in the West. (Boulder, Colorado, 1972).

2491. White, William C. A History of Military Music in America. (New York, 1945).

2492. Whittlesey, Joseph H. Report on National Military Education, with the Plan of a System for the United States Based on Existing Educational Agencies. (Washington, D.C., 1867).

2493. Whyte, James H. The Uncivil War; Washington During the Reconstruction, 1865-1878. (New York, 1958).

2494. Wilcox, Cadmus M. Rifles and Rifle Practice: An Elementary Treatise Upon the Theory of Rifle Firing. (New York, 1861).

2495. Williams, Rowan A. "Enter the Breechloaders." MR 45 (April 1965), 60- 4.

2496. Williams, Thomas Harry. "The Macs and the Ikes: America's Two Military Traditions." AMME 85 (October 1952), 32-39.

2497. Wilkinson, Norman B. Explosives in History; The Story of Black Powder. (Wilmington, Delaware, 1966).

2498. Wise, Jennings C. Empire and Armament; The Evolution of American Imperialism and the Problem of National Defense. (New York, 1915).

2499. Wish, Harvey. "American Slave Insurrections Before 1861." JNH 22 (July 1937), 299-320.

2500. Wolf, Simon. The American Jew as Patriot, Soldier and Citizen. Edited by Louis Edward Levy. (Philadelphia, Pennsylvania, 1895).

2501. Woodbury, Robert S. "The Legend of Eli Whitney and Interchangeable Parts." T&C 1 (Summer 1960), 235-53.

2502. Woodward, Arthur H. "Side Lights on Fifty Years of Apache Warfare 1836-1886." ARIZ 2 (Fall 1961), 3-14.

2503. Worcester, D.E. "The Weapons of American Indians." NMHR 20 (July 1945), 227-38.

2504. Wriston, Henry M. Executive Agents in American Foreign Relations. (Baltimore, Maryland, 1929).

2505. Wyeth, John A. History of LaGrange Military Academy and the Cadet Corps, 1857-1862, LaGrange College, 1830-1857. (New York, 1907).

2506. Yates, Bowling C. History of the Georgia Military Institute, Marietta, Georgia, Including the Confederate Military Service of the Cadet Battalion. (Marietta, Georgia, 1968).

See also: Part I: 91, 254; Part II: 115, 118, 126, 128, 993, 1087, 2033, 2067, 2079, 2086, 2103, 2123, 2124, 2152, 2157, 2158, 2160, 2171, 2179, 2183, 2202, 2211, 3484, 3525, 2532, 3541, 3542, 3554, 3568; Addendum: 1, 15, 16, 21, 31, 37, 41, 42, 50, 56, 58, 68, 76, 85, 90, 93, 94, 117, 120, 121, 137, 138, 139 144, 147, 169, 178, 180, 181.

AUTOBIOGRAPHIES, BIOGRAPHIES, DIARIES, LETTERS AND MEMOIRS

2507. Adams, Alexander B. Sitting Bull: An Epic of the Plains. (New York, 1973).

2508. Alexander, Charles. Battles and Victories of Allen Allensworth.... (Boston, Massachusetts, 1914).

2509. Alexander, Eveline M. Cavalry Wife: The Diary of Eveline M. Alexander, 1866-1867. Edited by Sandra L. Myres. (College Station, Texas, 1977).

2510. Allaben, Frank. <u>John Watts de Peyster</u>. (2 vols., New York, 1908).

2511. Allan, Carlisle. <u>Sergent Major Perry and Cadet Poe</u>. (West Point, New York, 1933).

2512. Alter, Judith M. "Rufus Zogbaum and the Frontier West." <u>MMWH</u> 23 (October 1973), 42-53.

2513. Ambrose, Stephen E. <u>Crazy Horse and Custer; the Parallel Lives of Two American Warriors</u>. (Garden City, New York, 1975).

2514. Ambrose, Stephen E. <u>Halleck: Lincoln's Chief of Staff</u>. (Baton Rouge, Louisiana, 1962).

2515. Ambrose, Stephen E. <u>Upton and the Army.</u> (Baton Rouge, Louisiana, 1964).

2516. Ames, Blanche A. <u>Adelbert Ames 1835-1933, General,,Senator and Governor</u>. (London, 1964).

2517. Anderson, Edward W. "Letters of a West Pointer, 1860-1861." Edited by Francis Sullivan. <u>AHR</u> 33 (April 1928), 599-617.

2518. Armes, Georges A. <u>Ups and Downs of an Army Officer</u>. (Washington, D.C., 1900).

2519. Ashford, Bailey K. <u>A Soldier in Science: The Autobiography of Bailey K. Ashford</u>. (New York, 1934).

2520. Athearn, Robert G. <u>William Tecumseh Sherman and the Settlement of the West</u>. (Norman, Oklahoma, 1956).

2521. Averell, William W. <u>Ten Years in the Saddle; The Memoirs of William Woods Averell, 1851-1862</u>. Edited by Edward K. Eckert and Nicholas J. Amato. (San Rafael, California, 1979).

2522. Baldwin, Alice (Blackwood). <u>Memoirs of the Late Frank D. Baldwin, Major General, USA</u>. (Los Angeles, California, 1929).

2523. Ballantine, George. <u>Autobiography of an English Soldier in the United States Army; Comprising Observations and Adventures in the United States and Mexico</u>. (2 vols., New York, 1953).

2524. Bandel, Eugene. <u>Life in the Army, 1854-1861</u>. Edited by Ralph P. Bieber. (Glendale, California, 1932).

2525. Barnes, William C. <u>Apaches and Longhorns: The Reminiscences of Will C. Barnes</u>. Edited by Frank Lockwood. (Los Angeles, California, 1941).

2526. Barnitz, Albert and Jennie. <u>Life in Custer's Cavalry; Diaries and Letters of Albert and Jennie Barnitz: 1867-1868</u>. Edited by Robert M. Utley. (New Haven, Connecticut, 1977).

2527. Bayard, Samuel J. Life of George Dashiell Bayard, Last Captain, U.S.A., and Brigadier General of Volunteers, Killed in the Battle of Fredericksburg, December, 1862. (New York, 1874).

2528. Bennett, James A. Forts and Forays; James A. Bennett, A Dragoon in New Mexico, 1850-1856. Edited by Clinton R. Brooks and Frank D. Reeve. (Albuquerque, New Mexico, 1948).

2529. Bent, George. Life of George Bent Written from His Letters by George E. Hyde. Edited by Savoie Lottinville. (Norman, Oklahoma, 1968).

2530. Berard, Augusta. Reminiscences of West Point in the Olden Time. (East Saginaw, Michigan, 1886).

2531. Biddle, Ellen (McGowan). Reminiscences of a Soldier's Wife. (Philadelphia, Pennsylvania, 1907).

2532. Bigelow, Donald N. William Conant Church and the Army and Navy Journal. (New York, 1952).

2533. Bisbee, William H. Through Four American Wars: The Impressions and Experiences of Brigadier General William Henry Bisbee, as Told to his Grandson, William Raymond Bisbee. (Boston, Massachusetts, 1931).

2534. Bishop, Joseph B. and Farnham. Goethals, Genius of the Panama Canal; A Biography. (New York, 1930).

2535. Blumenson, Martin. The Patton Papers. (2 vols., Boston, Massachusetts, 1972- 4).

2536.*Boening, Rose M., compl. "Bibliography of Isaac I. Stevens." WAHQ 9 (July 1918), 174-96.

2537. Boyd, Mrs. Orsemus Bronson. Cavalry Life in Tent and Field. (New York, 1894).

2538. Brimlow, George F. Cavalryman Out of the West; Life of General William Carey Brown. (Caldwell, Idahoe, 1944).

2539. Brininstool, Earl A. Dull Knife (A Cheyenne Napoleon). (Hollywood, California, 1935).

2540. Britt, Albert. Great Indian Chiefs; A Study of Indian Leaders in the Two Hundred Year Struggle to Stop the White Advance. (New York, 1938).

2541. Brodhead, Michael J. A Soldier-Scientist in the American Southwest; Being a Narrative of the Travels of Brevet Captain Elliott Coues, Assistant Surgeon, U.S.A....1864-1865. (Tucson, Arizona, 1973).

2542. Brown, Marion T. Letters from Fort Sill, 1886-1887. Edited by C. Richard King. (Austin, Texas, 1970).

2543. Brown, Richard C. "General Emory Upton--The Army's Mahan." MA 17 (Fall 1953), 125-31.

2544. Burdick, Usher L. The Last Days of Sitting Bull, Sioux Medicine Chief. (Baltimore, Maryland, 1941).

2545. Butler, Smedley D. as Told to Lowell Thomas. Old Gimlet Eye; The Adventures of Smedley D. Butler. (New York, 1933).

2546. Byrne, Bernard J.A. A Frontier Army Surgeon: An Authentic Description of Colorado in the Eighties. (Cranford, New Jersey, 1935).

2547. Calhoun, John C. The Papers of John C. Calhoun. Edited by W. Edwin Hamphill. (Columbia, South Carolina, 1963--).

2548. Canfield, Sarah E. "An Army Wife on the Upper Missouri: The Diary of Sarah E. Canfield, 1866-1868." Edited by Ray H. Mattison. NDH 20 (October 1953), 191-220.

2549. Carlson, Paul H. "William R. Shafter as a Frontier Commander." MHT&SW 12, No. 1 (1975), 15-29.

2550. Carpenter, John A. Sword and Olive Branch: Oliver Otis Howard. (Pittsburgh, Pennsylvania, 1964).

2551. Carr, Camillo. A Cavalryman in Indian Country. Foreward and Annotations by Dan L. Thrapp. (Ashland, Oregon, 1974).

2552. Carrington, Frances (Courtney). My Army Life and the Fort Phil Kearney Massacre with an Account of the Celebration of "Wyoming Opened." (Philadelphia, Pennsylvania, 1910).

2553. Carrington, Mrs. Margaret Irvin (Sullivant). Ab-sa-ra-ka, Home of the Crow; Being the Experiences of an Officer's Wife on the Plains.... (Philadelphia, Pennsylvania, 1868).

2554. Carter, William G.H. The Life of Lieutenant General Chaffee. (Chicago, Illinois, 1917).

2555. Catton, Bruce. U.S. Grant and the American Military Tradition. (Boston, Massachusetts, 1954).

2556. Charlton, John B. The Old Sergeant's Story; Winning the West from the Indians and Bad Men in 1870 to 1876. Edited by Robert G. Carter. (New York, 1926).

2557. Church, Albert E. Personal Reminiscences of the United States Military Academy, from 1824 to 1831. (West Point, New York, 1879).

2558. Claiborne, John F.H. Life and Correspondence of John A. Quitman, Major-General, U.S.A., and Governor of the State of Mississippi. (2 vols., New York, 1860).

2559. Clarke, Dwight L. Stephen Watts Kearny: Soldier of the West. (Norman, Oklahoma, 1961).

2560. Clark, Edward B. William L. Sibert: The Army Engineer. (Philadelphia, Pennsylvania, 1930).

2561. Clary, David A. "The Role of the Army Surgeon in the West: Daniel Weisel at Fort Davis, Texas 1868-1872." WHQ 3 (January 1972), 53-66.

2562. Claudy, Carl H. "Thomas E. Selfridge--An Appreciation." AERON 4 (April 1909), 143- 4.

2563. Cochise, Ciye, as Told to a Kinney Griffith. The First Hundred Years of Nino Cochise; The Untold Story of an Apache Indian Chief. (New York, 1971).

2564. Coffman, Edward M. The Hilt of the Sword; The Career of Peyton C. March. (Madison, Wisconsin, 1966).

2565. Colt, Katherine G. The Letters of Peter Wilson; Soldier, Explorer, and Indian Agent West of the Mississippi River. (Baltimore, Maryland, 1940).

2566. Conger, Arthur L. "The Military Education of Grant as General." WMH 4 (March 1921), 239-62.

2567. Cooke, Phillip St. George. Scenes and Adventures in the Army, or Romance of Military Life. (Philadelphia, Pennsylvania, 1857).

2568. Copley, Frank B. Frederick W. Taylor: Father of Scientific Management. (2 vols., New York, 1923).

2569. Corbusier, William H. Verde to San Carlos; Recollections of a Famous Army Surgeon and His Observant Family on the Western Frontier, 1869-86. Edited by William T. Corbusier. (Tucson, Arizona, 1971).

2570. Cortissoz, Royal. The Life of Whitelaw Reid. (2 vols., New York, 1921).

2571. Couper, William. Claudius Crozet; Soldier, Scholar, Educator, Engineer. (Charlottesville, Virginaa, 1936).

2572. Cox, John E. Five Years in the United States Army. (Owensville, Indiana, 1892).

2573. Crane, Charles J. The Experiences of a Colonel of Infantry. (New York, 1923).

2574. Crocchiola, Stanley F.L. (F. Stanley, pseudo.). Sumner; Major-General, United States Army, 1797-1863. (Borger, Texas, 1968).

2575. Crocchiola, Stanley F.L. (F. Stanley, pseudo.). Satanta and the Kiowas. (Borger, Texas, 1968).

2576. Crook, George. General George Crook; His Autobiography. Edited by Martin F. Schmitt. (Norman, Oklahoma, 1946).

2577. Cruse, Thomas. Apache Days and After. Edited by Eugene Cunningham. (Caldwell, Idaho, 1941).

2578. Cullum, George W. Biographical Register of the Officers and Graduates of the United States Military Academy at West Point, N.Y., from Its Establishment in 1802 to 1890. (Third Edition, 3 vols., Boston, Massachusetts, 1891).

2579. Custer, Elizabeth. "Boots and Saddles:" or, Life in Dakota with General Custer. (New York, 1885).

2580. Custer, Elizabeth. Following the Guidon. (New York, 1890).

2581. Custer, Elizabeth. Tenting on the Plains; or, General Custer in Kansas and Texas. (New York, 1887).

2582. Custer, George A. The Custer Story; The Life and Intimate Letters of General George A. Custer and his Wife Elizabeth. Edited by Marguerite Merington. (New York, 1950).

2583. Custer, George A. My Life on the Plains; or, Personal Experiences with Indians. (New York, 1874).

2584. Davidson, Homer K. Black Jack Davidson, a Cavalry Commander on the Western Frontier: The Life of General John W. Davidson. (Glendale, California, 1974).

2585. Davis, Jefferson. The Papers of Jefferson Davis. Edited by Haskell M. Monroe, Jr. and James T. McIntosh. (Baton Rouge, Louisiana, 1971--).

2586. DeForest, John W. A Union Officer in the Reconstruction. Edited by James H. Croushore and David M. Potter. (New Haven, Connecticut, 1948).

2587. Deutrich, Mabel E. Struggle for Supremacy; The Career of Fred C. Ainsworth. (Washington, D.C., 1962).

2588.* Dornbusch, Charles E., compl. Charles King American Army Novelist; A Bibliography from the Collection of the National Library of Australia, Canberra. (Cornwallville, New York, 1963).

2589. Dowdy, Clifford. Lee. (Boston, Massachusetts, 1965).

2590. DuBois, John VanDeusen. Campaigns in the West, 1856-1861; The Journal and Letters of Colonel John VanDeusen DuBois. Edited by George P. Hammond. (Tucson, Arizona, 1949).

2591. DuPont, Henry A. "West Point in the Fifties: The Letters of Henry A. DuPont." Edited by Stephen E. Ambrose. CWH 10 (September 1964), 291-308.

2592. Dupuy, Richard Ernest. Sylvanus Thayer: Father of Technology in the United States. (West Point, New York, 1958).

2593. Dutton, William S. DuPont; One Hundred and Forty Years. (New York, 1942).

2594. Dyer, Brainerd. Zachary Taylor. (Baton Rouge, Louisiana, 1946).

2595. Dyer, John P. From Shiloh to San Juan, the Life of"Fightin Joe" Wheeler. (Baton Rouge, Louisiana, 1961).

2596. Dyer, John P. The Gallant Hood. (Indianapolis, Indiana, 1950).

2597. Eastman, Charles A. Indian Heroes and Great Chieftains. (Boston, Massachusetts, 1918).

2598. Eaton, Clement. Jefferson Davis. (New York, 1977).

2599. Eaton, Rachel C. John Ross and the Cherokee Indians. (Menasha, Wisconsin, 1914).

2600. Eliot, George F. Sylvanus Thayer of West Point. (New York, 1959).

2601. Elkins, John M. Indian Fighting on the Texas Frontier. Written by Frank W. McCarty. (Amarillo, Texas, 1929).

2602. Elliot, Charles W. Winfield Scott: The Soldier and the Man. (New York, 1937).

2603. Ewell, Richard S. The Making of a Soldier; Letters of General R.S. Ewell. Arranged and Edited by Percy G. Hamlin. (Richmond, Virginia, 1935).

2604. Falk, Stanley L. "Soldier-Technologist: Major Alfred Mordecai and the Beginnings of Science in the United States Army." Ph.D. Dissertation, Georgetown University, 1959.

2605. Farmer, James E. My Life With the Army in the West; The Memoirs of James E. Farmer, 1858-1898. Edited by Dale F. Giese. (Santa Fe, New Mexico, 1967).

2606. Fish, Williston. Memories of West Point, 1877-1881. Edited by Gertrude Fish Ramsey and Josephine Fish Peabody. (3 vols., Batavia, New York, 1957).

2607. Fiske, Frank B. Life and Death of Sitting Bull. (Fort Yates, North Dakota, 1933).

2608. FitzGerald, Emily (McCorkle). An Army Doctor's Wife on the Frontier; Letters from Alaska and the Far West, 1874-1878. Edited by Abe Laufe. (Pittsburgh, Pennsylvania, 1962).

2609. Flipper, Henry O. The Colored Cadet at West Point. Autobiography of Lieutenant Henry Ossian Flipper, U.S.A., First Graduate of Color from the U.S. Military Academy. (New York, 1878).

2610. Flipper, Henry O. Negro Frontiersman: The Western Memoirs of Henry O. Flipper, First Negro Graduate of West Point. Edited by Theodore Harris. (El Paso, Texas, 1963).

2611. Forsyth, George A. _Thrilling Days in Army Life_. (New York, 1900).

2612. Fougera, Katherine (Gibson). _With Custer's Cavalry; From the Memoirs of the Late Katherine Gibson, Widow of Captain Francis M. Gibson of the Seventh Cavalry, U.S.A. (Retired)_. (Caldwell, Idaho, 1940).

2613. Freeman, Douglas S. _R.E. Lee, A Biography_. (4 vols., New York, 1934-35).

2614. Fremont, John C. _Memoirs of My Life...._ (New York, 1887).

2615. Friedel, Frank B. _Francis Lieber, Nineteenth Century Liberal_. (Baton Rouge, Louisiana, 1947).

2616. Frink, Maurice with Casey E. Barthelmess. _Photographer on an Army Mule_. (Norman, Oklahoma, 1965).

2617. Frost, Lawrence A. _The Court-Martial of General George Armstrong Custer_. (Norman, Oklahoma, 1968).

2618. Frost, Lawrence A. _General Custer's Libbie_. (Seattle, Washington, 1976).

2619. Gage, Duane. "Black Kettle: A Noble Savage." _COK_ 45 (Autumn 1967), 244-51.

2620. Garesche, Louis. _Biography of Lieut. Col. Julius P. Garesche, Assistant Adjutant-General U.S. Army_. (Philadelphia, Pennsylvania, 1887).

2621. Garrison, Fielding H. _John Shaw Billings; A Memoir_. (New York, 1915).

2622. Gibson, John M. _Physician to the World; The Life of General William C. Gorgas_. (Durham, North Carolina, 1950).

2623. Gibson, John M. _Soldier in White; The Life of General George Miller Sternberg_. (Durham, North Carolina, 1958).

2624. Glisan, Rodney. _Journal of Army Life_. (San Francisco, California, 1874).

2625. Goff, John S. _Robert Todd Lincoln; A Man in His Own Rights_. (Norman, Oklahoma, 1969).

2627. Gorgas, Marie D. and Burton J. Hendrick. _William Crawford Gorgas: His Life and Work_. (Garden City, New York, 1924).

2628. Graham, William A., ed. _The Custer Myth: A Source Book of Custeriana_. (Harrisburg, Pennsylvania, 1953).

2629. Grant, Ulysses S. _The Papers of Ulysses S. Grant_. Edited by John Y. Simon. (Carbondale, Illinois, 1967--).

2630. Grant, Ulysses S. _Personal Memoirs of U.S. Grant_. (2 vols., New York, 1885-6).

2631. Greely, Adolphus W. *Reminiscences of Adventure and Service, A Record of Sixty-five Years.* (New York, 1927).

2632. Griess, Thomas E. "Denis Hart Mahan: West Point Professor and Advocate of Military Professionalism, 1830-71." Ph.D. Dissertation, Duke University, 1969.

2633. Grinnell, George Bird. *Two Great Scouts and Their Pawnee Battalion. The Experiences of Frank J. North and Luther H. North, Pioneers in the Great West, 1856-1882, and Their Defence of the Building of the Union Pacific Railroad.* (Cleveland, Ohio, 1928).

2634. Hagedorn, Herman. *Leonard Wood, A Biography.* (2 vols., New York, 1931).

2635. Hamlin, Percy G. *"Old Bald Head" (General Richard S. Ewell), The Portrait of a Soldier.* (Strasburg, Virginia, 1940).

2636. Hancock, Almira R. *Reminiscences of Winfield Scott Hancock.* (New York, 1887).

2637. Harbaugh, William H. *Power and Responsibility: The Life and Times of Theodore Roosevelt.* (Revised Edition, New York, 1975).

2638. Harper, James W. "Hugh Lenox Scott: Soldier Diplomat, 1876-1917." Ed.D. Dissertation, University of Virginia, 1968.

2639. Hartje, Robert G. *Van Dorn; The Life and Times of a Confederate General.* (Nashville, Tennessee, 1967).

2640. Hein, Otto L. *Memories of Long Ago....* (New York, 1925).

2641. Helfers, Melvin C. "The Military Career of Edgar Allan Poe." M.A. Thesis, Duke University, 1949.

2642. Heth, Henry. *The Memoirs of Henry Heth.* Edited by James L. Morrison, Jr. (Westport, Connecticut, 1974).

2643. Heyman, Max L., Jr. *Prudent Soldier, A Biography of General E.R.S. Canby, 1817-1873....* (Glendale, California, 1959).

2644. Hinton, Harwood P. "The Military Career of John Ellis Wool, 1812-1863." Ph.D. Dissertation, University of Wisconsin--Madison, 1960.

2645. Hitchcock, Ethan A. *A Traveler in Indian Territory; The Journal of Ethan Allen Hitchcock, Late Maj.-Gen. in the U.S. Army.* Edited by Grant Foreman. (Cedar Rapids, Iowa, 1930).

2646. Hitchcock, Ethan A. *Fifty Years in Camp and Field, Diary of Major General Ethan Allen Hitchcock, U.S.A.* Edited by William A. Croffutt. (New York, 1909).

2647. Holden, Edward. *Biographical Memoir of William H.C. Bartlett.* (Washington, D.C., 1911).

2648. Hollon, William Eugene. Beyond the Cross Timbers; The Travels of Randolph B. Marcy, 1812-1887. (Norman, Oklahoma, 1955).

2649. Hood, John B. Advance and Retreat; Personal Experiences in the United States and Confederate States Army. (New Orleans, Louisiana, 1880).

2650. Howard, Oliver O. Autobiography of Oliver Otis Howard, Major General, United States Army. (2 vols., New York, 1907).

2651. Hughes, Nathaniel C., Jr. General William J. Hardee; Old Reliable. (Baton Rouge, Louisiana, 1968).

2652. Hull, Lewis B. "Soldiering on the High Plains: The Diary of Byram Hull, 1864-1866." Edited by Myra E. Hull. KANHQ 7 (February 1938), 3-53.

2653. Humphreys, Henry H. Andrew Atkinson Humphreys: A Biography. (Philadelphia, Pennsylvania, 1924).

2654. Hunt, Aurora. Major General James Henry Carleton, 1814-1873; Western Frontier Dragoon. (Glendale, California, 1958).

2655. Irving, Washington. The Adventures of Captain Bonneville. (New York, n.d.).

2656. Jackson, Andrew. The Correspondence of Andrew Jackson. Edited by John Spencer Bassett. (6 vols., Washington, D.C., 1926-33).

2657. James, Marquis. Andrew Jackson, The Border Captain. (Indianapolis, Indiana, 1933).

2658. James, Doris Clayton. The Years of MacArthur. Volume 1, 1880-1941. (Boston, Massachusetts, 1970).

2659. Jarvis, Nathan S. "An Army Surgeon's Notes on Frontier Serivce, 1833-1848." JMSI 39 (July-August 1906), 131- 5; (September-October), 275-86; (November-December 1906), 451-60; 40 (March-April 1907), 269-77; (May-June 1907), 435-53; 41 (July-August 1907), 90-105.

2660. Jenkins, James C. "Brigadier General Archibald Henderson, USMC." MCG 25 (June 1941), 18, 50- 4.

2661. Jessup, Philip C. Elihu Root. (2 vols., New York, 1938).

2662. Jocelyn, Stephen P. Mostly Alkalai. (Caldwell, Idaho, 1953).

2663. Johnson, Elliott L. "The Military Experiences of General Hugh A. Drum from 1898-1918." Ph.D. Dissertation, University of Wisconsin, 1975.

2664. Johnson, Richard W. Memoir of Major-General George H. Thomas. (Philadelphia, Pennsylvania, 1881).

2665. Johnson, Richard W. A Soldier's Reminiscences in Peace and War.
(Philadelphia, Pennsylvania, 1886).

2666. Johnson, Virginia W. The Unregimented General: A Biography of Nelson
A. Miles. (Boston, Massachusetts, 1962).

2667. Johnson, Charles H.J. Famous Indian Chiefs; Their Battles, Treaties,
Sieges, and Struggles with the Whites for the Possession of America.
(Boston, Massachusetts, 1909).

2668. Kahn, Ely J. McNair: Educator of an Army. (Washington, D.C.,1945).

2669. Kakar, Sudhir. Frederick Taylor: A Study in Personality and Innovation. (Cambridge, Massachusetts, 1970).

2670. Kaywaykla, James. In the Days of Victorio; Recollections of a Warm
Springs Apache. Edited by Eve Ball. (Tucson, Arizona, 1970).

2671. Kearny, Thomas. General Philip Kearny; Battle Soldier of Five Wars;
Including the Conquest of the West by General Stephen Watts Kearny.
(New York, 1937).

2672. Kershner, James W. "Sylvanus Thayer: A Biography." Ph.D. Dissertation,
West Virginia University, 1976.

2673. Keyes, Erasmus D. Fifty Years Observation of Men and Events, Civil
and Military. (New York, 1884).

2674. Kimball, Maria B. A Soldier-Doctor of Our Army, James P. Kimball....
(Boston, Massachusetts, 1917).

2675. King, James T. War Eagle; A Life of General Eugene A. Carr. (Lincoln,
Nebraska, 1963).

2676. Kip, Lawrence. Army Life on the Pacific: A Journal of the Expedition
Against the Northern Indians, The Tribes of the Coeur d'Orlenes, Spokans,
and Pelouzes, in the Summer of 1858. (New York, 1859).

2677. Kroeker, Marvin E. Great Plains Command; William B. Hazen in the Frontier West. (Norman, Oklahoma, 1976).

2678. Lane, Jack C. Armed Progressive: General Leonard Wood. (San Rafael,
California, 1978).

2679. Lane, Lydia Spencer. I Married a Soldier; or, Old Days in the Old
Army. (Philadelphia, Pennsylvania, 1893).

2680. Latrobe, John H.B. Reminiscences of West Point. (East Saginaw,
Michigan, 1887).

2681. Lavery, Dennis S. "John Gibbon and the Old Army: Portrait of an
American Professional Soldier, 1827-1896." Ph.D. Dissertation,
Pennsylvania State University, 1974.

2682. Lejune, John A. The Reminiscences of a Marine. (Philadelphia, Pennsylvania, 1930).

2683. Lewis, Charles L. Famous American Marines; An Account of the Corps: The Exploits of Officers and Men on Land, by Air and Sea, from the Decks of the Bonhomme Richard to the Summit of Mount Suribachi. (Boston, Massachusetts, 1950).

2684. Lewis, Lloyd. Captain Sam Grant. (Boston, Massachusetts, 1950).

2685. Lewis, Lloyd. Sherman; Fighting Prophet. (New York, 1932).

2686. Lockmiller, David A. Enoch H. Crowder; Soldier, Lawyer and States-man. (Columbia, Missouri, 1955).

2687. Loker, Donald E. Lewis Leffman, Ordnance Sergeant, United States Army. (Lockport, New York, 1974).

2688. Long, William W. "A Biography of Major General Edwin Vose Sumner, U.S.A., 1797-1863." Ph.D. Dissertation, University of New Mexico, 1971.

2689. Longacre, Edward G. Man Behind the Guns; A Biography of General Henry Jackson Hunt, Commander of Artillery, Army of the Potomac. (Cranbury, New Jersey, 1977).

2690. Lowe, Percival G. Five Years a Dragoon ('49 to '54) and Other Adventures on the Great Plains. (Kansas City, Missouri, 1906).

2691. MacArthur, Douglas. Reminiscences. (New York, 1964).

2692. McCall, George A. Letters from the Frontiers. Written During a Period of Thirty Years' Service in the Army of the United States. (Philadelphia, Pennsylvania, 1868).

2693. McClellan, Henry B. The Life and Campaigns of Major General J.E.B. Stuart, Commander of the Cavalry of the Army of Northern Virginia. (Boston, Massachusetts, 1885).

2694. McConnell, H.H. Five Years a Cavalryman; or, Sketches of Regular Army Life on the Texas Frontier Twenty Odd Years Ago. (Jackboro, Texas, 1889).

2695. McCrea, Tully. Dear Belle; Letters from a Cadet and Officer to His Sweetheart, 1858-1865. Edited by Catherine S. Crary. (Middletown, Connecticut, 1965).

2696. McKay, Robert H. Little Pills; An Army Story; Being Some Experiences of a United States Army Medical Officer on the Frontier Nearly a Half Century Ago. (Pittsburg, Kansas, 1918).

2697. McKenney, Thomas L. Memoirs, Official and Personal; With Sketches of Travel Among the Northern and Southern Indians; Embracing a War Excursion and Descriptions of Scenes Along the Western Borders. (2 vols., New York, 1846).

2698. Mackenzie, Ranald S. *Ranald S. Mackenzie's Official Correspondence Relating to Texas.* Edited by Ernest Wallace. (2 vols., Lubbock, Texas, 1967-68).

2699. McKinley, Silas B. and Silas Bent. *Old Rough and Ready, the Life and Times of Zachary Taylor.* (New York, 1946).

2700. McKinney, Francis F. *Education in Violence; The Life of George H. Thomas and the History of the Army of the Cumberland.* (Detroit, Michigan, 1961).

2701. Marcy, Randolph B. *Border Reminiscences.* (New York, 1872).

2702. Marcy, Randolph B. *Thirty Years of Army Life on the Border.* (New York, 1866).

2703. Mattes, Merrill J. *Indians, Infants, and Infantry: Andrew and Elizabeth Burt on the Frontier.* (Denver, Colorado, 1960).

2704. Maury, Dabney H. *Recollections of a Virginian in the Mexican, Indian, and Civil Wars.* (New York, 1894).

2705. Meade, George Gordon. *The Life and Letters of George Gordon Meade, Major General, United States Army.* Edited by George Gordon Meade. (New York, 1913).

2706. Meyers, Augustus. *Ten Years in the Ranks, U.S. Army.* (New York, 1914).

2707. Michie, Peter S. *The Life and Letters of Emory Upton, Colonel of the 4th Regiment of Artillery and Brevet Major-General U.S. Army.* (New York, 1885).

2708. Michie, Peter S. "Reminiscences of Cadet and Army Service" in *Military Order of the Loyal Legion of the United States, New York Commandery, Personal Recollections of the War of the Rebellion.* Second Series (New York, 1891-1912), 183-97.

2709. Miles, Nelson. *Personal Recollections and Observations.* (Chicago, Illinois, 1896).

2710. Miles, Nelson A. *Serving the Republic; Memoirs of the Civil and Military Life of Nelson A. Miles.* (New York, 1911).

2711. Millett, Allan R. *The General: Robert L. Bullard and Officership in the United States Army, 1881-1925.* (Westport, Connecticut, 1975).

2712. Mills, Anson. *My Story.* Edited by C.H. Claudy. (Washington, D.C., 1918).

2713. Mitchel, Frederick A. *Ormsby Macknight Mitchel, Astronomer and General.* (Boston, Massachusetts, 1887).

2714. Monaghan, Jay. *Custer; The Life of General George Armstrong Custer.* (Lincoln, Nebraska, 1959).

2715. Mordecai, Alfred. "The Life of Alfred Mordecai as Related by Himself." Edited by James A. Padgett. NCHR 22 (January 1945), 58-108.

2716. Moore, John H., ed. "Letters from a Santa Fe Army Clerk, 1855-1856." NMHR 40 (April 1965), 141-64.

2717. Morison, Elting E. Turmoil and Tradition: A Study of the Life and Times of Henry L. Stimson. (Boston, Massachusetts, 1960).

2718. Mott, Thomas Bentley. Twenty Years as Military Attache. (New York, 1937).

2719. Moulton, Gary E. "John Ross, Cherokee Chief." Ph.D. Dissertation, Oklahoma State University, 1974.

2720. Mulford, Ami F. Fighting Indians in the 7th U.S. Cavalry. (Corning, New York, 1878).

2721. Myers, William S. General George Brinton McClellan. (New York, 1934).

2722. Nalty, Bernard C. and Truman R. Strobridge. "Captain Emmet Crawford, Commander of Apache Scouts, 1882-1886." AZW 6 (Spring 1964), 30-40.

2723. Nevins, Allan. Fremont; Pathmaker of the West. (New York, 1939).

2724. Nichols, Edward J. Towards Gettysburg; A Biography of General John F. Reynolds. (University Park, Pennsylvania, 1958).

2725. Nichols, Roger L. General Henry Atkinson; A Western Military Career. (Norman, Oklahoma, 1965).

2726. Nohl, Lessing H., Jr. Bad Hand, The Military Career of Ranald Slidell Mackenzie, 1871-1889." Ph.D. Dissertation, University of New Mexico, 1962.

2727. North, Luther H. Man of the Plains: Recollections of Luther North, 1856-1882. Edited by Donald F. Danker. (Lincoln, Nebraska, 1961).

2728. O'Connor, Richard G. Black Jack Pershing. (Garden City, New York, 1961).

2729. O'Connor, Richard G. Hood, Cavalier General. (New York, 1959).

2730. Ostrander, Alson B. An Army Boy of the Sixties; A Story of the Plains. (Yonkers-on-Hudson, New York, 1924).

2731. Palmer, Frederick. Bliss, Peacemaker; The Life and Letters of General Tasker Howard Bliss. (New York, 1934).

2732. Palmer, Frederick. John J. Pershing, General of the Armies, A Biography. (Harrisburg, Pennsylvania, 1948).

2733. Parker, James. The Old Army: Memories, 1872-1918. (Philadelphia, Pennsylvania, 1929).

2734. Parks, Joseph H. General Kirby Smith, C.S.A. (Baton Rouge, Louisiana, 1954).

2735. Patrick, Rembert W. Aristocrat in Uniform; General Duncan L. Clinch. (Gainesville, Florida, 1963).

2736. Perkins, Jacob R. Trails, Rails and War; The Life of General G.M. Dodge. (Indianapolis, Indiana, 1929).

2737. Pogue, Forrest C. George G. Marshal; Education of a General, 1880-1939. (New York, 1963).

2738. Post, Marie C. The Life and Memoirs of Comte Regis de Trobriand.... (New York, 1910).

2739. Pratt, Richard H. Battlefield and Classroom: Four Decades with the American Indians, 1867-1904. Edited by Robert M. Utley. (New Haven, Connecticut, 1964).

2740. Preston, Walter C. Lee, West Point and Lexington. (Yellow Springs, Ohio, 1934).

2741. Preuss, Charles. Exploring with Fremont; The Private Diaries of Charles Preuss, Cartographer for John C. Fremont on His First, Second, and Fourth Expeditions to the Far West. Edited and Translated by Erwin G. and Elisabeth K. Gudde. (Norman, Oklahoma, 1958).

2742. Prickett, Robert C. "The Malfeasance of William Worth Belknap, Secretary of War." NDH 17 (January 1950), 5-52; (April 1950), 97-134.

2743. Pringle, Henry F. The Life and Times of William Howard Taft; A Biography. (2 vols., New York, 1939).

2744. Raymond, Dora N. Captain Lee Hall of Texas. (Norman, Oklahoma, 1940).

2745. Reavis, Logan U. The Life and Military Service of General William S. Harney. (St. Louis, Missouri, 1878).

2746. Recollections of the United States Army...by an American Soldier; Written During a Period in "the Service," since 1830. (Second Edition, Boston, Massachusetts, 1845).

2747. Remini, Robert V. Andrew Jackson and the Course of American Empire, 1767-1821. (New York, 1977).

2748. Revere, Joseph W. Keel and Saddle; A Retrospect of Forty Years of Military and Naval Service. (Boston, Massachusetts, 1872).

2749. Rice, Josiah M. A Cannoneer in Navajo Country; Journal of Private Josiah M. Rice, 1851. Edited by Richard H. Dillon. (Denver, Colorado, 1970).

2750. Rippy, James Fred. Joel R. Poinsett, Versatile American. (Durham, North Carolina, 1935).

2751. Rister, Carl Coke. Border Command, General Phil Sheridan in the West. (Norman, Oklahoma, 1944).

2752. Rodney, George B. As A Cavalryman Remembers. (Caldwell, Idaho, 1944).

2753. Roe, Francis M.A. Army Letters from an Officer's Wife, 1871-1888. (New York, 1909).

2754. Rogers, Fred B. Soldiers of the Overland: Being Some Account of the Services of General Patrick Edward Connor and His Volunteers in the Old West. (San Francisco, 1938).

2755. Roland, Charles P. Albert Sidney Johnston; Soldier of Three Republics. (Austin, Texas, 1964).

2756. Roosevelt, Theodore. Letters. Selected and Edited by Elting Morison, John M. Blum and John J. Buekley. (8 vols., Cambridge, Massachusetts, 1951- 4).

2757. Roosevelt, Theodore. Theodore Roosevelt; An Autobiography. (New York, 1913).

2758. Russell, Don. One Hundred and Three Fights and Scrimmages; The Story of General Reuben F. Bernard. (Washington, D.C., 1936).

2759. Sandoz, Mari. Crazy Horse, the Strange Man of the Ogalas; A Biography. (New York, 1942).

2760. Sanford, George B. Fighting Indians and Redskins; Experiences in Army Life of Colonel George B. Sanford. Edited by Edward R. Hageman. (Norman, Oklahoma, 1969).

2761. Scharf, Morris. The Spirit of Old West Point, 1858-1862. (Boston, Massachusetts, 1907).

2762. Schofield, John M. Forty Six Years in the Army. (New York, 1897).

2763. Schuon, Karl. U.S. Marine Corps Biographical Dictionary. (New York, 1963).

2764. Scott, Hugh L. Some Memories of a Soldier. (New York, 1928).

2765. Scott, Winfield. Memoirs of Lieutenant-General Scott, LLD. (2 vols., New York, 1864).

2766. Scott, Winfield. "Some Unpublished Letters of a Roving Soldier-Diplomat." Edited by Charles W. Elliott. MA 1 (Winter 1937-38), 165-73.

2767. Sedgwick, John. Correspondence of John Sedgwick, Major-General. (2 vols., New York, 1902-03).

2768. Settles, Thomas M. "The Military Career of John Bankhead Magruder." Ph.D. Dissertation, Texas Christian University, 1972.

2769. Sheridan, Philip H. Personal Memoirs of P.H. Sheridan.... (2 vols., New York, 1888).

2770. Sherman, William T. Memoirs of William T. Sherman. (2 vols., New York, 1875).

2771. Silver, James W. Edmund Pendleton Gaines, Frontier General. (Baton Rouge, Louisiana, 1949).

2772. Smith, Cornelius C., Jr. Don't Settle for Second: The Life and Times of Cornelius C. Smith. (San Rafael, California, 1977).

2773. Smith, William L.G. The Life and Times of Lewis Cass. (New York, 1856).

2774. Smythe, Donald. Guerilla Warrior; The Early Life of John J. Pershing. (New York, 1973).

2775. Spencer, Ivor D. The Victor and the Spoils; A Life of William L. Marcy. (Providence, Rhode Island, 1959).

2776. Spring, Agnes Wright. Casper Collins: The Life and Exploits of an Indian Fighter of the Sixties; Together with Casper Collins' Letters and Drawings, and Various Photographs and Documents Connected with His Career. (New York, 1927).

2777. Stanley, David S. Personal Memoirs of Major General D. S. Stanley, U.S.A. (Cambridge, Massachusetts, 1917).

2778. Stevens, Hazzard. The Life of Isaac Ingalls Stevens. (2 vols., Boston, Massachusetts, 1900).

2779. Stewart, George R. John Phoenix, Esq., The Veritable Squibob, A Life of Captain George H. Derby, U.S.A. (New York, 1937).

2780. Stover, Earl F. "Chaplain Henry V. Plummer, His Ministry and His Court-Martial." NEBH 56 (Spring 1975), 20-50.

2781. Strode, Hudson. Jefferson Davis. (3 vols., New York, 1955-64).

2782. Sully, Langdon. No Tears for the General; The Life of Alfred Sully, 1821-1879. (Palo Alto, California, 1974).

2783. Summerhayes, Martha. Vanished Arizona: Recollections of My Army Life. (Philadelphia, Pennsylvania, 1908).

2784. Sweeny, Thomas W. Journal of Lieutenant Thomas W. Sweeny, 1849-1853. Edited by Arthur Woodward. (Los Angeles, 1956).

2785. Swift, Eben. "An American Pioneer in the Course of Military Education." JMSI 44 (January-February 1908), 67-72.

2786. Swift, Eben. "The Military Education of Robert E. Lee." VMHB 35 (April 1927), 97-160.

2787. Swift, Joseph G. *The Memoirs of General Joseph Swift*. Edited by Harrison Ellery. (Worcester, Massachusetts, 1890).

2788. Talbot, Theodore. *Soldier in the West: Letters of Theodore Talbot During His Services in California, Mexico, and Oregon, 1845-53*. Edited by Robert V. Hine and Savoie Lottinville. (Norman, Oklahoma, 1972).

2789. Taylor, Emerson G. *Gouverneur Kemble Warren; The Life and Letters of an American Soldier, 1830-1882*. (New York, 1932).

2790. Terell, John U. and George Walton. *Faint the Trumpet Sounds: The Life and Trial of Major Reno*. (New York, 1966).

2791. Thomas, Benjamin P. and Harold M. Hyman. *Stanton; The Life and Times of Lincoln's Secretary of War*. (New York, 1962).

2792. Thomas, Lowell. *Woodfill of the Regulars: A True Story of Adventure from the Arctic to the Argonne*. (London, 1929).

2793. Thrapp, Dan L. *Al Sieber, Chief of Scouts*. (Norman, Oklahoma, 1964).

2794. Thrapp, Dan L. *Victorio and the Mimbres Apaches*. (Norman, Oklahoma, 1974).

2795. Tinkcom, Harry M. *John White Geary, Soldier-Statesman, 1819-1873*. (Philadelphia, Pennsylvania, 1940).

2796. Folman, Newton F. *The Search for General Miles; Biography of One of America's Most Extraordinary Military Heroes of the Civil War*. (New York, 1968).

2797. Trobriand, Phillippe Regis de. *Military Life in Dakota: The Journal of Phillippe Regis de Trobriand*. Translated by Lucille M. Kane. (St. Paul, Minnesota, 1951).

2798. Troubetzkoy, Ulrich. "Colonel Claudius Crozet." *VCAV* 12 (Spring 1963), 5-10.

2799. Tuchman, Barbara W. *Stilwell and the American Experience in China, 1911-45*. (New York, 1971).

2800. Turnley, Parmenas T. *Reminiscences of Parmenas Taylor Turnley from the Cradle to Three-Score and Ten; by Himself, from Diaries Kept from Early Boyhood*. (Chicago, Illinois, 1892).

2801. Twichell, Heath, Jr. *Allen: The Biography of an Army Officer, 1859-1930*. (New Brunswick, New Jersey, 1974).

2802. "Ulysses S. Grant's Pre-Civil War Military Education," in Grady McWhiney, *Southerners and Other Americans*. (New York, 1973), 61-71.

2803. Vandiver, Frank E. *Black Jack: The Life and Times of John J. Pershing*. (2 vols., College Station, Texas, 1977).

2804. Vestal, Stanley. Sitting Bull, Champion of the Sioux; A Biography.
(Boston, Massachusetts, 1932).

2805. Viele, Teresa. "Following the Drum": A Glimpse of Frontier Life.
(New York, 1858).

2806. Wallace, Edward S. General William Jenkins Worth, Monterey's
Forgotten Hero. (Dallas, Texas, 1953).

2807. Wallace, Ernest. Ranald S. Mackenzie on the Texas Frontier. (Lubbock,
Texas, 1964).

2808. Webb, Lester A. Captain Alden Partridge and the United States
Military Academy, 1806-1833. (Northport, Alabama, 1965).

2809. Webster's American Military Biographies. (Springfield, Massachusetts,
1978).

2810. Weigley, Russell F. Quartermaster General of the Union Army; A
Biography of M.C. Meigs. (New York, 1959).

2811. Weir, John Ferguson. "Memoirs of West Point During the Two Decades
Preceeding the Civil War." Edited by Theodore Sizer. NYHSQ 41
(April 1957), 109-41.

2812. Wessels, William L. Born to Be a Soldier; The Military Career of
William Wing Loring of St. Augustine, Florida. (Fort Worth, Texas,
1971).

2813. Wharton, Clarence. Satanta, the Great Chief of the Kiowas and His
People. (Dallas, Texas, 1935).

2814. Who Was Who in American History, The Military. (Chicago, Illinois,
1975).

2815. Willcox, Orlando B. ("Major March, pseudo.). Faca: An Army Memoir.
(Boston, Massachusetts, 1857).

2816. Williams, Thomas Harry. P.G.T. Beauregard; Napoleon in Gray. (Baton
Rouge, Louisiana, 1955).

2817. Wiltse, Charles M. John C. Calhoun, Nationalist, 1782-1828. (Indianapolis, Indiana, 1944).

2818. Wise, Frederic M. as Told to Meigs O. Frost. A Marine Tells It to You.
(New York, 1929).

2819. Wise, Jennings C. Personal Memoir of the Life and Services of Scott
Shipp. (Lexington, Virginia, 1915).

2820. Wood, Laura N. Walter Reed, Doctor in Uniform. (New York, 1943).

2821. Wood, Richard G. Stephen Harriman Long, 1784-1864; Army Engineer,
Explorer, Inventor. (Glendale, California, 1966).

2822. Wooden Leg. A Warrior Who Fought Custer. Interpreted by Thomas B. Marquis. (Minneapolis, Minnesota, 1931).

2823. Woodford, Frank B. Lewis Cass: The Last Jeffersonian. (New Brunswick, New Jersey, 1950).

2824. Wynne, James. Memoir of Major Samuel Ringgold, United States Army. (Baltimore, Maryland, 1847).

2825. Yellow Wolf. Yellow Wolf: His Own Story. Edited by Lucullus V. McWhortor. (Caldwell, Idaho, 1940).

2826. Young, Otis E. The West of Philip St. George Cooke, 1809-1895. (Glendale, California, 1955).

See also: Addendum: 18, 97, 101, 141.

MILITARY FORCES

2827. Abbot, Willis J. Soldiers of the Sea; The Story of the United States Marine Corps. (New York, 1918).

2828. Addington, Larry H. "The U.S. Coast Artillery and the Problem of Artillery Organization, 1907-1954." MA 40 (February 1976), 1-6.

2829. Adler, Bill, compl. The Black Soldier: From the American Revolution to Vietnam. Edited by Jay David and Elaine Carne. (New York, 1971).

2830. Albert, Alphaeus H. Record of American Uniform and Historical Buttons, with Supplement..., 1775-1973. (Boyertown, Pennsylvania, 1973).

2831. American Society of Military Insignia Collectors. Catalog of Distinctive Insignia of the U.S. Army. Edited by George S. Pappas. (Washington, D.C., 1960).

2832. Amos, Preston E. Above and Beyond in the West; Black Medal of Honor Winners, 1870-1890. (Washington, D.C., 1974).

2833. Anderson, George S. "Work of the Cavalry in Protecting the Yellowstone National Park." JUSCA 10 (March 1897), 3-10.

2834. Anderson, Thomas M. "Army Posts, Barracks and Quarters." JMSI 2, No. 5 (1881), 421-47.

2835. Andrews, Richard A. "Years of Frustration: William T. Sherman, The Army and Reform, 1869-1883." Ph.D. Dissertation, Northwestern University, 1968.

2836. Army Times, Washington, D.C. A History of the United States Signal Corps. (New York, 1961).

2837. Arthur, Robert. The Coast Artillery School, 1824-1927. (Fort Monroe, Virginia, 1928).

2838. Ashburn, Percy M. A History of the Medical Department of the United States Army. (Boston, Massachusetts, 1929).

2839. Axton, John T., Jr. Brief History of Chaplains in the U.S. Army. (Fort Leavenworth, Kansas, 1925).

2840. Ayars, Charles W. "Some Notes on the Medical Service of the Army, 1812-1839." MSUR 50 (May 1922), 505-24.

2841. Azoy, A.C.M. "Great Guns: A History of the Coast Artillery Corps." CARJ 84 (September-October 1941), 426-34; (November-December 1941), 573- 8.

2842. Baldwin, Kenneth H. Enchanted Enclosure: The Army Engineers and Yellowstone National Park; A Documentary History. (Washington, D.C., 1976).

2843. Ball, Eve. "The Apache Scouts: A Chiricahua Appraisal." AZW 7 (Winter 1965), 315-28.

2844. Baumer, William H. Not All Warriors; Portraits of 19th Century West Pointers Who Gained Fame in Other Than Military Fields. (New York, 1941).

2845. Boyne-Jones, Stanhope. The Evolution of Preventive Medicine in the United States Army, 1607-1939. (Washington, D.C., 1968).

2846. Beers, Henry P. "A History of the U.S. Topographical Engineers, 1813-1863." ME 34 (June 1942), 287-91; (July 1942), 348-52.

2847. Belden, Bauman L. United States War Medals. (New York, 1916).

2848. Bemis, Samuel F. "Captain John Mullan and the Engineer's Frontier." WAHQ 14 (July 1923), 201-5.

2849. Bender, Averam B. "The Soldier in the Far West, 1848-1860." PHR 8 (June 1939), 159-78.

2850. *Bentley, George R. A History of the Freedman's Bureau. (New York, 1970).

2851. Bergey, Ellwood. Why Soldiers Desert from the United States Army. (Philadelphia, Pennsylvania, 1903).

2852. Bernardo, C. Joseph and Eugene H. Bacon. American Military Policy; Its Development Since 1775. (Harrisburg, Pennsylvania, 1955).

2853. Bethel, Elizabeth. "The Military Intelligence Division: Origin of the Intelligence Division." MA 11 (Spring 1947), 17-24.

2854. Beyer, Walter F. and Oscar F. Keydel, eds. Deeds of Valor; How America's Heroes Won the Medal of Honor.... (2 vols., Detroit, Michigan, 1905).

2855. Binkley, John C. "A History of U.S. Army Force Structuring." MR 57 (February 1977), 67-82.

2856. Birkhimer, William E. Historical Sketch of the Organization, Administration, Material, and Tactics of the Artillery, United States Army. (Washington, D.C., 1884).

2857. Birkhimer, William E. The Law of Appointment and Promotion in the Regular Army of the United States. (New York, 1880).

2858. Blackburn, Forrest R. "Army Families in Frontier Forts." MR 49 (October 1969), 17-28.

2859. Blackburn, Forrest R. "The Army in Western Exploration." MR 51 (September 1971), 75-90.

2860. Blacks in the United States Armed Forces; Basic Documents. Edited by Morris J. MacGregor and Bernard C. Nalty. (13 vols., Wilmington, Delaware, 1977).

2861. Blakeney, Jane. Heroes, U.S. Marine Corps, 1861-1955, Armed Forces Award, Flags. (Washington, D.C., 1957).

2862. Bliven, Bruce, Jr. Volunteers, One and All. (Pleasantville, New York, 1976).

2863. Boatner, Mark M. Military Customs and Traditions. (New York, 1956).

2864. Boynton, Edward C. History of West Point, and Its Military Importance During the Revolution; And the Origin and Progress of the U.S. Military Academy. (New York, 1863).

2865. Brackett, Albert G. History of the United States Cavalry, From the Formation of the Federal Government to the 1st of June 1863. (New York, 1865).

2866. Brinckerhoff, Sidney B. Boots and Shoes of the Frontier Soldier, 1865-1893. (Tucson, Arizona, 1976).

2867. Brinckerhoff, Sidney B. Military Headgear in the Southwest, 1846-1890. (Tucson, Arizona, 1965).

2868. Brinckerhoff, Sidney B. Metal Uniform Insignia of the Frontier U.S. Army, 1846-1902. (Revised and Enlarged Edition, Tucson, Arizona, 1972).

2869. Britton, Jack and George Washington, Jr., compls. U.S. Military Shoulder Patches of the United States Armed Forces. (Tulsa, Oklahoma, 1975).

2870. Brower, Philip P. "The U.S. Army's Seizure and Administration of Enemy Records Up to World War II." AMAR 26 (April 1963), 191-207.

2871. Brown, Lisle G. "The Yellowstone Supply Depot." NDH 40 (Winter 1973), 24-33.

2872. Brown, Richard C. "Social Attitudes of American Generals, 1898-1940." Ph.D. Dissertation, University of Wisconsin, 1951.

2873. Brown, Stuart E., Jr. The Guns of Harpers Ferry. (Berryville, Virginia, 1968).

2874. Burdett, Thomas F. "Mobilizations of 1911 and 1913: Their Role in the Development of the Modern Army." MR 54 (July 1974), 65-74.

2875. Burg, Maclyn P. "Serving on the Vanishing Frontier, 1898-1922." MHT&SW 12, No. 4 (1976), 19-28.

2876. Butler, Benjamin F. The Military Profession in the United States. (New York, 1839).

2877. Caidin, Martin. Air Force: A Pictorial History of American Airpower. (New York, 1957).

2878. Callahan, Edward W., ed. List of Officers of the Navy of the United States and of the Marine Corps from 1775-1900. (New York, 1901).

2879. Campbell, Clark S. The '03 Springfield. (Beverly Hills, California, 1957).

2880. *Campbell, James D. and Edgar M. Howell. American Military Insignia 1800-1851. (Washington, D.C., 1963).

2881. Cantor, Louis. "The Creation of the Modern National Guard: The Dick Militia Act of 1903." Ph.D. Dissertation, Duke University, 1963.

2882. Carleton, William G. "Raising Armies Before the Civil War." CUH 54 (June 1968), 327-32, 363- 4.

2883. Carroll, John M., compl. The Black Military Experience in the American West. (New York, 1971).

2884. Carter, William G.H. The American Army. (Indianapolis, Indiana, 1915).

2885. Carter, William G.H. Creation of the American General Staff; Personal Narrative of the General Staff System of the American Army. (Washington, D.C., 1924).

2886. Carter, William G.H. "Elihu Root--His Services as Secretary of War." NAR 178 (January 1904), 110-21.

2887. Carter, William G.H. West Point in Literature. (Baltimore, Maryland, 1909).

2888. Cary, Norman M., Jr., compl. Guide to U.S. Army Museums and Historic Sites. (Washington, D.C., 1975).

2889. Casari, Robert B. "Powering Army Aircraft Through 1915." AAHSJ 22 (Summer 1977), 91-103.

2890. Cassel, Russell N. "Evolution of American Military Policy." MR 34 (July 1954), 40- 5.

2891. Castle, Henry A. "The Shelter Tent," in Military Order of the Loyal Legion of the United States, Minnesota Commandery, Glimpses of the Nation's Struggle. Third Series. (St. Paul, Minnesota, 1887-1909), 440-53.

2892. Catton, Bruce. "The Marine Tradition." AH 10 (February 1959), 24-35, 88-90.

2893. Catts, Gordon R. "Post Professional Libraries for Officers." JMSI 44 (January-February 1909), 84- 9.

2894. Chamberlain, Robert S. "The Northern State Militia." CWH 4 (June 1958), 105-18.

2895. Chandler, Charles D. and Frank P. Lahn. How Our Army Grew Wings; Airmen and Aircraft Before 1914. (New York, 1943).

2896. Chappell, Gordon. Brass Spikes and Horsehair Plumes: A Study of U.S. Army Dress Helmets, 1872-1903. (Tucson, Arizona, 1966).

2897. Chappell, Gordon. The Search for the Well-Dressed Soldier 1865-1890: Development and Innovations in United States Army Uniforms on the Western Frontier. (Tucson, Arizona, 1972).

2898. Chappell, Gordon. Summer Helmets of the U.S. Army, 1875-1910. (Cheyenne, Wyoming, 1967).

2899. Clemens, Al J. The American Military Armored Car. (Canoza Park, California, 1969).

2900. Clendenen, Clarence C. Blood on the Border; The United States Army and the Mexican Irregulars. (London, 1969).

2901. Clifford, Kenneth J. Progress and Purpose: A Developmental History of the United States Marine Corps, 1900-1970. (Washington, D.C., 1973).

2902. Claus, John W. "Some Remarks Upon the Army as a Pioneer of Civilization and as a Constructive Agency under Our Government," in Military Order of the Loyal Legion of the United States, New York, Commandery, Personal Recollections of the War of the Rebellion. Fourth Series. (New York, 1891-1912), 32-45.

2903. Coffman, Edward M. "Army Life on the Frontier, 1865-1898." MA 20 (Winter 1956), 193-201.

2904. Coffman, Edward M. The Young Officer in the Old Army. (Colorado Springs, Colorado, 1976).

2905. Colby, Elbridge. "Elihu Root and the National Guard." MA 23 (Spring 1959), 28-34.

2906. Collum, Richard S. History of the United States Marine Corps. (New York, 1890).

2907. Company of Military Historians. Military Uniforms in America. Edited by John R. Elting. (San Rafael, California, 1974--).

2908. Condit, Kenneth W., John H. Johnston and Ella W. Nargele. A Brief History of Headquarters Marine Corps Staff Organization. (Washington, D.C., 1971).

2909. Cooling, Benjamin Franklin. "A History of U.S. Army Aviation." AEH 21 (Summer 1974), 102-9.

2910. Cooper, Jerry M. "The Army and Civil Disorder: Federal Military Intervention in American Labor Disputes, 1877-1900." Ph.D. Dissertation, The University of Wisconsin, 1971.

2911. Corbin, Henry C. "The General Staff Corps," in Military Order of the Loyal Legion of the United States, New York Commandery, Personal Recollections of the War of the Rebellion. Third Series. (New York, 1891-1912), 281-91.

2912. Cornish, Dudley T. "To Be Recognized as Men: The Practical Utility of History." MR 58 (February 1978), 40-55.

2913. Cosmas, Graham A. "The Formative Years of Marine Corps Aviation, 1912-1939." AEH 24 (Summer 1977), 82-93.

2914. Cosmas, Graham A. "Military Reform After the Spanish-American War: The Army Reorganization Fight of 1898-1899." MA 35 (February 1971), 12-18.

2915. *Cresswell, Mary A. and Carl Berger, compls. United States Air Force History; An Annotated Bibliography. (Washington, D.C., 1971).

2916. Croghan, George. Army Life on the Western Frontier: Selections from the Official Reports Made Between 1826 and 1845. Edited by Francis P. Prucha. (Norman, Oklahoma, 1958).

2917. Croizat, Victor J. "The Development of MCS." MCG 38 (September 1954), 36-43.

2918. Cross, Osborne. The March of the Mounted Riflemen...from Fort Leavenworth to Fort Vancouver, May to October 1849. Edited by Raymond W. Settle. (Glendale, California, 1940).

2919. Croun, John A. "Tradition of Experts (Marksmanship)." MCG 38 (August 1954), 32- 9.

2920. Cunliffe, Marcus. "The American Military Tradition," in Harry C. Allen and Charles P. Hill, eds., British Essays in American History. (New York, 1957), 207-24.

2921. *Cunliffe, Marcus. <u>Soldiers and Civilians; The Martial Spirit in America, 1775-1865</u>. (Boston, Massachusetts, 1968).

2922. Davis, Carl L. and LeRoy H. Fischer. "Dragoon Life in Indian Territory, 1833-1846." <u>COK</u> 48 (Spring 1970), 2-24.

2923. Davis, Franklin M., Jr. and Thomas T. Jones. <u>The U.S. Army Engineers; Fighting Elite</u>. (New York, 1967).

2924. Davis, Gheradi. <u>The Colors of the United States Army, 1789-1912</u>. (New York, 1912).

2925. Davis, Rollin V., Jr. <u>U.S. Sword Bayonets, 1847-1865; A Compilation of Sword Bayonets Issued to the Military Services of the United States Prior to and During the Civil War</u>. (Pittsburgh, Pennsylvania, 1963).

2926. Dennison, George M. "Martial Law: The Development of a Theory of Emergency Powers, 1776-1861." <u>AJLH</u> 18 (June 1974), 52-79.

2927. Devol, Carroll A. "The Army in the San Francisco Disaster." <u>JUSIA</u> 4 (July 1907), 59-87.

2928. DeWeerd, H.A. "The Federalization of Our (U.S.) Army." <u>MA</u> 6 (Fall 1942), 143-52.

2929. Dibble, Ernest F. "Slave Rentals to the Military: Pensacola and the Gulf Coast." <u>CWH</u> 23 (June 1977), 101-13.

2930. *Dollen, Charles and the Library Staff of the University of San Diego. <u>Bibliography of the United States Marine Corps</u>. (New York, 1963).

2931. Dolph, Edward A. <u>"Sound Off!" Soldier Songs from the Revolution to World War II</u>. (New York, 1942).

2932. *Donnelly, Ralph W. <u>An Annotated Bibliography of United States Marine Corps Artillery</u>. (Washington, D.C., 1970).

2933. Donnelly, Ralph W. "Formosa Spy." <u>MCG</u> 52 (November 1968), 91- 4.

2934. Donovan, James A. <u>The United States Marine Corps</u>. (New York, 1967).

2935. *Dornbusch, Charles E., compl. <u>Histories of American Army Units. World Wars I and II and Korean Conflict, with Some Earlier Histories</u>. (Washington, D.C., 1956).

2936. *Dornbusch, Charles E., compl. <u>Histories, Personal Narratives, United States Army; A Checklist</u>. (Cornwallville, New York, 1967).

2937. Downey, Fairfax D. <u>The Buffalo Soldiers in the Indian Wars</u>. (New York, 1969).

2938. Downey, Fairfax D. <u>Fife, Drum and Bugle</u>. (Fort Collins, Colorado, 1971).

2939. Downey, Fairfax D. _Indian-Fighting Army_. (New York, 1944).

2940. Downey, Fairfax D. _Indian Wars of the U.S. Army, 1776-1865_. (Garden City, New York, 1963).

2941. Downey, Fairfax D. and Jacques N. Jacobson, Jr. _The Red/Bluecoats; The Indian Scouts, U.S. Army_. (Fort Collins, Colorado, 1973).

2942. Downey, Fairfax D. _The Sound of Guns; The Story of American Artillery from the Ancient and Honorable Company to the Atom Cannon and Guided Missle_. (New York, 1955).

2943. Drake-Wilkes, L.P. "United States Army: History and Traditions of the Corps of Engineers." _CAJ_ 6 (January 1953), 57-73.

2944. Driscoll, John A. _The Eagle, Globe and Anchor 1868-1969_. (Washington, D.C., 1971).

2945. Dudley, Edgar S. "Was 'Secession' Taught at West Point?" _CIMM_ 78 (August 1909), 629-35.

2946. DuMont, John S. _Custer Battle Guns_. (Fort Collins, Colorado, 1974).

2947. Dupuy, Richard Ernest. _The Compact History of the United States Army_. (New York, 1956).

2948. Dupuy, Richard Ernest. _Men of West Point; The First 150 Years of the United States Military Academy_. (New York, 1951).

2949. Dupuy, Richard Ernest. _The National Guard; A Compact History_. (New York, 1971).

2950. "Early Systems of Artillery." Ordnance Note No. 25, May 4, 1874, in United States, Ordnance Department, _Ordnance Notes._ (12 vols., Washington, D.C., 1873-84).

2951. Eller, Ernest M. "Launching U.S. Power from the Sea; The Saga of U.S. Combined Operations Since 1775." _AID_ 16 (July 1961), 44-55.

2952. Ellis, Richard N. _General Pope and U.S. Indian Policy_. (Albuquerque, New Mexico, 1970).

2953. Ellis, Richard N. "The Humanitarian Generals." _WHQ_ 3 (April 1972), 169-78.

2954. Ellis, Richard N. "The Humanitarian Soldiers." _JAZH_ 10 (Summer 1969), 55-62.

2955. Ellis, Richard N. "Volunteer Soldiers in the West, 1865." _MA_ 34 (April 1970), 53-6.

2956. Engle, Eloise. _Medic: America's Medical Soldiers, Sailors and Airmen in Peace and War_. (New York, 1967).

2957. Engleman, Rose C. and Robert J.T. Joy. 200 Years of Military Medicine. (Fort Detrick, 1975).

2958. Essin, Emmett M., III. "The Cavalry and the Horse." Ph.D. Dissertation, Texas Christian University, 1968.

2959. Essin, Emmett M., III. "Mules, Packs, and Packtrains." SWHQ 74 (July 1970), 52-63.

2960. Evans, Edward J. "Time on Target--177 Years (Artillery)." MCG 38 (February 1954), 36- 9.

2961. Ezell, Edward C. "The Development of Artillery for the United States Land Service Before 1861: With Emphasis on the Rodman Gun." M.A. Thesis, University of Delaware, 1963.

2962. Fahey, James C. U.S. Army Aircraft 1908-1946. (New York, 1946).

2963. Falk, Stanley L. "Artillery for the Land Service: The Development of a System." MA 28 (Winter 1964), 97-110.

2964. Faulk, Odie B. The U.S. Camel Corps; An Army Experiment. (New York, 1971).

2965. Fay, George E., ed. Military Engagements between United States Troops and Plains Indians; Documentary Inquiry by the U.S. Congress. (5 vols., Greeley, Colorado, 1972- 3).

2966. Feaver, Eric. "Indian Soldiers, 1891-95: An Experiment on the Closing Frontier." PROL 7 (Summer 1975), 108-18.

2967. Ferguson, S.W. "West Point Before the War." METM 28 (April 1908), 56-66.

2968. Fischer, Lawrence J. "Horse Soldiers in the Arctic: The Garlington Expedition of 1883." ANEP 36 (April 1976), 108-24.

2969. Fisher, Vincent J. "Mr. Calhoun's Army." MR 37 (September 1957), 52- 8.

2970. Fite, Gilbert C. "The United States Army and Relief to Pioneer Settlers, 1874-1875." JWEST 6 (January 1967), 99-107.

2971. Fleming, Thomas J. West Point; The Men and Times of the United States Military Academy. (New York, 1969).

2972. Fletcher, Henry C. Report on the Military Academy at West Point, U.S. (n.p., 187-).

2973. Fletcher, Marvin E. "The Black Bicycle Corps." AZW 16 (Autumn 1974), 219-32.

2974. Fletcher, Marvin E. The Black Soldier and Officer in the United States Army, 1891-1917. (Columbia, Missouri, 1974).

2975. Fletcher, Marvin E. "The Negro Volunteer in Reconstruction 1865-1866." MA 32 (December 1968), 124-31.

2976. Flick, Hugh M. "United States Campaign Medals." MA 6 (Winter 1942), 254- 6.

2977. Foner, Jack D. Blacks and the Military in American History: A New Perspective. (New York, 1974).

2978. Foner, Jack D. The United States Soldier Between Two Wars: Army Life and Reforms, 1865-1898. (New York, 1970).

2979. Forbes, Archibald. "The United States Army." NAR 135 (August 1882), 127-45.

2980. Forman, Sidney, ed. Cadet Life Before the Mexican War. Episodes in Cadet Life Drawn from the Manuscript Collections in the Library of the United States Military Academy Excerpted from Cadet Letters. (West Point, New York, 1945).

2981. Forman, Sidney. West Point; A History of the United States Military Academy. (New York, 1950).

2982. Forsyth, George A. The Story of the Soldier. (New York, 1900).

2983. Fowler, Arlen L. The Black Infantry in the West, 1869-1891. (Westport, Connecticut, 1971).

2984. Fowler, Harlan D. Camels to California; A Chapter in Western Transportation. (Stanford, California, 1950).

2985. *Frank, Emma L. The Chaplaincy in the Armed Services, A Preliminary Bibliography. (Oberlin, Ohio, 1945).

2986. Fratcher, William F. "History of the Judge Advocate General's Corp, United States Army." MLR 4 (March 1959), 89-122.

2987. Fratcher, William F. "Notes on the History of the Judge Advocate General's Department, 1775-1941." JAJ 1 (June 1944), 5-15.

2988. Frazer, Robert W. "Army Agriculture in New Mexico, 1852-53." NMHR 50 (October 1975), 313-34.

2989. Frost, John. The Book of the Army: Comprising a General Military History of the United States, from the Period of the Revolution to the Present Time. (Hartford, Connecticut, 1853).

2990. Fry, James B. Army Sacrifices: or, Briefs From Official Pigeon-Holes. (New York, 1879).

2991. Fry, James B. The Different Editions of Army Regulations.... (New York, 1876).

2992. Fry, James B. The History and Legal Effect of Brevets in the Armies of Great Britain and the United States From Their Origin in 1692 to the Present Time. (New York, 1877).

2993. Fugate, Robert T. "Chow Down." LENCK 37 (July 1954), 24-31.

2994. Fuller, Claud E. The Breech-loader in the Service, the Developments of One Hundred and One Years, 1816 to 1917; A Description of the Breech-loaders and Magazine Arms Tested by the Ordnance Boards; the Development of the Interchangeable System of Manufacture. (Topeka, Kansas, 1933).

2995. Fuller, Claud E., compl. Springfield Muzzle-loading Shoulder Arms; A Description of the Flint Lock Muskets, Musketoons and Carbines and the Muskets, Musketoons, Rifles, Carbines and Special Models from 1795 to 1865, with Ordnance Office Reports, Tables and Correspondence and a Sketch of Springfield Armory. (New York, 1930).

2996. Gabriel, Ralph H. "American Experience with Military Government." AHR 49 (July 1944), 630-43.

2997. Gamble, Richard D. "Army Chaplains at Frontier Posts, 1830-1860." HMPEC 27 (December 1958), 286-306.

2998. Gamble, Richard D. "Garrison Life at Frontier Military Posts, 1830-1860." Ph.D. Dissertation, University of Oklahoma, 1956.

2999. Ganoe, William A. The History of the United States Army. (Revised Edition, Ashton, Maryland, 1964).

3000. Generous, William T., Jr. Swords and Scales: The Development of the Uniform Code of Military Justice. (Port Washington, New York, 1973).

3001. Germain, Aidan H. Catholic Military and Naval Chaplains, 1776-1917. (Washington, D.C., 1929).

3002. Glassford, William A. Historical Sketch of the Signal Corps, United States Army. (New York, 1891).

3004. Glenn, Garrard. The Army and the Law. (New York, 1918).

3005. Glines, Carroll V., Jr. The Compact History of the United States Air Force. (New York, 1964).

3006. Gluckman, Arcadi, United States Muskets, Rifles and Carbines. (Buffalo, New York, 1948).

3007. Gluckman, Arcadi. United States Martial Pistols and Revolvers. (Buffalo, New York, 1944).

3008. Godson, William F.H. The History of West Point, 1852-1902. (Philadelphia, Pennsylvania, 1934).

3009. *Goetzman, William H. Army Exploration in the American West, 1803-1863. (New Haven, Connecticut, 1959).

3010. *Goldberg, Alfred, ed. A History of the United States Air Force, 1907-1957. (Princeton, New Jersey, 1957).

3011. Goldman, Henry H. "A Survey of Federal Escorts of the Santa Fe Trade, 1829-1843." JWEST 5 (October 1966), 504-16.

3012. Goode, Paul R. The United States Soldiers' Home: A History of Its First Hundred Years. (Washington, D.C., 1957).

3013. *Gordon, Martin K. "American Military Studies." ASTI 15 (Fall 1976), 3-16.

3014. Gould, Benjamin A. Investigation in the Military and Anthropological Statistics of American Soldiers. (New York, 1869).

3015. Graham, John R. A Constitutional History of the Military Draft. (Minneapolis, Minnesota, 1971).

3016. Graham, Stanley S. "Duty, Life and Law in the Old Army, 1865-1900." MHT&SW 12, No. 4 (1974), 273-81.

3017. Graham, Stanley S. "Life of the Enlisted Soldier on the Western Frontier, 1815-1845." Ph.D. Dissertation, North Texas State University, 1972.

3018. Graham, Stanley S. "Routine at Western Cavalry Posts, 1833-1861." JWEST15 (July 1976), 49-59.

3019. Grange, Roger T. "Treating the Wounded at Fort Robinson." NEBH 45 (September 1964), 273-94.

3020. Gray, Carl R. Railroading in Eighteen Countries; The Story of American Railroad Men Serving in the Military Railway Service, 1862-1953. (New York, 1955).

3021. Greely, Adolphus W. Three Years Arctic Service; An Account of the Lady Franklin Boy Expedition of 1881-84.... (New York, 1886).

3022. Greene, Duane M. Ladies and Officers of the United States Army; or, American Aristocracy, A Sketch of the Social Life and Character of the Army. (Chicago, 1880).

3023. Greene, Fred. "The Military View of American National Policy, 1904-1940." AHR 66 (January 1961), 354-77.

3024. Greene, Robert E. Black Defenders of America, 1775-1973. (Chicago, Illinois, 1974).

3025. Gardner, Charles K. A Dictionary of...the Army of the United States... Volunteers and Militia of the States... and of the Navy and Marine Corps. (Second Edition, New York, 1860).

3026. Grivas, Theodore. Military Governments in California, 1846-1850; With a Chapter on Their Prior Use in Louisiana, Florida, and New Mexico. (Glendale, California, 1963).

3027. *A Guide to the Sources of United States Military History. Edited by Robin Higham. (Hamden, Connecticut, 1975).

3028. Gurney, Gene. A Pictorial History of the United States Army in War and Peace, from Colonial Times to Vietnam. (New York, 1966).

3029. Hacker, Barton C. "The United States Army as a National Police Force: The Federal Policing of Labor Disputes, 1877-1898." MA 33 (April 1969), 255-64.

3030. Hagerman, Edward R. "The Professionalization of George B. McClellan and Early Field Command: An Institutional Perspective." CWH 21 (June 1975), 113-35.

3031. Hale, Henry. "The Soldier, the Advance Guard of Civilization," in Proceedings of the Mississippi Valley Historical Association for the Year 1913-14. Volume 7, 93- 8.

3032. Hall, Lt. Col. Robert H. "Early Discipline at the United States Military Academy." JMSI 2, No. 8 (1882), 448-74.

3033. Hamersly, Thomas H.S. Complete Regular Army Register of the United States: For One-Hundred Years (1779 to 1879). (Washington, D.C., 1880).

3034. Hamersly, Thomas H.S. General Register of the United States Navy and Marine Corps, Arranged in Alphabetical Order, for One-Hundred Years (1782 to 1882). (Washington, D.C., 1882).

3035. Hammer, Kenneth M. The Springfield Carbine on the Western Frontier. (Third Edition, Bellevue, Nebraska, 1970).

3036. Hammond, Paul Y. Organizing for Defense: The American Military Establishment in the Twentieth Century. (Princeton, New Jersey, 1961).

3037. Hampton, H. Duane. How the U.S. Cavalry Saved Our National Parks. (Bloomington, Indiana, 1971).

3038. Hampton, H. Duane. "The United States Army and the National Parks." MMWH 22 (July 1972), 64-79.

3039. Hancock, Harrie I. Life at West Point, the Making of the American Army Officer; His Studies, Discipline, and Amusements. (New York, 1902).

3040. Harris, Moses. "The Old Army," in Military Order of the Loyal Legion of the United States, Wisconsin Commandery, War Papers. Volume 2 (Milwaukee, Wisconsin, 1891-1900--), 331-44.

3041. Hawes, Joseph H.M. "The Signal Corps and the Weather Bureau." MA 30 (Summer 1966), 68-76.

3042. Hardin, Albert N. The American Bayonet, 1776-1964. (Philadelphia, Pennsylvania, 1964).

3043. Hardin, Albert N., Jr. and Robert W. Hedden. Light but Efficient; A Study of the M1880 Hunting and M1890 Intrenching Knives and Scabbards. (Pennsauken, New Jersey, 1973).

3044. Haydon, Frederick S. "First Attempts at Military Aviation in the United States." MA 2 (Fall 1938), 131- 8.

3045. Hayes, Norman B. "Major Photographers and the Development of Still Photography in Major American Wars." Ph.D. Dissertation, Syracuse University, 1966.

3046. Hazlett, James C. "The Napoleon Gun: Its Origin and Introduction into American Service." MC&H 15 (Spring 1963), 1-5.

3047. Heinl, Robert D. Soldiers of the Sea: The U.S. Marine Corps, 1775-1962. (Annapolis, Maryland, 1962).

3048. Heitman, Francis B. Historical Register and Dictionary of the United States Army, from its Organization, September 29, 1789, to March 2, 1903. (2 vols., Washington, D.C., 1903).

3049. Henry, Guy V. Military Record of Civilian Appointments in the United States Army. (2 vols., New York, 1873).

3050. Herbert, Craig S. "Gasbag Preferred." AEH 15 (Summer 1958), 39-51.

3051. Herr, John K. and Edward S. Wallace. The Story of the U.S. Cavalry, 1775-1942. (Boston, Massachusetts, 1953).

3052. Hewes, James E., Jr. From Root to McNamara: Army Organization and Administration, 1900-1963. (Washington, D.C., 1975).

3053. Hewes, James E., Jr. "The United States Army General Staff, 1900-1917." (With commentary by Edward M. Coffman). MA 38 (April 1974), 67-72.

3054. Hicks, James E. Notes on U.S. Ordnance. (2 vols., Mount Vernon, New York, 1940).

3055. Hill, Forest G. Roads, Rails and Waterways; The Army Engineers and Early Transportation. (Norman, Oklahoma, 1957).

3056. Hill, Jim Dan. The Minute Man in Peace and War; A History of the National Guard. (Harrisburg, Pennsylvania, 1964).

3057.*Hilliard, Jack B. and Harold A. Bivins, compls. An Annotated Reading List of United States Marine Corps History. (Revised Edition, Washington, D.C., 1971).

3058. Hints Bearing on the United States Army, with an Aim at the Adoption, Availability, Efficiency and Economy There of. (By August V. Kautz?) (Philadelphia, Pennsylvania, 1858).

3059. Hirsh, Joseph. "Notes on U.S. Army Medical Service Insignia (1818-1959)."
MMED 124 (July 1959), 491-6.

3060. Hitt, Parker. "A Brief History of the School of Musketry." MR 41 (July 1961),
86-90.

3061. Holabird, Samuel B. "Army Clothing." JMSI 2, No. 8 (1882), 355-87,
483-4.

3062. Holabird, Samuel B. "Army Wagon Transportation," Ordnance Note No. 189,
April 15, 1882, in United States, Ordnance Department, Ordnance Notes.
(12 vols., Washington, D.C., 1873-84).

3063. Holt, William S. The Office of the Chief of Engineers of the Army;
Its Non-Military History, Activities, and Organization. (Baltimore,
Maryland, 1923).

3064. Holt, William S. "The United States and the Defense of the Western
Hemisphere, 1815-1940." PHR 10 (March 1941), 29-38.

3065. Honeywell, Roy J. Chaplains of the United States Army. (Washington,
D.C., 1958).

3066. Hopkins, Richard E. Military Sharps; Rifles and Carbines. (Campbell,
California, 1967).

3067. Howell, Edgar M. and Donald E. Kloster. United States Army Headgear
to 1854. (Washington, D.C., 1969).

3068. Huber, Edward F. "Crossed Sword and Pen--and Other Trade Marks of
the Judge Advocate." JAJ 2 (March 1945), 43- 5.

3069. Huidekoper, Frederic L. The Military Unpreparedness of the United
States; A History of American Land Forces from Colonial Times Until
June 1, 1915. (New York, 1915).

3070. Hume, Edgar E. Ornithologists of the United States Army Medical Corps,
Thirty-six Biographies. (Baltimore, Maryland, 1942).

3071. Hume, Edgar E. Victories of Army Medicine: Scientific Accomplishments
of the Medical Department of the United States Army. (Philadelphia,
Pennsylvania, 1943).

3072. Humphreys, Edward R. Education of Officers: Preparatory and Professional. (Boston, Massachusetts, 1862).

3073. Hunt, Elvid. History of Fort Leavenworth, 1827-1927. (Ft. Leavenworth,
Kansas, 1926).

3074. Huntington, Roy T. Hall's Breechloaders; John H. Hall's Invention and
Development of a Breechloading Rifle with Precision-Made Interchangeable
Parts and Its Introduction Into the United States Service. Edited by
Nancy Bagby. (York, Pennsylvania, 1972).

3075. *Huston, James A. The Sinews of War: Army Logistics, 1775-1953. (Washington, D.C., 1966).

3076. Hutchins, James S. "The Army Campaign Hat of 1872." MC&H 14 (Fall 1964), 65-73.

3077. Hutchins, James S. Boots and Saddles at the Little Big Horn; Weapons, Dress, Equipment, Horses, and Flags of General Custer's Seventh U.S. Cavalry in 1876. (Fort Collins, Colorado, 1976).

3078. Hutchins, James S. "The Cavalry Campaign Outfit at the Little Big Horn." MC&H 7 (Winter 1956), 91-101.

3079. Hutchins, James S. "Mounted Riflemen: The Real Role of Cavalry in the Indian Wars," in Conference on the History of Western America, 1st, Santa Fe, New Mexico, 1961, Probing the American West; Papers from the Santa Fe Conference. Edited by Kenneth Ross Toole. (Santa Fe, California, 1962), 79-85.

3080. Hyman, Harold M. "Johnson, Stanton, and Grant: A Reconsideration of the Army's Role in the Events Leading to Impeachment." AHR 66 (October 1960), 85-100.

3081. "Infantry Equipments," Ordnance Note No. 67, June 1, 1877, in United States, Ordnance Department, Ordnance Notes. (12 vols., Washington, D.C., 1873-84).

3082. "The Infantry of the Regular Army." MA 11 (Summer 1947), 103-115.

3083. Ingersoll, Lurton D. A History of the War Department of the United States. (Washington, D.C., 1879).

3084. Irvine, Dallas. "The Archive Office of the War Department: Repository of Captured Confederate Archives, 1865-1881." MA 10 (Spring 1946), 93-111.

3085. Irvine, Dallas. "The Genesis of the Official Records." MVHR 24 (September 1937), 221- 9.

3086. Itschner, Emerson C. The Army Engineers' Contribution to American Defence and Advancement. (New York, 1959).

3087. Jackson, William Turrentine. Wagon Roads West; A Study of Federal Road Survey and Construction in the Trans-Mississippi West, 1846-1869. (Berkeley, California, 1952).

3088. Jacobs, Bruce. Heroes of the Army; The Medal of Honor and its Winners. (New York, 1956).

3089. James, Joseph B. "Life at West Point One Hundred Years Ago." MVHR 31 (June 1944), 21-40.

3090. Jenkins, Walworth. Q.M.D.; or, Book of Reference for Quartermasters. (Louisville, Kentucky, 1865).

3091. Johnson, Charles, Jr. "Black Soldiers in the National Guard, 1877-1949." Ph.D. Dissertation, Howard University, 1976.

3092. Johnson, David F. Uniform Buttons: American Armed Forces, 1784-1948. (2 vols., Watkins Glen, New York, 1948).

3093. Johnson, Edward C. Marine Corps Aviation: The Early Years, 1912-1940. Edited by Graham A. Cosmas. (Washington, D.C., 1977).

3094. Johnson, Leslie L. Notes on U.S. Cavalry 1865-1890. (Little Rock, Arkansas, 1960).

3095. *Kaplan, Stephen S. "The Use of Military Force Abroad by the United States Since 1798; An Annotated Bibliography of Unclassified Lists of Incidents Prepared by the U.S. Government." JCR 19 (December 1975), 708-12.

3096. Karsten, Peter. "The American Democratic Soldier; Triumph or Disaster?" MA 30 (Spring 1966), 34-40.

3097. Karsten, Peter. Soldiers and Society; The Effects of Military Service and War on American Life. (Westport, Connecticut, 1978).

3098. Kautz, August V. Customs of Service for Non-Commissioned Officers and Soldiers as Derived from Law and Regulations and Practiced in the Army of the United States. (Philadelphia, Pennsylvania, 1864).

3099. *Kemble, Charles Robert. The Image of the Army Officer in America. (Westport, Connecticut, 1973).

3100. Kerksis, Sydney C. Plates and Buckles of the American Military 1795-1874. (Kenesaw, Georgia, 1974).

3101. Kerrigan, Evans E. American Badges and Insignia. (New York, 1967).

3102. Kerrigan, Evans E. American War Medals and Decorations. (New York, 1964).

3103. Kilbourne, Henry S. "The Physical Proportions of the American Soldier." JMSI 22 (January 1898), 50-61.

3104. Kloster, Donald E. "Uniforms of the Army Prior and Subsequent to 1872." MC&H 14 (Winter 1962), 103-12; 15 (Spring 1963), 6-14.

3105. Knight, Oliver. Life and Manners in the Frontier Army. (Norman, Oklahoma, 1978).

3106. Kofmehl, William Earl, Jr. "Non-Military Education and the United States Army: A History." Ph.D. Dissertation, University of Pittsburgh, 1973.

3107. Kredel, Fritz and Frederick P. Todd. Soldiers of the American Army, 1775-1941. (Revised Edition, Chicago, Illinois, 1954).

3108. Kreidberg, Marvin A. and Merton G. Henry. History of Military Mobilization in the United States Army 1775-1945. (Washington, D.C., 1955).

3109. Kurtz, Henry I. "A Soldier's Life." AHI 7 (August 1972), 24-35.

3110. Laffin, John. Americans in Battle. (New York, 1973).

3111. LaFollette, Robert M., ed. Army and Navy. (Volume 9 in The Making of America). (Philadelphia, Pennsylvania, 1905).

3112. Laframboise, Leon. History of the Artillery, Cavalry, and Infantry Branch of Service Insignia. (Steelville, Missouri, 1976).

3113. Lammons, Frank B. "Operation Camel: An Experiment in Animal Transportation in Texas, 1857-1860." SWHQ 61 (July 1957), 20-50.

3114. Langellier, John Phillip. Parade Ground Soldiers; Military Uniforms and Headdress, 1837-1910, in the Collections of the State Historical Society of Wisconsin. (Madison, Wisconsin, 1978).

3115. Langellier, John Phillip. They Continually Wear the Blue; U.S. Army Enlisted Dress Uniforms 1865-1902. (San Francisco, California, 1974).

3116. Langellier, John Phillip. Uniforms of the Seacoast Soldiers, 1851-1902. (San Rafael, California, 1978).

3117. Laurent, Francis W. Organization for Military Defense of the United States, 1789-1959. (Madison, Wisconsin, 1960).

3118. Lawton, Eba A., ed. History of the "Soldiers' Home," Washington, D.C. (New York, 1914).

3119. Lenney, John J. Caste System in the American Army: A Study of the Corps of Engineers and the West Point System. (New York, 1949).

3120. Leckie, William H. The Buffalo Soldiers; A Narrative of the Negro Cavalry in the West. (Norman, Oklahoma, 1967).

3121. Leckie, William H. The Military Conquest of the Southwest Plains. (Norman, Oklahoma, 1963).

3122. *Leonard, Thomas C. Above the Battle; War-Making in America from Appomattox to Versailles. (New York, 1978).

3123. Leonard, Thomas C. "America's Armed Vision: Soldiers, Weapons, and Violence, 1870-1920." Ph.D. Dissertation, University of California-- Berkeley, 1973.

3124. Leonard, Thomas C. "Red, White and the Army Blue: Empathy and Anger in the American West." AMQT 26 (May 1974), 176-90.

3125. Lewis, Berkeley R. Small Arms and Ammunition in the United States Service, 1776-1865. (Washington, D.C., 1956).

3126. Lewis, George G. and John Mewha. History of Prisoner of War Utilization by the United States Army 1776-1945. (Washington, D.C., 1955).

3127. Lewis, Waverly P. U.S. Military Headgear, 1770-1880. (Devon, Connecticut, 1960).

3128. Lieber, Guido Norman. Remarks on the Army Regulations. (Washington, D.C., 1977).

3129. Logan, John A. The Volunteer Soldier of America. (Chicago, Illinois, 1887).

3130. London, Lena. "The Militia Fine, 1830-1860." MA 15 (Fall 1951), 136- 8.

3131. Long, Capt. Oscar F. Changes in the Uniforms of the Army, 1774-1895. (Washington, D.C., 1896).

3132. Lyon, Clarence C. Experiences of A Recruit in the U.S. Army. (Washington, D.C., 1916).

3133. *Lyons, Gene M. andJohn W. Masland. Education and Military Leadership; A Study of the R.O.T.C. (Princeton, New Jersey, 1959).

3134. Lyons, Gene M. and John W. Masland. "The Origins of the R.O.T.C." MA 23 (Spring 1959), 1-12.

3135. McBarron, H. Charles. "U.S. Marine Corps, 1859-1875." MC&H 1 (December 1949), 1-2.

3136. McBarron, H. Charles. "U.S. Marine Corps Field Service, 1859-1868." MC&H 5 (June 1953), 47-8.

3137. McClellan, Edwin N. Uniforms of the American Marines, 1775 to 1932. (Washington, D.C., 1932).

3138. McClellan, Edwin N. The United States Marine Corps Band. (n.p., 1925).

3139. McClendon, R. Earl. The Question of Autonomy for the United States Air Arm, 1907-1945. (2 vols., Maxwell Air Force Base, Alabama, 1950).

3140. McClernand, Edward J. Historical Notes on the Drill Regulations of the U.S. Cavalry. (n.p., n.d.).

3141. McConnell, Roland C. Negro Troops of Antebellum Louisiana; A History of the Battalion of Free Men of Color. (Baton Rouge, Louisiana, 1968).

3142. McKinley, Silas B. Democracy and Military Power. (New York, 1934).

3143. McLaughlin, Patrick D. "Soldiers and Symbols: The Origins of the Army Shoulder Patch." PROL 3 (Fall 1971), 79-87.

3144. McWhiney, Grady. "Jefferson Davis and the Art of War." CWH 21 (June 1975), 101-12.

3146. Maass, Arthur A. Muddy Waters: The Army's Engineers and the Nation's Rivers. (Cambridge, Massachusetts, 1951).

3147. Mahon, Dennis H. Advanced Guard, Out-Post, and Detachment Service of Troops. (New York, 1863).

3148. Mahon, John K. "A Board of Officers Considers the Conditions of the Militia in 1826." MA 15 (Summer 1951), 85-94.

3149. Mahon, John K. and Romana Danyash. Infantry. Part 1. (Revised and Enlarged Edition, Washington, D.C., 1972).

3150. Marshall, Max L., ed. The Story of the U.S. Army Signal Corps. (New York, 1965).

3151. "Making Muskets at Springfield (1852)." ARF 107 (August 1959), 40- 4.

3152. Mansfield, Edward D. The Utility and Services of the United States Military Academy. (New York, 1847).

3153. "Manufacturing at the National Armory." Ordnance Note No. 97, February 19, 1879, in United States, Ordnance Department, Ordnance Notes. (12 vols., Washington, D.C., 1973-84).

3154. Marsh, George P. The Camel; His Organization, Habits, and Uses, Considered with Reference to his Introduction Into the United States. (Boston, Massachusetts, 1856).

3155. *Masland, John W. and Laurence I. Radway. Soldiers and Scholars: Military Education and National Policy. (Princeton, New Jersey, 1957).

3156. Mason, Joyce E. "The Use of Indian Scouts in the Apache Wars, 1870-1886." Ph.D. Dissertation, Indiana University, 1970.

3157. *Matloff, Maurice, ed. American Military History. (Washington, D.C., 1969).

3158. Matthews, William and Dixon Wecter. Our Soldiers Speak, 1775-1918. (Boston, Massachusetts, 1943).

3159. Mattison, Ray H. The Army Post on the Northern Plains, 1865-1885. (Gering, Nebraska, 1962).

3160. Mayhew, Capt. Walter L. "The Regimental System in the United States Army: Its evolution and Future." M.M.S. Thesis, Command and General Staff College, Fort Leavenworth, Kansas, 1976.

3161. Meredith, Roy. The American Wars: 1775-1953, A Pictorial History from Quebec to Korea. (New York, 1955).

3162. Merillat, Louis A. and Delwin M. Campbell. Veterinary Military History of the United States; With a Brief Record of the Development of Veterinary Education, Practice, Organization and Legislation. (2 vols., Kansa City, Missouri, 1935).

3163. Merlin, John R. "Critique of the Army Ration, Past and Present." MSUR 50 (January 1922), 38-60; (February 1922), 163-87.

3164. Merrill, James M. "The Greely Relief Expedition, 1884." USNIP 77 (September 1951), 969-976.

3165. Merrill, James M. Spurs to Glory; The Story of the United States Cavalry. (Chicago, Illinois, 1966).

3166. Metcalf, Clyde H. A History of the United States Marine Corps. (New York, 1939).

3167. Metcalfe, Henry. Ordnance and Gunnery, U.S.M.A. (West Point, New York, 1889).

3168. Metcalfe, Henry and C.W. Whipple. The Ordnance Department, U.S. Army, at the International Exhibition, 1876. (Washington, D.C., 1884).

3169. Metts, Albert C. "U.S. Army Strength, 1789-1900." MC&H 24 (Summer 1972), 48-9.

3170. Miewald, Robert D. "The Army Post Schools: A Report from the Bureaucratic Wars." MA 39 (February 1975), 8-11.

3171. Miller, Duane E. "Soldiers of the Renaissance; The U.S. Army in the 1880's." MR 52 (June 1972), 27-39.

3172. *Military History Symposium, 7th, U.S. Air Force Academy, 1976, The American Military on the Frontier: The Proceedings of the 7th Military History Symposium. Edited by James P. Tate. (Washington, D.C., 1978).

3173. Miller, William M. A Chronology of the United States Marine Corps. (Washington, D.C., 1965--).

3174. Millett, Allan R. Military Professionalism and Officership in America. (Columbus, Ohio, 1977).

3175. Millis, Walter, ed. American Military Thought. (Indianapolis, Indiana, 1966).

3176. Millis, Walter. Arms and Men; A Study of American Military History. (New York, 1956).

3177. Montrose, Lynn. The United States Marines: A Pictorial History. (New York, 1959).

3178. Mooney, Chase L. and Martha E. Layman. Organization of Military Aeronautics, 1907-1935 (Congressional and War Department Action). (Washington, D.C., 1944).

3179. *Moran, John B., compl. Creating a Legend. Descriptive Catalog of Writing About the U.S. Marine Corps. (Chicago, Illinois, 1973).

3180. Morgan, Arthur E. Dams and Other Disasters; A Century of the Army Corps of Engineers in Civil Works. (Boston, Massachusetts, 1971).

3181. Morgan, Joseph M. Military Medals and Insignia of the United States. (Glendale, California, 1941).

3182. Morrison, James L., Jr. "Educating the Civil War Generals: West Point, 1833-1861." MA 38 (October 1974), 108-111.

3183. Morton, Louis. "Army and Marines on the China Station: A Study in Military and Political Rivalry." PHR 29 (February 1960), 51-73.

3184. Morton, Louis. "The Origins of American Military Policy." MA 23 (Summer 1958), 75-82.

3185. Moskin, J. Robert. The United States Marine Corps Story. (New York, 1977).

3186. Murray, Robert A. The Army on Powder River. (Bellevue, Nebraska, 1969).

3187. Nalty, Bernard C. A Brief History of U.S. Marine Corps Officer Procurement. (Washington, D.C., 1962).

3188. Nalty, Bernard C. Certain Aspects of Manpower Utilization in the Marine Corps. (Washington, D.C., 1959).

3189. Nalty, Bernard C. Inspection in the U.S. Marine Corps, 1773-1957; Historical Background. (Washington, D.C., 1960).

3190. Nastri, A.P. "USMC Artillery, 1900-1941." FARJ 45 (July-August 1977), 32-6.

3191. National Museum of History and Technology, United States Army Headgear, 1855-1902. By Edgar M. Howell. (Washington, D.C., 1975).

3192. Neff, Jacob K. and Thomas H. Burrowes. The Army and Navy of America... (Revised Edition, Lancaster, Pennsylvania, 1866).

3193. Nelson, Harold L. "Military Roads for War and Peace, 1791-1836." MA 19 (Spring 1955), 1-14.

3194. Nelson, Otto L., Jr. National Security and the General Staff. (Washington, D.C., 1946).

3195. Nelson, William H. and Frank E. Vandiver. Fields of Glory: An Illustrated Narrative of American Land Warfare. (New York, 1960).

3196. *Nenninger, Timothy K. The Leavenworth Schools and the Old Army: Education, Professionalism, and the Officer Corps of the United States Army, 1881-1918. (Westport, Connecticut, 1978).

3197. *Neufeld, Jacob, compl. United States Air Force History; A Guide to Monographic Literature 1943-1974. (Washington, D.C., 1977).

3198. *Ney, Virgil. Evolution of the United States Army Field Manual: Valley Forge to Vietnam. (Fort Belvoir, Virginia, 1966).

3199. Ney, Virgil. The United States Army in a Nonviolent Role; An Historical Overview. (Fort Belvoir, Virginia, 1967).

3200. Nichols, Roger L. "The Army and the Indians 1800-1830--A Reappraisal: The Missouri Valley Example." PHR 41 (May 1972), 151-68.

3201. Nichols, Roger L. "Army Contributions to River Transportation, 1818-1825." MA 33 (April 1969), 242- 9.

3202. Nichols, Roger L. "Soldiers as Farmers: Army Agriculture in the Missouri Valley, 1818-1827." NEBH 52 (Fall 1971), 239-54.

3203. Norton, Herman A. Struggling for Recognition; The United States Army Chaplaincy 1791-1865. (Washington, D.C., 1977).

3204. Offutt, Milton. The Protection of Citizens Abroad by the Armed Forces of the United States. (Baltimore, Maryland, 1928).

3205. Olejar, Paul D. "Rockets in Early American Wars." MA 10 (Winter 1946), 16-34.

3206. Oliva, Leo E. "The Army and the Indian." MA 36 (October 1974), 117- 9.

3207. Oliva, Leo E. Soldiers on the Santa Fe Trail. (Norman, Oklahoma, 1967).

3208. Olsen, Stanley J. "The Development of the U.S. Army Saddle." MC&H 7 (Spring 1955), 1-7.

3209. Olsen, Stanley J. "Variations in the M-1858 McClellan Saddle." MC&H 8 (Summer 1956), 48-50.

3210. Otis, George A. A Report to the Surgeon General on the Transport of Sick and Wounded by Pack Animals. (Washington, D.C., 1877).

3211. Palliser, Edward. United States Artillery. (London, 1879).

3212. Palmer, Frederick. The Ways of the Service. (New York, 1901).

3213. Palmer, John McAuley. America in Arms: The Experience of the United States with Military Organization. (New Haven, Connecticut, 1941).

3214. Pappas, George S. Prudens Futuri; The U.S. Army War College, 1901-1967. (Carlisle Barracks, Pennsylvania, 1967).

3215. *Pappas, George S., compl. U.S. Army Unit Histories (Bibliography). (Carlisle Barracks, Pennsylvania, 1971).

3216. Park, Roswell. A Sketch of the History and Topography of West Point and the U.S. Military Academy. (Philadelphia, Pennsylvania, 1840).

3217. Parker, William D. A Concise History of the United States Marine Corps 1775-1969. (Washington, D.C., 1970).

3218. Parkinson, Russell J. "United States Signal Corps Balloons, 1871-1902." MA 24 (Winter 1960-61), 189-202.

3219. Patterson, C. Meade. "The Military Rifle Flasks of 1832 and 1837." MC&H 5 (March 1953), 7-12.

3220. Perry, Ralph B. The Platsburgh Movement. (New York, 1921).

3221. Petersen, William J. "Troops and Military Supplies on the Upper Mississippi River Steamboats." IJH&P 33 (July 1935), 260-86.

3222. Peterson, Harold L. The American Sword 1775-1945; A Survey of the Swords Worn by the Uniformed Forces of the United States from the Revolution to the Close of World War II. (New Hope, Pennsylvania, 1954).

3223. Peterson, Harold L. (N.E. Beveridge, pseudo.). Cups of Valor. (Harrisburg, Pennsylvania, 1968).

3224. Peterson, Harold L. The Fuller Collection of American Firearms: America's Military Longarms. (Fort Oglethorpe, Georgia, 1967).

3225. Peterson, Harold L. Round Shot and Rammers; An Introduction to Muzzle-loading Land Artillery in the United States. (Harrisburg, Pennsylvania, 1969).

3226. Peterson, Mendel L. "American Army Epaulettes 1814-1872." MC&H 3 (March 1951), 1-14.

3227. Peterson, Mendel L. "American Epaulettes 1775-1820." MC&H 2 (June 1950), 17-21.

3228. Pfanz, Harry W. "Soldiering in the South During the Reconstruction Period, 1865-1877." Ph.D. Dissertation, Ohio State University, 1958.

3229. Phillips, Helen C. "Dedication of the Signal Corps Museum." MA 19 (Winter 1955), 204-5.

3230. Phillips, Thomas D. "The Black Regulars: Negro Soldiers in the U.S. Army, 1866-1891." Ph.D. Dissertation, University of Wisconsin, 1970.

3231. Pohl, James W. "The General Staff and American Military Policy: The Formative Period, 1898-1917." Ph.D. Dissertation, University of Texas at Austin, 1967.

3232. Porter, Kenneth W. "The Seminole Negro-Indian Scouts, 1870-1881." SWHQ 55 (January 1952), 358-77.

3233. Powe, Marc B. "American Military Intelligence Comes of Age: A Sketch of a Man and His Times." MR 55 (December 1975), 17-30.

3234. Powe, Marc B. The Emergence of the War Department Intelligence Agency: 1885-1918. (Manhattan, Kansas, 1974).

3235. Powe, Marc B. and Edward E. Wilson. The Evolution of American Military Intelligence. (Fort Huachuca, Arizona, 1973).

3236. Powe, Marc B. "A Great Debate: The American General Staff (1903-16)." MR 55 (Spril 1975), 71-89.

3237. Powell, James W. Customs of the Service. The Army, National Guard, and Volunteers. (Revised Edition, Kansas City, Missouri, 1899).

3238. Powers, Ramos S. and Gene Younger. "Cholera and the Army in the West: Treatment and Control in 1866 and 1867." MA 39 (April 1975), 49-54.

3239. Pratt, Julius W. America's Colonial Experiment; How the United States Gained, Governed, and, in part, Gave Away a Colonial Empire. (New York, 1950).

3240. Pratt, Julius W. Expansionists of 1898: The Acquisition of Hawaii and the Spanish Islands. (Baltimore, Maryland, 1936).

3241. Prucha, Francis Paul. Broadax and Bayonet; The Role of the United States Army in the Development of the Northwest 1815-1860. (Madison, Wisconsin, 1953).

3242. Prucha, Francis Paul. "Distribution of Regular Army Troops Before the Civil War." MA 16 (Winter 1952), 169-73.

3243. *Prucha, Francis Paul. The Sword of the Republic: The United States Army on the Frontier, 1783-1846. (New York, 1969).

3244. Prucha, Francis Paul. "The United States Army as Viewed by British Travelers, 1825-1860." MA 17 (Fall 1953), 113-24.

3245. Quattlebaum, Charles B. "Military Highways." MA 8 (Fall 1944), 225-31.

3246. Raines, Edgar F., Jr. "Major General J. Franklin Bell and Military Reform: The Chief of Staff Years, 1906-1910." Ph.D. Dissertation, University of Wisconsin, 1976.

3247. Rankin, Robert H. Uniforms of the Army. (New York, 1968).

3248. Rankin, Robert H. Uniforms of the Marines. (New York, 1970).

3249. Ranson, Edward. "American Military Policy and Civil-Military Relations, 1865-1904." Ph.D. Dissertation, University of Manchester, 1964.

3250. Ranson, Edward. "The Endicott Board of 1885-1886 and the Coast Defenses." MA 31 (Summer 1967), 74-84.

3251. Ranson, Edward. "The Investigation of the War Department, 1898-99." HST 34 (November 1971), 78-99.

3252. Ranson, Edward. "Nelson A. Miles as Commanding General, 1895-1903." MA 29 (Winter 1965-66), 179-200.

3253. Reddick, L.D. "The Negro Policy of the United States Army, 1775-1945." JNH 34 (January 1949), 9-29.

3254. Reed, Hugh T. _Cadet Life at West Point_. (Chicago, Illinois, 1896).

3255. Reedstrom, Ernest L. _Bugles, Banners and War Bonnets_. (Caldwell, Idaho, 1977).

3256. Reese, Calvin L. "The United States Army and the Indian: Low Plains Area 1815-1854." Ph.D. Dissertation, University of Southern California, 1963.

3257. Reese, Michael, II. _U.S. Test Trials, 1900 Luger_. (Gretna, Louisiana, 1970).

3258. Reeves, Ira L. _Military Education in the United States_. (Burlington, Vermont, 1914).

3259. Reichley, Marlin S. "Federal Military Intervention in Civil Disturbances." Ph.D. Dissertation, Georgetown University, 1939.

3260. Reid, Jasper B., Jr. "Russell A. Alger as Secretary of War." _MICH_ 43 (June 1959), 225-39.

3261. *Reilly, Robert M. _United States Military Small Arms, 1816-1865; The Federal Firearms of the Civil War_. (Baton Rouge, Louisiana, 1970).

3262. "Reports of Experiments with Small Arms at the National Armory Made by Capt. John E. Greer, Under the Direction of Lt. Col. James G. Benton." Ordnance Note No. 104, May 10, 1879, in United States, Ordnance Department, _Ordnance Notes_. (Washington, D.C., 1873-84).

3263. Reynolds, Alfred. _The Life of an Enlisted Soldier in the United States Army_. (Washington, D.C., 1904).

3264. Reynolds, Mary T. "The General Staff as a Propaganda Agency, 1908-1914." _POQ_ 3 (July 1939), 391-408.

3265. Rhodes, Charles D. "The Utilization of Native Troops in Our Foreign Possessions." _JMSI_ 30 (January 1902), 1-22.

3266. Rice, James M. "Military Education and the Volunteer Militia." _CIMM_ 35 (October 1888), 1939-43.

3267. *Rickey, Don, Jr. _Forty Miles a Day on Beans and Hay; The Enlisted Soldier Fighting the Indian Wars_. (Norman, Oklahoma, 1963).

3268. Rickey, Don, Jr. _War in the West; The Indian Campaigns_. (Crow Agency, Montana, 1956).

3269. Riker, William H. _Soldiers of the State: The Role of the National Guard in American Democracy_. (Washington, D.C., 1957).

3270. *Risch, Erna. _Quartermaster Support of the Army: A History of the Corps, 1775-1939_. (Washington, D.C., 1962).

3271. Robie, William R. "The Court-Martial of a Judge Advocate General: Brigadier General David G. Swaim (1884)." MLR 56 (Spring 1972), 211-40.

3272. Robinson, Fayette. An Account of the Organization of the Army of the United States; with Biographies of Distinguished Officers of all Grades. (2 vols., Philadelphia, Pennsylvania, 1848).

3273. Robles, Philip K. United States Military Medals and Ribbons. (Rutland, Vermont, 1971).

3274. Roddis, Louis H. "Naval and Marine Corps Casualties in the Wars of the United States." MSUR 99 (October 1946), 305-10.

3275. Rodenbough, Theophilus F. and William L. Haskin, eds. The Army of the United States. Historical Sketches of Staff and Line with Portraits of Generals-in-Chief. (New York, 1896).

3276. Rodenbough, Theophilus F., ed. Sabre and Bayonet; Stories of Heroism and Military Adventure. (New York, 1897).

3277. Rodenbough, Theophilus F., ed. Uncle Sam's Medal of Honor; Some of the Noble Deeds for Which the Medal Has Been Awarded, Described by Those Who Have Won It, 1861-1886. (New York, 1886).

3278. Roe, Thomas G. A History of Marine Corps Roles and Missions, 1775-1962. (Washington, D.C., 1962).

3279. Rollman, Robert O. "Of Crime, Courts-Martial and Punishment--A Short History of Military Justice." AFJAG 11 (Spring 1969), 212-22.

3280. Root, Elihu. The Military and Colonial Policy of the United States; Addresses and Reports. (Cambridge, Massachusetts, 1916).

3281. *Ropp, Theodore. "War From Colonies to Vietnam," in William H. Cartwright and Richard L. Watson, Jr., eds. American History and Culture. (Washington, D.C., 1973), 207-26.

3282. Rosengarten, Joseph G. The German Soldier in the Wars of the United States. (Philadelphia, Pennsylvania, 1886).

3283. Russell, Don. "How Many Indians Were Killed? White Man versus Red Man: The Facts and the Legend." AMERW 10 (July 1973), 42-47, 61- 3.

3284. Schoenfeld, Seymour J. The Negro in the Armed Forces, His Value and Status, Past and Present, and Potential. (Washington, D.C., 1945).

3285. Schoonover, Thomas. "Manpower, North and South, in 1860." CWH 6 (June 1960), 170- 3.

3286. Schreier, Konrad F., Jr. "U.S. Army Field Artillery Weapons, 1866-1918." MC&H 20 (Summer 1968), 40- 5.

3287. Schubert, Frank N. "The Fort Robinson Y.M.C.A., 1902-1907: A Social Organization in a Black Regiment." NEBH 55 (Summer 1974), 165-79.

3288. Schuon, Karl. Home of the Commandants. (Washington, D.C., 1966).

3289. Schwartz, Rudolph. "Non-Military Education in the United States Army and Air Force, 1900-1960." Ed.D. Dissertation, New York University, 1963.

3290. The Scouts. By the Editors of Time-Life Books with Text by Keith Wheeler. (Alexandria, Virginia, 1978).

3291. Seaman, Louis L. "Native Troops for Our Colonial Possessions." NAR 171 (December 1900), 847-60.

3292. *Sefton, James E. The United States Army and Reconstruction, 1865-1877. (Baton Rouge, Louisiana, 1967).

3293. Self, Zenobia. "Court-Martial of J.J. Reynolds." MA 37 (April 1973), 52- 6.

3294. Semsch, Philip L. "Elihu Root and the General Staff." MA 27 (Spring 1963), 16-27.

3295. Seymour, Truman. Military Education: A Vindication of West Point and the Regular Army. (n.p., 1864).

3296. Shapard, John. "The United States Army, Camel Corps: 1856-66." MR 55 (August 1975), 77-89.

3297. Shaughnessy, Thomas E. "Beginnings of National Professional Military Education in America, 1775-1825." Ph.D. Dissertation, Johns Hopkins University, 1957.

3298. Shields, Joseph W., Jr. From Flintlock to M1. (New York, 1954).

3299. *Shiley, Harry A. "A Select Bibliography of Articles on Military and Indian Conflicts on the American Frontier," in Raymond Brandees,ed., Troopers West: Military and Indian Affairs on the American Frontier. (San Diego, California, 1970), 189-206.

3300. Shindler, Henry and Erving E. Booth. History of the Army Service Schools, Fort Leavenworth, Kansas. (Fort Leavenworth, Kansas, 1908).

3301. Shindler, Henry. History of the United States Military Prison. (Fort Leavenworth, Kansas, 1911).

3302. Shockley, Philip M. The Krag-Jorgensen Rifle in the Service. (Aledo, Illinois, 1960).

3303. Shockley, Rhilip M. The Trap-Door Springfield in the Service. (Aledo, Illinois, 1958).

3304. Sibbald, John R. "Camp Followers All." AMERW 3 (Spring 1966), 56-67.

3305. Simmons, Edwin H. The United States Marine. (London, 1974).

3306. Skelton, William B. "The United States Army, 1821-1837; An Institutional History." Ph.D. Dissertation, Northwestern University, 1968.

3307. Skelton, William B. "Army Officers' Attitudes Towrad Indians, 1830-1860." PACNWQ 67 (July 1967), 113-24.

3308. Skelton, William B. "The Commanding General and the Problem of Command in the United States Army, 1821-1841." MA 34 (December 1970), 117-22.

3309. Skelton, William B. "Professionalization in the U.S. Army Officer Corps During the Age of Jackson." AFS 1 (August 1975), 443-71.

3310. *Slonaker, John, compl. The U.S. Army and Domestic Disturbances. (Bibliography). (Carlisle Barracks, Pennsylvania, 1970).

3311. *Slonaker, John, compl. The U.S. Army and the Negro. (Bibliography). (Carlisle Barracks, Pennsylvania, 1971).

3312. Smith, Carlton B. "The United States War Department, 1815-1842." Ph.D. Dissertation, University of Virginia, 1967.

3313. Smith, Francis Henney. West Point Fifty Years Ago. (New York, 1879).

3314. *Smith, Merritt R. Harpers Ferry Armory and the New Technology; The Challenge of Change. (Ithaca, New York, 1977).

3315. Snedeker, James. A Brief History of Courts-Martial. (Annapolis, Maryland, 1954).

3316. The Soldiers. By the Editors of Time-Life Books with Text by David Nevin. (New York, 1973).

3317. Soley, John C. "The Naval Brigade." USNIP 6, No. 13 (1880), 271-94.

3318. Spaulding, Oliver L. The United States Army in War and Peace. (New York, 1937).

3319. Stacey, May Humphreys. Uncle Sam's Camels: The Journal of May Humphreys Stacey Supplemented by the Report of Edward Fitzgerald Beale (1857-1858). Edited by Lewis Burt Lesley. (Cambridge, Massachusetts, 1929).

3320. Stansfield, George J. "A History of the Judge Advocate General's Department, United States Army." MA 9 (Fall 1945), 219-37.

3321. *Stallard, Patricia. Glittering Misery: Dependents of the Indian-Fighting Army. (Fort Collins, Colorado, 1978).

3322. Steele, James W. Frontier Army Sketches. (Chicago, Illinois, 1883).

3323. Steere, Edward. "Genesis of American Graves Registration 1861-1870." MA 12 (Fall 1948), 149-61.

3324. Steffen, Randy. The Horse Soldier, 1776-1943, The United States Cavalryman: His Uniforms, Arms, Accoutrements, and Equipment. (Norman, Oklahoma, 1977--).

3325. Steffen, Randy. United States Military Saddles, 1812-1943. (Norman, Oklahoma, 1973).

3326. Stevens, Phillip H. Search Out the Land; A History of American Military Scouts. (Chicago, Illinois, 1969).

3327. Stewart, Theophilus, ed. Active Service; or, Religious Work Among U.S. Soldiers, a Series of Papers by Our Post and Regimental Chaplains. (New York, 189-?).

3328. Stewart, Theophilus. The Colored Regulars in the United States Army. (Philadelphia, Pennsylvania, 1904).

3329. Stillman, Richard J., ed. The U.S. Infantry: Queen of Battle. (New York, 1965).

3330. Stohlman, Robert F., Jr. The Powerless Position: The Commanding General of the Army of the United States, 1864-1903. (Manhattan, Kansas, 1975).

3331. Stover, Earl F. Up From Handymen; The United States Army Chaplaincy, 1865-1920. (Washington, D.C., 1977).

3332. Stratton, David H. "The Army and the Gospel in the West." WEHUR 8 (Summer 1954), 247-62.

3333. Strong, George C. Cadet Life at West Point. (Boston, Massachusetts, 1862).

3334. Strait, Newton A. Alphabetical List of Battles, 1754-1900: War of the Rebellion, Spanish-American War, Philippine Insurrection, and all Old Wars with Dates; Summary of Events of the War of the Rebellion, 1860-1865; Spanish-American War, Philippine Insurrection, 1898-1900; Troubles in China, 1900, with other Valuable Information.... (Washington, D.C., 1900).

3335. Stubbs, Mary Lee, Stanley R. Connor and Janice E. McKenney. Armor-Cavalry. (2 vols., Washington, D.C., 1969-72).

3336. Stunkel, Kenneth R. "Military Scientists of the American West." ARMY 13 (May 1963), 50- 8.

3337. Swanborough, F.G. and Peter M. Bowers. United States Military Aircraft Since 1909. (New York, 1963).

3338. Swett, Morris. "The Forerunners of Sill." FARJ 28 (November-December 1938), 453-63.

3339. Symons, Thomas W. "The Army and the Exploration of the West." JMSI 4 (September 1883), 205-49.

3340. Tapson, Alfred J. "The Sutler and the Soldier." MA 21 (Winter 1957), 175-81.

3341. Tate, Michael L. "Soldiers of the Line: Apache Companies in the U.S. Army, 1891-1897." <u>AZW</u> 16 (Winter 1974), 343-64.

3342. Thoburn, Joseph B. "The Dragoon Campaigns to the Rocky Mountains." <u>COK</u> 8 (March 1930), 35-41.

3343. Thompson, Gerald. <u>The Army and the Navajo; The Bosque Redondo Reservation Experiment, 1863-1868</u>. (Tucson, Arizona, 1976).

3344. Tierney, Richard. <u>The Army Aviation Story</u>. (Northport, Alabama, 1963).

3345. Tobey, James A. <u>The Medical Department of the Army; Its History, Activities and Organization</u>. (Baltimore, Maryland, 1927).

3346. Todd, Frederick P., et. al. <u>American Military Equipage 1851-1872</u>. (Providence, Rhode Island, 1974--).

3347. Todd, Frederick P. <u>Cadet Gray: A Pictorial History of Life at West Point as Seen Through its Uniforms</u>. (New York, 1955).

3348. Tone, Theobald W. <u>School of Cavalry; or, System of Organization, Instruction, and Manoeuvres, Proposed for the Cavalry of the United States</u>. (Washington, D.C., 1917).

3349. *Toomey, Noxon. <u>The History of the Infantry Drill Regulations of the United States Army</u>. (St. Louis, Missouri, 1917).

3350. Townsend, F.C. and Frederick P. Todd. "Branch Insignia of the Regular Cavalry, 1833-1872." <u>MC&H</u> 8 (Spring 1956), 1-5.

3351. Tripp, William H. <u>A Guide to West Point and the United States Military Academy Giving the Location and History of All Public Buildings, Monuments and Principle Points of Interest, Together with the Hours for all Drills and Formations</u>. (Philadelphia, Pennsylvania, 1906).

3352. United States, Adjutant General's Office. <u>Circular Showing the Distribution of Troops of the Line of the United States Army, January 1, 1866 to June 30, 1909</u>. (Washington, D.C., 1909).

3353. United States, Adjutant General's Office. <u>Federal Aid in Domestic Disturbances, 1787-1903</u>. By Frederick T. Wilson. (Washington, D.C., 1903).

3354. United States, Adjutant General's Office. <u>Legislative History of the General Staff of the Army of the United States...from 1775 to 1901</u>. By Raphael P. Thian. (Washington, D.C., 1901).

3355. United States, Adjutant General's Office. <u>List of Military Posts, etc., Established in the United States From Its Earliest Settlement to the Present Time</u>. (Washington, D.C., 1902).

3356. United States, Adjutant General's Office. Notes Illustrating the Military Geography of the United States, 1813-1880. Compiled by Raphael P. Thian. (Washington, D.C., 1881).

3357. United States, Adjutant General's Office. Office Memoranda... Chronological List of Actions, &c., with Indians, January 1, 1866, to January, 1891. (Washington, D.C., 1891).

3358. United States, Adjutant General's Office. Regimental History of the United States Regular Army. Chronological Outline 1866-1918. (Washington, D.C., 1918).

3359. United States, Armed Forces Information School, Carlisle Barracks, Pennsylvania. The Army Almanac; A Book of Facts Concerning the Army of the United States. (Washington, D.C., 1950).

3360. United States, Army, Alaska. Building Alaska with the U.S. Army, 1867-1962. (Seattle, Washington, 1962).

3361. United States, Army, Alaska. The U.S. Army in Alaska. (Fifth Edition, Fort Richardson, ?, 1972).

3362. United States, Army, Military Division of Missouri. Record of Engagements with Hostile Indians within the Military Division of the Missouri, from 1868 to 1882. (Washington, D.C., 1882).

3363. United States, Army, Pacific Division. Earthquake in California, April 18, 1906. Special Report...on the Relief Operations Conducted by the Military Authorities of the United States at San Francisco and Other Points, with Accompanying Documents. (Washington, D.C., 1906).

3364. United States, Army Medical Museum. A History of the United States Army Medical Museum, 1862-1917. (Washington, D.C., 1917).

3365. United States, Army War College. The Army War College: A Brief Narrative, 1901-1952. (Carlisle Barracks, Pennsylvania, 1953).

3366. United States, Arsenal, Rock Island, Illinois. Descriptive Catalogue of the Ordnance Museum. (Rock Island, Illinois, 1909).

3367. United States, Congress. American State Papers: Documents, Legislative and Executive, 1789-1838. Military Affairs. (38 vols., Washington, D.C., 1832-1861).

3368. United States, Department of the Army. A Brief History of the United States Army Chaplain Corps. (Washington, D.C., 1974).

3369. *United States, Department of the Army. Civilian in Peace, Soldier in War: A Bibliographic Survey of the Army and Air National Guard. (Washington, D.C., 1967).

3370. *United States, Department of the Army. The Role of the Reserve in the Total Army. (Bibliography). (Washington, D.C., 1977).

3371. *United States, Department of the Army. The Writing of American Military History; A Guide. (Washington, D.C., 1956).

3372. United States, Department of the Army, Office of Military History. Demobilization in the United States Army. By John C. Sparrow. (Washington, D.C., 1951).

3373. United States, Department of the Army, Office of Military History. The Personnel Replacement System in the United States Army. By Leonard L. Lerwill. (Washington, D.C., 1954).

3374. United States, Engineer School. History and Traditions of the Corps. (Fort Belvoir, Virginia, 1953).

3375. United States, Engineer School. Occassional Papers, No. 16. Historical Papers Relating to the Corps of Engineers and to Engineers and to Engineer Troops in the U.S. Army. (Washington, D.C., 1904).

3376. United States, Engineer School. U.S. Army, Stations of Engineer Units, Regular Army, 1846-1937. (Washington, D.C., 1938).

3377. *United States, Engineer School, Library. Early American Wars; A Bibliography. (Fort Belvoir, Virginia, 1956).

3378. *United States, Engineer School, Library. Engineer Troops; References to Their Organization, Equipment, Training and Duties Together with a Short List of Books and Pamphlets of Interest to the Engineer Service. (Washington, D.C., 1911).

3379. United States, Engineer School, Museum. Geneses of the Corps of Engineers, Including Portraits and Profiles of Its Forty Chiefs, with An Introductory Sketch of Events from 1745 to 1953. (Fort Belvoir, Virginia, 1953).

3380. United States, General Staff, Second Section. American Campaigns. By Matthew F. Steele. (2 vols., Washington, D.C., 1909).

3381. United States, Infantry School, Fort Benning, Georgia. Selected Readings in American Military History... (2 vols., Fort Benning, Georgia, 1953).

3382. United States, Judge-Advocate General's Department (Army). Federal Aid in Domestic Disturbances, 1903-1922. (Washington, D.C., 1922).

3383. United States, Marine Corps. A Brief History of Marine Corps Aviation. (Washington, D.C., 1960).

3384. United States, Marine Corps. A Brief History of the Marine Corps Recruit Depot, Paris Island, South Carolina, 1891-1956. (Revised Edition, Washington, D.C., 1960).

3385. United States, Marine Crops. A Brief History of Marine Corps Staff Organization. (Washington, D.C., 1961).

3386. United States, Marine Corps. Marine Corps Aircraft, 1913-1960. (Washington, D.C., 1961).

3387. United States, Marine Corps. One Hundred Eighty Landings of United States Marines, 1800-1934. By Harry A. Ellsworth. (Washington, D.C., 1934).

3388. United States, Marine Corps. Marine Corps Aircraft, 1913-1965. (Revised Edition, Washington, D.C., 1967).

3389. United States, Marine Corps. Marine Corps Lore. (Washington, D.C., 1960).

3390. *United States, Military Academy, West Point. The Centennial of the United States Military Academy at West Point, New York, 1802-1902. (2 vols., Washington, D.C., 1904).

3391. United States, Military Academy, West Point, Department of Economics, Government, and History. Military Policy of the United States, 1775-1944. (West Point, New York, 1944).

3392. United States, Military Academy, West Point, Department of Military Art and Engineering. The West Point Atlas of American Wars. By Vincent J. Esposito. (2 vols., New York, 1959).

3393. United States, National Armed Forces Museum Advisory Board. The Armed Forces of the United States as Seen by the Contemporary Artist. (Washington, D.C., 1968).

3394. United States, National Park Service. Soldier and Brave; Historic Places Associated with Indian Affairs and the Indian Wars in the Trans-Mississippi West. (New Edition, Washington, D.C., 1971).

3395. United States, Ordnance Department. Artillery for the United States Land Service, as Devised and Arranged by the Ordnance Board. By Alfred Mordecai. (2 vols., Washington, D.C., 1849).

3396. United States, Ordnance Department. Reports of Experiments on the Strength and Other Properties of Metals for Cannon: Description of the Machines for Testing Metals, and of the Classification of Cannon in Service. (Philadelphia, Pennsylvania, 1856).

3397. United States, Ordnance Department. Reports of Experiments with Small Arms for the Military Service. (Washington, D.C., 1856).

3398. United States, Pay Department (War Department). A Compendium of the Pay of the Army from 1785 to 1888. Compiled Under the Direction of Thomas M. Exley. (Washington, D.C., 1888).

3399. United States, Public Buildings Service. Executive Office Building (State, War and Navy Building). (Revised Edition, Washington, D.C., 1970).

3400. United States, Quartermaster's Corps. Illustrations of Chevrons. (Washington, D.C., 1914).

3401. United States, Quartermaster's Corps. <u>Illustrations of Silken Colors, Guidons and Standards</u>. (Washington, D.C., 1914)

3402. United States, Quartermaster's Department. <u>The Army of the United States</u>. Text by Henry L. Nelson and Drawings by Henry A. Ogden. (Washington, D.C., 1888).

3403. United States, Quartermaster's Department. <u>Uniform of the Army of the United States (Illustrated) from 1774 to 1889, 1898 to 1907</u>. (2 vols., New York, 1890-1909).

3404. United States, Signal Office. <u>History of the United States Signal Service....</u> (Washington, D.C., 1883).

3405. United States, Solicitor of the Department of State. <u>Right to Protect Citizens in Foreign Countries by Landing Forces</u>. (Third Revised Edition, Washington, D.C., 1934).

3406. United States, Surgeon General's Office. <u>The Medical Department of the United States Army from 1775 to 1873</u>. Compiled Under the Direction of Harvey E. Brown. (Washington, D.C., 1873).

3407. United States, Surgeon General's Office. <u>Report on Epidemic of Cholera in the Army of the United States, During the Year 1866</u>. By Joseph J. Woodward. (Washington, D.C., 1867).

3408. United States, Surgeon General's Office. <u>A Report on the Hygiene of the United States Army with Descriptions of Military Posts</u>. (Washington, D.C., 1875).

3409. United States, War Department. <u>Annual Report of the Secretary of War</u>. (Washington, D.C., 18-- to 19--).

3410. United States, War Department. <u>Five Years of the War Department Following the War with Spain, 1899-1903, As Shown in the Annual Reports of the Secretary of War</u>. (Elihu Root). (Washington, D.C., January 1904).

3411. United States, War Department. <u>Fortifications. Letter from the Secretary of War in Reference to Fortifications, December 11, 1851</u>. (Washington, D.C., 1851).

3412. United States, War Department, General Staff. <u>Report on the Organization of the Land Forces of the United States</u>. (Washington, D.C., 1912).

3413. "U.S. Army Bugle Calls--Echoes of History." <u>AID</u> 21 (October 1966), 19-21.

3414. *<u>The United States Army in Peacetime: Essays in Honor of the Bicentennial, 1775-1975</u>. Edited by Robin Higham and Carol Brandt. (Manhattan, Kansas, 1978).

3415. <u>United States Marine Corps Ranks and Grades, 1775-1969</u>. By Bernard C. Nalty and Others. (Revised Edition, Washington, D.C., 1969).

3416. Upton, Emory. The Military Policy of the United States. (Washington, D.C., 1904).

3417. Uselding, Paul L. "Technical Progress at the Springfield Armory, 1820-1850." EXEH 9 (Spring 1972), 291-316.

3418. Utley, Robert M. and Wilcomb E. Washburn. The American Heritage History of the Indian Wars. (New York, 1977).

3419. Utley, Robert M. "A Chained Dog: The Indian-Fighting Army." AMERW 10 (July 1973), 18-24, 61.

3420. *Utley, Robert M. Frontier Regulars; The United States Army and the Indian 1866-1891. (New York, 1973).

3421. *Utley, Robert M. Frontiersmen in Blue; The United States Army and the Indian, 1848-1865. (New York, 1967).

3422. Vaughn, William P. "West Point and the First Negro Cadet." MA 35 (October 1971), 100-102.

3423. Wade, Arthur P. "The Military Command Structure: The Great Plains, 1853-1891." JWEST 15 (July 1976), 5-22.

3424. Wade, Arthur P. "Roads to the Top--An Analysis of General-Officer Selection in the United States Army, 1789-1898." MA 40 (December 1976), 157-63.

3425. Wagner, Arthur L. A Catchism of Outpost Duty. (Kansas City, Missouri, 1895).

3426. Wagner, Arthur L. and James D. Jerrold. Our Country's Defensive Forces in War and Peace. The United States Army and Navy; Their Histories from the Era of the Revolution to the Close of the Spanish-American War.... (Akron, Ohio, 1899).

3427. Wainwright, Jack D. "Root Versus Bliss: The Shaping of the Army War College." P 4, No. 2 (1974), 52-65.

3428. Walker, John G. and Oliver L. Shepard. The Navajo Reconnaissance; A Military Exploration of the Navajo Country in 1859. (Los Angeles, California, 1964).

3429. Walker, Henry P. "When the Law Wore Army Blue." MC&H 29 (Spring 1977), 4-14.

3430. Wallace, Edward S. The Great Reconnaissance, Soldiers, Artists and Scientists on the Frontier, 1848-1861. (Boston, Massachusetts, 1955).

3431. Walton, William, ed. Asa Bird Gardiner and H.C. Taylor, ass't. eds. The Army and Navy of the United States from the Period of the Revolution to the Present Day; A Record of the Formation, Organization, and General Equipment of the Land and Naval Forces of the Republic. (2 vols., Boston, 1889-95).

3432. Ward, John W. "The Use of Native Troops in Our New Possessions." JMSI 31 (November 1902), 793-805.

3433. Ward, Robert D. "A Note on General Leonard Wood's Experimental Companies." MA 35 (October 1971), 92-93.

3434. Webb, George W. Chronological List of Engagements Between the Regular Army of the United States and Various Tribes of Hostile Indians Which Occured During the Years, 1790-1898. (St. Joseph, Missouri, 1939).

3435. Wecter, Dixon. When Johnny Comes Marching Home. (Cambridge, Massachusetts, 1944).

3436. Weigley, Russell F., ed. The American Military; Readings in the History of the Military in American Society. (Reading, Massachusetts, 1969).

3437. Weigley, Russell F. "A Historian Looks at the Army." MR 52 (February 1972), 25-36.

3438. *Weigley, Russell F. History of the United States Army. (New York, 1967).

3439. Weigley, Russell F. "The Military Thought of John M. Schofield." MA 23 (Summer 1959), 77-84.

3440. *Weigley, Russell F. Towards an American Army; Military Thought from Washington to Marshall. (New York, 1962).

3441. Weinert, Richard P., Jr. The Guns of Fort Monroe. (Fort Monroe, Virginia, 1974).

3442. Weinert, Richard P., Jr. "The Year McClellan Studied War in Europe." CWTI 2 (May 1963), 38-41.

3443. Welch, M.L. "Early West Point French Teachers and Influences." JASFLH 26 (Spring 1955), 27-43.

3444. Welty, Raymond L. "The Army and the Mining Frontier (1860-1870)." FRO 12 (March 1932), 261- 9.

3445. Welty, Raymond L. "The Army Fort of the Frontier (1860-70)." NDH 2 (April 1928), 155-67.

3446. Welty, Raymond L. "Supplying the Frontier Military Posts." KANHQ 7 (May 1938), 154-69.

3447. Welty, Raymond L. "The Policing of the Frontier by the Army, 1860-1870." KANHQ 7 (1938), 246-57.

3448. Welty, Raymond L. "The Western Army Frontier, 1860-1870." Ph.D. Dissertation, University of Iowa, 1925.

3449. Wharfield, H.B. With Scouts and Cavalry at Fort Apache. Edited by John A. Carroll. (Tucson, Arizona, 1965).

3450. White, William B. "The Military and the Melting Pot: The American Army and Minority Groups, 1865-1924." Ph.D. Dissertation, University of Wisconsin, 1968.

3451. Whiteley, John F. Early Army Aviation: The Emerging Air Force. (Manhattan, Kansas, 1974).

3452. Whitman, Sidney E. The Troopers: An Informal History of the Plains Cavalry, 1865-1890. (New York, 1962).

3453. Whitmore, Earle. "Artists at West Point before 1865." A 32 (December 1973), 16- 9, 34-5.

3454. Williams, R. "Army Organization in the United States." G 24 (November 1877), 594-602.

3455. Williams, R. "The Staff of the United States Army." ATLM 42 (March 1878), 376-80.

3456. *Williams, Thomas Harry. Americans at War; The Development of the American Military System. (Baton Rouge, Louisiana, 1960).

3457. Winton, George P., Jr. "Ante-Bellum Military Instruction of West Point Officers and Its Influence upon Confederate Military Organization and Operations." Ph.D. Dissertation, University of South Carolina, 1972.

3458. Wood, Robert L. Men, Mules and Mountains; Lieutenant O'Neil's Olympic Expedition. (Seattle, Washington, 1976).

3459. Wormser, Richard E. The Yellowlegs; The Story of the United States Cavalry. (Garden City, New York, 1966).

3460. Wyllie, Robert E. Orders, Decorations, and Insignia, Military and Civil; With the History and Romance of Their Origin and a Full Description of Each. (New York, 1921).

3461. Wyman, Walker D. "The Outfitting Posts." PHR 18 (February 1949), 14-23.

3462. Young, Otis E. The First Military Escort on the Santa Fe Trails, 1829; From the Journal and Reports of Major Bennet Riley and Lieutenant Philip St. George Cooke. (Glendale, California, 1952).

3463. Young, Otis E. "Military Protection of the Santa Fe Trail and Trade." MOHR 49 (October 1954), 19-32.

3464. Youngberg, Gilbert A. History of Engineer Troops in the United States Army, 1775-1901. (Washington, D.C., 1910).

3465. "Your Patton Museum." ARMOR 73 (May-June 1964), 50-2.

3466. Zeitlin, Richard H. "Brass Buttons and Iron Rails: The United States Army and American Involvement in Mexico, 1868-1881." Ph. D. Dissertation, University of Wisconsin, 1973.

> See also:Part I: 244; Part II: 1366, 1608, 2093, 2151, 2156; Addendum: 4, 20, 28, 48, 55, 65, 91, 109, 124, 132, 133, 157, 158, 166, 173, 179.

REPUBLIC OF TEXAS, 1835-1845

3467. Barton, Henry W. "The Problem of Command in the Army of the Republic of Texas." SWHQ 62 (January 1959), 299-311.

3468. Binkley, William C. The Expansionist Movement in Texas, 1836-1850. (Berkeley, California, 1925).

3469. De Shields, James T. Border Wars of Texas.... (Tiogo, Texas, 1912).

3470. Hefter, Joseph. The Army of the Republic of Texas. (Bellvue, Nebraska, 1971).

3471. Hefter, Joseph. Early Texas Uniforms. (n.p., 1969).

3472. Koury, Michael J. and Joseph Hefter. Arms for Texas; A Study of the Weapons of the Republic of Texas. (Fort Collins, Colorado, 1973).

3473. Nackman, Mark E. "The Making of the Texan Soldier, 1835-1860." SWHQ 78 (January 1975), 231-53.

3474. Nance, Joseph M. After San Jacinto; The Texas-Mexican Frontier, 1836-1841. (Austin, Texas, 1963).

3475. Pierce, Gerald S. Texas Under Arms: The Camps, Forts, and Military Towns of the Republic of Texas, 1836-1846. (Austin, Texas, 1969).

PACIFIC ISLANDS

3476. Allardyce, W.L. "The Fijians in Peace and War." MAN 4, No. 5 (1904), 69-73.

3477. Brookes, Jean I. International Rivalry in the Pacific Islands, 1800-1875. (Berkeley, California, 1941).

3478. Dodge, Ernest S. Islands and Empires; Western Impact on the Pacific and East Asia. (Minneapolis, Minnesota, 1976).

3479. Ellison, Joseph W. Opening and Penetration of Foreign Influence in Samoa to 1880. (Corvallis, Oregon, 1938).

3480. Gordon, Leonard H.D. "Taiwan and the Powers, 1840-1895," in Taiwan: Studies in Chinese Local History. Edited by Leonard Gordon. (New York, 1970), 93-116.

3481. Masterman, Sylvia. The Origins of International Rivalry in Samoa, 1845-1884. (London, 1934).

3482. United States, Adjutant General's Office, Military Information Division. Report of the Island of Guam. By Joseph Wheeler. (Washington, D.C., 1900).

See also: Part I: 719.

PHILIPPINE ISLANDS

3483. Cavanna y Manso, Jesus Maria, C.M. Rizal and the Philippines of His Day; An Introduction to the Study of Dr. Rizal's Life, Works, and Writings; Historical Notes.... (Manila, 1957).

3484. Coats, George Y. "The Philippine Constabulary: 1901-1917." Ph.D. Dissertation, Ohio State University, 1968.

3485. Craig, Austin. The Filipinos' Fight for Freedom; True History of the Filipino People During Their 400 Years' Struggle Told After the Manner of Jose Rizal. (Manila, 1933).

3486. Craig, Austin. Rizal's Life and Minor Writings. (Manila, 1927).

3487. Craig, Austin. The Story of Jose Rizal, the Greatest Man of the Brown Race. (Manila, 1909).

3488. Elarth, Harold H., ed. The Story of the Philippine Constabulary. (Los Angeles, California, 1949).

3489. Elliott, Charles B. The Philippines to the End of the Military Regime. (Indianapolis, Indiana, 1917).

3490. Eyre, James K., Jr. "Military History of the Filipino People." ME 34 (June 1942), 283- 6.

3491. Gleeck, Lewis E., Jr. Over Seventy-Five Years of Philippine American History (The Army and Navy Club of Manila). (Manila, 1976).

3492. Guerrero, Leon Ma. The First Filipino; A Biography of Jose Rizal.
      (Manila, 1963).

3493. Johnston, William H. "Employment of Philippine Scouts in War."
      JMSI 38 (January-February 1906), 67-77; (March-April 1906), 289-98.

3494. Krieger, Herbert W. The Collection of Primitive Weapons and Armor
      of the Philippine Islands in the United States National Museum.
      (Washington, D.C., 1926).

3495. McKinley, William E.W. "A Brief Summary of Historical Accounts
      Respecting the Spanish Military Operations Against the Moros, from
      the Year 1578 to 1898," in United States, War Department, Annual
      Report of the Secretary of War, 1903. Volume 3, Appendix VII.
      (Washington, D.C., 18-- to 19--), 379-98.

3496. Morton, Louis. "Defense of the Philippines During the War Scare of
      1907." MA 13 (Summer 1949), 95-104.

3497. Parker, T.C. "The Army-Navy Club of Manila." USNIP 83 (April 1957),
      408-15.

3498. Rizal y Alonso, Jose. Rizal's Own Story of His Life. Edited by
      Austin Craig. (Manila, 1918).

3499. Salamanca, Bonifacio S. Filipino Reaction to American Rule, 1901-1913.
      (Hamden, Connecticut, 1968).

3500. Storey, Morrfield and Marcial P. Lichanco. The Conquest of the
      Philippines by the United States, 1898-1925. (New York, 1928).

3501. Sturtevant, David R. Popular Uprisings in the Philippines, 1840-1940.
      (Ithaca, New York, 1976).

3502. White, John R. Bullets and Bolos; Fifteen Years in the Philippine
      Islands. (New York, 1928).

3503. United States, Adjutant General's Office, Military Information Division.
      Military Notes on the Philippines. (Washington, D.C., 1898).

3504. United States, Division of the Philippines. Report on the Military
      Government of the City of Manila, P.I., from 1898 to 1901. By
      George W. Davis. (Manila, 1901).

      See also: Addendum: 8, 33, 58.

HAWAIIAN ISLANDS

3505. Dutton, C.E. "The Hawaiian Islands and People." Ordnance Note No. 343,
      April 23, 1884, in United States, Ordnance Department, Ordnance Notes.
      (12 vols., Washington, D.C., 1873-84).

3506. "Hawaii's Army Guard: From Royal Volunteers to Modern Minutemen." HAG 17 (Fall 1971), 18-21.

3507. Judd, Walter F. Palaces and Forts of the Hawaiian Kingdom; From Thatched to American Florentine. (Palo Alto, California, 1975).

3508. Kenn, Charles W. "The Army and Navy of Kamehameha I." USNIP 71 (November 1945), 1335- 9.

3509. Rolle, Andrew F. "California Filibustering and the Hawaiian Islands." PHR 19 (August 1950), 251-63.

3510. Gowen, Herbert H. The Napoleon of the Pacific, Kamehameha the Great. (New York, 1919).

3511. Mellen, Kathleen D. The Lonely Warrior; The Life and Times of Kamehameha the Great of Hawaii. (New York, 1949).

3512. Warfield, Charles L. The History of the Hawaii National Guard from Feudal Times to June 30, 1935. (Honolulu, Hawaii, 1935).

SOUTH AMERICA

3513. Arcaya, Pedro M. The Gomez Regime in Venezuela and Its Background. (Washington, D.C., 1936).

3514. Brinckerhoff, Sidney B. and Pierce A. Chamberlain. Spanish Military Weapons in Colonial America, 1700-1821. (Harrisburg, Pennsylvania, 1972).

3515. Burr, Robert N. "The Balance of Power in Nineteenth-Century South America: An Exploratory Essay." HAHR 35 (February 1955), 37-60.

3516. Bushnell, David. The Santander Regime in Gran Colombia. (Newark, Delaware, 1954).

3517. Chapman, Charles E. "The Age of the Caudillos: A Chapter in Hispanic American History." HAHR 12 (August 1932), 281-300.

3518. *Chapman, Charles E. "List of Books on Caudillos." HAHR 13 (February 1933), 143- 6.

3519. Chapman, Charles E. "Melgarejo of Bolivia: An Illustration of Spanish American Dictatorships." PHR 8 (March 1939), 37-45.

3520. Corbett, Charles D. The Latin American Military as a Socio-Political Force: Case Studies of Bolivia and Argentina. (Coral Gables, Florida, 1972).

3521. Davis, Harold E. Makers of Democracy in Latin America. (New York, 1945).

3522. Douglas, Wadsworth C. "Patterns of Indian Warfare in the Province of Santa Marta (Colombia)." Ph.D. Dissertation, The University of Wisconsin-Madison, 1974.

3523. *Einaudi, Luigi and Herbert Goldhamer, compls. An Annotated Bibliography of Latin American Military Journals. (Santa Monica, California, 1965).

3524. *Einaudi, Luigi and Herbert Goldhamer. "An Annotated Bibliography of Latin American Military Journals." LARR 2 (Spring 1967), 95-122.

3525. Geisler, Richard A. "Measures for Military Collaboration Between the United States and Latin America: The Record, 1826-1951." Ph.D. Dissertation, New York University, 1955.

3526. George Washington University, Washington, D.C., Seminar Conference on Hispanic American Affairs. South American Dictators During the First Century of Independence. Edited by Alva Curtis Wilgus. (Washington, D.C., 1937).

3527. *Gilmore, Robert L. Caudillism and Militarism in Venezuela, 1810-1910. (Athens, 1964).

3528. Graham, Robert B. Cunninghame. Jose Antonio Paez. (London, 1929).

3529. Graham, Robert B. Cunninghame. Portrait of a Dictator, Francisco Solano Lopez. (London, 1933).

3530. Haigh, Roger M. "The Creation and Control of a Caudillo (Martin Guemes)." HAHR 44 (November 1964), 481-90.

3531. Haring, Clarence H. The Spanish Empire in America. (New York, 1947).

3532. Hill, Lawrence F. "Confederate Exodus to Latin America." SWHQ 39 (October 1935), 100-34; (January 1936), 161-99.

3533. Ingersoll, Hazel M.B. "The War of the Mountain, A Study of Reactionary Peasant Insurgency in Guatemala, 1837-1873." Ph.D. Dissertation, The George Washington University, 1972.

3534. Ireland, Gordon. Boundaries, Possessions, and Conflicts in Central and North America and the Caribbean. (Harvard, Cambridge, Massachusetts, 1941).

3535. Ireland, Gordon. Boundaries, Possessions, and Conflicts in South America. (Cambridge, Massachusetts, 1938).

3536. Johnson, John J. The Military and Society in Latin America. (Stanford, California, 1964).

3537. Lieuwen, Edwin. Arms and Politics in Latin America. (New York, 1960).

3538. Lieuwin, Edwin. "The Changing Role of the Military in Latin America." JI-AS 3 (October 1961), 559-69.

3539. *McAlister, L.N. "Recent Research and Writings on the Role of the Military in Latin America." LARR 2 (Fall 1966), 5-36.

3540. Matthews, Robert P., Jr. "Rural Violence and Social Unrest in Venezuela, 1840-1858; Origins of the Federalist War." Ph.D. Dissertation, New York University, 1974.

3541. Militarists, Merchants and Missionaries; United States Expansion in Middle America. Edited by Eugene R. Huck and Edward H. Moseby. (University, Alabama, 1970).

3542. *Naylor, Bernard. Accounts of Nineteenth-Century South America: An Annotated Checklist of Works by British and United States Observers. (London, 1969).

3543. Nichols, Madaline W. The Gaucho: Cattle Hunter, Cavalryman, Ideal of Romance. (Durham, North Carolina, 1942).

3544. North, Lisa. Civil-Military Relations in Argentina, Chile, and Peru. (Berkeley, California, 1966).

3545. Nunn, Frederick, M. "Effects of European Military Training in Latin America: The Origins and Nature of Professional Militarism in Argentina, Brazil, Chile, and Peru, 1890-1940." MA 39 (February 1975), 1-7.

3546. *Nunn, Frederick M. "The Latin American Military Establishment: Some Thoughts on its Origins and an Illustrative Bibliographical Essay." AMERS 27 (October 1971), 135-51.

3547. Padelford, Norman J. The Panama Canal in Peace and War. (New York, 1942).

3548. Ropp, Steve C. "The Honduran Army in the Sociopolitical Evolution of the Honduran State." AMERS 30 (April 1974), 504-28.

3549. Rozman, Stephen L. "The Evolution of the Political Role of the Peruvian Military." JI-AS 12 (October 1970), 539-65.

3550. Rourke, Thomas. Gomez, Tyrant of the Andes. (New York, 1936).

3551. Spence, James M. The Land of Boliva; or, War, Peace and Adventure in the Republic of Venezuela. (2 vols., London, 1878).

3552. Wise, George S. Caudillo, A Portrail of Antonio Guzman Blanco. (New York, 1951).

See also: Part II: 2196, 2475; Addendum: 168.

ARGENTINA

3553. Argentine Republic, Laws, Statutes, etc. Laws and Regulations Respecting General Enrollment in the Argentine Republic, Enacted in 1911. (London, 1913).

3554. Cady, John F. Foreign Intervention in the Rio de la Plata, 1838-50; A Study of French, British, and American Policy in Relation to the Dictator Juan Manuel Rosas. (Philadelphia, Pennsylvania, 1929).

3555. Ferrer, Jose. "The Armed Forces in Argentine Politics to 1930." Ph.D. Dissertation, University of New Mexico, 1966.

3556. Goldwert, Marvin. "The Rise of Modern Militarism in Argentina." HAHR 48 (May 1968), 189-205.

3557. Gomez, Ben I. The Role of the Military in Governing Argentina 1868-1968. (Maxwell Air Force Base, Alabama, 1970).

3558. Jeffrey, William H. Mitre and Argentina. (New York, 1952).

3559. King, John A. Twenty-four Years in the Argentine Republic; Embracing Its Civil and Military History and an Account of Its Political Condition, Before and During the Administration of Governor Rosas.... (New York, 1846).

3560. Perry, Richard O. "Warfare on the Pampas in the 1870's." MA 36 (April 1972), 52- 8.

3561. *Robinson, John L. "Bartolome Mitre: A Historiographical Study." Ph.D. Dissertation, Texas Christian University, 1970.

3562. Schiff, Warren. "The Influence of the German Armed Forces and War Industry on Argentina, 1880-1914." HAHR 52 (August 1972), 436-55.

See also: Part II: 3544, 3545.

BRAZIL

3563. Dudley, William S. "Reform and Radicalism in the Brazilian Army, 1870-1889." Ph.D. Dissertation, Columbia University, 1972.

3564. Estep, Raymond. The Military in Brazilian Politics, 1821-1970. (Maxwell Air Force Base, Alabama, 1971).

3565. Hahner, June E. Civilian-Military Relations in Brazil, 1889-1898. (Columbia, South Carolina, 1969).

3566. Hahner, June E. "The Paulistas' Rise to Power: A Civilian Group Ends Military Rule." HAHR 47 (May 1967), 149-65.

3567. Hayes, Robert A. "The Formation of the Brazilian Army and Its Political Behavior (1807-1930)." Ph.D. Dissertation, University of New Mexico, 1969.

3568. Hill, Lawrence F. "Confederate Exiles to Brazil." HAHR 7 (May 1927), 192-210.

3569. McBeth, Michael C. "The Politicians vs. the Generals: The Decline of the Brazilian Army During the First Empire, 1822-1831." Ph.D. Dissertation, University of Washington, 1972.

3570. Morton, F.W.O. "The Military and Society in Bahia, 1800-1821." JLAS 7 (November 1975), 249-69.

3571. Nunn, Frederick M. "Military Professionalism and Professional Militarism in Brazil, 1870-1970; Historical Perspectives and Political Implications." JLAS 4 (May 1972), 29-54.

3572. Perspectives on Armed Politics in Brazil. Edited by Henry H. Keith and Robert A. Hayes. (Tempe, Arizona, 1976).

3573. Prince, Howard M. "Slave Rebellion in Bahia, 1807-1835." Ph.D. Dissertation, Columbia,University, 1972.

3574. Simmons, Charles W. "The Rise of the Brazilian Military Class, 1870-1890." MID-A 39 (October 1957), 227-40.

3575. Stepan, Alfred C. The Military in Politics; Changing Patterns in Brazil. (Princeton, New Jersey, 1971).

3576. Wachholz, Paul F. "Brazil's Army." AID 14 (September 1959), 48-52.

3577. Williams, Mary W. Dom Pedro the Magnanimous, Second Emperor of Brazil. (Chapel Hill, North Carolina, 1937).

See also: Part II: 3545; Addendum: 39.

CHILE

3578. Burr, Robert N. By Reason or Force; Chile and the Balancing of Power in South America, 1830-1905. (Berkeley, California, 1965).

3579. Hillmon, Tommie J. "A History of the Armed Forces of Chile from Independence to 1920." D.S.S. Dissertation, Syracuse University, 1963.

3580. Johnson, John J. "The Telegraph in Chile, 1852-1872; An Economic History; With a Chapter on the Telegraph System of the Military Frontier, 1870-1875." Ph.D. Dissertation, University of California-- Berkeley, 1947.

3581. Nunn, Frederick M. "Civil-Military Relations in Chile, 1891-1938." Ph.D. Dissertation, The University of New Mexico, 1963.

3582. Nunn, Frederick M. "Emil Korner and the Prussianization of the Chilean Army: Origins, Process, and Consequences, 1885-1920." HAHR 50 (May 1970), 300-22.

3583. Nunn, Frederick M. The Military in Chilean History; Essays on Civil-Military Relations, 1810-1973. (Albuquerque, New Mexico, 1976).

See also: Part II: 3544, 3545.

Corrections of Errors

Part II: 91, Cave, Laurence T. The French in Africa. (London, 1859),should come before Part II: 88.

Part II: 800, Helmreich, E.C. "Documents--An Unpublished Report on Austro-German Military Conversations of November 1912." JMH 5 (June 1933), 197-207, should come before Part II: 797.

Part II: 834, Wickham-Steed, Henry. The Hapsburg Monarchy. (London, 1914), should come before Part II: 829, because the author's name is actually Wickham, Henry Steed.

Part II: 1023, Guttery, Thomas E. Zeppelin, An Illustrated Life of Count Ferdinand Von Zeppelin, 1838-1917. (Aylesburg, England, 1973), should come after Part II: 1028.

Part II: 2023, Beach, Thomas M. (Henri LeCaron, pseudo.). Twenty-Five Years in the Secret Service; The Recollections of a Spy. (London, 1892), is a correct citation and should replace Part II: 1276.

Part II: 2265, Calhoun, John C. The Papers of John C. Calhoun. Edited by Robert L. Meriweather, et.al. (Columbia, South Carolina, 1959), is a correct citation and should replace Part II: 2547.

Part II: 2413, Russell, Carl P. Guns on the Early Frontier; A History of Firearms from Colonial Times through the Years of the Western Fur Trade. (Berkeley, California, 1957), should come after Part II: 2424.

Part II: 2433, Schmitt, Martin F. and Dee A. Brown. Fighting Indians of the West. (New York, 1948), is a correct citation and should replace Part II: 2254.

Part II: 2488, Western Apache Raiding and Warfare, from the Notes of Grenville Goodwin. Edited by Keith H. Basso with the assistance of E.W. Jernigan and W.B. Kessell. (Tucson, Arizona, 1971), is a correct citation and should replace Part II: 2265.

Part II: 3025, Gardner, Charles K. A Dictionary of...the Army of the United States...Volunteers and Militia of the States... and of the Navy and Marine Corps. (Second Edition, New York, 1860), should come before Part II: 3000.

Part II: 3042, Hardin, Albert N. The American Bayonet, 1776-1964. (Philadelphia, Pennsylvania, 1964), and Part II: 3043, Hardin, Albert N. and Robert W. Hedden. Light but Efficient; A Study of the M1880 Hunting and M1890 Intrenching Knives and Scabbards. (Pennsauken, New Jersey, 1973), should come before Part II: 3040.